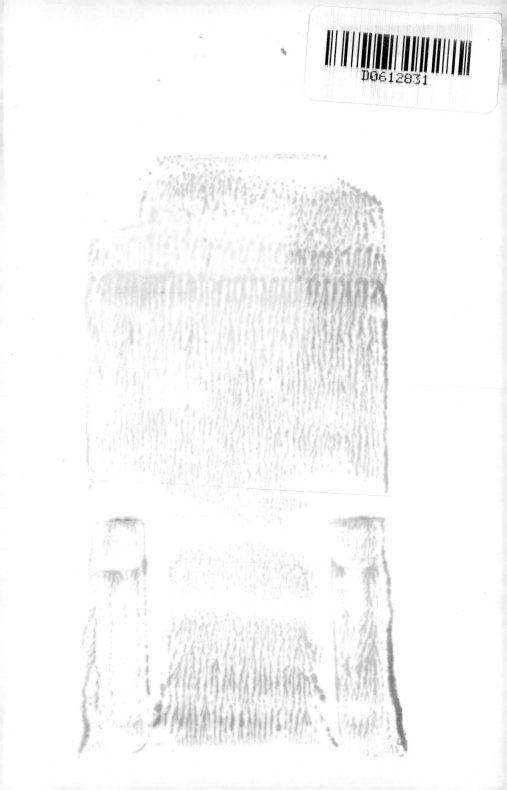

EMERSON'S PLUTARCH

PLUTARCH's
MORALS.

Tranſlated from the *Greek*

BY

SEVERAL HANDS.

VOLUME V.

𝔗𝔥𝔢 𝔉𝔦𝔣𝔱𝔥 𝔈𝔡𝔦𝔱𝔦𝔬𝔫 ℭ𝔬𝔯𝔯𝔢𝔠𝔱𝔢𝔡.

LONDON:

Printed for W. TAYLOR at the *Ship*
in *Pater-noſter Row,* 1718.

EMERSON'S PLUTARCH

Edmund G. Berry

Cambridge, Massachusetts

HARVARD UNIVERSITY PRESS

1961

Publication of this book has been aided by a grant from the Ford Foundation

Library of Congress Catalog Card Number 61-7389

Printed in the United States of America

FOR A.M.B. AND V.G.B.

PREFACE

A number of studies of Emerson's sources and of the influence of other writers on his work have been published. He read widely and drew concepts, illustrations, and even literary expressions from a wide field. Anyone who reads Emerson closely will soon notice that he refers frequently to Plutarch; that is not surprising since everyone in England and America in the eighteenth and nineteenth centuries knew Plutarch's lives of the great Greeks and Romans. But Plutarch's moral essays, not read at all in the twentieth century, were not much more familiar to Emerson's contemporaries than they are to readers today; and yet Emerson knew these essays very well indeed in translation and there are very few of his writings which do not contain a reference to or a quotation or expression drawn from Plutarch, the Plutarch of both *Lives* and *Morals*. This present study endeavors to explore the exact extent of the influence of Plutarch on Emerson and to show that this influence is not only one of borrowed anecdotes and expressions drawn from repeatedly "raffling the pages of Plutarch" but is also one of literary form. For his essay topics Emerson often turned to the topics of Plutarch's essays. He thought of himself as a moral essayist and at one time expressed the wish to be a modern Plutarch, portraying the essential character of the great men of his own day. When he criticized contemporary Christianity he more than once called for the restoration of the "Stoicism" which he found in Plutarch's heroes.

I have used the Latin title *Moralia* throughout to indicate the moral essays of Plutarch; volume numbers and page references are to the revised version of the seventeenth-century "Several Hands" translation which was made by Professor Goodwin of Harvard

(*Plutarch's Morals*, 5 vols., Boston, 1870), and for which Emerson wrote the introductory essay. Until the publication of this revision, Emerson used the unrevised version of the "Several Hands" translation but this is scarce nowadays; few readers will have access to it and the changes made by Goodwin are often slight. Since the Loeb Classical Library translation of the *Moralia* is still incomplete, Goodwin's is the most accessible and throughout this study quotations from the *Moralia* are given in Goodwin's version. Also for reasons of availability, I give quotations from the *Lives* in the Dryden translation, revised by A. H. Clough; quotations from Montaigne are given in Cotton's version, which Emerson used. I have found Webster's distinction between "Stoic" and "stoic" and between "Stoicism" and "stoicism" too precise, especially since these terms deal with such imprecise ideas. One of the points I wish to make is that Emerson's "stoicism" is in reality "Stoicism," that is, that it is based upon a knowledge of classical Stoicism; I have therefore (except in quotations, where I adhere to the original) capitalized "Stoic" and "Stoicism."

I am grateful to the John Simon Guggenheim Memorial Foundation for a fellowship in 1951–52 which enabled me to examine the manuscripts of Emerson's journals, notebooks, lectures, and sermons and the volumes from his own library in the Houghton Library of Harvard University. I owe thanks to Harvard College Library and the Houghton Library for permission to do this, and to Professor W. A. Jackson, Mr. W. H. Bond, and Miss Carolyn Jakeman for assistance. I am grateful also to the Canada Council for a subvention in aid of publication; the fact that a grant has been made does not imply, however, that the Canada Council endorses or is responsible for the statements or views expressed. I wish to thank President Saunderson and the University of Manitoba for research grants; the library of the University of Manitoba has helped me on a number of occasions.

Professor Stephen E. Whicher of Cornell and Professor Robert E. Spiller of Pennsylvania, expert authorities on Emerson, have given very valuable advice and comment on my manuscript, have saved a classicist from many errors of interpretation, and have introduced me to works with which I was unacquainted. Their publication of the first volume of Emerson's early lectures was of material help to me in the final stages of the completion of this book. For any errors I alone am responsible. I owe thanks also to Professors Harold Cherniss, C. L. Gohdes, G. P. Goold, William Chase Greene, Werner Jaeger, J. P. Pritchard, and R. L. Rusk for assistance of various kinds. I am grateful to Harvard University Press for its courtesy and to its Editorial Department for its careful and competent editing.

I also express my thanks to Professor Edward Waldo Forbes and the Emerson Memorial Association for permission to use and quote from Emerson's works, journals, letters, notebooks, and sermons, published and unpublished, and to reproduce a page of one of Emerson's volumes of the *Moralia*; to Houghton Mifflin Company for permission to quote from *The Journals of Ralph Waldo Emerson* (1909–14), and from his *Complete Works* (Centenary Edition, 1903–04); to Columbia University Press for permission to quote from *The Letters of Ralph Waldo Emerson*, ed. Ralph L. Rusk (1939); to Cambridge University Press for permission to quote from E. V. Arnold, *Roman Stoicism* (1910); and to Kenneth W. Cameron for permission to use material from his *Ralph Waldo Emerson's Reading* (Raleigh, N.C., 1941) and *Emerson the Essayist* (Raleigh, N.C., 1945).

The abbreviation *Journals* refers to *The Journals of Ralph Waldo Emerson* (ed. E. W. Emerson and W. E. Forbes, 10 vols., Boston, 1909–14); *CW* to the Centenary Edition of *The Complete Works of Ralph Waldo Emerson* (ed. E. W. Emerson, 12 vols., Boston, 1903–04); *Letters* to *The Letters of Ralph Waldo Emerson* (ed. R. L. Rusk, 6 vols., New York, 1939).

Winnipeg, July 1960   E. G. B.

CONTENTS

EMERSON'S PLUTARCH

Plutarch cannot be spared from the smallest library; first because he is so readable, which is much; then that he is medicinal and invigorating. The lives . . . are what history has of best. . . . But Plutarch's Morals is less known, and seldom reprinted. Yet such a reader as I am writing to can as ill spare it as the Lives.

"Books"

Plutarch charms by the facility of his associations; so that it signifies little where you open his book, you find yourself at the Olympian tables. His memory is like the Isthmian Games, where all that was excellent in Greece was assembled. . . .

"Books"

Plutarch's memory is full, and his horizon wide. Nothing touches man but he feels to be his; he is tolerant even of vice, if he finds it genial; enough a man of the world to give even the Devil his due. . . . He is a philosopher with philosophers, a naturalist with naturalists. . . .

"Plutarch"

[Plutarch] is not a profound mind; not a master in any science; not a lawgiver . . . not a leader of the mind of a generation, like Plato or Goethe. But if he had not the highest powers, he was yet a man of rare gifts. He had that universal sympathy with genius which makes all its victories his own.

"Plutarch"

I

PLUTARCH AND THE PLUTARCHAN TRADITION

*Go with mean people and you think life is mean. Then
read Plutarch, and the world is a proud place, peopled with
men of positive quality, with heroes and demigods standing
around us, who will not let us sleep.*

"Books"

*I know not where to find a book — to borrow a phrase of
Ben Jonson's — "so rammed with life."*

"Plutarch"

Anyone who is curious to trace the history of the influence of
Plutarch in the thought and literature of the Western world soon
becomes aware that the task is by no means a simple one, for
Plutarch is a prolific writer who attempts several different literary
forms and a variety of themes.[1] He is not always completely consistent in his ideas or in the philosophy which lies behind his writing.
Indeed there seem to be several Plutarchs, and in the history of the
rise and fall of his popularity over two thousand years it is not
always possible to determine exactly which Plutarch is indicated in
a literary tribute to him, or which aspect is foremost in a writer's
mind when he criticizes and abuses him. For while we can find
tributes to Plutarch like those of Montaigne or Henry IV of France
or Emerson, we can also find vigorous criticisms of Plutarch and
of the Plutarch cult, as in Ben Jonson or Carlyle or Macaulay.

Admirers of Plutarch seem to be extravagant in their admiration, but his critics are seldom apathetic and their expressions sometimes seem unduly strong.

At times literature seems to be devoted to Plutarch and the Plutarchan and in other periods turns away from him, but even in the same generation readers of Plutarch often find different aspects to cherish and value in a knowledge and reading of his works. The age of hero worship can find models for the military hero in the *Lives* of the Greeks and Romans, while even among these hero-worshippers there are the conservatives who will point to the men who stabilized or enlarged the Greek or Roman states like Solon and Pericles and Fabius, while the radicals and revolutionaries will point out Phocion and Timoleon who liberated their own countries and others from tyranny and oppression. The idealists who take Plato as their master can find in Plutarch a devotion to Plato in which they can share. On the other hand, those who find Plato impractical and not sufficiently devoted to ethics see in Plutarch a keen interest in the practical ethics of everyday life, an interest which was largely Stoic in origin. When Hellenism is in the ascendancy as in the time of the Renaissance, Plutarch the biographer of heroes and the historian of Greece (to the extent to which biography can be called history) is read with extravagant expressions of admiration. When the Roman element in Western cultures receives fresh emphasis, again Plutarch is appealed to and the lives of Fabius and Cicero and Caesar are regarded as the best source of a knowledge of Roman history. Plutarch with the *Lives* of the Greeks and Romans, with the *Moralia* or moral essays (both those properly moral or concerned with human character and morale and the others which deal with questions in natural science or history or philosophy or religion), covers so many fields of human culture that at almost any time in the history of literature some aspect of Plutarch is appreciated and his name can be adduced as a great teacher or moralist, a philosopher or theologian or biographer. In an age of few books and especially in one in which the classical world is held in esteem, Plutarch is a bible and encyclopedia, a handbook in psychology, a guide for princes and ordinary men.

But a sharp decline in enthusiasm for Plutarch begins somewhere in the middle of the nineteenth century when the vaguely laudatory remarks by Browning or Sainte-Beuve only serve to indicate that they are exceptions to the general neglect of Plutarch. The decline gains momentum after the death of Emerson, the last great devotee of Plutarch. The twentieth century is not the age for Plutarch. He is little read now and what reading of him there is is done by classical scholars who look warily for his version of historical events or for his picture of the Greek religion of a Hellenist living under the Roman Empire, or perhaps even for the fragments of lost Greek authors embedded in the *Lives* or the *Moralia*. One of the reasons for this decline in interest in Plutarch is in the recent discovery that he is unreliable as a recorder of Greek history and Greek thought; this was first pointed out by the new scientific school of ancient historians in the nineteenth century. He portrays the great heroes and military leaders and has little or nothing to say about the Greek and Roman nations, the ordinary people; in fact he is writing biography and not history. This attitude will not retain the interest of a time which stresses the rise of the national spirit, which sees always the crowds behind the leader. Even as a chronicler of events he is unreliable, for he is writing the history of happenings some of which occurred several centuries before his own time and he is often biased or erroneous. In the same way his Platonism was once taken to be genuine Platonism and by some Plutarch was regarded as giving an outline of the Platonic philosophy. But we now know that this philosophy is not simply Platonic but is overlaid with the results of four hundred years of changing interpretation, of borrowings from other schools, of ideas grafted on to the Platonic system, concepts which turn Plutarch in the direction of Stoicism or even of mysticism. At one time his list of the doctrines of the Greek philosophers constituted a convenient handbook of Greek philosophy before Plato, but we know now that his statements are over-simplified and the constant reinterpretation of the doctrines has changed the meaning of the statements; scholars are now more interested in how the doctrines developed and how this development changed for each age the meaning of the philosophical terms.

These discoveries have diminished the value of Plutarch for scholars, but he was always read more by ordinary people than by scholars until the decline begins. Plutarch's world seemed close to preceding generations when education was largely based on the Greek and Roman classics. Today a doctrine which is to exert an influence, or a theory of politics or education which is to spread widely, must bear the witness of recent authorities and the latest research to suit the modern age. Plutarch's theory of education in "A Discourse concerning the Training of Children" and in other moral treatises contains sound principles which survived longer than most other Plutarchan elements and his ideas can still be found in modern textbooks on education. But it has long been forgotten that these apparently new ideas are as old as the second century, and references to modern authorities have long since replaced quotations from Plutarch. His "Discourse to an Unlearned Prince" was also once an educative force, but absolute monarchy has disappeared from the Western world, and long ago Plutarch's principles were re-expressed in later writers who usurped his place as an instructor of kings.

His writings contain many moral anecdotes and apothegms of the classical heroes. They occur often in the *Lives* and in a number of the essays, and the ethical principle behind them is often Stoic. There are in the *Moralia* two collections, "Apothegms of the Spartans" and "Apothegms of Kings and Great Commanders," which were probably assembled from his works by someone after his own time. They constitute one of the first of the great number of collections of maxims and anecdotes which have come down to us, and which were so popular in the Renaissance. Anecdotes and apothegms enforce moral principles in a vivid and memorable way and in an age when the classics were the basis of education these extracts from Plutarch made fine schoolbooks. They showed a sound morality and at the same time they provided some wholesome ancient history for the student. There must be many hundreds of volumes of extracts from the *Lives*, used for instructing children over five hundred years. The nineteenth century, especially in its first half, was prolific in abridgments of or extracts from the *Lives* and one such, *The Beauties of Plutarch*, is in Emerson's library. For many boys of the first half of the nineteenth century the heroes were those of the classical world, known to them from Plutarch. In Emerson's youth there must have been few households which did not have a Dryden or a Langhorne, and probably also a volume of extracts. The career of the translations of the *Moralia* is equally significant for the Plutarchan tradition. It was first translated into English by the "master translator" Philemon Holland, and the "Several Hands" version for which Dryden wrote the introduction was published between 1684 and 1694. The *Moralia* found no Langhorne in the eighteenth century and Emerson and his contemporaries who knew the *Moralia* used the "Several Hands" version in one of its many editions, faulty as it was and varying greatly in the quality of the translations.[2] Emerson himself was anxious to see a new and improved version of these familiar essays but it was not until 1870 that the old version was revised and it was as an introduction to this revision that he wrote his Plutarch essay.

But now the apogee of the popularity of Plutarch is long past and he has given up the predominant place he once occupied in Western thought and education. The *Lives* have not been given a modern translation since Clough revised that of Dryden almost a century ago and it is difficult now to appreciate the enormous popularity of Amyot's French translation, or of North's translation of Amyot into English, or of the later Dryden or Langhorne versions. Only within the last few years has a new edition and translation of the *Moralia* been undertaken, the most accurate yet made,

but it is still very unlikely to achieve the popularity or the wide
reading which it would have received a century and a half ago.

ii

If Plutarch, biographer and essayist, was popular for so long and
yet was read with such diverse objects in mind, it may well be
asked if there is any real Plutarch whose nature can be grasped
and surveyed comprehensively and whose philosophy can be traced
in his writing. It should be possible to straighten out some of the
tangled themes of Plutarch, or at least to point out several consistent
strains of thought, though these tend to be obscured by interest in
some of his more immediately striking elements such as his anecdotes and epigrams. There are among the *Moralia* two chief groups
of essays which give a consistent outline of Plutarch's ideas. These
are the essays which deal with human character and morals, and
those which treat of religion. The essays in these two groups have
generally been more consistently popular and have been quoted
more often than the other essays during the long history of the
Plutarchan tradition and it was to these that Emerson turned most
frequently. In addition, the *Lives* show something more of Plutarch's
ideals for human conduct and for life in the world.

In the first place it is important to note that Plutarch is a Hellenist,
a lover and admirer of things Greek. But it is equally significant
that he lived at a time when Greece had become no more than a
province of the Roman Empire, when Hellenism was giving way
before the cosmopolitan and ecumenical influences which contributed so much to the spread of Christianity. The Roman Empire
was now at its zenith and Plutarch is well aware that the great age
of Greece is past, for he was born at Chaeroneia, the scene of the
last battle for Greek freedom against Macedon. After Plutarch
there would be other important Greek writers but these are the
Neoplatonists and their thought is much different from the Platonism of Plato or even from the Platonism of Plutarch.

To what extent is Plutarch a Platonist? For this title is often given him. He is not a Platonist in the sense that he subscribes to all of Plato's doctrines, for many of them had long been discarded even by the Academy. But through all of Plutarch runs the fundamental Platonic idea that there are two worlds, the material world and the spiritual or transcendental world, the realm of ideas. This has its implications for metaphysics and for ethics. For Plutarch the Platonist, God is eternal, pure, and absolute being; he is also the idea of the good, and fate and destiny; the world is created after the model of the idea of the good. Plutarch is emphatic that there is no room for chance or luck in the world. Everywhere Fate guides mankind; what is apparently chance happening or the work of human contrivance is also guided behind and unseen by Fate and Providence. Nothing happens without a cause, and the ultimate cause is God. In ethics, there is in Plutarch the Platonic concept that virtue is knowledge and can be taught, and that vice is ignorance. On this basis rest the several didactic essays on moral qualities. The dominant position given to reason and philosophy is also Platonic and here Plutarch would go even farther than Plato, even while using a Platonic theory. For mind and reason are divine; sometimes (perhaps borrowing from Aristotle) God is reason, while being at the same time a personal God who by reason knows men's minds. All things are open to reason and philosophy, and reason must examine all things. All the ancient and modern views of God must be examined for "philosophy is the mystagogue of theology." Hence Plutarch's ethical treatises are always reasonable and logical, and it is the straightforward common sense approach to problems which gave him so much appeal.

This is what is meant by Plutarch's "Platonism" and those who are acquainted with Emerson's ideas and with Transcendentalism will immediately see that there is a kinship between Plutarch and Emerson, for Emerson too has a basic dualism, the world of sense and the world of the Over-Soul and one description of Plutarch's aim in teaching might equally well be that of Emerson: "La tendance dominante de Plutarque sera d'affranchir l'esprit de la matière, de l'élever du monde sensible au monde des idées, ce qui est proprement platonicien." [3] It goes without saying that we cannot claim that Emerson's Transcendentalism is derived from Plutarch, for there are many influences which worked on Emerson and most of them were nearer in time than Plutarch. But in Plutarch Emerson, like many serious thinkers before him, could find these apparently novel concepts reinforced and reaffirmed in an ancient moral essayist whom he held in special regard.

I have tried in the above paragraphs to separate out only the elements in Plutarch which can be called Platonic. But what I have said is only a very incomplete outline of Plutarch's metaphysics and ethics; there are several basic elements yet unmentioned. Plutarch is an eclectic — he draws his ideas from many sources, being in this a real child of his time.

For example, Plutarch dislikes the Stoic school and devotes several essays to a refutation of specific doctrines. But these doctrines are usually on minor and technical points. In his larger general concepts Plutarch is often genuinely Stoic and occasionally Plutarch the Stoic is in direct contradiction to Plutarch the Platonist. His Stoicism can perhaps be divided into two parts — those elements which he borrowed from the Greek Stoics, the original founders of the school, and those elements which show a kinship with later Roman Stoicism, especially with that of Seneca.

Plutarch was faced with the same problem which the Greek Stoics saw in Platonism; it is the problem of how to bridge the gap between God and man, for everywhere there was a new interest in human conduct and a lessening appeal in a cold metaphysic. Plato's God is not even the creator of the universe; to make him so would be to detract from his complete blessedness and self-sufficiency. The Stoics chose a monism and for its basis went back to Heraclitus and his theory of a single basic substance, a "fire" or "fiery breath," which underlies all nature, man and God. It is thus a pantheistic monism, and occasionally Plutarch seems to approach this pantheism and man is made to share in the attributes of God. More often, however, he adopts a more Platonic solution by which he can preserve the best of monism, dualism, and the Hellenic polytheism. He adopts the theory of "spirits" or "daemons," part man and part God, a concept which frequently appears in Greek thought with different variations of meaning in Homer, Xenocrates, Plato, the Pythagoreans, and the Stoics. The daemons are controlled by fate, the cycle of things, and through the divine part of their nature they are able to reveal fate or the divine purpose to man by means of oracles, prophecies, dreams, and omens. But they contradict neither natural causality nor reason; they can assist the man who uses reason by making him more receptive to their revelations. Plutarch's theory of demonology also helps to preserve the old Hellenic polytheism and even its divination; the old oracles are not silent now because they were not true in the past but because Providence has given us other means of foretelling the future; there are many instruments of divine revelation. In his essay "Of Isis and Osiris" Plutarch takes over from the Stoics the allegorical method of interpreting myths, and uses this method to show (in the form of a Platonic dialogue) that the religion of Egypt is really Platonism in a different guise. This demonstration of the universality of the same religion is also a Stoic concept.

Such is Plutarch's debt to the old Stoicism and it is not extensive. I do not think that these are the elements which Emerson thinks of when he calls Plutarch a Stoic or speaks of his Stoic heroes. He is rather thinking of the still more practical turn taken by Roman Stoicism, the increased emphasis on ethics, which, especially as recorded by Seneca, exerted such a strong influence on Western thought from Plutarch on.

Seneca takes over the entire Greek Stoic metaphysic with its one substance, now called Reason or the World Soul, and with it the Stoic divination; Fate becomes still more personal and its providential aspect comes to the forefront. The Stoic ethic springs from this, for man has a rational nature common in origin with the reason that controls and creates the cosmos. Morality is the affair of this "inward part" in man. Seneca maintains the Stoic fatalism, a belief in an inflexible, unchanging destiny. All things happen according to Fate; he and Plutarch also share the current Roman concept of fortune or chance but point out that chance happenings are not without a cause; they are controlled by Fate, and only *appear* to an individual's deficient viewpoint to be chance. They are the operations of an unseen cause. It is from this Stoic determinism that the Stoic indifference to the accidents of life arises; fatalism produces resolution and calmness; disaster is merely an opportunity for virtue to display itself. There is also the increasing prominence given to the idea of a universal law which protects man and lifts him above circumstances. The universal law is the law of nature and the highest goal is life according to nature, in fact man is a microcosm and contains in himself the whole universe in miniature.

These are the main tenets of Roman Stoicism and they are accompanied in Seneca and other Stoic writers by many familiar ethical commonplaces and by a cosmopolitanism and concept of human brotherhood which commended itself to many generations. All these Stoic elements are adopted by Plutarch, especially when they can easily be reconciled with Platonism, and hence Plutarch, especially in his ethics, can reasonably be called a Stoic, emphasizing the practical and useful and stressing the tranquillity and serenity which Stoicism should bring. The titles of some of the essays in the *Moralia* given to them by the translators of the "Several Hands" version seem to show that Plutarch's aim was practical and applicable to the ordinary man — "How to Know a Flatterer from a Friend," "Of the Tranquillity of the Mind" — but the Stoicism of Plutarch also appears readily in the *Lives*. The heroes (except in the case of bad men like Demetrius Poliorcetes and Antony) are made to conform to the ideal Roman, Stoic type. They are calm, self-reliant, strong, and silent men, who when they speak do so in terse epigram. They are all made attractive and wise. They have the qualities inculcated by the Roman Stoics, especially by Seneca. Plutarch himself would probably deny that they are Stoic but they are certainly so, for even the Greeks are made to act and talk like Romans and for Plutarch's time "Roman" and "Stoic" are inseparably interwoven and often almost identical.

iii

It is not difficult to account for the long interest in Stoicism in the Western world. In the first place its spread is contemporaneous with the growth and development of Christianity and closely connected with it. The Church Fathers early realized that many of the Stoic virtues resemble the Christian ones, even while resting upon an entirely different basis. A good Stoic would act very much like a good Christian. There are indeed Stoic as well as Christian martyrs. A Stoic faces the accidents of life bravely because all is fated; he dies cheerfully because death is inevitable. The Christian dies cheerfully because he has the promise of another life hereafter. Both Stoic and Christian lay stress on the brotherhood of man; the Stoics point out that all partake equally of the same soul, the Christian, that Jew and Gentile alike are sons of the same God. The Stoic "daemons" have certainly some connection — we cannot be more precise than this — with the Christian angels. Stoicism implanted a "natural" religion in Christianity — Justin Martyr entitles his faith a "philosophy," Jesus is a "teacher" as well as a savior. So the Church Fathers reinforced their own Christian ethics by drawing upon the writings of the pagan moralists; Seneca's brother Gallio presided over the court examination of St. Paul in Corinth and the legend of a correspondence between St. Paul and Seneca arose. This affinity between Stoicism and Christianity is never completely forgotten and from time to time, as in England in the seventeenth century, the divines of the Church again adopt a Stoic tone and quote Seneca and Plutarch. The affinity can be seen, I think, in Emerson the Christian minister, reading the seventeenth-century divines and the Stoic writers at the same time. He is doing nothing new; he is perfectly aware of the kinship between Stoicism and Christianity. But besides this connection there is also another. Stoicism can become, for those who dislike dogma or individual dogmas such as the Incarnation of the Christians, a wholly adequate substitute for Christianity. Emerson was again not the first to find Stoicism increasingly attractive after he had left the ministry because he felt a distaste for its dogma, its gloom, its ritual. The Stoicism of Seneca plays down metaphysics, does away with theology, discards dogma and ritual, and yet leaves a believer who has all the virtues of Christianity without its encumbrances in creed and ritual. This is the element in Stoicism which attracts Montaigne and Bacon as well as, later on, Emerson. It is practical and realistic, it does not require a weak humility but gives sanction for a cheerful pride. It gives high place to reason and common sense and provides full play for the spreading belief in a "natural religion." It is not otherworldly but on the contrary is cosmopolitan and world-wide. It has a strong appeal for a great variety of minds and even today, though the name is little used, there are those who might be called Stoics not inaccurately.

Because of this close similarity between the ethical doctrines of Stoicism and of Christianity (and sometimes perhaps in spite of the similarity), with the revival of classical learning in the Renaissance, Seneca and Stoicism, and Plutarch also, receive new respect. Again Christianity is reinforced by pagan learning and the Renaissance pagan as well as the Christian was intensely interested in morals. The new morality of the Renaissance is to a great extent Senecan and Stoic. In the sixteenth century Montaigne and Lipsius are largely responsible for the "Neostoic" movement, and the fact that today we are all familiar with the loose sense of the word "Stoic" with the meaning of "resolute and firm before adversity" may be largely due to Lipsius, who wrote the *De Constantia*, a work on Stoic philosophy, emphasizing this Roman aspect of Stoicism; about 1595, when this work was translated into English, Neostoicism began to flourish in England, and it is indicative of the connection between Neostoicism and Christianity that Joseph Hall, the chief exponent of the new philosophy, was a bishop in the Church of England.[4] The influence of Seneca on literary style, on drama and on moral philosophy in England in the seventeenth century is all-pervasive, and for some time the influence of Stoic thought is widely spread, though often unrecognized, in the belief in natural law and the immortality of the soul, in the microcosm-macrocosm theory, and in the concept of natural religion, of the brotherhood and equality of man. It has been said that Descartes, Spinoza, and Leibniz are really Stoic in their ethical attitudes. In England later, the Platonism of the Romantic Movement has many resemblances to Stoicism; Wordsworth knew Plutarch well and his interest in this loose kind of Stoicism can be clearly seen in his "Ode to Duty."

But besides reinforcing theology with philosophy as in the Church Fathers, the new paganism also helped to divorce morality from religion. The popular new morality, without a doctrine of revealed sanctions, is Stoic and Donne speaks as if Plutarch were prominently identified with Stoicism; he calls Plutarch "the oracle of moral men." The anecdote and epigram of Plutarch and Seneca almost had for the Neostoics the place which the Bible had for orthodox Christians. So pervasive was the influence of Stoicism upon the philosophy of the time that the term "philosopher," while retaining its old meaning, also acquired in addition the meaning of "one who can endure pain."

Strictly, then, the term "Stoicism" is the title of the philosophy which originated in Greece, became most popular in the Roman Empire, and is expressed in the writings of Seneca, Plutarch, and Marcus Aurelius. We have seen that its chief characteristic in the view of later ages seemed to be in the qualities of character which it demanded — equanimity, complete and calm self-control, restraint in every aspect of emotion and feeling as well as in every action. These are only one aspect of Stoicism — the personal marks of a Stoic — and it will be well to remember that when the nineteenth-century writers, like Emerson, speak of Stoicism, this is really all that is referred to; there is very seldom any implication of Stoic pantheism; the term might almost be summed up as "calm endurance." This is primarily what Emerson means when he talks of Stoicism or calls Plutarch a Stoic. He uses the term loosely, in the same way in which many of his contemporaries did and in the same way in which it is used loosely today. But deeper down in Emerson's thought there can be discerned close coincidences between several aspects of his thought and ancient Stoic concepts. He is much more closely akin to the Stoics than he ever specifically indicates; he has, as we shall see, an unconscious or only partly conscious "affinity" for Stoicism and for Stoic ways of looking at man and at the universe in which man lives.

There is still another philosophical strand which can occasionally be found in Plutarch. Emerson is said sometimes to be heavily in debt to the Neoplatonists and he himself occasionally seems to include Plutarch among them. This is not strictly accurate but still the title is not entirely without justification, for Plutarch's teacher, the Platonist Ammonius, and Plutarch himself are part of a philosophical movement of the early second century which began to study the Pythagorean theory of daemons and which gave current philosophy a religious and mystical coloring; the Neoplatonists developed this daemonic theory farther in the direction of mysticism. They solved the problem of the distance separating man and God in still another way — man can achieve unity with God by means of a mystical experience, a union more direct and intense than that mediated by the daemons. Plutarch would not go so far as this but at the same time his own philosophy is a halfway step between Platonism and Neoplatonism. Emerson knew the Neoplatonists well and in his expression of Transcendentalism sometimes indicates that mystical experience is a way of achieving unity with God or nature; as his critics observed, he approaches pantheism and occasionally this pantheism is Neoplatonic as well as Stoic. At other times he will not go so far, but rather elaborates and confirms Plutarch's demonology, widening its meaning to include many new forms of divination.

Such are the strains of Plutarch which make it possible to call him a Platonist or a Stoic or a Neoplatonist. In ages when Platonism is a vital tradition, as in Italy in the sixteenth century, Plutarch is usually also in the forefront; he also makes an appearance when Stoicism or Neostoicism is flourishing, as in England in the seventeenth century, and he receives new attention when Neoplatonism is in vogue as in the same century in the English Neoplatonists, More and Cudworth. To those who find, often unconsciously, that they are Platonists or idealists, or Stoics, or Neoplatonists with a mystic tendency, Plutarch can and does exert an appeal and an influence.

i v

But this is Plutarch the philosopher and for every reader who values this side of his character there are ten who find something else to admire and to imitate — some quality of literary style or moral character or political attitude which has a wider appeal than his religion or philosophy. Some of these outstanding elements appear repeatedly in the history of the Plutarchan tradition. Plutarch the lover of anecdote and epigram has been mentioned already, but there is also Plutarch the teacher and moralist, Plutarch the portrayer of history as the lives of great men, Plutarch the essayist. Each of these Plutarchs has his day from time to time and it is significant that only at the end of a long period of devotion to these various aspects of Plutarch does there appear a writer and thinker who seems to appreciate all of them, who goes to him for confirmation, by quotation and illustration, of his own themes, who is aware that Plutarch has a universal value and appeal. That writer is Emerson.

Plutarch was widely read from the Renaissance on. It was realized that he portrayed almost every aspect of classical life and thought, now dominant in education. A list of his illustrious admirers and imitators includes many great literary figures over several centuries — dramatists, essayists, historians, biographers. He was a familiar name to kings and statesmen; he was read and used by conservatives and revolutionaries; he was known to schoolboys and to the most eminent scholars. But in general the admiration for Plutarch was an admiration for one or other of the aspects mentioned above.

The first appearance of an interest in Plutarch after his works were first printed and translated into Latin [5] does not seem to have extended to all of his writings. Certain individual works had a more practical and immediate usefulness for the fifteenth and sixteenth centuries. There were few systematic handbooks of education available but there was the revived interest in the classical authors, many of whom were used in this way; they were interesting not merely for their portrayal of ancient life and thought but it was also felt that the ideas of the Greeks and Romans on most topics were sound, or were indeed the only correct ideas. Quintilian's work on rhetoric and the training of the orator was held in high regard but it dealt specifically with the education of the orator; Plutarch's treatise on the education of the young is more general and more practical. He educates the whole man, not merely the orator, and this systematic treatment with its fairly acute observation of psychology could be profitably used. Erasmus did much to spread acquaintance with Plutarch, especially with his ideas on education. He also was one of the first to perceive that several other essays dealing with human character and virtue could be used in the same way, as educational textbooks. He presented to Henry VIII a translation of "How to Know a Flatterer from a Friend," saying that it ought to be read by all rulers. No doubt the various "mirrors for princes" and to some degree the books on the courtier go back to a reading of some of the *Moralia*, including of course the "Discourse to an Unlearned Prince." The French kings too were reading Plutarch and Emerson quotes in his Plutarch essay Henry IV's letter to his wife with its tribute to Plutarch. The king indicated that his mother gave him Plutarch as a boy; it was an educational book; she would not wish, she said, to see her son "an intellectual dunce." He had found Plutarch useful and practical. Emerson quotes the king: "It has been like my conscience, and has whispered in my ear many good suggestions and maxims for my conduct and the government of my affairs." Amyot's translations of the *Lives* (1559) and of the *Moralia* (1572) were everywhere received with great acclaim and with Amyot there began with a flourish the long and deep popularity of Plutarch in France; his version was that used by Montaigne, Racine, Rousseau, Herder. "Amyot" came to be synonymous with "Plutarch" and it was now observed that the *Lives*, as well as the essays, had an educative function. So Montaigne found Plutarch's version of Greek history with his "moral insights" invaluable in the field of education. The great Greeks and Romans were very vivid to Renaissance man, and the modern statesman, it was felt, could do no better than to imitate these noble ancients — loyal, patriotic, restraining sentiment and emotion, giving supremacy to reason, adopting a wide, humane, Stoic viewpoint. A remark of Montaigne helps to explain this growing popularity of Plutarchan heroic anecdotes and their use in education. In his own essay "On the Education of Children" he admires the way in which Plutarch can pick out a trivial incident in a human career and use it as a means of illuminating character. Plutarch likes economy of language and sharpness of rhetorical effect, the sort of thing for which the Spartans were famous; this is also a feature of the writing of the Roman Stoics, who advocated laconic speech and wrote in maxims.

Montaigne was in many ways a typical man of the later Renaissance, who admired the epigrammatic and proverbial statement almost as much as did the Roman Stoics. Indeed Plutarch played a prominent part in the rhetorical theory of the sixteenth century, while the moral discourses of the age (and hence the moral essay which developed from them) owed more to Plutarch than has been generally appreciated; in England, Lyly may be adduced as an example of this, for besides writing moral theses he also made extensive use of Plutarch's treatise on education.[6] For many genera-

tions it was taken for granted that the young could best be educated
by maxims and proverbs; and moral principles are best confirmed
by illustration and example. Thus both the moral essays and the
Lives came to play a prominent part in education. The moral
precepts of the essays are illustrated in a specific individual in the
Lives and given a greater pedagogic force. Montaigne saw the value
of this method clearly. It was his aim to apply maxims to life and
here he was aided by Plutarch and Seneca; he believed that the
Lives are history taught by a moralist and that the *Moralia* are
ethical dissertations in which almost all of the concepts are based
on, and are strengthened by, historical examples. "Tous deux,"
writes Villey, "lui présentaient le mélange intime d'expériences
psychologiques avec la réflexion morale." [7] Montaigne too observes
Plutarch's function as a teacher. "He is a philosopher that teaches
us virtue," he writes in the "Defence of Seneca and Plutarch" and
says in "Of Coaches" that Plutarch "of all the authors I ever con-
versed with, is he who has best mixed art with nature, and judgment with knowledge."

It is well known that Bacon was in the tradition of Montaigne
and that, for example, he adopted the term "essays" from Montaigne;
both his essays and his longer works owe much to Plutarch and
display use of him as a teacher and moralist. That Bacon's essays
may correctly be described as "moral essays" is indicated by the fact
that when they were put into Latin they were entitled "opera
moralia," that is, works dealing with human actions and human
mores. "They handle those things whereof a man shall find much
in experience, little in books." [8] Bacon wished to make them guides
to living rather than collections of maxims. He indicated in the
De Augmentis Scientiarum that he was well aware of the old collections of adages and that he himself had originally made such collections, like those of Erasmus, Machiavelli, and Giucciardini, and
had from them progressed to the fully developed "essay" in which
aphorism and anecdote fill merely the role of examples to illustrate
personal judgments and comments.

Bacon makes only a single direct acknowledged quotation from Plutarch (at the end of "Of Fortune" the *Lives* are quoted) but the essays contain very many anecdotes and apothegms which come from Plutarch directly or through some other writer. Often the other writer is Montaigne. It is curious to observe, for instance, that in his single acknowledged quotation from Montaigne in the first essay of the last author's edition, "Of Truth," Bacon with characteristic inaccuracy attributes to Montaigne an apothegm which Montaigne himself says he read in "an ancient writer"; the ancient writer is Plutarch in the life of Lysander.[9] Many of the parallels between Bacon and Montaigne can of course be explained by the use of a common store of epigram and anecdote which was also used by many others, but it is evident, too, that Bacon read Montaigne and noted relevant classical phrases for use in his own essays.

In English preaching in the seventeenth century, the great age of the sermon, the classical ethic of Plutarch does not disappear. He was a favorite of Jeremy Taylor, and Archbishop Trench observed that the index to his works contains 256 allusions or direct references to Plutarch's writings; Taylor's sermons show that as the Church Fathers had done he continually philosophized Christian counsels by means of the ethical wisdom of the pagans like Plutarch and Seneca.[10] The Neoplatonist Cudworth (whose *True Intellectual System of the Universe* was perhaps the first book to draw Emerson's attention to Neoplatonism) is, as Emerson himself observed (*Journals* 7.95), "a magazine of quotations, of extraordinary ethical sentences, the shining summits of ancient philosophy" and shows a close acquaintance with the *Moralia*. But at the same time the *Lives* retained their interest for many, an interest which in England produced the new translation towards the end of the century; when we hear of Plutarch being known to schoolboys it is usually the *Lives* which are indicated and they retained their predominant place throughout the eighteenth and at least part of the nineteenth centuries. The *Moralia* were still available though they achieved nothing like the popularity of the lives of the Greek and Roman heroes.

But we shall see that Emerson knew the *Moralia* well and that he knew them as moral essays and valued them so; he points out in his Plutarch essay that Plutarch's moral sentiment is always "pure." Even his "superstitions are poetic, aspiring, affirmative." Emerson seems to mean that even when Plutarch's religious ideas are simply wrong, yet he is constructive, always aiming at the purification of religion and rendering it accessible to reason and philosophy. He is interested in, believes in, progress and in the improvement of the human character. Plutarch has something of Emerson's own optimism.

v

Emerson then is in the old tradition of Plutarch the moralist, teaching by moral anecdotes and epigrams. But he also seems definitely to subscribe to another doctrine of Plutarch, that history consists of the lives of great men. This Plutarchan attitude has a long history. Plutarch himself expressly disclaims to be writing history; he uses the historians, when he found them of use, in a new literary genre, the moral biography. He says at the beginning of the life of Alexander: "Therefore as portrait-painters are more exact in the lines and features of the face, in which the character is seen, than in the other parts of the body, so I must be allowed to give my more particular attention to the marks and indications of the souls of men, and while I endeavour by these to portray their lives, may be free to leave more weighty matters and great battles to be treated of by others." At the beginning of the life of Timoleon he tells us that he had begun to write lives for the sake of others, but gradually came to write for himself and his own good, "the virtues of these great men serving me as a sort of looking-glass in which I may see how to adjust and adorn my own life." If biography is not history, it still has a moral purpose.

After Plato or rather after Socrates, when ethics and practical virtue began to claim men's attention rather than metaphysics, the new literary type, biography, developed and was from the first separate and distinct from history of the old annalistic type. It displayed a special interest in the human character and gradually developed a moral purpose, as Plutarch says. Throughout the Middle Ages, chronicles and lives were written side by side — lives of saints, ecclesiastics, and good rulers; but gradually the lives were idealized and moralized to fit in with the traditional purpose of biography — to show the heights to which the human soul can attain. Then with the new knowledge of the classics which appeared in the Renaissance and with the Renaissance great men ruling the great states, the distinction between history and biography was obliterated and the lives were read as if they were real history. For the Renaissance, history was biography and had a ethical purpose. (Amyot, who said that the *Lives* and the essays have the same moral and didactic purpose, must be typical of many of his contemporaries.) The best study for princes who would be heroes was the lives of the Greeks and Romans and the Elizabethan hero in England tended to model himself on the Plutarchan great man.

The interest in Plutarch had not a little to do with the new development of biography which appears as early as the sixteenth century. It became fashionable in France and often took the pattern of parallel lives. For example, Perrault wrote his "Parallèle des Anciens et des Modernes," Racine compared St. Louis and Romulus, Pascal composed a "Comparaison d'Épictète et de Montaigne." North's version of Amyot made the *Lives* familiar in English and his book has been said to be "perhaps the greatest vehicle of the Greek past in our language." [11] But still it must be conceded that the formal influence of Plutarch's *Lives* was slight; it was rather the material on the ancient world and not the form which the lovers of Plutarch borrowed. If the seventeenth and eighteenth centuries are rich in biography, they vary from the short sketch to the full-dress biography, and the only feature which might perhaps be called Plutarchan is the tendency which sometimes appears to idealize the subject and raise him to heroic stature. The name of

Francis Bacon must inevitably be mentioned in this connection also, for Bacon has a deep appreciation of the value of Plutarch as a historian and he is well aware that history is moral. In "Of Studies" he writes that "history makes men wise: it fashions and molds its readers." Again, "history is a globe of precepts" and he finds it "strange that these times have so little esteemed the virtues of the times, as that the writings of lives should be no more frequent." Bacon makes this remark in the *Advancement of Learning*, a work which is filled with allusions to and quotations from Plutarch; and Bacon himself wrote a number of brief portraits which he called "Imagines," and which are almost condensed Plutarchan lives with a moral purpose; the chief biographers of the century like Isaak Walton are in the Plutarchan tradition, demonstrating the strength rather than the weakness of their subjects.

The concept of the ethical nature of history prevails everywhere in England in the seventeenth century. Dryden says in the life of Plutarch, which was prefixed to the "Dryden" translation of the *Lives* (1683–1686), "All history is but the precepts of moral philosophy reduced into examples" and he thus agrees with Amyot's description of the *Lives* as "histories." Some writers combined the two genres, precept and example; and there can be no doubt that they were strongly influenced by the example of Plutarch and by the connection which they saw between the purpose of the *Lives* and that of the *Moralia*. It has been pointed out that in Fuller's *Holy and Profane States* (which Emerson knew well) "the closing paragraph of the Favorite, which introduces the pattern lives, shows that Fuller's characters are the 'precepts of doctrine,' his biographies the 'examples' of famous men, both ancient and modern." [12] His use of two lives together and parallelled is an imitation of Plutarch. The Puritans looked more often to the Old Testament than to Plutarch and the pagan authors for their heroes, and Milton for example, although he owes much to classical authors and especially to Vergil for some epic elements in *Paradise Lost*, shows little indication of the influence of Plutarch.[13] But still it was natural that the Puritans of the New World should bring with them to America the current moralistic concept of history and "they liked especially the moralistic tone of some of the Greeks and Romans." [14] To Cotton Mather, Plutarch was "incomparable" and he duly listed Plutarch among the historians whom "a person of good sense" should know.[15]

The same concept of Plutarch at once the moral biographer of heroes and the historian seems to dominate in the eighteenth century. By now the influence of Plutarch's *Lives* has spread far beyond the royal courts; he is used to inspire heroic conduct in everybody. Not only the great men but also the ordinary man can be heroic in the ancient pattern. Plutarch is the wise benefactor of humanity, portraying for us examples of good human character like Socrates or Solon, Aristides or Epaminondas. The monarchs and emperors may be flattered to be called heroes but more and more often it is pointed out that many of them are not heroes at all, since they lack humanity. Plutarch, it is now felt, was supreme in portraying both the hero and the man, in making the hero human — not a superman, but an ordinary human being whom others in any estate might copy. A new philanthropy is in the wind, or a new humanism. In France this "humanity" of Plutarch is pointed out by Mably, in England by Pope and by Thomson of "The Seasons." Along with "humanity" the term "philanthropy" itself is frequently employed, and this may have been borrowed from Plutarch. Plutarch's humanity can inspire the men of the revolution against tyranny as his heroes had once inspired princes and monarchs. Rousseau tells us how when young he was drawn away by Plutarch from the exotic Oriental romances, which were then so popular, and Agesilaus, Brutus, and Aristides took the place of Orondates, Artamenes, and Juba. It was Plutarch who taught him to see through the false heroes of the older generation and to perceive rather the men who are truly great in their natural simplicity; Plutarch led him to read the history of the free countries; Madam Roland loved Plutarch in the same way and for the same qualities. In Italy, Gioberti com-

pared Plutarch with Dante, Leopardi knew Plutarch the revolutionary well, and there are traces of Plutarch, the hero of revolution
and liberty, in Metastasio's *Catone* and *Artaserse*. So too for Alfieri,
Plutarch was a favorite, and in 1847 Emerson noted in his journal
that Alfieri was "a dear lover of Plutarch and Montaigne." In the
Greek war of independence Plutarchan mottoes and parallels were
used frequently (Ali Pasha was the modern Pyrrhus), parallel lives
of the heroes of the revolution appeared, and Koraïs, the hero of
the new Hellas, translated the *Lives*.

There are several references to Plutarch and recurrences of Plutarchan themes in the dramas of Schiller, who said that he was led
to write *Fiesko* by a remark of Rousseau that only one man in later
ages, Fiesko of Genoa, was worthy of the pen of Plutarch, the
biographer of great men. He outlined the plan for a drama on
Themistocles, and his treatise on the lawmaking of Solon and
Lycurgus drew material obviously from Plutarch. Probably the
greatest influences upon the young Goethe were those of Shakespeare, Rousseau, and Plutarch. Goethe read both *Lives* and *Moralia*
constantly, and in the *Lives* he valued the morality and ethical
principles which have an eternal validity. For him Plutarch is "ein
weiser, gelehrter Mann von Chäronea." [16]

Since Plutarch was held in such high regard, it is not surprising
that his example exerted an extensive influence on contemporary
biography. "Plutarch" meant "biography" at this time, and there
were plans for a modern Plutarch for each nation, a "Volksplutarch"
and a German Plutarch, a Plutarch for women, a Westphalian
Biography. *The British Plutarch* went through several editions and
was enlarged with each edition. It contained "the lives of the most
eminent statesmen, patriots, divines, warriors, philosophers, poets
and artists of Great Britain and Ireland from the accession of Henry
VIII to the present time." Its object, as stated in the introduction,
was to create a type of character: "by having before our eyes the
principles of men of honour and probity, enforced by *example*, we
shall be animated to fix upon some great model to be the rule of

our conduct." [17] Thus "Plutarch" became merely the standard name for any collection of biographies. At the same time universal histories such as those of Müller and Rollin were also popular, and for their accounts of the ancient world they leaned heavily on Plutarch for anecdotes and followed his custom of inserting moral reflections at appropriate places.

In the *Lives*, Phocion, Dion, and Timoleon seem to have been among the most popular in the eighteenth century, as later they are among Emerson's favorite heroes. Their names were adduced frequently as parallels, and this in itself presupposes a fairly thorough acquaintance with these lives. There was almost a Timoleon cult among the radicals and liberals of the late eighteenth and early nineteenth centuries. He was revered as the liberator of Sicily and along with him the lives of other liberators and champions of freedom were widely familiar — Brutus, Demosthenes, and the Gracchi. But while the revolutionaries could point to these ancient heroes of liberty, Phocion's name often occurs as a model of the conservative and the mirror of virtue. These names were bandied about everywhere in a way which is hard for us to appreciate today, and oratory and pamphlet are full of references and knowing allusions to the classical *Lives* of Plutarch. Of the *Lives* in the eighteenth century it has been said, "seldom has a philosopher had such a powerful educational and moral effect, at such a remove in space and time." [18]

If the Plutarch of the *Lives* was claimed as an apostle of liberty by the revolutionaries in France, by the radicals in England, and by the founding fathers in America, it is natural that Plutarch the radical should be also attacked by the conservatives; nor were all his admirers above criticising various aspects of Plutarch. As the nineteenth century advanced these criticisms of Plutarch the biographer became more frequent. The popularity of the *Lives* began to decline and the names of the Greek and Roman heroes occur less frequently in pamphlets and oratory. Two new ways of thought are responsible for this. In the first place, for the first time the concept of history as biography was severely criticized. Already, Lessing had been well aware of Plutarch's shortcomings as a historian but still, near the beginning of the *Laokoön*, drew from Plutarch an epigram of Simonides, "the Greek Voltaire." [19] Voltaire too had pointed out Plutarch's unreliability as a historian, while Rousseau had made fun of his addiction to anecdotes. Macaulay became impatient with the constant appeal by the radicals to the name of Timoleon; while they enjoyed greater freedom than any society had ever known they kept calling for a Brutus or Timoleon to remove their oppressor; and Timoleon's assassination of his brother was a shocking affair; it was only these recent historians who had discovered that it was really a noble and glorious act. Finally he said in "History" that "the heroes of Livy are the most insipid of all beings, the heroes of Plutarch always excepted." Then too in history the nation and its destiny were becoming the object of interest rather than the nation's great leaders. For the study of ancient history, Herodotus, Thucydides, and Demosthenes took the place of Plutarch, since for them, it seemed, history was fact and not, as Plutarchan history seemed to be, something which came second to morals.

In the second place, the mystical overtones which now appear in the concept of the hero himself lead to a different heroic portrait. This view is not entirely new for it was foreshadowed early in the eighteenth century in Vico, whose belief in an age of heroes and whose love of the great individual also sprang from the old Plutarchan concept of history. Vico's hero, however, becomes a demigod, surrounded by a misty aura of superhuman greatness. Though Vico's concept of the hero was temporarily overwhelmed by the more general view of the humane, good, humble, manly hero of eighteenth-century humanism, soon the divine hero returns. His power, indeed his omnipotence, are stressed. Wordsworth's Plutarchan "Dion" of 1816 is almost a landmark in the change of the heroic concept for here the poet, who was always devoted to the *Lives* and who himself had always been strong on the side of liberty, or even of revolution to achieve liberty, warns that the hero who loses his humanity, succumbing to love of power and as a consequence trampling on human freedom, is doomed. Wordsworth seems to be pointing to the new romantic hero and no moral could be plainer than that which the tale of Dion, once regarded almost as a deity by his people, enshrines:

> Him only pleasure leads and peace attends,
> Him, only him, the shield of Jove defends,
> Whose means are fair and spotless as his ends.

The new concept of the heroic, that of the Romantic Movement, has little of Wordsworth's humanity about it. The hero is far from the simple, manly Plutarchan character who always lets duty control his emotions. The romantic hero is sensitive and gives his emotions full play; he is "the man of feeling." So while Fichte at the very beginning of the century uses Plutarch, his heroes are not great individuals but are mastered and conquered by a great idea. They are not even conscious of themselves, but are merely manifestations of God, the infinite will, the absolute life.

From Fichte's answer to the problem of the relation between man and the absolute, springs the heroism and hero worship of Carlyle. Some of Carlyle's ideas seem superficially to resemble those of Plutarch, for example his concept of Providence and the vengeance of Providence and Fate on man. In some points his heroism and hero worship resemble those of Plutarch's admirers, but nothing more. He is not interested in heroes as individuals, but, in heroes as the embodiment of a great idea. If for him history is still the biography of great men, it treats of great men in whom great ideas and energies have taken form. His heroes are not noble, serene, restrained, but vigorous, wild, and not too moral — figures like Danton, Mirabeau, Napoleon. They are inspired supermen carrying out what Carlyle calls "the Divine Idea of the World." The tyrant Dion of Wordsworth's poem would be a hero in Carlyle's eyes, for the end justifies the means. In his hero worship Carlyle is completely undemocratic and has no interest in the human traits of the individual, for the heroes themselves are but the instruments of divine will. The relation of hero-worshipper to hero is that of obedience rather than imitation. Hence Carlyle has little use for Plutarch; indeed he said, "Away with this obsolete ethnic heroism of a Pericles and Epaminondas"; he can show far greater heroes in his own times.[20] Yet in the very concept that history is biography the old influence of Plutarch and the reading of the *Lives* must have made a strong, if early, impression upon Carlyle. His question in *The French Revolution*, "Where are the Plutarchs?" is purely rhetorical when we know of Carlyle's slight regard for Plutarch; but we can hear in many places the complaint which Emerson echoes, that there are now no great men and hence no Plutarchs to write about them. It is expressed as early as 1788 by Charlotte von Lengefeld; it is echoed by Immerman and Sainte-Beuve as well as by Emerson.[21]

If the new kind of heroism, that of the Romantic period, worked against the Plutarchan hero, so also did the new concept of "humanism," a different humanism from that which idolized the simple, humane, Plutarchan man. Winckelmann, who published an edition of Plutarch's "Of Love" and the "Five Tragical Histories of Love" which were of more obvious appeal to the cult of the romantic, was largely responsible for Plutarch's decreasing popularity, with his belief that not morals but beauty is admirable, not the deeds of heroes but works of art. As the Greeks advanced to the front of the stage now, the Romans withdrew and the Greeks who attracted most attention were no longer Plutarch's heroes but Plato and Homer. Instead of the brave military actions of the heroes, readers looked for the calm balance of powers which Winckelmann saw in ancient art and which Schiller and von Humboldt developed in thought. Plutarch was now valued less highly and soon the sphere of his influence had shrunk to the formal side, the occasional use of parallel lives in writing; Sainte-Beuve proposed a new "Plutarch" for France and placed a very high value on Plutarch as a portrayer of character.[22] We might expect that with the decline of the popularity of the *Lives*, the moral essays might come back into their own, especially in an age in which much emphasis is laid on "morals" or "the moral sentiment," but the diminishing number of references to Plutarch are still to the biographer of the heroes, not to the moral essayist.

v i

But there is still another aspect of the influence of Plutarch which can be traced over the centuries between the Renaissance and Emerson and Emerson himself was powerfully attracted by it. This is a formal aspect of the *Moralia* — for here we turn again from the *Lives* to the moral essays — the spread of the practise of the moral essay in the Plutarchan mode. Here again the influence is most strong in the three great devotees of Plutarch — Montaigne, Bacon, and Emerson. At the outset it must be observed that in the classical age Seneca was also a writer of the moral essay, and the chief later moral essayists were acquainted with Seneca as well as with Plutarch. But most of them compared the two and found Seneca too strict and too much of a Stoic; he is a moralist, no doubt, but he is not pleasant or agreeable. He is heavier and more stern. Plutarch is both edifying and enjoyable. In "Of Books" Montaigne contrasted the two, "their instruction is the cream of philosophy"; but Plutarch is easygoing; his opinions are "accomodated to civil society." Seneca's principles are too exacting, too much divorced from what the ordinary man can achieve. Seneca "pushes us on," while Plutarch "guides us."

In the development of the moral essay we should place first chronologically the homilies of the Christian church. At first these were meditations and simple explications of the Scripture but very early it seems that they turned to ethical instruction and hundreds of examples of this sort of thing are found in the Church Fathers, from St. Paul onward. Very early too the Fathers supplemented and elaborated their ideas with ideas taken from pagan ethical

writers like Seneca and Cicero, as we have seen above. With the
Renaissance there arose a new interest in the moral principles of
the pagan world, at first with the collections of classical moral
anecdotes and adages. Pierre Villey has analysed in detail the extent
of the influence of Plutarch on Montaigne.[23] He shows that many
predecessors of Montaigne had written dissertations of an essay form
which multiplied examples of conduct and morality and which were
weighed down with learning and with evidence of wide reading.
Many of the classical anecdotes which these writers employed Montaigne also used, though they wrote with a strong Christian and
authoritative viewpoint. While Montaigne himself in his earlier days
wrote impersonal moral discourses, he gradually achieved a more
personal style. We shall see how closely parallel to this development
was that of Emerson, as he turned away from the orthodox sermon to
pagan morality and ethics, especially to the endurance and hardiness
of an ethic like Plutarch's which he calls "Stoicism."

Montaigne read Plutarch constantly. There are over four hundred
passages in the *Essays* which are derived from Plutarch; he often
acknowledges his debt to him and mentions him sixty-eight times.
He reads both the *Lives* and the *Moralia* and is drawn not only
to the moral judgments but also to the way in which these judgments are presented, in an informal, easy, readable manner. Plutarch's style is casual, employing frequent digressions, and always
genial and natural. It is the style which Montaigne most admires
and which he cultivates himself. Indeed, he admits in "On Some
Verses of Virgil", he goes continually to Plutarch for illustrative
aphorism and anecdote; Plutarch is "so universal and so full" and
"holds out a liberal and not to be exhausted hand of riches and
embellishments." It may not be extravagant to think that the "riches"
are the moral concepts and ideas, the "embellishments" are the
digressions, the anecdotes, the elements of Plutarchan form and
style. So, inspired largely by the *Moralia*, Montaigne invents a new
literary form which he calls the "essai," the reflective essay dealing
with human character. Although this literary type is a new inven-

tion, the essays still show by references and occasionally by title that the *Moralia* constitute their prototype.

His reading and rereading of the *Moralia* render Montaigne's essays simple, vivid, practical, and real. While the *Lives* deal with the great men of the ancient world, the *Moralia* are applicable to all humanity. From the *Moralia* too Montaigne obtains his polemic tone against academic philosophy, be it Stoicism or Epicureanism; from the same source he obtains his eclecticism, drawing from any school whatever is useful to him.

Villey thinks that it was also Plutarch who trained Montaigne in the art of observation of life about him, something which is characteristic of all moral essayists after him. Such observations he used as Plutarch did, for examples of action and guides of conduct. Villey points out that except for the "Apothegms" and the essay "Brute Beasts," Montaigne used most frequently the genuinely moral essays of Plutarch — "Of Hearing," "How to Know a Flatterer from a Friend," "Of the Tranquillity of the Mind," "Concerning Such Whom God Is Slow to Punish," "Of Anger," "Of Curiosity."

But if Montaigne turned the essay toward reflection and a personal and casual tone, employing digression and personal asides as well as classical and Plutarchan borrowings, there were still in the sixteenth century many examples in Italy, France, and England of the older type of essay in the pattern of Erasmus and Guevara, filled with epigrams, adages, and anecdotes, indeed with little other material. In England, Sir Thomas Elyot's *The Governour* is a conspicuous example and here belong also many of the works of Lyly. But between these two something of development can be seen, for Elyot's ethics are stern and solemn, while Lyly stresses rhetoric, demonstrating its prominence in Elizabethan England and laying more emphasis on wit and on eloquence than on ethics in the makeup of the courtier.[24]

Bacon himself composed several collections of apothegms and his early essays as published in 1597, like the early essays of Montaigne, are really selections of his commonplace books, making full use of apothegms, proverbs, and classical examples. Later however, as is well known, he developed a freer style and was perfectly aware that in this he was following the new mode. In the *Advancement of Learning* he wrote that it had become the fashion "out of a few axioms or observations upon any subject, to make a solemn and formal art, filling it with some discourses, and illustrating it with examples, and digesting it into a sensible method." In other words, Bacon (although he did not mention Montaigne until the edition of 1625) went through the same development as the French inventor of the "essai." And there are in other writers such as Elyot, not a few various anticipations of the Baconian essay. Upon the development of these early essays it is now to be recognized that Plutarch's *Moralia* and Aristotle's *Ethics* exerted almost as much influence as Cicero and Seneca, who for long have been given the greater part of the credit in the development of the English essay.[25]

Both contemporaneous with and shortly after Bacon there are a fair number of writers of the essay, both of the older type, the collection of adages, and also of the new, personal, carefully digested, and organized style. Robert Johnson's *Essais*, 1601, are examples of the first type and Sir William Cornwallis' *Essays*, 1601–1602, of the second school of essay writing. Plutarch's name is occasionally cited with commendation for his style, easy and flowing in contrast with that of Seneca, which is attractive but leaves no permanent impression. Dryden, in his introduction to the new translation of the *Lives*, says the same thing as Montaigne: "The arguments of the Grecian, drawn from reason, work themselves into your understanding, and make a deep and lasting impression in your mind." But the list of those who cultivate the moral essay in England would be comparatively small. It almost appears as if this genre has begun to take second place to the sermon, which also borrows from Plutarch and Stoicism. Plutarch's morality is cherished but his essay form is not much imitated.[26]

As the century closes and the Queen Anne period begins, the names of the great essayists of the eighteenth century appear. Addison is a moralist and *The Spectator* and *The Tatler* aim at being moral forces, but the moral qualities inculcated are usually the lesser ones, the qualities which lend themselves to satire rather than to serious teaching. Steele is still more of a moralist; at least Thackeray pointed out his high respect for religion in the home, for women and children. His general tone is moral and he is gentler and kinder than Addison. In general the essayists of this age aim at wholesome entertainment; the instruction occupies a minor role. Many of these essayists show their classical training by quotations and anecdotes, occasionally Plutarchan, but ethical instruction is left either to the systematic philosopher or to the clergyman's sermon. We would find it difficult to point out among writers of the nineteenth century in England a single important practitioner of the moral essay of the type of Montaigne or Bacon. Sermons seem to dominate the field of ethics, while for the Romantics poetry and romances far outshine the essay on morals or character. It is left to a writer on the other side of the ocean to revive for a short time the cult of the Plutarchan moral essay.

vii

Such approximately are the chief strands in the Plutarchan tradition in Western thought, before the time of Emerson. After Emerson, the interest in Plutarch seems to fade out gradually. Emerson's Plutarch essay of 1870 is the last essay on him by a well-known figure. Three years later Archbishop Trench of Dublin published a few lectures on Plutarch; in the eighteenth-century tradition, he considers the greatest lives those of Dion and Timoleon: "the life of Timoleon, as told by Plutarch, waits but a poet's hand, and offers capabilities of poetical treatment at least equal to that of Dion. It is a story of deepest tragical interest, and as told by him, is in some sort a poem already." [27] The poet for whom Timoleon was waiting was not a great poet; it was Herman Melville in America in 1891. Melville knew the story of Timoleon's assassination of his brother

and "Timoleon" is the title poem in a volume which Melville published privately in the year of his death. He was prompted by
Balzac's story, *The Two Brothers*, and "checked the passage describing the mother's marked preference for the flashy older son
over his unspectacular and often unkempt younger brother." [28] This
was the situation in Melville's own family in his youth and in
making it the subject for a poem he perhaps transferred the story
of his own youth to Plutarch's story of Timoleon and Timophanes.
A reference in Canto 6 indicates that Phocion was also known to
Melville, in all probability from Plutarch. Perhaps one of the last
references to the *Moralia* in modern times in the reading of any
well-known figure is a passing reference by Theodore Roosevelt
in a letter to Henry Cabot Lodge; in 1903 he says that he has been
reading "Aristotle's politics and Plutarch's miscellany." [29] Today
the word "Plutarch" makes most people think of the *Lives*, which
are sometimes referred to and which are still available in several
editions; the *Moralia* are unknown except to a few students of the
classics. Today is not Plutarch's day, but perhaps in the future he
may, as Emerson foretold, be rediscovered and read once more.

II

EMERSON'S ACQUAINTANCE
WITH PLUTARCH

*Plutarch, the elixir of Greece and Rome, that is the book
which nations went to compose. If the world's library were
burning, I should as soon fly to rescue that, as Shakspeare
and Plato, or next afterwards.*

Journals

AT the beginning of the nineteenth century when Emerson was
in his boyhood, "Plutarch" means the *Lives* and usually the lives
in the Dryden or Langhorne translation. If boys began Greek early,
it would not be with Plutarch but Xenophon and later Plato. If
we are to try to answer the questions, "How well did Emerson
know Plutarch? What did he specially like in Plutarch?" we should
begin by noticing that he was not particularly precocious in his study
of Greek, but that like his contemporaries he early obtained some
acquaintance with the *Lives* in translation. It is doubtful if he had,
like Theodore Parker, read Homer and Plutarch by the time he
was eight years old, but certainly he met the *Lives* when he was
still a boy. His son Edward tells us that his father made him read
the *Lives* when he was fourteen; that it was at first irksome, but
that Lycurgus, Archimedes, Hannibal, Scipio, Caesar, and Cato
soon came to be liked and that the personality of the author starts
to make some impression even on the young reader, as when, for
instance, Plutarch interrupts the narrative to censure Cato's inhu-

manity in selling slaves when they had outlived their usefulness.[1] Emerson himself probably read the *Lives*, and probably these same ones, when he was a boy. In several passages he speaks of boys relieving their serious study surreptitiously at home or in school with Plutarch and in one of these passages he indicates that it was the anecdotes which remained in his own memory and there even replaced the great figures of history. Emerson was finding, like many generations before him, that the anecdotes of Plutarch are often his most attractive characteristic and that they teach more than direct ethical instruction can do; when he himself became a teacher he wrote out Plutarchan anecdotes for his pupils and he recommended Plutarch for schoolboys.[2]

The names of some of the Greek and Roman heroes, then, came to mean something for these boys of the early nineteenth century. One of Emerson's earliest attempts at writing is dated by Rusk as of 1815; it is a poem entitled "Poetical Essay" and tells of the historical fights led by "Independence." [3] The examples from ancient history include Phocion and Demosthenes against Philip of Macedon, and it is most probable that he knew both either from the *Lives* or from some general history like that of Rollin or Goldsmith, the two most popular ones, which made use of Plutarch.

By the time he was ready to enter Harvard College, however, Emerson was fully aware that the classics were not everything. He wrote then to his older brother: "I do not think it necessary to understand Mathematicks & Greek thoroughly, to be a good, useful, or even *great* man"; but he adds, "do not be afraid, for I do mean to study them, though not with an equal interest to the other studies." [4] He still read Plutarch when he had leisure; he may be thinking of his own college days when he writes years later again to his brother about the education of his nephew: "What if he has gone through the course at Columbia? It will only permit him to be a better & more thoroughly-grounded scholar, & allow him time for Plutarch & Gibbon, or whatever subsidiary studies." [5] Again "Plutarch" here means "Langhorne" in all probability, for Emerson's attitude towards reading the original Latin and Greek and reading translations is well known; he gained sufficient Greek to copy phrases or verses into his journals and, in his old age, to compare Goodwin's translation with the original, but after he left college, almost all his reading of the classics or of French or German writers was done in translation; so he read Montaigne in Cotton's translation, the Neoplatonists in that of Thomas Taylor, the *Lives* in Langhorne and in the "Dryden" version, the *Moralia* in the "Several Hands" translation.[6]

We may be certain, I think, that Emerson was still not acquainted with Plutarch's *Moralia* when he wrote his two college prize essays, "A Dissertation on the Character of Socrates" in 1820, and "A Dissertation on the Present State of Ethical Philosophy" in 1821.[7] Surely if he had read Plutarch's "Discourse Concerning Socrates's Daemon" he would have mentioned it in his first essay along with Xenophon and Plato as a source of our knowledge of ancient opinion about the operations of the mysterious thing which Socrates called his "daemon" or "daemonion." This omission becomes pointed when Emerson mentions Diogenes Laertius; the choice of this recorder of anecdotes and opinions is the more significant because Plutarch is the only other extant source of such matters. Further, had Emerson read the *Moralia* he would not have concluded the outline of ancient ethical thought in "The Present State of Ethical Philosophy" with the remark: "With Seneca and Marcus Aurelius closes the line of ancient moralists, and with them the chief praise of human ingenuity and wisdom." Surely he would also have included Plutarch, one of the greatest moralists of the ancient world, if he were acquainted with the *Moralia*; in later life, when listing thinkers, and especially ethical thinkers, Emerson would not for a moment omit his name. Instead, the only possible reference to Plutarch in these essays is an oblique one to the *Lives*.[8] Thus we can conclude that to Emerson by 1821 "Plutarch" meant the author of the *Lives* only.

Although he did not yet know Plutarch's moral essays, Emerson's two prize essays were a landmark in his development and, in a

roundabout way, may be said to have led him to his later devotion
to Plutarch. Perhaps the fact that his ability at essay writing was
thus recognized led him to make further acquaintance with the
greatest practitioners of the moral essay, Plutarch, Montaigne, and
Bacon; this acquaintance gradually proved to him that he himself
had an affinity, a natural ability in the writing of moral essays of
the classical type. After his college days the occasional references
to passages or anecdotes in the *Lives* continue to appear in journals
and letters and have some interest in that they show that he is still
very much in the eighteenth-century Plutarchan tradition, now
beginning to decline, when tags and anecdotes from Plutarch were
commonly quoted and the average reader or audience would be
likely to be acquainted with them; there is no strong feeling yet
that such quotations are old fashioned or out-of-date. The earliest
journal reference to Plutarch occurs in 1822 and a little later in that
same year there is a passage which seems to come from the life of
Antony; occasionally in the journals of the next few years there
are random indications of a reading of the *Lives* — those of Aristides, Cato, Aemilius Paulus — but some of these are tags which
could have been met in a variety of books.[9]

So far Emerson is doing much the same as many of his contemporaries, to whom as boys the *Lives* were fairly well known. But
soon we see that he seems to have met the *Moralia* also and this
point is significant because the *Moralia* were rarely read and evoked
very little interest. The record of books borrowed by the Emerson
family from the Boston Library Society shows that the third volume
of the fifth edition of the "Several Hands" translation was borrowed
in 1825, the second, third, and fourth volumes in 1828, the fourth
and fifth in 1829.[10] We can trace Emerson's reading of the *Moralia*
still further, for in 1826 he borrowed from Harvard College Library
the fifteenth volume of Amyot's *Oeuvres de Plutarque*, a volume
containing some of the *Moralia*.[11] This does not mean that he had
forsaken the *Lives*, however. References to them continue and become more specific while his knowledge of Plutarch widens to

include the *Moralia*. By August 1827, for example, we can tell definitely for the first time that he is using Langhorne's version of the *Lives*; he transcribes the following passage from the life of Agesilaus in Langhorne's rendering (*Journals* 2. 216): "Whenever Agesilaus made an excursion, he lodged in the temples most renowned for sanctity; and whereas upon many occasions we do not choose that men should see what we are about, he was desirous to have the gods themselves inspectors and witnesses of his conduct." [12] In 1827 Emerson borrowed from Harvard Amyot's fourth volume, containing the *Lives* from Philopoemen to Sulla; [13] the next year he borrowed the fourteenth and nineteenth volumes, which include some of the *Moralia*. Letters of 1828 mirror this reading. When saying that the writer must abandon himself, he probably draws on the life of Pericles for the figure, "Like Pericles let him thunder and lighten." Another letter of the same year mentions the life of Marcellus, in which Emerson met one of his favorite heroes, Archimedes. The year 1828 also provides us for the first time with definite evidence of his use of the *Moralia*; Emerson writes (*Journals* 2. 228): "Demades told the Athenians that he had observed that they never treated of peace except in black clothes; so, says Plutarch, men never reduce their diet except amidst cataplasms, clysters and medicines; so also men do not turn for enjoyment to another world till their hopes in this have failed them." [14] The last clause seems to be Emerson's own but the rest is derived from the "Rules for the Preservation of Health" (*Moralia* 1. 259). He was now able to write to his brother Charles: "Much obliged to you for the Plutarch tis fine reading though I have seen most of this volume before in French." [15]

The year 1830 is another landmark in the development of Emerson's love of Plutarch. Of the Greek philosophers, he had already met Socrates and Plato; that would be sufficient for the ordinary college graduate and for the ordinary man's acquaintance with Greek philosophy. It is an age of Plato and idealism and few except historians of philosophy would know more than the names of the

Greek pre-Socratic philosophers. But in 1830 Emerson made numerous notes on the cosmic ideas of the early philosophers — Thales, Anaximander, Pythagoras, Xenophanes, Anaximenes, Heraclitus, Anaxagoras, Democritus, Empedocles, Zeno. He met them in Gérando's *Histoire Comparée des Systèmes de Philosophie*, which made extensive use of Plutarch's collection of short statements (scarcely more than notes themselves) on the views of the Greek philosophers.[16] This is to use Plutarch for a purpose rather different from the common one at the time — it is to use him as a historian of Greek thought on the universe. The statements are short and bald, so compressed that nowadays we should say that they are almost valueless. But still it is interesting that Emerson, before he has formulated his own philosophy and at a time when he has just become acquainted with the German Transcendentalists and with Coleridge, is surveying the field. He is no Platonist yet and he indicates that he appreciates the fact that there were philosophers before Plato. But he does not seem drawn to any one of them in particular unless he shows perhaps a little more interest in Heraclitus and his theory of flux than in the other pre-Socratic cosmic theories. Xenophanes and Empedocles with their stress on unity amid diversity also attracted him and while the ideas of Heraclitus made frequent subsequent appearances in his writing, Gérando's remarks on Xenophanes and Empedocles duly made their way, along with those on Heraclitus, into the poems "Xenophanes," "Empedocles," "Each and All," and "Rhodora." [17]

In the journals Emerson's predilection for the *Moralia* is immediately evident. The indications of his reading of the *Moralia* (at least when the journals are used as guides) far outnumber traces of the influence of the *Lives*, even though Emerson was strongly addicted to biography. To the journal references must be added "lustres" from Plutarch which he incorporated directly into lectures and sermons, both published and unpublished. To these references must also be added the numerous anecdotes and quotations whose sources have not formerly been identified but which can now be shown to come from Plutarch. They would not bulk large in the complete volume of all the journals, it is true, but the striking thing about this devotion to Plutarch is that the indications of it are scattered through the writing of many years, from Emerson's youth until not long before his death, and the same is true of the letters.

The journals show that Emerson had his favorite works within both the *Lives* and the *Moralia*; when he had a choice, as in the case of the life of Demosthenes and the much shorter version in the "Lives of the Ten Attic Orators" in the *Moralia*, it was to the *Moralia* that he resorted; because he found here anecdotes and quotations, rather than the detailed and dull history of events, Plutarch's moral essays soon became familiar to him and were valued highly.

According to the journals and letters Emerson's notes on Plutarch from 1830 on run something like this: 1830, "Political Precepts" and "Of Those Sentiments concerning Nature . . ." (but indirectly, in Gérando); 1831, "Of Garrulity" (but indirectly, in Jeremy Taylor and similarly the "Laconic Apothegms," in Montaigne); 1832, "Whether Vice Is Sufficient to Render a Man Unhappy," the lives of Pericles, Phocion, and Dion; 1833, "Of Tranquillity"; 1834, "Lives of the Ten Attic Orators," "Of Isis and Osiris," "Why the Oracles Cease to Give Answers," "Why the Pythian Priestess Ceases Her Oracles in Verse," "Of Inquisitiveness"; 1835, "Laconic Apothegms," "Of Banishment," "Why the Pythian Priestess Ceases Her Oracles in Verse," the life of Lycurgus; 1836 "Symposiacs"; in 1837 he is "raffling the pages of Plutarch's 'Morals,' " and makes numerous extracts from three volumes of the *Moralia*, from "Of Love," "Concerning Such Whom God Is Slow to Punish," "Of Common Conceptions against the Stoics," "Discourse to an Unlearned Prince," "Of Isis and Osiris," "Of Brotherly Love," "Why the Pythian Priestess Ceases Her Oracles in Verse," "Symposiacs," "Consolation to Apollonius," "Concerning the Cure of Anger," "Of Banishment." The life of Brutus is quoted and Margaret Fuller borrows a volume of the *Moralia* from him; 1838, "Why the Oracles Cease to Give Answers," "A Discourse concerning Socrates's Daemon"; 1839, perhaps the lives of Fabius and Dion, "Why the Oracles Cease to Give Answers," "How a Man May Praise Himself without Being Envied," "Of Isis and Osiris"; 1841, lives of Cleomenes, the Gracchi, Demosthenes, Dion, Demetrius, Aratus, "Apothegms of Kings," "That Pleasure Is Not Attainable According to Epicurus"; 1845, life of Lycurgus, "Symposiacs"; 1847 shows the motto for his journal from "Why the Pythian Priestess Ceases Her Oracles in Verse," perhaps the life of Pericles and "Of Those Sentiments concerning Nature . . ."; 1848, the life of Marcellus, "That Pleasure Is Not Attainable According to Epicurus," "A Discourse concerning Socrates's Daemon"; 1850, "Of Those Sentiments concerning Nature . . . ," the life of Marcellus; 1852, life of Demetrius, the life of Alexander, "Whether the Athenians Were More Warlike . . ."; in 1857 he is awaiting the announcement of the Bohn translation of the *Moralia*; some time between 1860 and 1866, "How a Man May Be Sensible of His Progress in Virtue," "How a Young Man Ought to Hear Poems"; 1862, life of Pericles or "Whether an Aged Man Ought to Meddle in State Affairs," the life of Aemilius Paulus; 1862–1863, the life of Alcibiades; 1868, "Whether an Aged Man Ought to Meddle in State Affairs"; in 1869, perhaps "Of Isis and Osiris" and in this year he is going to give a series of readings in Boston and some extracts are to come from "Plutarch's Morals"; in this year he was reading the *Moralia* fairly thoroughly for he was writing his introduction to Goodwin's revision of the "Several Hands" translation; 1870, "Whether an Aged Man Ought to Meddle in State Affairs," "Of Envy and Hatred," "Of the Cure of Anger," "Of the Tranquillity of the Mind." He compares several passages in Goodwin with the old version and consults the original Greek; one of the last journal entries which refers to Plutarch, in 1873, refers to "Of the Tranquillity of the Mind." It is difficult to date at all the later journals and notebooks but they refer to or quote from "Customs of the Lacedaemonians," "Of the Tranquillity of the Mind," "Parallels between Greeks and Romans," "Whether an Aged Man Ought to Meddle in State Affairs," "Against Running in Debt," "Symposiacs," "How a Young Man Ought to Hear Poems," "Why the Oracles Cease to Give Answers," "Why the Pythian Priestess Ceases Her Oracles in Verse," "Of the Eating of Flesh."

This chronological list shows the predominance of the *Moralia* over the *Lives* and it also shows again in a rough way which essays of the *Moralia* were most read by Emerson. The omissions are also significant. He finds nothing in and probably has not read the more technical essays in the *Moralia*, that is, the essay on the face in the moon, the "Platonic Questions," or the essay on the Timaeus, the essay on music. He prefers the genuinely moral essays, those which deal with men, character, and morals. We might expect the essay entitled "On Moral Virtue" to attract him; he seems to have known it but it never rated highly with him. The reason seems obvious. It is philosophical and rather technically philosophical. It contains a few quotations of Greek poetry, but at the most only one or two anecdotes. It abandons the dialogue form, the setting and the portrayal of the participants, the preliminary byplay and argument which made other essays of the *Moralia* so attractive.

We have seen that notes on Plutarch are fairly evenly distributed over many years. Several modifying factors in connection with this chronological listing, however, should be kept in mind. First, Emerson does not always quote directly from his reading. He may be recalling something which he has read some time before; occasionally an error or a wrong attribution indicates this. Or he may be quoting from another devoted Plutarchan like Montaigne, Bacon, Sir Thomas Browne, or Cudworth; for example, as we have seen, he obtains most of his knowledge of the pre-Socratic philosophers from Plutarch but he met them first not in Plutarch but at second hand, in Gérando. Sometimes too a familiar anecdote of classical times stems from other classical writers besides Plutarch; thus a reference to Dion need not necessarily indicate that Emerson has been reading Plutarch's biography. Thirdly, if he transcribes an aphorism or anecdote from Plutarch we cannot always assume that he has read the entire work in which he found it. His lists of books "to be read" or of books borrowed from libraries are long, but it is doubtful whether he read many of them thoroughly. As Oliver Wendell Holmes put it, Emerson does not often tackle "profound study." He reads for "a few brilliant and suggestive glimpses," [18] and as Emerson himself says in "The American Scholar," the discerning reader, even in Plato or Shakespeare, will read "only the authentic utterances of the oracle." He rejects the remainder, "were it never so many times Plato's and Shakspeare's." Finally, Emerson's published works often contain passages from Plutarch which do not occur in the journals. While he often looks through his journals and notebooks for illustrations and parallels, he sometimes uses the *Moralia* directly when he is composing an essay. This is specially striking in Emerson's essay "Love"; only once in his journals (in 1837) does Emerson make a quotation from Plutarch's "Of Love"; yet, as we shall see, he uses Plutarch's essay very closely when he comes to write on the same topic.

By 1837 Emerson was well acquainted with both *Lives* and *Moralia*. In that year he made fairly extensive notes, mostly of quotations from Greek poetry, in his journals from the latter; from this time on few volumes of the journals are without a quotation from Plutarch or a reference to him or to one of his great men. Again and again Emerson turned to Plutarch for quotations from poetry, for notes on the views of the Greek philosophers, for anecdotes and aphorisms of the Greek and Roman heroes. Although he read constantly in a great variety of writings his predominant taste was for "old and famed" books; among the classical authors he recommended (in "Books") Plutarch along with Herodotus, Aeschylus, Aristophanes, and Plato. Livy also was included "but one of the short English compends, some Goldsmith or Ferguson, should be used, that will place in the cycle the bright stars of Plutarch." Here as always Emerson finds history specially useful when it is expressed with the illuminating anecdotes and the personal biographical treatment which Plutarch furnished. This bias towards biography, which puts Emerson in the "history is biography" tradition which was at this time on the decline, comes out again in the same essay, "Books," when he discusses the important books of the Middle Ages and of modern times. When he gives examples of the great history of great individuals, Plutarch's name appears; books "impart sympathetic activity to the moral power. Go with mean people and you think life is mean. Then read Plutarch, and the world is a proud place, peopled with men of positive quality, with heroes and demigods standing around us, who will not let us sleep." Here we see Emerson accepting another element in the traditional view of history in the form of lives. He seems to feel that man has a natural instinct towards morality and goodness but that by the very possession of this he is sometimes made to feel alone and unable to struggle against conformity, against fate. The history of great men can inspire and raise up the solitary individual, for he can then perceive that others, even the greatest, have felt as he feels. They can inspire the reader with something of their own courage and perseverence. We may observe in passing that the phrase "who will not let us sleep" echoes Themistocles' remark, quoted in Plutarch several times, that the trophies of Miltiades would not let him sleep. Emerson noticed it and here his almost unconscious borrowing of a Plutarchan apothegm shows neatly how he reads his Plutarch.[19] He does the same thing in "Heroism." Here he says of the *Lives*, "we need books of this tart cathartic virtue more than books of political science or of private economy. Life is a festival only to the wise." Even while writing about the *Lives* (for he is talking of heroes and heroism), a "lustre" from the *Moralia* is at the back of his mind, for the last sentence is a clear reminiscence of Plutarch's "to the good man every day is a festival," from one of Emerson's favorite essays in the *Moralia*, "Of the Tranquillity of the Mind." [20]

In "Books," one of the last essays which he himself published,

Emerson gives a longer statement than usual of what he finds valuable in Plutarch and here for the first time we see him differentiate between the biographies and the essays, affirming what he cherishes in each. He restates his debt to the *Lives*: they are "readable" and "invigorating," but they are still easily accessible; so he passes on to the less familiar "Morals" and since they are unfamiliar he goes into some detail in outlining their value to him. He singles out a few individual essays for special mention and they are the ones which we know he uses most frequently — "A Discourse concerning Socrates's Daemon," "Of Isis and Osiris," "Of Progress in Virtue," "Of Garrulity," and "Of Love." He stresses the variety of Plutarch's style, probably thinking of the "riches and embellishments" which Montaigne found in him, the inspiring poetry, the philosophical opinions (which we have seen he knew as early as 1830), the picturesque details which give the setting of the dialogue in a Greek household, or a Greek temple, the background for the dialogues on moral conduct. The omissions or the topics which Emerson passes over briefly are also a good key to what he values in Plutarch. He does not read Plutarch as a philosopher and he knows that as a historian he is unreliable, but it is the "lustres," the phrases, the vignettes, the small descriptive details which attract him and which for him turn what otherwise would have been dry moral discourses into small fragments of life, bright and vivid. He compares the three classical banquet scenes, the *Symposium* of Plato, the same work of Xenophon, and Plutarch's "Banquet of the Seven Wise Men." Again it is the setting and the life which he observes. Plutarch's banquet is "a charming portraiture of ancient manners and discourse, and is as clear as the voice of a fife, and entertaining as a French novel." This emphasis on the simple, natural picture of Greek life rather than on the deeper content of Plutarch is characteristic of Emerson's attitude to the Greeks and it too is part of the common Hellenism of his time everywhere; it is again of the eighteenth century; for the young Goethe, for instance, exhibits exactly the same attitude and shows the same preferences in his interest in the classical world.

But Emerson finds Plutarch not only inspiring in a lofty sense but also on a more ordinary plane. He stimulates thinking and provides the initial impulse to writing; in "Inspiration" Emerson says that it makes no difference what man or person gives him this initial impulse or however far from his topic the impulse is; a random remark may start a chain of thought; and we are told repeatedly that Plutarch gives such an impulse frequently; in *Journals* 10. 101 Emerson says that Marcus Aurelius or Plato or Plutarch are "agreeable and suggestive books to me" while St. Paul and St. John are not; and in 1841 he calls such a book "spermatic" and gives as examples Plato and Plotinus and Plutarch (*Journals* 5. 508); again he called Plutarch "his tuning-key when he was about to write." [21]

We thus get to know how Emerson, at least on occasion, started an essay; he found the title in another work, or an epigram met his eye as a suitable beginning for the first paragraph and he was off on his essay, sometimes following his original no farther, at other times following it fairly closely for several pages or returning to it from time to time for a quotable "sentence."

When he had thus discovered Plutarch and proved the value to himself of both *Lives* and *Moralia*, it is not surprising that we find him telling his friends about Plutarch and urging them to read him; he lends the *Moralia* to Margaret Fuller and persuades one of his English acquaintances to read them also.[22] It has been said that it was Emerson who persuaded Arthur Hugh Clough to translate some of the *Lives* once more; perhaps it was at Emerson's instigation that it was published in America at a time when as Clough himself said, England "thinks Plutarch an old fool." [23] He was specially attracted to other writers if they appreciated Plutarch. This was the case with Montaigne and Cudworth and later with Alfieri. It may well be chiefly Montaigne's devotion to Plutarch which drew

Emerson to him, for he could never read Montaigne far without coming across the Plutarchan element. Because of this he liked Montaigne's short essay on books with its tribute to Plutarch and he echoes perhaps unconsciously another such tribute of Montaigne. He wrote to his brother William in 1841 (*Letters* 2. 444): "Do you never read Plutarch? I can never have done with him. Only yesterday I read the life of Cleomenes & of the Gracchi & Demosthenes: and I keep the 'Morals' always near me. They are admirable Prayer books." In this striking tribute to both aspects of Plutarch's work surely "they are admirable Prayer books" is an echo of Montaigne's tribute to Amyot's Plutarch which Emerson himself quoted many years later in his Plutarch essay: "Montaigne, in 1589, says: 'We dunces had been lost, had not this book raised us out of the dirt. By this favor of his we dare now speak and write. The ladies are able to read to schoolmasters. 'T is our breviary.'" So across the years one Plutarch devotee echoes another.

In "Books," Emerson draws attention once more to Plutarch's moral essays and reinforces the already widespread interest in the *Lives*, which he shows are not merely wholesome schoolbooks for boys. It was perhaps also Emerson's pointing out that Plutarch was not merely useful and entertaining as biographer but also a delightful essayist which aroused, after a century or more, fresh interest in the *Moralia*. So in the 1860's, Professor Goodwin of Harvard revised the old familiar seventeenth-century "Several Hands" translation. Since his devotion to these essays must have been well known at Harvard, it was natural that Emerson should be asked to contribute the introductory essay. Here then almost at the end of his writing career he had a further opportunity to write about one of his favorite authors and to acknowledge his debt to Plutarch.

In this essay we might expect that Emerson would come out with a lively, penetrating study of the Plutarch of the *Moralia*. It is a readable, useful introduction to the work — which after all was Emerson's aim — but it has little of the inspiration and none of the vigor which we associate with the younger Emerson. The factual,

down-to-earth treatment is filled out with the sort of quotation
which always caught the writer's eye. Comments on, and occasional
criticisms of, Plutarch are to a great extent repetitions of remarks
published in former essays, or used in lectures and journals. Even
so, Emerson does put together a statement of what he found valuable in Plutarch, and occasionally we are given fresh light on the
reasons for his lifelong devotion to him.

Emerson outlines something of the history of the popularity of
Plutarch in France and England from Amyot on. There is a paragraph on Plutarch's talent which Oliver Wendell Holmes thought
might serve as a portrait of Emerson himself. Emerson observes
that Plutarch's gifts were not intellectual, but were rather gifts of
sympathy, universality, objectivity, and morality. This is the same
sort of thing that Montaigne had already said, but we cannot doubt
that Emerson recalls his own long use of Plutarch when he mentions Plutarch's value as a source of classical stories and anecdotes
conveniently put together — "a compend of all accepted traditions."
Here he is once again in the old tradition of Plutarch readers — he
finds Plutarch to be a sort of handbook of classical antiquity, of
history, mythology, religion, philosophy. Towards the end of this
section he says, "But what specially marks him, he is a chief example
of the illumination of the intellect by the force of morals." These
two elements sum up well what Emerson found in him. Not only
does Plutarch provide illustrative anecdote and "precious sentences
. . . of authors whose books are lost," thus giving the reader the
pleasure of recognizing the original sources of expression which
have become proverbial, but his morality is always sound and
applicable today. His thought and philosophical ideas are always
tinged with the ethical view, with an emphasis on good conduct. In
Plutarch there is always the natural "moral sentiment" which Emerson prizes wherever he finds it.

Emerson comes at this again from a different angle. Plutarch
is a cultured gentleman, what we would call a well-rounded man,
mixing easily with all types of human society, and with wide in-

terests. He can range over all aspects of life, from the court and
the camp to "the forge, farm, kitchen and cellar and every utensil
and use," with the wise eye of a poet; like Emerson himself, he can

> Give to barrows, trays and pans
> Grace and glimmer of romance.

He is "tolerant even of vice, if he finds it genial." In addition to the
moralist whose themes are all noble, great, and good, Emerson
discerns the man who is aware of the mixture of good and evil
in every man and does not neglect the darker aspects of human
character. But always Plutarch's religious nature saves him from
Montaigne's "wantonness." He is plain spoken but his "moral
sentiment is always pure." Emerson also sees the kinship between
himself and Plutarch in their eclectic natures. He likes Plutarch's
freedom from dogmatism; he does not adhere to any extreme viewpoint. Nature and common sense are always dominant. In this
Emerson seems to show his kinship with another Plutarchan tradition, that of the Neostoics of the seventeenth century, when philosophy without the dogmatism of religion was a better consolation
for mortals than that furnished by the religion of creed and
revelation.

He soon returns to Plutarch's attractive style, to his "striking
similes" and "happy anecdotes." Plutarch in a rich and varied style
describes what he sees; and his keen, objective eyes see "everything
that moves, shines or threatens in nature or art, or thought or
dreams." His style is rapid and exciting as though he had at his
finger tips more anecdotes than he could ever use. To Emerson
these elements account for Plutarch's readability and spontaneity;
Plutarch, he says, "prattles history."

Emerson's remarks on the philosophical essays of Plutarch,
especially on "Of those Sentiments concerning Nature . . . ," which
gives the opinions of the philosophers on various philosophical problems, have more interest than other sections of the essay since they
show almost for the first time a development, or at least a change,

in his attitude to one aspect of Plutarch. Originally he had set a high value on these opinions of the philosophers and had observed several times that they anticipated the theories of modern thinkers. Now however, years later, he can see that they are for the most part, "very crude," even "puerile." He qualifies this opinion, however, by adding, "when Thales, Anaximenes or Anaximander are quoted, it is really a good judgment." This is vague, but he seems to mean that the opinions of these philosophers are, in spite of their age, still close to modern theories. This commendation of Thales and Anaximander does not mean that Emerson is becoming less interested in Heraclitus and the Stoics who draw on him, for in several of the opinions the views of Thales or Anaximander and the Stoics are made by Plutarch to coincide, and at least two of these passages are marked in Emerson's own copy of the *Moralia*.

This section of the essay indicates another area in which Emerson's interests are closely kindred to those of Plutarch — the phenomena of natural science. Plutarch displays great interest in the physical aspects of the operation of oracles, the various theories about the universe and natural phenomena held by the Greek philosophers, and the *curiosa* of nature. Similarly, no reader of Emerson can fail to be impressed by his awareness of the latest developments of science and nature study and his skill in the acute observation of nature. Inevitably, because of scientific development, he had come to consider many of Plutarch's theories "crude opinions." Thus, to him, Plutarch's natural history "is that of a lover and poet, and not of a physicist" and he seems drawn more to Plutarch's remarks on the virtues of animals and the indications of his all-embracing kindness and humanity. Despite this gap between them, Emerson and Plutarch have much in common in this field. Although the chief interests of both men are moral and ethical, they consider natural phenomena of vital and perennial interest as part of the operation of nature and natural law.

Plutarch's interest in stories of travel and in antiquarianism also has its parallel in Emerson, who read books of travel extensively and turned repeatedly to works on antiquities and archaeology. Each lived in a town where history had been made by a battle; therefore local history and local heroes had a natural appeal to both.

Emerson ventures a brief paragraph of contrast between Seneca and Plutarch, saying what Montaigne [24] and Dryden had said before him. He finds Seneca less humane, drier, and more didactic than Plutarch. Plutarch has the greater sympathy, he enjoys life and is more contented than Seneca, who is harder and sterner, more given to preaching. He seems to mean that Seneca is a Stoic while Plutarch is a Platonist, taking from Stoicism only its happier, less ascetic element. Approving Plutarch for wearing his garb of a philosopher lightly, Emerson gives a disguised quotation from the *Moralia* on the merit of philosophizing by means of mirth, which at the same time has a serious objective beneath it.[25]

Then for several pages he strings together a number of quotations from the *Moralia* to illustrate the moral ideas of Plutarch — on the gods, on immortality, on heroism, against fortune, on virtue.[26] They depict Plutarch's amiability and human kindness, which Emerson compares with that of Charles Lamb. Although he is well aware that Plutarch has nothing good to say of the Stoic school of thought, Emerson is equally aware that there is a Stoic element in Plutarch — he is "Stoic in his fight with Fortune, with vices, effeminacy and indolence." He gives a roll call of heroic names — Leonidas, Agesilaus, Aristides, Phocion, Themistocles, Demosthenes, Epaminondas, Caesar, Cato. Along with the heroic stories of these great men in the *Lives* and the *Moralia* Emerson places the essays on the fortune of Alexander which treated Alexander as a Greek hero who introduced civilization to the East. He looks up and uses again a passage from one of these essays which he had paraphrased in 1838 for his essay, "War." [27] Thus he finds his heroic stories in the *Moralia* as well as in the *Lives* themselves, and his concept of the hero, if it is Plutarchan, is drawn just as much from the moral essays as from the biographies.

In his peroration he mentions two of his favorite works in the collection of the *Moralia*, the "Laconic Apothegms" and the "Apothegms of Kings and Great Commanders."

Thus, in one of Emerson's last published works, he pays his tribute to the Plutarch of the *Moralia*. The essay is not entirely satisfactory. A great part of it consists of a string of quotations, many of which he had noted and used many years before. There are errors of carelessness — the incorrect attribution of an epigram to Seneca which really belongs to Plutarch; the incorrect dating of the first printed edition of the works of Plutarch; [28] the occasional use of the old edition rather than the new revised edition which this essay was to introduce. Yet still the Plutarch essay serves as the final effective piece of evidence of his devotion to the *Moralia* which we have traced bit by bit through his writings.

We can now see something of the history of Emerson's acquaintance with Plutarch. Like his contemporaries, when he was a boy he knew the *Lives* in translation and by 1828 he seems to have become acquainted with the *Moralia*; in 1830 he met Plutarch the historian of pre-Socratic Greek philosophy and here perhaps begins his interest in Heraclitus and Stoicism. From this time on all his writing shows traces of random reading of both the *Lives* and the *Moralia*. No particular pattern is evident in this reading; his constant use of old journals and of old essays in the fashioning of new ones prevents us finding a pattern. He seems often to have glanced through Plutarch looking for a "lustre." His two longest tributes to Plutarch both belong to his last years as an author, but they sum up attitudes which he had felt for many years and had expressed in journals and letters. They confirm the statement that he valued the *Moralia* just as highly, or more highly than the *Lives*.

We can also see something of Emerson's aim in reading Plutarch. He finds this Greek, writing about the Greeks, simple, natural, and readable. Plutarch's morality is inspiring, invigorating, and encouraging to the ordinary man living many centuries after him. He inspires the moral power by the great examples he adduces. In this Emerson is in the old tradition of Plutarchans like Montaigne.

Occasionally also he uses Plutarch as a handbook of ancient philosophy and classical antiquity and at the same time for a vivid, lively portrayal of the picturesque background of Greek life, the element which his stage setting and anecdotes and dialogue provide. Here again Emerson is in the old Plutarchan tradition which used him as a handbook of Greek antiquity, a picture of the life of Greek gentlemen. He also appreciates fully Plutarch's literary style, casual and lively, using to the full the resources of anecdote, epigram, and digression. Plutarch is in this aspect inspiring in another sense — he sets the writer to work by giving him a "lustre" which can provide a theme for an essay or even supply a thought or an epigram which starts another train of thought.

Several of these elements which put Emerson in debt to Plutarch must be examined further in the subsequent chapters. Specifically we shall examine Emerson's attitude towards the classical world, the particular nature of his concept of the hero, the source of his knowledge of Greek philosophy and the classical element in his own thought, the way in which he uses Plutarch in his own writings, and finally the connection between his own essays and the classical moral essays like those of Plutarch. For Emerson valued Plutarch much more than the record of his reading and his published tributes to Plutarch, which we have described above, might indicate.

III

GREEK SIMPLICITY

*The Grecian state is the era of the bodily nature, the per-
fection of the senses, — of the spiritual nature unfolded in
strict unity with the body. . . . The manners of that period
are plain and fierce. . . . Luxury and elegance are not
known.*

"History"

In his many references to the classical world we can see Emerson's
predilection for the Greeks over the Romans; the Romans whom
he selects for special reference or whom he includes in his lists of
great names are usually Stoics, as the Greeks are often Spartans. In
this liking for the Greeks he is by no means outside the stream of
tradition, but on the contrary, besides exhibiting an interest in
Plutarch which is a hold over from the eighteenth century, he is also
a typical follower of the Neo-Hellenic school, which also began in
the eighteenth century but flourished and was omnipresent in the
early nineteenth century and in the Romantic Movement. His attitude toward the Greeks is derived both from his reading of Plutarch
and from the prevalent view of his time.

The Augustan age in England and indeed the eighteenth century
in Europe and America gave as much place to Romans as to Greeks
in the ancient world and the Stoicism which the Augustans advocated and tried to emulate was that of Cato — Addison's tragedy
treated a hero whose name and philosophy must have been fairly

widely familiar. Later the Plutarchan heroes of liberty, Phocion and Timoleon, take the place of Cato. At the same time, it is sometimes said, the eighteenth-century classicism begins to fade before the influence of themes from the Middle Ages and from chivalry. But it is the Roman side of classicism only which begins to fade out of the picture; Hellenism remains, stronger than ever, if a little less close to the surface and less immediately obvious. The Romantic Movement is strongly allied to Greek philosophy and takes over completely the Neo-Hellenic view of Greek expressiveness.

The new movement, really a second renaissance in Greek studies, is initiated by Winckelmann and springs from the new study of Greek art and the new cultivation of the Greek aesthetic which Winckelmann created. Winckelmann discovered the symbolism of Greek art, as he called it, the art of conveying much in a little, of suggesting the deepest truth, the greatest moral and spiritual ideas by touches of artistic and yet apparently artless simplicity. A line of poetry suggests a whole picture or series of pictures, a whole way of life; a single detail in a Greek sculpture contains in essence the whole spirit of the artist, the whole Greek spirit, for those who can perceive it. This new awareness of the symbolic nature of Greek art produced two other important conclusions. Greek art in sculpture or poetry or drama conveys more than the beauty of nature; it has an ideal beauty, a transcendental beauty, the sort of beauty the Transcendentalists spoke of as coming from God and as sometimes displayed to those who can rise above the material to the world of the Over-Soul. Traces of this beauty, clues for our guidance, are visible sometimes in nature. Winckelmann described the sign of a masterpiece as "a noble simplicity and a calm grandeur," [1] both in pose and expression. A Greek poem or a Greek work of art contains within it the entire universe and exemplifies an ideal unity with nature; in the form of allegory it conveys a great spiritual truth. Classical mythology was reinterpreted in the same way — it conveys to us in allegory the greatest desires or qualities and characteristics of mankind.

This view of the Greeks is that of most of the great Romantics, of Wordsworth, Byron, Keats, Shelley; of Goethe — and of Emerson. In Wordsworth it appears in his concept of nature, in his pastoral themes; in his admiration for the Greek and Roman liberators, in his political poetry; in his Greek and Roman philosophy, in his devotion to the Stoic Seneca, in his Platonism, and in his Stoic control of emotion. In Byron it is evident in his taste for the classical, formal style and in his fight for Greek freedom in his own day. It is in Keats' emphasis on spiritual beauty underlying the physical, in his symbolism, and in the universality of the "Ode to a Grecian Urn," to take only one example. In Shelley it is in the Greek eloquence, the Platonism, the classical form of "Adonais" and the dramas, above all in his admiration for Greek freedom — freedom of thought, freedom from tyranny, freedom from religious dogma. But it was in Germany that the Neo-Hellenic influence exerted the greatest power. Here Lessing illustrated Winckelmann's theory in his famous essay on the "Laocoön" sculpture, pointing out its dignity and restraint. If the modern attitude to Hellenistic art has changed since the time of Lessing, yet it must be conceded that he did create a new appreciation for Greek things. Gilbet Highet puts it well. Winckelmann and Lessing taught men to see Greek art "not with the cool and sometimes patronising eye of the Enlightenment, but with the enthusiasm and love which make great criticism." [2] But of the Germans, Emerson knew Goethe best and Goethe was the one who took Winckelmann's view of Greek simplicity and naturalness and established, elaborated, and worked it out in philosophy and in drama. Goethe is a Hellenist through and through, owing and often acknowledging in his writing his enormous debt to Greece and the Greek view of life, reading Plutarch among the many Greek authors whom he knew well. Goethe embraces many traditions and diverse strains of thought, but the Hellenic is always one of the strongest, and Goethe's Hellenism may be taken, if not as typical of the Romantic view, at least as so comprehensive that there is no prevalent attitude to the Greeks in

the time of the Romantic Movement which cannot be exemplified
at some time in his work.

Goethe's relation to Hellenism is a many-sided and changing
element in a many-sided man who never ceased developing and
assimilating new ideas and refashioning old ones, formerly cherished; brought up in the rococo pseudoclassicism of eighteenth-
century Germany, he went over completely to the side of Winckelmann and is replete in the earlier years with admiration for the
natural simplicity of the Greeks. But he soon saw more, that the
Greeks were sundered as he himself was by the daemonic, the
restless spirit of the Dionysian disordered passion; the Greek heroes
hurl defiance and blasphemy at the gods. Then he coveted the order,
the nearness to basic values, the humanity of Aeschylus and Pindar,
and the vitality of their mythology. Later, according to one modern
view of Goethe's attitude to the Greeks, in Weimar he still valued
the Greek revelation of beauty but came to doubt the validity of the
Greek concept of Goodness and Truth; it seemed crude and un-
forgiving, with too much place given to vengeance. He turned then
to Italy and there perhaps discovered that the Greek view of the
world was right after all; man is helpless before the forces of nature,
life is callous and the Greeks had rightly seen this; they had depicted
the world as it is, not as it might be. Then came what has been
called his period of full Hellenism when he had discovered what the
Greeks were really like and tried to live in the Greek way; every
faculty was allowed to develop freely according to the laws of its
nature; the Greeks had been perfect men, working as a whole, with
every part of their nature, content with this world which they could
master and not straining after another unattainable world; feeling
and thought were at one and had not yet separated as they seemed
to have done in the modern world. The Greek wholeness which
he cultivated meant freedom from moral conflict, and ability to
develop all sides of the personality. Hellenism is civilization, with
its goals of form and order and wholeness, of self-control and perfect
coordination. It cannot be made one's own, cannot be really assimi-

lated, but we can see it and then go our own way with our abilities
and whole nature heightened and purified.[3]

It would be useless to try to claim that the Neo-Hellenic movement of the late eighteenth and early nineteenth centuries with its
stress on wholesomeness, simplicity, and naturalness is Plutarchan,
for it is based on no single author. Its idealism is Platonic, and the
new way of looking at the Greeks, of seeing the spiritual significance under a physical object is certainly the Platonic method. In
Goethe and Wordsworth it is often, perhaps under the influence
of study of the Neoplatonists, given a mystical direction. But still
Plutarch above all other Greek writers best confirms the correctness
of the Neo-Hellenic view; he is in spirit a Neo-Hellene himself.
He seems to confirm in his own words the simple, ideal, natural
simplicity of Winckelmann. His heroes are Stoic and Spartan, men
of simple good sense, restraint, and natural nobility; they speak
simply but their simplest statements convey by a symbol a great
truth; Plutarch himself allegorizes myth. His Greeks are uncomplicated and natural, living in the greatest age of the world, before
the turbulence of the Middle Ages, the complexities of the modern
age, put us off the right road. So even if the Neo-Hellenic movement is not Plutarchan, and even if Plutarch is read less in the nineteenth century, his heroes to those who knew them, and his views
of life, confirm the correctness of the Neo-Hellenic attitude towards
Greece. Among those who knew Plutarch and his heroes well were
Wordsworth and Shelley and Goethe, and all of these three were
acquainted with at least some of the moral essays, those which
seemed truly Platonic or which allegorized mythology in the current mode. Plutarch was brought to the front from time to time as
illustrating the symbolism in Greek art and life or the natural and
simple spiritual beauty of the Greeks.

It would have been strange if Emerson, reading Plutarch, Plato,
the Neoplatonists, Wordsworth, and Goethe and especially so
ready to take to himself ideas in others for which he feels an
affinity, had managed to resist the Neo-Hellenic flood. As his view

of nature and its connection with man resembles in many ways other contemporary or recent views, those of Goethe or Hölderlin or Kant or of the English Romantics, so his view of Greece is always colored by the contemporary preoccupation with the simple, natural nobility of the Greeks. It is always not far from the surface, under-lying Emerson's remarks on the ancient world. But while he is influenced by this current attitude he also retains something of the older eighteenth-century classical tradition which gave him Plu-tarch when he was a boy — the didactic tone, the desire to use the lessons of the Greeks for his own time, to try to get the men of today to adopt the Greeks as models.

He is quite aware that the Romantic Movement is not anti-classical and he dismisses as pedantic any differentiation between roman-ticism and classicism. Both are devotees of the ancient world and variations in point of view make no significant difference; the im-portant thing is that the Greeks make one feel "the eternity of man, the identity of his thought." [4] Because of our identity with the men of two thousand years ago, we can come close to them. We can admire them near at hand and — here is the Transcendental note — can share in their humanity, their naturalness.

"Every man passes personally through a Grecian period," Emer-son says. He means by this that there is in every man's life a time when the bodily nature and the spiritual nature develop in health and naturalness together. This comes in youth, when "childlike genius" is combined with "inborn energy." [5] But Emerson is well aware that education is as important as natural ability, and for him and his generation this simple inborn genius which he finds in the child is reinforced and cultivated by the current education with its classical basis and its Plutarchan picture of the simplicity and hon-esty of the men of the classical world, and with the implication or direct injunction that these are the proper models for the youth of the time. Emerson's own Grecian period is dominated by the old Plutarchan tradition. When he meets Goethe and the other German writers or the Romantic poets, he finds this same viewpoint, and the Neo-Hellenism now at its zenith merely confirms and strengthens his own attitude; the Greeks were the best and most civilized people after all. They knew perfection and attained it; they were the most sensible and wisest people in the world. He turns to Plutarch to illustrate this, and if he tends to overemphasize the simplicity of the Greeks and treats every Greek as if he were a Plutarchan hero, it is because his view is colored first by Plutarch and then also by Winckelmann, Goethe, Wordsworth, and others who revered and admired what they thought was the Greek view of life and who cherished the Greek part in our own civilization.

Emerson thinks with Goethe that even if we can feel our identity with the Greeks, they are still far superior to us lesser and later mortals; the Greeks saw things more clearly than we do; when he speaks of classical and romantic art he goes back to a sentence from his journals (*CW* 12. 304-305): "When I read Plutarch, or look at a Greek vase, I incline to accept the common opinion of scholars, that the Greeks had clearer wits than any other people." They did not separate the physical world from that of thought and imagination; to them the cosmos was a unity; hence gods, heroes, and men were all one and were all equally vivid. In 1836 (*Journals* 4. 141-142) to illustrate this from Plutarch, he singles out picturesque details from a passage in the "Symposiacs" which show that the Greek gods act completely as human beings; their world is regarded as if it were this world. "They charm me with their taste, their wantonly beautiful superstitions." The banquet scenes of the gods are treated by Plutarch as if they are those of civilized Greeks, and the details which elaborate the picture are attractive, simple, and natural. He adds significantly that the Greeks "seem to be no transcendentalists, — to rest always in the spontaneous consciousness." For him as for Goethe the Greeks are not otherworldly, nor are their natural instincts restrained or repressed by a confining doctrine or dogma; they live naturally and simply, governed by supreme good sense rather than by an ethical code imparted by some divine means. Picturesque small details in Plutarch's description of the Greek gods and of the Greek men attract Emerson by their poetic beauty. They make the Greeks real and vivid, and they make us see that gods and men are treated alike; no elaborate metaphysical barrier separates them. As he wrote about the Greeks in 1855, " 'T is strange what immortality is in their very rags: so much mentality about the race has made every shred durable." [6]

To Emerson "art" means classical art, and in the journals he pays several high tributes to Greek art in particular. In the same way "tragedy" means Greek tragedy to him. Greek mythology as the source of the tragic themes has a lively appeal to him, both because of the creative and imaginative element involved in it and because he feels that mythology has a symbolic meaning, is able to express a natural law through a symbol. For Emerson, mythology expresses eternal verities. The Greek myths convey symbolic truth; they head the list of mythologies in "Books" and are mentioned again in "History." The story of Prometheus has a whole "range of meanings" and a "perpetual pertinence" (*CW* 2. 30). Prometheus is "the Jesus of the old mythology," while the myths of Antaeus, of Orpheus, of Proteus, of Tantalus are all symbolic representations of facts with which every man is personally acquainted. In *Journals* 3. 412–413 he comments on the "obscure and slender thread of truth" that "runs through all mythologies." He notes that the story of Isis and Osiris which he knew from Plutarch has a parallel in the Greek story of Eros and Anteros, indeed "a singular correspondence is also to be remarked in the fables themselves." "Old Knurre Murre is dead" is paralleled by "the great god Pan is dead" in Plutarch's "Why the Oracles Cease to Give Answers."

In the lecture "The Age of Fable" in 1835 Emerson tells the story of Prometheus in detail and points out that it seems to be "a collection of pleasing allegories." "In the beautiful creations of the Grecian muse every fable, though related as religious truth and believed by the multitude as history, is, at the same time a fine allegory conveying a wise and consistent sense." [7] The Greek myths are designed primarily to convey the allegory, while the "Gothic

Fables" or the fables of "our Romantic Literature" are primarily literature and it is the reader who discovers, or rather invents, the hidden meaning. This attitude to the classical myths is in the best tradition of the Neo-Hellenists, for it indicates a perception of the poetical symbolism of mythology and, whether Emerson's remark about Romantic literature is correct or not, it resembles the Romantic attitude, exhibited specially in Shelley, that myths express a truth under a symbol.

But at another time, mythology appears to have a still greater significance to Emerson. He writes in his Journals in 1853: "Yet when I think of the robust Greek mythology and what a cosmic imagination — I wish to say astronomic imagination — they had, a power, I mean, of expressing in graceful fable the laws of the world, so that the mythology is beautiful poetry on one side, at any moment convertible into severe science on the other, — then, the English verse looks poor and purposeless, as if written for hire, and not obeying the grandeur of Ideas." [8] Here Emerson is saying with Plutarch that myth conceals a historical fact, or even a scientific fact. His attitude is not only the Romantic, the Goethean one, but is also that of the older generation, the "speculative mythologists" of the age of enlightenment, who felt that the myths contained truth which is revealed when they are rationalized. It is also one of Plutarch's points of view and is a cardinal Stoic tenet and Emerson probably in this perception owes more to Plutarch than to the Neo-Hellenists.

But the main elements of Emerson's Hellenism can easily be identified with the widespread view of his time. According to this, the Greeks are a simple, childlike people, living in the morning of the world. They look with clear and reasonable eyes on everything, uncomplicated by introspection. They have a simple nobility and manliness. They are all heroes like those described by Plutarch. In "History," for example, Emerson admires the independence and self-reliance of the Greek hero as represented in Homer's Agamemnon and Diomedes and in Xenophon's Greeks in the *Anabasis*.[9]

He also uses Greek tragedy as an example to stress the simplicity and naturalness of the Greeks. His statement that "the Greeks are not reflective" may well give us pause, but he appears to mean that for the Greeks the contemplative life is not the main object, since it must be linked with physical perfection, too. He believes that the characters in Greek tragedy speak simply, "speak as persons who have great good sense without knowing it, before yet the reflective habit has become the predominant habit of the mind." "Adults," he goes on to say, "acted with the simplicity and grace of children." Or, recalling a sentence of Coleridge's *Friend* which he had used not long before in his lecture on Burke,[10] Emerson puts it, "The Greeks combine the energy of manhood with the enjoying unconsciousness of childhood." Or he says of the Greeks of the Expedition of the Ten Thousand, "Who does not see that this is a gang of great boys, with such a code of honour and such lax discipline as great boys have?" When he speaks of the simplicity of Greek tragedy he is apparently thinking of Sophocles' *Philoctetes*. He is reasonably correct in his observation of the simplicity of Sophocles' style, but it is the simplicity of superb artistry and careful technique on the part of a skilled dramatist. In addition, to identify the Greeks or a Greek with a character of Sophoclean drama is to make a long leap in thought which cannot well be justified. The statement would not be valid if made of Greek tragedy in general, for Aeschylus and Euripides are in a number of ways more subtle or at least more complex than Sophocles.

While all the Greeks are simple and uncomplicated, Emerson found Sparta and the Spartans of greater interest and inspiration than the Athenians. Less intellectual, they were soldiers above everything else and the military hero is immediately evident in their generals. They led the simplest kind of life, even if their simplicity was based on a very strict discipline. In reading the essays Emerson observed Plutarch's "love of Sparta" and it was from his reading of Plutarch that he derived most of his acquaintance with the Spartans, as his journal extracts on Sparta indicate. In 1845 he set

down in journal "Y" a number of disjointed selections from and
notes on Plutarch's life of Lycurgus; Spartan laws were not written;
their houses were simply wrought; their king offered sacrifice to
the Muses before a battle; Emerson himself comments that they
were "terrific prefourierites"; he concludes with a Plutarchan sentence used in "Eloquence": "Other nations asked of them no other
aid than a Spartan general. So Gylippus by the Sicilians, Brasidas
by the Chalcidians; Lysander, Agesilaus, by the people of Asia."
Some of these extracts reappear in various essays, and among the
notes which Emerson made on the *Moralia* when he was preparing
to write the introduction for Goodwin's revised translation there
appears a page of Spartan anecdotes taken from the "Laconic Apo
thegms." Both these collections of extracts show why the Spartans
attracted him. Above all else they furnished him with inspiring
examples of military heroism, of self-reliance and a combination of
common sense and practical idealism. They were manly pioneers,
using language briefly and effectively, conveying a whole attitude
to life in a simple remark. Yet they were poetic enough to sacrifice
to the Muses before a battle.

In "Goethe" Emerson returns to the theme of Greek simplicity
and writes, "We conceive Greek or Roman life, life in the Middle
Ages, to be a simple and comprehensive affair," and in the essay
on Plato he says that the Greek genius is "not yet chilled by any fore-
sight of the detriment of an excess." The Greeks had "no sinister
political economy," no "pitiless subdivision of classes." "The understanding was in its health and prime. Art was in its splendid
novelty." He goes on to speak of the ease with which Greek sculpture and architecture were constructed. This too is part of a fallacy
which frequently appears in Romantic Hellenism; [11] no mention
is made of the fact that the Greeks originated the term "political
economy" and certainly knew a far from simple form of it themselves; that they had a class structure more rigid than that of the
nineteenth century and that to speak of the ease of construction of a
Greek work of architecture is very far from accurate. Emerson's

belief, which can also be seen in his remark on the language of Sophocles, arises from confusion between the impression which the work gives the beholder and the artistic skill which went into its creation — something with which he was not entirely unacquainted, but which he ignored when he wrote of the Greeks.

An early journal passage, of 1822, illustrates another aspect of the same fallacy (1. 157–158):

What imparted that impulse to Greece which may be said to have created literature, which has been communicated through Rome to the world? It is a curious spectacle to a contemplative man to observe a little population of twelve or twenty thousand men for a couple of generations setting their minds at work more diligently than men were accustomed, and effecting something altogether new and strange; to see them lie quietly down again in darkness, while all the nations of the world rise up to do them a vain reverence; and all the wisest among them exhausting their powers to make a faint imitation of some one excellence of Greece in her age of glory; to see this admiration continued and augmented as the world grows older, and with all the advantages of an experience of 6000 years to find those departed artists never paralleled.

This attitude to Greek history and the belief that two generations mark the sudden flowering of Greek culture, which arose out of nothing and went back to nothing, were not Emerson's alone, but were quite commonly held in his time. Interestingly enough, Emerson said something quite contradictory to this two years later (*Journals* 1. 388): "The Grecian genius did not start into life with the victories of Salamis and Plataea, but was born and disciplined before Homer sang." In this acute perception he was ahead of most of his classics-trained contemporaries, but he never seems to have returned to this statement and developed it; he saw it one day but then forgot that he had ever observed this new phenomenon in the development of the Greek mind.

Emerson considers the Greeks undisciplined or "wild" as well as simple and uncomplicated. In Plutarch's *Lives* he likes the heroes with their "wild wisdom and an elegance as wild and handsome as sunshine." [12] The *Lives* have a "wild courage, a Stoicism not of the schools but of the blood." [13] Once more he tends to identify the Greeks with the Spartans when he writes in "History": "The manners of that period are plain and fierce. The reverence exhibited is for personal qualities; courage, address, self-command, justice, strength, swiftness, a loud voice, a broad chest. Luxury and elegance are not known. A sparse population and want make every man his own valet, cook, butcher and soldier, and the habit of supplying his own needs educates the body to wonderful performances." This picture with its emphasis on "wildness" seems to bear little resemblance to the rigorous military discipline of Sparta, but Emerson's linking of "wild courage" with "a Stoicism not of the schools but of the blood" shows that, as often, he is using the word in a special sense. His concept of the "Greek wildness" is freedom from a discipline based on dogma or theory. It is the Spartan discipline and it is Stoic, self-imposed, and regulated by the "spontaneous consciousness." It is a military discipline, not a social or moral one, but it is still natural. Spartan soldiers served under Spartan generals. All had the same patriotic aim and hence in a sense their discipline can be described as "self-imposed." In "The Superlative" this wild, simple courage is called "moderation" and he writes specially about moderation in speech, showing his Plutarchan, Stoic, and Spartan dislike for exaggeration. He likes the moderation of the Greek speech, and clearly indicates that when he speaks of moderation he means not "a middle way" but has a strong bias toward restrained, laconic, extremely simple speech. He thinks of the Spartan apothegms: "Spartans, stoics, heroes, saints and gods use a short and positive speech. They are never off their centres." In the original lecture from which this essay was formed (*CW* 10. 544–545) Emerson mentions the Greeks and the Spartans to illustrate what he means by moderation, and uses some of the material which he had copied from the life of Lycurgus into his journals, adding Plutarchan anecdotes.[14] But he is not an orthodox Stoic any more than Plutarch was; perhaps he feels that he is leaning here too far to the Spartan side and he sometimes modifies this call for Spartan restraint. He appeals for the superlative, for Platonic enthusiasm, provided it is aroused by the proper objects — "the superlative is as good as the positive, if it be alive."

Thus for Emerson the simplicity of the Greeks is a natural simplicity. There is never any sense of strain, and their simplicity is not based upon tradition or discipline imposed by some alien power. The Greeks act rightly not because they have been trained or regulated in that direction, but because they are born good and upright. They are all heroic. Hence all their actions are instinctively right and good. I think it was belief in this ethical simplicity which made Emerson note in his journals in 1870 (10. 321–322) what he calls the "recoil" of the Athenians against moral evil: "I cannot but please myself with the recoil when Plutarch tells me that 'the Athenians had such an abhorrence of those who accused Socrates that they would neither lend them fire, nor answer them any question, nor wash with them in the same water, but commanded the servants to pour it out as polluted, till these sycophants, no longer able to bear up under the pressure of this hatred, put an end to their own lives'." [15] The Athenians had such simple and good common sense, such a natural horror of injustice, that they instinctively chose a simple but very effective way of indicating that they would have no part with evildoers.

To the romantic Hellenists the Greek heroes are still heroic and rise far above the common man, and very far above the common man of the nineteenth century; their world is a noble, ideal world, far removed from the ordinary one. But not long before the romantic Hellenism brought in this elevated concept of the Greeks, there had been complaints that heroes must resemble us if they are to have any significance for us today; the later eighteenth century had been stressing the humanity of the hero, his oneness with all other men. The Emersonian theory of nature could easily be accommodated to this viewpoint; the heroes make us *feel* their identity with us because they *are* identical with us. It is this which makes Emerson feel the attraction of the humanity which Plutarch shows in his description of the heroes. They are not demigods but men. Thus in spite of his kinship with Goethe, when Emerson reads him and "these German Weimarish art friends" he says that they are radicals, rejecting tradition and convention; but still they are no nearer the truth. They exert no strong influence, for they are not heroic and they "fail in sympathy with humanity. . . . They do not illuminate me: they do not edify me. Plutarch's heroes cheer, exalt. . . . The roots of what is great and high must still be in the common life."[16] The great men are great in their humanity, not in their superhuman quality; they are men and should appeal to us because we also are human. Plutarch especially conveys this identity of all men — "I cannot read Plutarch without perpetual reminders of men and women whom I know," or even more strongly, "Plutarch's heroes are my friends and relatives" (*Journals* 6. 82). This humanity too was the secret of ancient democracy. It was real democracy, for everyone. It was government of the people, not of the aristocrats or the wealthy only, and the great men were still of the people and not above them. In reading the life of Gaius Gracchus, Emerson, turning to Rome for once, used in a lecture on "American Civilization" a note which expressed this briefly and neatly: "*Democracy.* Gaius Gracchus, Plutarch says, first among the Romans turned himself in addressing the people from facing the senate-house, as was usual, and faced the Forum."[17] The symbolism of this is vivid to Emerson; the popular leader does not lead his people in begging or requesting popular rights from those in authority, from the king or aristocracy; instead he leads the people by facing them and persuading them to claim their own rights.

Over and over again Emerson returns to the Neo-Hellenic discovery of the Greek "naturalness." The Greeks inspire us with morality without the dogma and preaching of the modern church. Their "sentences" reach us directly and immediately. "God never cants," he says in *Journals* 4.266, "and the charm of Plutarch and Plato and Thucydides for me, I believe, is that there I get ethics without cant." The stories of the Greeks which Emerson prizes most are those which show their simple, natural humanity and the "moral common sense" which rebukes arbitrary power or artificiality or mere ingenuity. Such anecdotes he considers better teachers than the dry facts which usually make up history, for these sketches bring the tedious narrative to life and show us the unity of all mankind, Christian and pagan, Greek and American. In this vein, Emerson, in *Journals* 3. 552–553, refers tacitly to the Greek storytellers like Plutarch whom he admired for their moral quality imparted simply by anecdote; when the important facts of history have disappeared from memory, it is a few anecdotes of a moral quality or some momentary act or word which survives, because of its "simple element of humanity or moral common sense." He notes in his journal in 1835 (3. 565) two Plutarchan anecdotes, Pyrrhus and the nightingale and Hannibal's answer to Antiochus' remark that the entrails of the sacrificial animal forbade a battle — "You are for doing what the flesh of a beast, not what the reason of a wise man, adviseth" — as instances of "the putting down reverend folly by childish reason." Artificial cleverness or strict attention to vain superstition and useless convention is refuted by Plutarch's heroes by a terse and natural simplicity. The childish answer is correct because it has an instinctive correctness of native reason.

Emerson commended the Greek combination of the active with the contemplative life and considered that the Greek clarity comes from instinct rather than reflection. For his own time however, he felt the need of emphasizing the contemplative side which tended to be neglected in America. Here again the Greeks could provide an example, and it was most probably from Plutarch that Emerson drew his repeated references to the Pythagorean injunction of silence, in "Literary Ethics," "Fate," "Culture," and "Inspiration." Plutarch had written of the merit of silence in "Of Garrulity," "Of Inquisitiveness," "Of the Training of Children"; in the second he says: "Pythagoras thought fit to check the too early loquacity of his scholars, by imposing on them five years' silence from their first admission." Similarly Emerson wrote in "Literary Ethics" that the scholar must "embrace solitude as a bride" and urged, "Let us sit with our hands on our mouths, a long, austere, Pythagorean lustrum"; then he continued:

Let us live in corners, and do chores, and suffer, and weep, and drudge, with eyes and hearts that love the Lord. Silence, seclusion, austerity, may pierce deep into the grandeur and secret of our being, and so diving, bring up out of secular darkness the sublimities of the moral constitution. How mean to go blazing, a gaudy butterfly, in fashionable or political *salons*, the fool of society, the fool of notoriety, a topic for newspapers, a piece of the street, and forfeiting the real prerogative of the russet coat, the privacy, and the true and warm heart of the citizen!

Emerson's picture of the "butterfly" of society is drawn in general terms; Plutarch's reference to Pythagoras follows a passage (*Moralia* 2. 434) in which he commends the simple, honest sincerity of the rustic and contrasts him with the man-about-town, who is described wittily and vividly, in bright colors and with an air of realism as he asks eagerly for news of the city and for the latest gossip. Emerson's term "butterfly" would sum up Plutarch's description neatly and he may have read this lively paragraph and turned it into more general terms for his own purposes — terms which make it more serious and also more applicable to modern America and the modern American. But both Emerson and Plutarch are saying the same thing — many men lead a superficial life, vainly busy about nothing. Both mention the good which comes from silence and contemplation.

There is something of the Puritan strain in this stress on silence; it fits in with Emerson's dislike of exaggeration or extravagance and makes one think of the traditional New England taciturnity and laconic speech, but in "Culture" Emerson elevates it and gives it a philosophical scope by appealing to the classical example (*CW* 6. 156):

"In the morning, — solitude;" said Pythagoras; that nature may speak to the imagination, as she does never in company, and that her favorite may make acquaintance with those divine strengths which disclose themselves to serious and abstracted thought. 'T is very certain that Plato, Plotinus, Archimedes, Hermes, Newton, Milton, Wordsworth, did not live in a crowd, but descended into it from time to time as benefactors; and the wise instructor will press this point of securing to the young soul in the disposition of time and the arrangements of living, periods and habits of solitude.

In this passage of "Culture" Emerson handles an old classical and conventional theme. He seems to have combined and adapted some of Plutarch's remarks. Plutarch had written in "Of the Training of Children," (*Moralia* 1. 24): "For it is a point of wisdom to be silent when occasion requires, and better than to speak, though never so well. And, in my judgment, for this reason the ancients instituted mystical rites of initiation in religion, that, being in them accustomed to silence, we might thence transfer the fear we have of the Gods to the fidelity required in human secrets." Plutarch's general reference to the initiations of "ancient" religion recalled to Emerson the familiar specific example, the dictum of Pythagoras and his requirement of five years of silence on the part of his initiates, and he sharpened it into the phrase "in the morning, solitude." His reference to "the wise instructor" sounds like a handbook on education like that of Plutarch from which the above extract comes. Plutarch also wrote in the same work (*Moralia,* 1. 18):

But those of all men I count most complete, who know how to mix and temper the managery of civil affairs with philosophy; seeing they are thereby masters of two of the greatest good things that are, — a life of public usefulness as statesmen, and a life of calm tranquillity as students of philosophy. . . . Wherefore we are to apply our utmost endeavor to enable ourselves for both; that is, to manage public employments, and withal, at convenient seasons, to give ourselves to philosophical studies. Such statesmen were Pericles and Archytas the Tarentine; such were Dion the Syracusan and Epaminondas the Theban, both of whom were of Plato's familiar acquaintance.

Plutarch inevitably mentions Plato, and so does Emerson; his name would naturally come to mind, and Emerson further recalls him when he says that these men did not live in a crowd "but descended into it from time to time as benefactors"; he is obviously thinking of Plato's myth of the cave into which the philosophers descend to instruct their fellows after they visited the upper world of the spirit.

In his advocacy and praise of silence and contemplation, then, Emerson turns again to the Greeks and to his familiar Plutarch,[18] for confirmation and example. Although he advises Greek austerity and silence, as Pythagoras does, action is also imperative. Therefore Plato is mentioned, to enjoin a mixture of action and contemplation. Significant however is the presence of the inevitable Plutarchan hero Archimedes, repeatedly mentioned by Emerson as the supreme example of concentration, whose presence in this paragraph of "Culture" serves to modify the Platonic call to action.

Emerson also has much to say on the topic of wealth and poverty and knowing how he tends to use antiquity as a model, and how fully he adopts the contemporary portrait of Greek simplicity we should expect him to commend poverty, with words of admiration for Greek moderation and Spartan restraint. He does so, drawing once more on Plutarch's heroes for examples. In "Domestic Life" he tells us that the greatest man in history was the poorest and cites "the captains and sages of Greece and Rome," Socrates, Epaminondas, Aemilius Paulus, and Cato, and gives a Plutarchan comment on the poverty of Aristides. For most of these examples he is thinking of specific passages in Plutarch. In "Manners" he treats classical poverty again, pointing out that gentlemanly bearing and wealth are by no means synonymous and the same examples are used again and several of the anecdotes are Plutarchan.[19]

Plutarch's attitude towards wealth in both of his treatises, "Of the Love of Wealth" and "Against Running in Debt," is one of hostility; In the first essay, wealth is treated as in the orthodox Stoic diatribe — it does not free its possessor from love of more wealth, for it is insatiable; poverty is more desirable, he says, echoing Seneca (*Moralia* 2. 295); "no man is poor as to what nature requires and what suffices it"; when men run into debt it is for extravagant luxuries, for things which are quite unnecessary for a happy life. His main theme throughout is the insatiability of riches. Those who pile up wealth which they cannot use are merely handing it on to future generations until by an informer or tyrant it is taken away or "diverted into another channel." The miser's motto is "Gain as much and spend as little as may be; value yourself according to what you are worth"; and the children of such misers will be miserly and covetous like their parents. The proper use of riches, Plutarch says, is "the enjoyment of what suffices nature" and in this the wealthy have no advantage over those who have just sufficient for living. The reader is instructed not to give up all toil and labor but to do without superfluities and to banish all useless things.

Plutarch's other essay on wealth, entitled "Against Running in Debt," is a diatribe against debt. Again debt is incurred for luxuries. His advice now is to make fullest possible use of one's own resources, borrowing only as the final resort. Debtors are a slave to their debts; rather than incur debts, a man must contract his desires in the Stoic fashion: "God gives us a table of wood, vessels of earth, and garments of coarse cloth, if we desire to live and continue in freedom."

Here again Emerson is in the classical tradition and there are echoes of Stoicism and of Plutarch. Emerson treats wealth in two passages. In "Man the Reformer" he feels that every man should work for himself, manufacture his own food and implements; this is the classical point of view, the self-sufficiency of the Stoics or of the Cynics—which in "History" Emerson attributes to all the Greeks —and Plutarch. "Every man," Emerson says, "ought to have this opportunity to conquer the world for himself." He who inherits wealth only inherits misery and he elaborates in vivid Emersonian language and style the "difference between the first and second owner of property." The man who supplies all his own needs lives happily and is self-reliant; his son who inherits all that his father has accumulated, has his hands full not using these things but merely preserving them intact. He is "converted from the owner into a watchman or watch-dog." Emerson paints a vivid picture of the change in temperament which then occurs; instead of the father's active, happy self-reliance, the son becomes a wealthy recluse, the servant of his property. The mixture of generalization and of detail, brought down to earth and made concrete by lists of material things, is characteristically Emersonian. But it is equally Plutarchan, for Plutarch (*Moralia* 2. 301–302) had written in a similar vein of misers and their sons who inherit their wealth. In both the theme is the same — "the difference between the first and second owner of property." But they characterize the "first owner" differently. In Plutarch he is "the covetous man," a conventional type, and it is his fault that his son receives the wrong training and becomes a wretched miser like his father. The "first owner" is different to Emerson; he is the man of good humor, power, fertility of resource, with "strong and learned hands, piercing and learned eyes, supple body, mighty and prevailing heart" whom nature knew and feared, loved and served. When Emerson describes "the second owner," he is thus able to use the power of contrast — the son is the complete opposite of his father. As he puts it again in "Manners" (*CW* 3. 128): "the working heroes . . . are the sowers, their sons shall be the reapers, and *their* sons, in the ordinary course of things, must yield the possession of the harvest to new competitors with keener eyes and stronger frames." This is an adaptation and alteration of Plutarch's contrast between the son before he inherited the wealth (and Plutarch gives him some of the traits which Emerson assigns to the father) and the same son after his father's death and his acquisition of the ancestral property. In this description of the son in his changed state Emerson may well have followed Plutarch — the son becomes "grave, severe, morose" in Plutarch, "is made anxious" in Emerson, in both he has lost interest in physical well-being; in both he is surrounded by servants and has to spend his time supervising them; in Plutarch his kindness and humanity shrivel up, in Emerson he loses sight of one of the ends of wealth, "the prosecution of his love; the helping of his friend."

But here, besides Plutarch, a movement much closer to Emerson in time and place must receive credit. One of the key points of the contention between the Whigs and Democrats in the age of Jackson was the debate on property and the rights of ownership. The Democrats argued that the Whig "aristocracy," inspired by Hamilton, had given to "fictitious property," bank paper and stocks, the value which rightly belonged to honest property, land or wages created by labor. The power of the Democrats was strongest in the South where an agrarian movement developed, claiming to be inspired by Jefferson. Emerson was vaguely interested in agrarianism, even if his interest was more easily aroused by the sturdy Concord farmers than by a developed theory about land tenure versus paper money. He usually glorifies farming and the work of the farmer, close to nature; the distinction he makes between the wages of toil and income derived from inheritance and his decided preference for "the first owner" may to some extent be a reflection of this contemporary debate in his own country.[20]

In another part of "Man the Reformer" Emerson inculcates "the lesson of self-help"; too many people require others to serve their need for luxuries; yet, he adds, he will not be understood as advocating such complete self-reliance that isolation from society will inevitably result. Plutarch also (*Moralia* 2. 303) explains in self-defence that he does not mean to advocate idleness and stop commerce, but only the labor and the commerce which aim at the introduction of unnecessary luxuries.

But there are also in "Man the Reformer" some indications that Emerson has read at this point Plutarch's other essay, on debt and debtors. His indictment of the business world is much more general than Plutarch's indictment of usury, which attacks only usury and usurers. Plutarch's remedy for debt, (*Moralia* 5. 413) however, is exactly what Emerson advocates in his essay — simplicity and self-help — and his portrait of the simple life is almost a compressed version of a much longer and elaborate description which Emerson presents in three pages (*CW* 1. 243–246). For both Plutarch and Emerson, the goal of economy is liberty — liberty from the slavery and captivity which debt produces. Occasionally there is a correspondence in terminology which seems to be more than coincidence. Emerson's references to "parched corn," to "gods and heroes," to the "Furies of Lacedaemon," and to the "narrow tenements" of the Romans indicate that when he advocates simplicity and self-help the Spartans and Romans occur readily to his mind and these references give the whole paragraph a classical tone.[21] Emerson tends to express briefly and concisely a remark which Plutarch puts in general terms, and then to elaborate passages of description which are strictly limited and shortened in Plutarch.

Emerson sets the same slight value upon wealth in this lecture as any Stoic or Platonic rhetorician or essayist does; both Emerson and Plutarch advocate simplicity and Emerson adds emphasis upon the dignity of manual labor, for this lecture was written for delivery to the Mechanics' Apprentices' Literary Association in Boston. Emerson advocates an equality of wealth, or at least a fair share for all; this is only to be attained by a new love which "would put a new face on this weary old world." In his peroration he describes the man who has this steady flow of love and a "prospective prudence" which subordinates the immediate present to a lifetime. Plutarch's cure for the love of wealth, at the end of the essay of that title, is attention to "temperance or philosophy or such knowledge of the Gods as is requisite." These are the things which bring the greatest joy to the soul. "Such a thing is truth, virtue, or the beauty of geometrical and astrological sciences." In short, Plutarch advocates the simple life of the philosopher and thinker; and Emerson with his remark above on "thought" and "want of thought" seems to agree with Plutarch. We feel that in a moment he will say that the life of the philosopher is better than riches. But here he stops following Plutarch and instead of advocating withdrawal he becomes militant and advocates a kind of Christian socialism, inspired by love.

"Man the Reformer" belongs to about 1841. By the time he writes his essay "Wealth" in *The Conduct of Life*, several years later, Emerson's attitude has in some respects changed; his mind has developed along lines farther away from the Greek simplicity, the self-sufficiency of the Stoic philosophers and their advocacy of poverty, away also from the Spartan pioneering age of early America. Indeed, now Emerson commends wealth, saying that every man ought to add something to the common wealth, for wealth is natural since it arises "in applications of the mind to nature" — bringing fruit from the orchard to the market, bringing all produce to the place where it is sold and used. He thinks now of the Plato of the *Republic* rather than of Plutarch, and life begins with the articles of necessity — nature requires that each man feed himself. Plutarch would stop here, with the simple needs which can be easily satisfied, with life according to nature. But Emerson follows Plato on, and so he explains that after this point of bare livelihood has been reached, "then, less peremptorily, but still with sting enough, she [Nature] urges him to the acquisition of such things as belong to him. Every warehouse and shop-window, every fruit-tree, every thought of every hour opens a new want to him which it concerns his power and dignity to gratify." The theory that primitive nature has no use for wealth, but that the individual is inevitably led to build up a society and private property and that society's needs become more complex as that society itself increases in size and complexity, is Platonic but it is also American and nineteenth-century American. Emerson admires sturdy American individualism and hard work, and does not dislike the wealth which the work produces. His country, he realizes, has progressed from the simple, pioneering state of the Spartan New England farmers. It is exuberant, wealthy, and expansive. Indeed in the next sentence Emerson seems to refute Plutarch: "It is of no use to argue

the wants down: the philosophers have laid the greatness of man
in making his wants few, but will a man content himself with a
hut and a handful of dried pease? He is born to be rich." Plutarch
had said that only extreme simplicity and freedom from wealth
and debt produce freedom. Emerson seems to challenge this too
and to feel that only the wealthy man is completely free (*CW* 6.
89). Economy mixes itself with morals, Emerson says. Independence
is a great virtue; poverty demoralizes. Plutarch sets the same high
value on liberty and independence when he speaks, like Emerson,
of the slavery of the debtor. Emerson's "poverty demoralizes" (*CW*
6. 90) shows a dislike of poverty, a feeling that it is an evil, which
at first seems to indicate a very different point of view from that
of Plutarch. But on the other hand, if Plutarch would not say this,
he actually goes even farther than Emerson, for to Plutarch "no
man is poor as to what nature requires" — poverty is not an evil,
for it does not really exist; it is only an appearance. No man is
poor in regard to necessities.

Emerson goes on to indicate that a reputation for integrity accom-
panies wealth. In poverty, "the chances of integrity are frightfully
diminished; as if virtue were coming to be a luxury which few
could afford. . . . He may fix his inventory of necessities and of
enjoyments on what scale he pleases, but if he wishes the power
and privilege of thought, the chalking out his own career and having
society on his own terms, he must bring his wants within his proper
power to satisfy." Emerson still approves of wealth, but he can
accommodate Plutarch neatly to his own attitudes. Where Plutarch
and the later Stoic philosophers would enjoin limitation of one's
desires to a few necessities, Emerson finds a middle way without
having to approve debt or usury: "he must bring his wants within
his proper power to satisfy." This is an ingenious compromise and
it makes one feel that Emerson may well be trying here to fit the
classical philosophers' or the Stoic's attitude to wealth to the nineteenth-century American attitude, that every man should have the
opportunity to acquire wealth.

There is much in Plutarch that Emerson can use on this topic
in spite of the difference in attitude. Like Plutarch he dislikes what
he calls "fops who never did anything." He agrees with Plutarch
that labor is not degrading. The workman cannot afford the grace
or elegance which comes from an easy life but he can replace it
with the merit of work well done. All men alike can feel pride in
their work. He agrees again with Plutarch that wealth for the
purpose of ostentation is an evil (*CW* 6. 92–93); wealth can be
useful and even good when certain rules for its acquisition and
employment are kept in mind.

The first of the "measures of economy" which Emerson gives in
"Wealth" is the rule that "man's expense must proceed from his
character." It can also be expressed, "spend for your expense, and
retrench the expense which is not yours." This is the Emersonian
self-reliance but it is not as stringent as the Plutarchan type. Emerson mentions the older generation of New England farmers who
had a sort of "Arcadian fanaticism" and tried to combine literature
and learning with farming. They failed because a farmer becomes
a slave to his land. Leave farming to the farmer and literature to
the man of letters. When a man has found, Emerson says, something which he can do, he should concentrate on that and "relieve
himself of all vague squandering on objects not his." This is not
as confining as Plutarch's Stoic limitation of desires nor as limited
as Emerson's own earlier attitude to wealth and expenditure, but
Emerson would relax his rules only a little more than Plutarch. We
must still buy only necessities, but we must also remember that what
are luxuries for one are necessities for another. What he opposes
is "vague squandering," the result of an excessive regard for appearances; it is Plutarch's "ostentation" expressed more moderately.
To elaborate his meaning Emerson distinguishes between vanity
which costs much in money and labor and is still worthless, and
pride, a sense of one's own real worth, which can go anywhere,
into any society, and which is found alike in poverty and wealth.
His second "measure of economy" is "spend after your genius and

by system"; he is simply repeating Plutarch's "buy what you need," limiting your needs by your ability to satisfy them, by your income.

In writing of poverty and wealth, Emerson tends first in "Man the Reformer" to feel that every man should work for himself and practise self-help; he elaborates this with the aid of the classical and conventional themes of the moral essay on wealth — the contrast of wealth inherited and wealth earned by labor, the diatribes against luxury, the ability of nature to satisfy our needs. Later on, in "Wealth," modifications are made, but we are never carried far away from the Plutarchan, Stoic view or the view of the classical moralists, for example of the Plutarchan Montaigne in "Of Solitude." For Plutarch's limitation of desires Emerson substitutes bringing one's desires within one's power to satisfy them; desires are still to be restricted but not as rigidly as the Stoics would prescribe. Still the classical "sentences" appear in the diatribes against society of the city and the ostentatious use of wealth, in the emphasis on need as the standard of measure. In reading Emerson on poverty and wealth we feel that although he admires the simplicity of the Greeks and would like to use them as the great examples of self-reliance, times have changed and even self-reliance cannot be carried to the extreme advocated by the classical moralists. Even Thoreau's experiment was not completely successful.[22] Men have to live in society, and society in nineteenth-century America set a high value on ability to get ahead and to progress; what Emerson could draw from Plutarch and the Stoics, however, was the emphasis on the dignity of toil, something which appealed to his countrymen, and on the need to devote one's efforts to the common wealth. Emerson's modifications of the Plutarchan view were far more akin to the spirit of the time; America had passed through its Spartan period in Colonial days.

Emerson's view of the Greeks is traditional and conventional; traditional in that it relies upon the eighteenth-century mode of using them as patterns for today, as schoolboy heroes; conventional in that he adopts the Neo-Hellenic view of the Greeks as simple, natural, and noble, living in the Golden Age. The simplicity of the New England background, the "Arcadian" period of the colonies and the pioneers, and the restraint of New England Puritanism all would tend to turn his thoughts in the direction of simplicity, rigor, and the Spartan way. But a large part of the responsibility for this tone in Emerson's thought must be attributed to Plutarch. The Neo-Hellenists all knew the *Lives* and used the names of the great Greeks in familiar terms; but Emerson was also influenced by the *Moralia*; when he writes of the simple, childlike nature of the Greeks he recalls and sets down illustrative anecdotes from the *Moralia*; when he expresses his liking for the Spartans he illustrates this again by anecdotes from the *Moralia*; when he wishes to indicate that the Greeks inspire him it is usually evident that he is thinking of particular passages and quotations from the *Moralia*; and when he speaks of Greek austerity and poverty he fails to realise that they are not Greek but Plutarchan and are stressed by Plutarch only because they illustrate aptly some of the tenets of Plutarch's own philosophy and are part of his debt to Stoicism. Emerson's Hellenism is Plutarchan and is separated by five hundred years of changing ideas and attitudes from that of Greece's great flowering, the Periclean age.

IV

THE PLUTARCHAN HERO

But if we explore the literature of Heroism we shall quickly come to Plutarch, who is its Doctor and historian.

"Heroism"

For the eighteenth century, ancient history was the story of the heroes of Greece and Rome; it was a series of great battles led by military heroes or of peaceful reforms instituted and carried through by great individuals like Solon or Lycurgus or the Gracchi. The cult of the great man was visible everywhere and through Carlyle and Nietzsche it would continue to exert a strong influence. Inevitably the admiration for the great men of the hour, for Frederick the Great or Napoleon, was extended back into the period of classical civilization by an age which valued Plutarch and which read Langhorne. In the first half of the nineteenth century, too, most writers on the ancient world put Plutarch on an equal basis with Herodotus, Thucydides, and Livy; he was regarded as a historian, indeed quite often as the best ancient historian, and finally as synonymous with history itself.

The young Emerson readily accepted this attitude to history, for he was brought up on the history books of this earlier period, on Goldsmith and Rollin. So for Emerson, the history of Greece and Rome was a record of the heroes; history, he said, is biography and he read his Langhorne. Behind every great event, he felt, there stood a great individual who singlehanded advanced his nation to

supremacy on the battlefield or gave his country a new legal code
or at a single blow advanced his people from oligarchy to democracy. In this identifying Greek or Roman history with the biographies of Plutarch he was by no means unique and it was almost
inevitable that when he spoke of the unity of history he selected
the history of Greece and the lives of the Greek heroes for an
example of both the unity of the past with the present and the
unity of the various facets which can "represent" the same period.
Thus for an example of "civil history" he took the Plutarchan
account of the death of Phocion, rather than a passage of Herodotus
or Thucydides. Pindar, he said, the Pantheon, a marble faun,
Phocion's death are all diverse objects or events which unite to
portray the Greek genius (*CW* 2. 14–15).

But, as we have seen, even in the eighteenth century there were
those who found fault with the adulation of Plutarch and with the
search for the heroic; the criticisms became more frequent as time
passed. It was at last generally observed that Plutarch himself disclaims to be writing history, that he neglects vast areas of human
culture and society which must now claim to be considered as part
of the story of Greece or Rome. There was a new movement arising
which viewed history as the history of a culture and of a people,
not as a list of great men. In Germany, the famous Niebuhr was the
leading representative of this school and Emerson knew the writings
of Niebuhr and of others in the same new mode of historiography.
The theme of the essay "History" is the unity and permanence of
the human soul throughout all history and all cultures. This stress
on identity (and Emerson specially mentions our identity with
the Greeks and Romans) indicates that he feels with Niebuhr that
history is intensely relevant today; Rome, for example, is a guide
for the modern state. In three or four passages in this essay, too,
Emerson follows Niebuhr's method of drawing conclusions about
ancient institutions, or buildings, or about the mind of the Romans
from later survivals; he seems to sum up this method when he
writes, "all public facts are to be individualized, all private facts

are to be generalized. Then at once History becomes fluid and true, and Biography deep and sublime." But except for these remarks and a few direct tributes to Niebuhr, Heeren, and Fustel de Coulanges, Emerson remains faithful to the older, traditional view current in his youth and inherited from a past generation. He still tends to identify Greece with its leaders and great men. His interest is always focused on the great individual and on his traits of human character. His training and background have directed him down a different road and Plutarch's heroes continue to be the real representatives of the man of the ancient world.

We have seen that the first extant journal reference to Plutarch speaks of his "heroes" and it is interesting to observe Emerson's earliest references to the individual Greeks who seem to have been his favorite Plutarchan heroes. In 1815 we find Phocion mentioned along with Demosthenes in a youthful poem; Aristides appears in 1822; in 1833 Timoleon is mentioned twice in letters from Sicily and in 1834 Phocion is referred to three times.[1] We can see that Aristides was an early favorite, probably because the great and good Aristides was often singled out in school histories; later Phocion and Timoleon, who fought against tyranny, were mentioned more often and even seem to have been Emerson's favorite examples of the heroic Greek. We know that these names were familiar to many, indeed were the favorite Greek heroes at the end of the eighteenth century and had often been used in France, Greece, and America during the struggles of revolution. They may therefore well have had special significance for Emerson, living as he did near the scenes of the first battle for American independence. His liking for them shows the older, traditional type of heroism; the simple, sensible, human heroism; but devotion to this type still lingered among strong classicists in the nineteenth century, along with the superhuman hero of Carlyle and later Nietzche. Landor, for example, was a thorough and complete classicist, and Emerson himself observed that Landor thought the three greatest men in history are Washington, Phocion, and Timoleon (*CW* 5. 8). To those in this tradition the classical world of Plutarch was the most vivid in history and the *Lives* one of the best books ever written.

We have now to look more closely at Emerson's concept of the hero. "Great men," he says, "are excellent" and I take it that he is here using the term in its classical sense of "outstanding." He also says that it is natural to believe in great men, indeed that "life is sweet and tolerable" only if we believe in their existence. Their name and their works are everywhere and even religion "is the love and cherishing of these patrons." Great men are utterly different from ourselves; they inhabit a different world from the world in which we live, and a higher sphere of thought. The great man does not remind us of others. These remarks, even though they occur in *Representative Men*, show nothing of Emerson's theory of representation. Indeed it may be doubted whether they express his own developed view of the hero; he may well be merely stating the common view of the great man which he is going to develop and emend.

Emerson still supports the old heroic tradition in his feeling that the essential use of great men is moral: "I cannot even hear of personal vigor of any kind, great power of performance, without fresh resolution." The heroes inspire us very directly to follow their example. This is in the spirit of those who valued Plutarch the educator; indeed it is Plutarch himself; he tells us at the beginning of the life of Timoleon that the virtues of the heroes serve as models for his own character: "My method is, . . . by the study of history, and by the familiarity acquired in writing, to habituate my memory to receive and retain images of the best and worthiest characters. I am thus enabled to free myself from any ignoble, base, or vicious impressions, contracted from the contagion of ill company that I may be unavoidably engaged in; by the remedy of turning my thoughts in a happy and calm temper to view these noble examples." In other words, Plutarch considers that the heroes are examples to follow; Emerson has really little new to add to what he already found in Plutarch; he merely summarizes the Plutarchan view of history when he says, "we owe to biography the fortification of our hope" and "we are emulous of all that man can do." This educational purpose of biography comes out occasionally, especially in the introductory or concluding sentences of several lectures of the series "Biography" of 1835. Michelangelo teaches us love of beauty and hence how we may approach the great source of beauty, "Perfect Goodness." The life of Luther conveys a "salutary truth," that simple honesty can accomplish much and can win everlasting fame. Milton kindles love and emulation in his nineteenth-century readers, for not only does his epic of man elevate the concept of mankind, but Milton is able to communicate his great feelings and ideas — hope, self-reverence, piety, delight in beauty — to others: "For are we not the better; are not all men fortified by the remembrance of the bravery, the purity, the temperance, the toil, the independence, and the angelic devotion of this man . . . ?" George Fox shows us how much nature, in a common man, can do by itself, and the Quaker devotion to principle and to simplicity find an echo in all of us; so nobody can look at Fox's life "without thinking better and hoping better of the race of Man." Burke in his life and oratory "instructs the present and future ages." In the same year, in his lecture on Bacon, Emerson restates this cardinal concept, that great men "exhilarate the spirit by the scope they give to admiration and hope." When we are depressed, he says, and when our opinion of men is low, the great men encourage us and make us feel our community with them.

Stressing Plutarch's moral influence, Emerson speaks (*CW* 2. 248) of the "tart cathartic virtue" of his stories of the heroes; indeed all history "is as severely moral in its teaching as the straitest religious sect" (*Journals* 3. 442). In "Literary Ethics" he bases his advocacy of self-reliance strongly upon Plutarch and takes Plutarch's heroes as examples of this quality (*CW* 1. 160); the whole value of history and biography is to increase the reader's own self-trust; "this is the moral of the Plutarchs, the Cudworths, the Tennemanns, who give us the story of men or of opinions." In "The

Uses of Great Men," the inspiring quality of Plutarch who instills in us intelligence and determination is again mentioned. Biography, Emerson says with Plutarch, teaches us "how needlessly mean our lives are" and makes us wish to acquire regal splendor and noble principles. So over a number of years he still adheres to the old method of using Plutarch as a schoolbook, to inspire good qualities.

But there is also another strain in "Literary Ethics" — he explains how the heroes inspire self-reliance. First, they prevent despondency in the present unheroic age; they fortify our faith by showing that others in the past have mastered despondency by courage and resolution. If nature produced Shakespeare and Plato and Milton, "then I dare; I also will essay to be." But secondly, they inspire us only to the extent to which, inspired by them, we then stand on our own feet. The heroes themselves are self-reliant and teach us self-reliance. Every heroic soul must be "spontaneous." Culture itself, especially the culture based on book knowledge, can impede spontaneity or self-reliance, and this idea too is echoed over a number of years. In *Representative Men* it is mentioned briefly, "excellent is culture for a savage; but once let him read in the book, and he is no longer able not to think of Plutarch's heroes." However, books, Emerson says, are only for the scholar's idle times; the stories of ancient authors do not guarantee the possession of heroic opinions. The ancient writers are ransacked for examples of heroism, but a man's fortune is the result of his character. This theme recurs in the early 1850's in "Fate" and in the late 1860's in "Books"; Emerson thinks that even Plutarch can be used too much to inspire us with examples of virtue. In fact, Emerson's admiration for the heroes of antiquity is often accompanied by the feeling (which he shared with Carlyle) that we have as great men around us at present as ever lived in Greece or Rome; he says, for example (*Journals* 9. 236): "We go to Plutarch and Montaigne for our examples of character, but we might as well go to Pliny and Varro for oaks and firs, which grow as well in our own dooryards and cow-pastures." There are, he continues, "domestic graces" and fine qualities about us, in our own home circle, but they are overlooked in favor of an ancient author. Emerson is not really disparaging Plutarch's heroes or turning away from the youthful liking for Plutarch; he is merely saying what he has often said, that natural conduct of one's own is better than blindly copying a heroic model of the past. The two opposing strains of thought which one writer finds summed up in the poem "Grace" and in "Self-Reliance" [2] are always present, in spite of occasional attempts to reconcile them. On the one hand Emerson writes in the poem of the "defences," provided by example and custom and on the other advocates self-reliance and the overthrow of the conventional. Even when he is at the high point of his advocacy of the strongest individualism, he still writes in his journals tributes to his ancestry and his upbringing, to the old-fashioned education.

There are present, then, what may be called strong traditional elements in Emerson's doctrine of the hero and, if they are persistent, they appear most strongly in the earlier years when he is still largely under the influence of eighteenth century heroism; he has not yet been inspired to rebel against tradition. At the same time his heroes and his view of heroism are moral; he admires the great men who acted morally or advanced morality or discovered a moral truth. He has difficulty with Byron, Wordsworth, and Goethe during this period, before he has arrived at a theory which will permit him to include them also among the great. While the early lectures demonstrate the educative and formative purpose of history and biography, they also inevitably show Emerson's close attention to the ethical principles or the absence of them in the men whom he chooses as subjects. If in his lecture on Bacon, Emerson finds much that is commendable in the great statesman, he had thought of including a "censure of Bacon" in his "British Plutarch" (*Journals* 2. 504) and he indicates throughout that Bacon's merit is intellectual rather than ethical and grieves that a statesman, so highly endowed, has serious "deformities in the moral character." Goethe is denied greatness because of his defective morality; on

the other hand the opening sentences of the lecture on Michelangelo in 1835 commend the fact that his life contains "no in-
jurious influence." Luther for all his iron temperament and his
vigorous loves and hates is still "poor, loyal, abstemious, of irre-
proachable life" and the principles which govern all his militant
action are based on a love of right and goodness. With his lecture
on George Fox, Emerson is completely at home; it is not necessary
to comment on his moral character specifically since the whole man
breathes forth an aura of piety, devotion, and goodness; his Quaker
followers are in the forefront of philanthropic and charitable move-
ments. If Burke the statesman has less appeal for Emerson than a
religious leader like Luther or Fox and is lauded chiefly as the
philosopher in action, Emerson still finds space in his lecture on
Burke to mention in passing that this "adorner of existing institutions" possessed also "a fire of affection, and a depth of virtuous
sentiment that add heroism to his wisdom." The central thought
of the lecture on Milton is that he added "the genius of the Christian sanctity" to "antique heroism" and therefore becomes identified with "all select and holy images"; [3] even in his old age
Emerson contrasts the elevated, pure morality of Plutarch with
that of Montaigne (*CW* 10. 299–300).

When he formulates "Self-Reliance" about 1839–40 Emerson has
not yet arrived at his theory of representative men; he cannot yet
say with confidence, trust yourself because you and the hero are
one; instead he reiterates simply the command to avoid the conformity which is stifling America and turning its people into
whimpering, timid creatures. Emerson has however by this time
formulated his philosophy of nature and his theory of the unity
of nature leads to his doctrine of the hero. Thus he can reaffirm
that there are no greater men today than there ever were. All great
men are alike, at whatever time in the history of the world they
live, and by great men he still means men of the Plutarchan mold.
All our modern progress cannot, he says, give us heroes greater
than those of Plutarch. "Phocion, Socrates, Anaxagoras, Diogenes,

are great men, but they leave no class." Instead, those who really
follow the heroes will be no followers but will be themselves and
will found a new line of heroes modeled on themselves. Emerson
is simply saying that the heroes are self-reliant. Plutarch's heroes
can teach us this and so can the Stoics. "Let a Stoic," Emerson
writes, "open the resources of man and tell men they are not leaning
willows, but can and must detach themselves." This Stoicism will
show us a new independence which in turn will give us the strength
to overthrow timid conformity.

But during these early years Emerson was gradually and with
difficulty evolving his theory of the great man which was to find
its complete expression in *Representative Men.* Various influences
were working here. Sampson Reed's "Oration on Genius" showed
Emerson the distinction which he adopted between understanding
and reason, between talent and genius; the one possessed by the
masses, the other only by the truly great man.[4] Coleridge also aided
Emerson's perception and helped him toward a new theory of
genius by indicating a correspondence between mind and nature —
genius is moral and is allied to the divine in nature. In the period
when he was reading Sampson Reed and Coleridge, Emerson was,
like the ancient Stoics, seeking unity in diversity. This is sometimes
described as Emerson's Neoplatonic period and Coleridge's Neoplatonism is stressed as an influence on Emerson at this point; but
the Stoics also sought for unity in the midst of diversity and there
is a distinct Stoic element in Coleridge, as influential as the Neoplatonic. It is true that he has no use for pantheism, which is to
him only atheism under another guise, but self-examination and
self-knowledge are fundamental to Coleridge and when he is reading Coleridge, Emerson several times notes down from this source
the mottoes, "gnōthi seauton" and "ne te quaesiveris extra" (prefixed as a motto to "Self-Reliance") so that as McCormick puts it
they become "almost daily invocations" in the journals. These are
of course cardinal Stoic tenets and expressions of a Stoic self-
reliance.[5] Coleridge's emphasis on the individual will on the ground

that it is dependent on the Supreme Will certainly sounds Stoic enough. Emerson's view of greatness at this point has been expressed in these terms: "The greatest man is not man at all, for he merges his human will in the Divine and becomes the image of God"; this too is at the same time Coleridgean and perfectly Stoic.[6]

The Platonic and Neoplatonic influences upon the younger Emerson have often been stressed, but Stoicism is by no means lacking; even his reading of the pre-Socratics in Gérando must have made him observe the pre-Stoic Stoicism in the philosophers who were to give classical Stoicism its initial impetus. The pre-Socratics, especially Heraclitus, foreshadow the dualism of Plato and some of them, like Pythagoras, tend towards a monism; or towards a moral theism, as in Thales and Anaximander. All of them, but especially Pythagoras and Heraclitus, pointed the way to Stoic pantheism, for the boundary between theism and pantheism is not always clearly marked. This is true even of Emerson himself; as a man he is a theist but what he writes about men in general in *Journals* 9. 45 is also applicable to himself: "In the woods, this afternoon, it seemed plain to me that most men were Pantheists at heart, say what they might of their theism. No other path is, indeed, open for them to the One, intellectually at least." And other writings give good ground for the accusation of pantheism frequently made against him. The same lack of clarity, or rather lack of firm boundaries, is by no means absent from some of his ancient predecessors. For Heraclitus could inspire quite as well as Plato the conviction that man and nature are one and from this concept it is not a long step to the conclusion that great men "represent" nature and the entire human race. Thus we can say that if Emerson's earliest hero worship is Plutarchan and to that extent Stoic, we can also say that a little later, when he is evolving the theory of representative men, the Stoic influence is not absent, even if the men whom he finally chooses as examples of the representative man are not in the Plutarchan, Stoic mold; for by the time of the composition of *Representative Men*, the heroes of the *Lives* no longer attract him to quite the same degree as they had done earlier. But still the Stoic cosmopolitanism is attractive; it can be seen clearly and simply in the last sentences of "Michael Angelo": "he was not a citizen of any country; he belonged to the human race"; such a man, Emerson says, is kin to all those, wherever they are, who love beauty and nature. The Stoic ideal of world citizenship, of the brotherhood of man, is attractive to thinking people in many ages; here in art, it exerts its appeal to Emerson and provides another stone for the foundations of the doctrine of representative men.

McCormick thinks that Cousin "crystallised for Emerson" all the influences which before 1831 had helped him towards his formulation of the correspondence between man and nature which provided the theory of representative men. Cousin's philosophy is primarily that the great man is the spirit of his times or "the soul of his culture." The great man is the representative of the common type which any multiplicity creates; he is not a great individual, but by being typical he is great. The history of the great man is the history of the human race. Cousin too identifies nature, God, and man as the Stoics did. His only fresh discovery is that the great man appears "in order to represent an idea 'at the precise time when that idea is worth representing, and neither before nor after it. . .'" [7]

McCormick has demonstrated that Emerson is found formulating his theory of representative men as early as 1826–27, before he has met Cousin or Carlyle. Emerson writes then (*Journals* 2. 101) that "geniuses are the organs, mouthpieces of their age; do not speak their own words, nor think their own thoughts." This anticipation of Cousin is also in the old tradition of heroism — that history is biography, that the nation is the great man. To Emerson the Greek genius is Phocion and Timoleon and Demosthenes. They do not merely lead their people, they are the spirit of the people. Plutarch is right after all and so also is the idea that we must all partake of greatness and that the hero is and must be human and like other men.

Finally, among the influences which promote the theory of representative men in place of the old heroism and hero worship we must also reckon with the American political scene and with the practical problem of how to live intelligently in a democracy. By making genius democratic, Emerson solved the problem of the evil and the faults in the political men he saw about him in America. It was the theory of representation, Perry Miller thinks, which saved Emerson from the leader-principle, the reactionary attitude of Carlyle. The individual genius, even the lawless one, is fitted into the pattern.[8] This aspect of heroism is not at all inconsistent with the Stoic trend in Emerson's thinking. It is frankly pragmatic and the practical reasoning behind it is Stoic and coheres well with the Stoic feeling that theories are adequate only if they provide a solution to the problems of living. It is perhaps specially Stoic because it solves the problem in a democratic way, preserving the natural equality of men. It is Stoic also in admitting the existence of evil instead of denying its existence on the one hand or resorting to despair on the other. For the Stoics as for Emerson, Nature or Necessity furnishes the evil but furnishes also the power to use it for good, so that both are eventually brought into harmony with the divine nature of man.

Even after he has formulated his own theory and when he has called for heroes who will destroy all heroes, Emerson is impressed by a passage in Plutarch which combines hero and people and yet which preserves the heroic uniqueness; in 1850 he notes from the life of Marcellus: "All the rest of the Syracusans were no more than the body, in the batteries of Archimedes, while he himself was the all moving and informing soul." [9] The hero and the ordinary man are one as body and soul are one, but the crowd is the body while Archimedes is the soul. This strain, which preserves the earlier uniqueness and "excellence" of the hero is never entirely lost in the destruction of individualism which *Representative Men* calls for. The hero always in Emerson stands out from ordinary mortals by an "energy," a "fire," a "genius," a grandeur. There is

thus always something of the traditional in Emerson. But long
before the appearance of *Representative Men* occurs the other concept that we and the heroes are of the same substance and that
there can arise an innate sympathy between ourselves and the heroes,
a sympathy which can annihilate the barrier which separates us
from the great. The sympathy is often illustrated in connection with
the Greeks, for it is with them (as portrayed by Plutarch) that we
can most readily feel this uniting sympathy.

The trait in the hero which separates him from ordinary men is
described in various terms. Sometimes, as in *Representative Men*,
he is a tremendous man, a man at the height of his powers, giving
full expression to that which in others is cramped and confined.
"There is fire enough to fuse a mountain of ore." There are various
heroes, military, statesmanly, and literary; they excel others by
their vigor and inward fire. In "Power," again Emerson writes of
the powerful individual and his "inward force" and, drawing on
Plutarch, points out that in Greek democracy the clumsy, awkward
character of democratic government with its disagreements and lack
of harmony is compensated for by the spirit and energy which it
awakens.[10] He illustrates this inspiring fire by the example of
Archimedes from Plutarch. In the lecture "Greatness" he quotes
from Plutarch an apothegm about Scipio to illustrate this outstanding excellence which elevates the hero above others: "Cato said
of the Roman commanders in Africa that 'Scipio was the wise
man, — the rest were flying shadows'."[11] That there is in this
concept of the hero something of Stoicism may perhaps be seen
in the Stoic term "the wise man," even if the use of the term
"fire" to describe this quality may not necessarily be an echo of
the Heraclitean, Stoic element. Sometimes this vague heroic quality
is nothing more than a sort of grandeur; Emerson quotes in a
journal of 1850–51 a Plutarchan passage which tells how even his
enemies were impressed by the beauty and grandeur of the enormous ships and deadly machines which were directed against their
own city by Demetrius Poliorcetes.[12] Emerson never really out-

grows his liking for the great man of overwhelming power and grandeur.

Emerson's admiration for the soldier, the military hero, appears clearly; not one of the subjects of the lecture series "Biography" is a soldier, but after reading almost any one of them it is Emerson's stress on the military aspect, the manly virtues, of the hero which remains with the reader. Michelangelo is for a time the heroic engineer of the fortifications of Florence, but more indicative of the soldier is his endurance of fatigue and labor which is compared with that of Julius Caesar or Charles XII; as an old man he carries on "with the heat and determination of manhood" against obstacles and enemies; his bold demand for complete freedom to go his own way in the design and building of St. Peter's is compared with the terms which George Washington demanded for leading the American armies; he faced death with his "habitual heroism." Luther's "boldness" and "confidence" and "terrible determination" are mentioned: "Never . . . did the human Will clothe itself in more fit expression than in this man's words"; resolution is seen in all his words and acts; his will is that of Attila or Napoleon. He is portrayed as a soldier fighting against evil with spiritual weapons, unmoved by threat of prison and fire, confident of victory like the Hebrew prophets. Military metaphors occur and recur to describe his action — he is summoned by God to battle with the hosts of evil. The military figures do not occur so strikingly in the lecture on Milton, rather it is the heroic stature of the man and of his work, his manliness, which comes out — he "stands erect, commanding"; "no man, in these later ages, and few men ever, possessed so great a conception of the manly character." In the controversies of the time he is a strong fighter for liberty, brave and courageous, undeterred by labor or danger. Fox is a hero of a different kind; his meekness and quietness tend to make metaphors of battle inappropriate, but still he too fights for the liberty of the subject and for freedom of religion. Burke too is a thinker and orator rather than a soldier, but the wholeheartedness of his devotion to a cause has a military ring about it and he also is oblivious to labor or fear or pride.

This concept of the hero as a soldier and a fighter very probably stems in part from Emerson's youthful acquaintance with, and liking for, Plutarch; again in 1837 he is reading Plutarch and the composition of the essay "Heroism" stems from a lecture series of that year. Here Plutarch's influence appears more clearly in a variety of ways. The hero described is the Plutarchan military hero and the poem which is prefixed to the essay as a motto contains a couplet derived from Plutarch.[13] At the beginning of the essay Emerson does not, as we might expect, go back to Greece and Rome; to show that heroism belongs to every age he chooses the time of Beaumont and Fletcher for his example of "noble behavior," but the long quotation from "The Triumph of Honor" is on a Roman theme with Greek overtones. Immediately afterwards we notice the name of one of Plutarch's heroes; although, he says, few works can approach the nobility of this play, Wordsworth's "Dion" is one of the few. A few sentences further on he writes, "In the Harleian Miscellanies there is an account of the battle of Lutzen which deserves to be read." In a letter of 1839 (*Letters* 2. 235) on this same theme the last phrase concludes, "it is as fine as Plutarch." In the published essay, however, Emerson keeps back the name of Plutarch for a grander entry on the stage. Another example of "prodigies of individual valour" from Ockley's *History of the Saracens* helps to build up the atmosphere of military heroism and warriors' valor. All this leads up to Plutarch: "But if we explore the literature of Heroism we shall quickly come to Plutarch, who is its Doctor and historian. To him we owe the Brasidas, the Dion, the Epaminondas, the Scipio of old, and I must think we are more deeply indebted to him than to all the ancient writers. Each of his 'Lives' is a refutation to the despondency and cowardice of our religious and political theorists." Man must be armed, Emerson says, and fearlessly fight as a warrior. He must be "self-collected" and must disregard life and reputation in his pursuit of truth and rectitude.

Emerson's heroism is primarily militant. He describes it in military terms: "the breast assumes a warlike attitude"; "to this military attitude of the soul we give the name of Heroism"; it has "a contempt for safety and ease, which makes the attractiveness of war."

Over and over again Emerson returns to this military aspect of heroism. In 1834 when he sets down in his journals (3. 418–419) his debt to Greek thought, he refers especially to Greek biography and to "the brave anecdotes of Agesilaus, Phocion, and Epaminondas." It is significant that these are all drawn from Plutarch and still more significant that all are soldiers and military heroes. Emerson's hero worship always retained something of the admiration of the schoolboy for the hero of the battlefield. In "War" this point of view is reinforced, for there we are told that war is the subject of all history, that it tests the mettle of men and of nations. Once again the leaders whom Emerson mentions are more than a little reminiscent of Plutarch's Stoic heroes; they are picked men "of a courage and vigor tried and augmented in fifty battles" and they try to outdo each other in "new merits, as clemency, hospitality, splendor of living." Here are two of the elements of Stoic virtue, and also the grandeur of the great, extraordinary hero. The last phrases might be suggested by Plutarch's description of the clemency of Caesar, the splendor of living of Lucullus. On the benefits of war Emerson makes the additional comment that when a country has advanced to great heights of culture and prosperity, its achievements are disseminated and spread over the world by its invading armies. He quotes at some length Plutarch's comment on the spread of Greek culture and civilization in Asia, which was the result of the invasions of Alexander the Great.[14] This evidently attracts Emerson strongly, for he uses this Plutarchan passage again in "Considerations by the Way" on much the same topic, the value of apparent evil.

Emerson treats militant heroism in still another essay, "Aristocracy," which belongs to 1848. This is after the formulation of *Representative Men*, but still the military hero survives. He speaks of the universal respect for war; soldiers are respected and even in civil life those who have a military mind, who "engineer in sword and cannon style, with energy and sharpness," are those who prosper. The reason for this admiration for the military is that "courage never loses its high price" and the first faculty which determines a true aristocracy is "a commanding talent." He comments on the ancient concept of the hero as someone gigantic in power and strength. But by this time other qualities must be added to the purely military one; "genius" is also outstanding and for examples of this he goes to the eloquence of Greece and Rome. A man possessed of eloquence, Emerson thinks, has an extraordinary ability which ennobles him; he can neglect trifles, and this apparently leads him to the third quality of the hero, "elevation of sentiment," "the beautiful scorn, the elegant simplicity, the directness, the commanding port" which is universally admired. Here again he seems to be thinking of another quality of the Plutarchan hero with his simple and direct apothegms, his noble actions, his freedom from restraint.

Even in *Representative Men* itself, Emerson does not conceal his admiration for the overwhelming hero. He likes all types, he says, but the examples are military heroes once more — Caesar, Charles V of Spain, Charles XII of Spain, Richard Plantaganet, Bonaparte. The military epithets or military terms best convey the heroic type: "I applaud a sufficient man, an officer equal to his office; captains, ministers, senators." He adds, "Sword and staff, or talents sword-like or staff-like, carry on the work of the world." But Emerson will now add that greater than such heroes is the man who can abolish all heroes, "by letting in this element of reason, irrespective of persons" which destroys individualism: "Then he is a monarch who gives a constitution to his people; a pontiff who preaches the equality of souls and releases his servants from their barbarous homages; an emperor who can spare his empire." Emerson's hero is still the military hero, even if it is his mental and moral qualities which deserve admiration. He stems from Plutarch's hero — the great king or statesman or general. And even the mental and moral qualities which Emerson admires are Plutarchan; there is a cosmopolitanism about *Representative Men*, not merely the self-conscious cosmopolitanism which made him find heroes lacking in America, but also a higher kind, the Stoic cosmopolitanism which stresses equality and the brotherhood of all men, which is seen in Emerson's term "irrespective of persons," a cosmopolitanism which abolishes all individuality. The Stoicism of Plutarch is a hardy perennial in Emerson's thought.

Occasionally, such is Emerson's admiration for Plutarch's heroes that he cannot quite determine why some of them who are not primarily men of war should have such a tremendous following or be regarded as of heroic stature; he begins his essay "Character" (1841–42) with this idea, that the facts of a biography do not always justify the real estimate of a man's "genius." Narrative will give only so much; the real genius must remain latent, hidden in the man's character: "The Gracchi, Agis, Cleomenes, and others of Plutarch's heroes, do not in the record of facts equal their own fame" (*CW* 3. 89). Emerson seems to mean that it is hard to see why Plutarch chose such men as these for biographies; he does not make them seem really great; they must have latent character or genius. It is significant that these subjects of Plutarch's biographical art are not the ones whom Emerson usually singles out as the greatest. He instinctively prefers Phocion, Timoleon, and Epaminondas, who stand out for some noble quality which Emerson thinks of as typical of the "ancients" who were warlike heroes, at the head of the armies of a great nation. At first he cannot understand why the practical reformers, with less romantic characters, are so famous. Emerson's answer to this problem is that these heroes of reform have "character" or "genius." By their innate nature they rise above their fellows in every quality; they see in large terms, they are not petty or mean, they never succumb to the charm of popularity.

It appears that the virtues which constitute "character" are less outstanding and more easily attainable than those which go to make up the hero. There is also a Stoic ring about a journal passage on character in 1828; we must not exhibit anxiety about events or the consequences of action; they have no importance for us. "They have another Director, controller, guide. The whole object of the universe to us is the formation of character." Another passage, four years later, indicates that character is self-sufficiency and self-reliance, based on the soul's "absolute command of its desires." [15] This will produce a decreased concern about what other men do and the language here inevitably reminds us of the classical Stoic apathy and its small regard for philanthropy. Whicher describes Emerson's concept of character as "a combination of probity and practical competence in coöperation with, rather than in defiance of, the order of society" and thinks that it assumes more and more the place of a practical ideal for Emerson as he increasingly realized "the futility of reform." [16] It seems to mark a retreat from the higher demands of heroism to a simpler, more easily attainable ideal, an ideal which has a number of Stoic traits about it. The essay on character and other passages on character usually require some of the old qualities of the hero — character depends somehow on the heroic "reserve of power" and its outward sign is heroic action or "greatness"; will is part of it, the power to overlook the personal profit or loss of an action; it also requires heroic self-sufficiency, but here self-sufficiency is only a negative virtue, "the impossibility of being displaced or overset," or it is a simpler, less strenuous quality, "the habit of fronting the fact, and not dealing with it at second hand, through the perceptions of somebody else." The second essay on character, published in 1866, obviously contains old material. Here character means simply giving the sovereignty to ethics, and its qualities are the same, "habitual self-possession," "a balance not to be overset or easily disturbed by outward events and opinion." The military metaphors and the names of the heroes are almost entirely missing; instead there are references to Heraclitus and Marcus Aurelius, the Stoic philosopher. Character is a mark of the presence of "majestic perception and command"; it is "the presence of the Eternal in each perishing man" and when he elaborates this idea Emerson's words bear a close resemblance to the terms of Stoic pantheism, as when he says that "the Divine Mind imparts itself to the single person." Character is not limited only to the great and the heroes. Anyone who has a devotion to moral principles can acquire character. If the outstanding heroic qualities of "Heroism" are toned down here, so are the rewards. Emerson speaks no longer of fame, the power to influence history, change the direction of an age, and fortify other men; character, it seems, will not provide these, but it brings rather a protection against outward events, "a superiority to all the accidents of life"; rather than a great and lofty height, character is a safe middle way, the way of Stoicism.

To Emerson at a later time character and heroism seem to be synonymous. In a journal passage Emerson mentions some of the Plutarchan heroes who have this intangible quality called character (*Journals* 10. 458–459):

In history we appreciate it [character] fully. We all read Plutarch with one mind, and unanimously take sides with Agesilaus in Sparta, with Aristides, Phocion, Demosthenes, in Athens, with Epaminondas in Thebes, and wonder how the Athenians could be such fools as to take such bravos as the Cleons against these grave, just and noble heroes. In Rome, we give our suffrages again to Scipio, Regulus, Paulus Aemilius, and Cato, and Trajan, and Marcus Aurelius against their profligate rivals.

These heroes are of the Stoic pattern and in the last list the names of Cato and Marcus Aurelius are of special significance, for they are two of the great representatives of the classical Stoic school. These heroes reform their country or lead it against the enemy out of devotion to a principle. They are distinguished for justice; they are capable of dying for a principle; like Demosthenes they will uphold that principle in the face of unpopularity and go against the strong tide as a "minority of one." These are all aspects of the Stoic self-reliance, and Emerson in *English Traits* describes an English hero in similar terms (*CW* 5. 136): "There is an English hero superior to the French, the German, the Italian, or the Greek. When he is brought to the strife with fate, he sacrifices a richer material possession, and on more purely metaphysical grounds. He is there with his own consent, face to face with fortune, which he defies. On deliberate choice and from grounds of character, he has elected his part to live and die for, and dies with grandeur." Like the classical Stoic, the English hero strives against fate and fortune. When he also says of Englishmen, "half their strength they put not forth," we are reminded again of Emerson's Greek heroes who have the easy nonchalance which comes from their "reserve of power."

Self-reliance seems almost to be the one common quality which unites the heroes who are subjects of the lecture series, "Biography." It is in Michelangelo's "almost savage independence," in his demand for absolute freedom in the designing of St. Peter's, in his refusal to accept gifts since thereby he would be obligated to the giver. Luther's self-confidence is based on a confidence in God and in the power of the truth. Emerson speaks of his "sublime reliance on the simple force of truth" and this reliance springs from the conviction that he has the truth and that he is the instrument of God; "No man in history ever assumed a more commanding attitude or expressed a more perfect self-reliance." He abhors dependence and servility. Self-reliance in Emerson's sense of the term appears least in the lectures on Milton and Fox, but Milton speaks of his own "honest haughtiness and self-esteem" which prevented any charge of loose living being a true indictment. In the case of Fox, the Quaker meekness would oppose any self-reliance except that which is based on his conviction that God is within man; it would run strongly contrary to reliance on any human quality or on any merely human self. Yet there is something of the Stoic self-confidence about both Milton and Fox — they trust in the inner light or fire which shows them to be part of God, or to have God within them.

In "Greatness" (*CW* 8. 303) Emerson says, "Self-respect is the early form in which greatness appears" (and here "greatness" seems to be to Emerson synonymous with heroism): "The man in the tavern maintains his opinions, though the whole crowd takes the other side; we are at once drawn to him." Emerson has no use for the masses and he has great difficulty in reconciling his sympathy with the leader principle and his attachment to the modern popular principle of democracy. We must judge a country not by the majority but by the minority; the malefactors always outnumber the benefactors. The really great man, or the man who is on the way to greatness, is persistent in the face of opposition; "the characteristic of heroism is its persistency. . . . "Adhere to your own act," Emerson advises us (*CW* 2. 260), "and congratulate yourself if you have done something strange and extravagant and broken the monotony of a decorous age." He says this again in "The Progress of Culture": "In politics, mark the importance of minorities of one, as of Phocion, Cato, Lafayette, Arago." Emerson here again goes back to Plutarch, where the lives of Phocion and the Stoic Cato are paired as they are here; the reference to Phocion is apparently to be connected with an anecdote used in "Heroism" which draws the moral that a simple manly character need never make apology; he should look at the past with the calmness of Phocion, who admitted that a battle had turned out successfully but did not regret the fact that he had urged against the battle.[17] Here we see the old Stoic calmness in a classical apothegm used long before Emerson, by Montaigne, in "Of Repentance."[18]

The whole concept of the wise minority seems Plutarchan; in "Of Man's Progress in Virtue" Plutarch inculcates self-reliance in the same way and also indicates its presence in the man who will vote against the majority; a sure sign of proficiency in virtue is there "if he hath voted right against a majority of biassed suffragans." Such a man, "who can prove and try himself by himself," shows that "his reason looks inward and is well-rooted within him." This idea is not only Plutarchan but Stoic too, for the Stoics always maintained that the standard for one's guidance is "what the wise man would do." If one follows that guiding rule one can disregard the opinions of all other men.

The essay "War," we have said, stresses military heroism, but the main part of this military heroism is self-reliance; the real significance of war in human history is that it illustrates and instills self-help. In this scheme of things even peace must be an active peace which will employ the resources available for war: "the manhood that has been in war must be transferred to the cause of peace." The attractiveness of war lies in the conviction which it brings "that a man should be himself responsible, with goods, health and life, for his behavior." With the classical hero in mind, Emerson also says, "What makes to us the attractiveness of the Greek heroes? Of the Roman? . . . It is their absolute self-dependence." In the journals (6. 41) he remarks on Sparta, whose whole system was military, "the whole history of Sparta seems to be a picture or text of self-reliance." His conclusion is that peace must be made as attractive as war is to the hero. If peace is to be maintained, it must be by brave men of heroic stature, who will stake everything, including their lives, for a principle. That these ideas are related to Plutarch in Emerson's mind is shown by the placing of a similar passage (CW 3. 274) immediately after a passage borrowed from Plutarch [19] and by references to Plutarchan heroes — Cimon, Themistocles, Alcibiades, Alexander, Caesar — in this particular connection.

"Spontaneity" is sometimes another Emersonian term for self-reliance; more often, however, it is a quality which is a part of self-reliance, and is opposed to thought and logical reasoning. As an example of this quality also Emerson names a Plutarchan hero; in "Spiritual Laws" (CW 2. 133) he says: "We love characters in proportion as they are impulsive and spontaneous. The less a man thinks or knows about his virtues the better we like him. Timoleon's victories are the best victories, which ran and flowed like Homer's verses, Plutarch said." This reference to the life of Timoleon is another favorite of Emerson, occurring also in the letters, the journals, and in "Milton," [20] while Timoleon, as we have seen, was one of the favorite heroes of the eighteenth century and of Emerson's youth. This attribute of self-reliance, too, is the result of the universal humanity of the hero; as Emerson says in "Literary Ethics," "the vision of genius comes by renouncing the too officious activity of the understanding, and giving leave and amplest privilege to the spontaneous sentiment." This is of course a facet of the theory of representative men — spontaneity is as valuable as careful reasoning because it is shared by the individual with all men and comes to him from his universal humanity. But it is also in the strain of the eighteenth century, with its complaints that the heroes of the time are not human but superhuman, embodiments of some overriding spirit or *Geist*.

Another aspect of self-reliance is simplicity or self-denial. Simplicity or self-denial appears in some of the "heroes" of the lectures on "Biography." It is in Michelangelo's simple way of life, in the unsophisticated mind of Luther, contrasted with today's "imitative and artificial society," in the austerity and simplicity of Milton and George Fox. In "Self-Reliance" Emerson says, "The heroic soul does not sell all its justice and nobleness." In other words, the hero does not seek material comforts. "The essence of greatness is the perception that virtue is enough. Poverty is its ornament." As often before, Emerson illustrates this aspect by referring to Plutarchan heroes and echoing Plutarchan passages. In "Heroism," he refuses to accept the story that, after Philippi, Brutus quoted Euripides, "O virtue! I have followed thee through life, and I find thee at last but a shade." [21] Emerson goes on to indicate that if virtue is enough, the hero reckons that opinion, success, and life are cheap, and here his example is Scipio tearing up his account books when challenged by the Roman Senate. On another occasion he notes that Plutarch's Demosthenes is a similar example of self-denial (*Journals* 6. 45): "In Plutarch's Life of Demosthenes it is quoted from the philosopher that through all his orations runs one idea, that Virtue secures its own success." Plutarch gives the name of this anonymous philosopher: it is Panaetius, one of the leading Stoics, and the self-sufficiency of virtue is a familiar Stoic paradox; it is given by Seneca in the proverb "virtue is its own reward"; it is stressed by Epictetus and is the chief theme of Marcus Aurelius. In "Heroism" also the hero acts out of service and love, not for show; no classical example is given here but a phrase shows that Emerson is thinking of Plutarch's Demosthenes.[22] Further classical examples of self-sacrifice occur in "Courage" — Socrates, Aristides, Phocion, Quintus Curtius, Cato, and Regulus — all except the last one known to him from Plutarch, and in several instances we can tell which anecdote in Plutarch Emerson is thinking about when he sets down these particular names.[23]

Prudence or caution is also allied to self-reliance. This is not the common prudence which Emerson mentions in the essay of that title, but the "prudence of a higher strain" which he calls for at the end of the same essay — a caution which does not consist in evasion or flight but in courage. It is based upon reason rather than foolhardiness. In his notebook "War" in 1862 Emerson notes from his Plutarch that it was Pericles' policy to avoid a battle and he refers in the same passage to Aemilius Paulus in Plutarch, who similarly refused battle when his men were weary and those of the enemy fresh. Even the great heroes did not take chances; there is such a thing as a heroic caution, and the Stoics give it a place in their categories of the virtues.[24]

Since the hero is self-reliant, he should be subject to no other restraint. This idea occurs in a number of passages in Emerson, beginning about 1835 and McCormick finds in this concept a new stage in the development of Emerson's attitude to the great man; he is getting away from his religious and moral preconceptions about greatness, away from emphasis on unity, to stress on diversity.[25] But this new concept is, as Emerson knows, really as old as Plutarch. It occurs in "New England Reformers" with Plutarch's sanction: the great reformer will not have undue regard for conventions or even for law, and Plutarch furnishes the apt illustration (*CW* 3.280): "The wise Dandamis, on hearing the lives of Socrates, Pythagoras, and Diogenes read, 'judged them to be great men in every way, excepting that they were too much subjected to the reverence of the laws, which to second and authorize, true virtue must abate very much of its original vigor'." Convention and law must take second place to the energy and vigor of the heroic reformer. This is an old illustration; occurring first in Plutarch's life of Alexander, it was quoted by Bacon in *The Advancement of Learning* and by Montaigne in "Of Utility and Honesty," and here Emerson is using the words of Cotton's Montaigne. He returns to this theme in "Politics," beginning with the idea that "every law and usage was a man's expedient to meet a particular case"; this is the classical Greek concept, debated all through Greek political thought and still current in the eighteenth century, that the state and law exist by "convention," a mutual agreement between men, rather than by "nature." Emerson does not use the term "conventional" but he indicates clearly that he believes that the state is the creation of its citizens and that it is not superior to them. In fact he refers to the Greek tyrant Peisistratus as if to show that he is thinking of the Greek debate here. He puts the theme of the Dandamis apothegm quite boldly and without qualification, "Good men must not obey the laws too well." This aspect of heroism is therefore also Plutarchan, but it is not peculiar to Plutarch or Emerson. It is prominent in Winckelmann and from Winckelmann it passes to Goethe; Goethe's attitude to morality during his classical period, "the ideal of the naturally moral man, who is above the constraints of the laws of conventional morality, who possesses the restraining forces in his own character," [26] is close to that of Emerson. This aspect of heroism is very much in the air in Emerson's own time and its prevalence again illustrates the Plutarchan background of the eighteenth-century doctrine of heroism, still alive in Emerson's time.

"Health" is another quality of the Emersonian hero. The hero of *Representative Men* with his inward fire and without restraint proclaims his "health or fortunate constitution." In "Power" it is the capacity to resist illness, a sort of buoyancy, which produces strength, serenity, and power. In "Courage" it is "the right or healthy state of every man, when he is free to do that which is constitutional to him to do"; it is "organic action." Emerson explains what he means by referring to a passage from Plutarch: "On organic action all strength depends. . . . Plutarch relates that the Pythoness who tried to prophesy without command in the Temple at Delphi, though she performed the usual rites, and inhaled the air of the cavern standing on the tripod, fell into convulsions and died." There is a leap in thought here which makes the anecdote obscure. Emerson appears to mean that the legend can be rationalized to show that heroic strength and courage depend on the organic state of the individual and that an endeavor to do something for which one's nature is not suited can only lead to disaster. When we turn to the passage in Plutarch and read the anecdote in its context, we immediately see its relevance, for Plutarch states (*Moralia* 4. 62–63) that "enthusiasm" or "divine fury" depend upon the existence of a proper proportion between the imaginative part of the soul and the prophetic exhalation; in other words, prophetic ability depends upon the temperament of the prophet as well as upon the spell of the shrine.[27] Courage or heroism, Emerson means, is an organic expression of the whole human constitution. According to him every creature has a courage of his own particular kind and in one passage he alludes to another familiar classical story to explain his theory (*CW* 7. 270): "Every creature has a courage of his constitution fit for his duties: — Archimedes, the courage of a geometer to stick to his diagram, heedless of the siege and sack of the city; and the Roman soldier his faculty to strike at Archimedes. Each is strong, relying on his own, and each is betrayed when he seeks in himself the courage of others." In the essay on courage other classical names appear — Leonidas, Scipio, Caesar, who were all military heroes and whose names could be expected to occur in this connection. The reference to Archimedes is more puzzling, but Emerson regards his concentration as contributed by a healthy, balanced constitution. Nature protects him by giving him concentration or "aridity" as she protects all men of extraordinary talent.[28]

In "Power" Emerson says that concentration is "the secret of strength" in politics, in war, in all kinds of human action. Again his illustration is another Plutarchan hero, Pericles: "Or if you will have a text from politics, take this from Plutarch: 'There was, in the whole city, but one street in which Pericles was ever seen, the street which led to the market-place and the council house. He declined all invitations to banquets, and all gay assemblies and company. During the whole period of his administration he never dined at the table of a friend'." Emerson manages to make this sound modern, as if he were writing about a President of the United States, but the language is actually that of Langhorne, here used verbatim. In *Representative Men* Emerson goes to Plutarch to illustrate another type of concentration, that which makes a speaker keep to his topic and avoid digression and verbiage. Writing of Swedenborg's "theologic determination" and incongruous importation of a foreign rhetoric, he says: "The more coherent and elaborate the system, the less I like it. I say, with the Spartan, 'Why do you speak so much to the purpose, of that which is nothing to the purpose?'" He found this in Plutarch's life of Lycurgus, and another earlier reference to Lycurgus in the same essay again indicates Emerson's Stoic predilection, for "Spartan" and "Stoic" mean roughly the same thing to him, as they did to Plutarch. It is not mere coincidence that Plutarch admires the Spartans almost more than the Athenians — they are the Romans of the pre-Roman world, the Stoics before the term "Stoicism" had been used for the first time.

There is another classical heroic element which Emerson seems to apply to his own concept of the hero. This is the hero as the eloquent speaker. Emerson as a youth fell under the spell of

Daniel Webster, and all his life, as Matthiessen puts it, "an exquisitely modulated human voice, uttering man's convictions, seemed to him . . . the greatest of God's gifts." [29] He found this respect for the orator a characteristic of the ancient world and of Plutarch and this common attachment shared by both Emerson and the ancients probably is the reason for his special interest in anecdotes about Demosthenes, which recur in journals and essays. If the 1835 lecture on Burke lauds him primarily as the statesman-philosopher, the admiration for Burke the orator and lover of Demosthenes finds fairly full scope and the Plutarchan anecdotes about the Greek orator are compared with similar ones about his modern counterpart. To Emerson society became civilized only with the advent of the orator. Emerson's later essay on eloquence in *Letters and Social Aims* is largely a reworking of the earlier in *Society and Solitude*, but the fact that there are two essays on this subject indicates his great interest in oratory and the orator. He regards the orator in the classical, Plutarchan manner, as a man of power with great qualities, who subdues the audience to himself and conquers his hearers. He is an orator-statesman-soldier like Demosthenes. With his audience at his feet, "he is the true potentate; for they are not kings who sit on thrones, but they who know how to govern" (*CW* 7. 63). Plutarch also helps to form Emerson's belief that eloquence itself is an ennobling influence; as Emerson wrote, "Plutarch says 'Eloquence strengthens the nobler parts of the body'." It is not simply "powers of speech" but the heroic "power" which perfects the orator. This "appropriate organ of the highest personal energy" is the same quality, whether it be called fire, power, or energy, which makes the hero. In reality Emerson adopts the Platonic definition of eloquence, "the art of ruling the minds of men," and for other definitions of it he quotes the Platonist Plutarch. [30] Oratory is "a triumph of pure power" which can sway men and nations, and he begins his second essay by picturing oratory as a battle in which is an element of surprise, even though the audience can calculate the weapons, "the armies, the cannon, the musketry, the cavalry, and the character and advantages of the ground." The prime quality of the orator is manliness and the metaphor of the battle is extended over a fairly long passage (*CW* 8. 115) most of which is classical in attitude, and which owes more than a little to Plutarch's portrait of Demosthenes.[31] The same essay on eloquence adds two other illustrations from Plutarch's "Lives of the Ten Attic Orators"; when Emerson wants to indicate that in most civilizations the orator is regarded as a hero and rewarded accordingly he turns to Plutarch;[32] when he speaks of the power of the human voice he cites Plutarch; and when he enumerates the other qualities of the orator they also are classical: "These are ascending stairs, — a good voice, winning manners, plain speech, chastened, however, by the schools into correctness; but we must come to the main matter, of power of statement, — know your fact; hug your fact." If Emerson had lived in ancient Greece, he shows clearly that he would have chosen the best elements of both classical schools of oratory; simplicity rather than ornateness, but also "correctness" in the sense of following the rules developed by the oratorical schools rather than complete freedom; the emphasis on simplicity may further point out to us that he thinks of the Stoics, the directness and terseness of the Stoic hero of Plutarchan Greece. His concept of oratory is completely classical in nature. Again and again when reading Emerson's remarks on oratory we come across references to Demosthenes and in his first essay on eloquence (*CW* 7. 73) both Demosthenes and Pericles appear in two aphorisms which are borrowed from Plutarch.[33]

In three other passages in the first essay on eloquence Emerson uses Plutarch to illustrate the power of the orator. Two of them are anecdotes of Julius Caesar.[34] He considers the orator "a match for events, one who has never found his match, against whom other men being dashed are broken." Equal to any emergency, the orator is a Napoleon or Caesar. He implies that the orator has all the qualities of Caesar: "A man this is who cannot be disconcerted, and so can never play his last card, but has a reserve of power when he has hit his mark. With a serene face, he subverts a kingdom. What is told of him is miraculous; it affects men so. The confidence of men in him is lavish, and he changes the face of the world, and histories, poems and new philosophies arise to account for him." The orator, Emerson indicates again and again, has all the qualities of the hero. He "stands on his own feet." Emerson ends the long paragraph which compares the orator with Julius Caesar with another pro-Spartan passage, based on Plutarch, which reinforces the picture of the orator as a soldier.[35]

What Emerson finds in Demosthenes and to a lesser degree in Cicero, as in all his Plutarchan heroes, is self-reliance; they are great men, fighting for the right, as in a battle, with the weapons of the trained orator.[36] When Emerson thinks of oratory and the orator his mind goes back to the classical examples; and just as Plutarch fashions all his heroes in one mold, so Emerson makes Luther, Burke, Webster, Chatham, Calhoun, and Adams over into examples of the modern Demosthenes or of the modern Cicero, with whom Demosthenes is paired in Plutarch. The complaint that Sumner's speeches were written out is answered by Emerson with an aphorism of Demosthenes.[37] When we have examined the various qualities which, according to Emerson, go to make up the orator, it becomes plain that he is not thinking of a man skilled primarily at speech but of the orator-statesman of Greece and Rome. Endowed with all the attributes of the classical hero, he is in fact the hero under another guise, fighting, in civil life as well as on the battlefield, for a matter of principle.

The essays on eloquence, therefore, seem to repeat much of the material of "Heroism" or "Self-Reliance." They show to how great an extent Emerson was dominated by the concept of the Plutarchan hero. In his *Lives* Plutarch always lays strong stress on the speech of his heroes; they are all orators, speaking in aphorisms and declaiming naturally, and, of the orators, Plutarch shows a marked predilection for Demosthenes, fighting for the liberty of his country. In addition, Emerson's liking for the moral essay with its quotable "sentences" drew him to the short life of Demosthenes in the *Moralia*. There, in addition to several less familiar anecdotes about Demosthenes, he found the brief lives of other orators which gave him evidence of the high regard for oratory and the part of eloquence in the public life of the ancient world. If Emerson turns the orator into another hero it is because Plutarch had done so before him.

It is significant that most of the heroic traits which Emerson mentions fit in well with what he and his contemporaries mean by "stoicism" or "Stoicism." "The Greek battle-pieces are calm," he says in "Culture," "the heroes, in whatever violent actions engaged, retain a serene aspect." In some degree the entire essay is a classical Stoic treatise on education and manners, advocating "quiet manners," and Emerson names Epaminondas along with others as an example to follow, "who never says anything, but will listen eternally." Once more familiar ingredients are at hand. Epaminondas is a calm, serene Greek soldier, concentrating on the task before him and again the anecdote comes from Plutarch.[38] Equanimity and calm have a famous Roman exemplar also and Emerson probably thinks of the life of Fabius when he speaks in his journals in 1839 (5. 248–249) of the "great action and great passiveness of Fabius," of his equanimity before the animosity of the people.

According to Emerson, the self-reliant hero possesses military and masculine virtues, embodying what is essentially Stoicism; indeed "the doctrine of Zeno and the Stoic Sect" may be reduced to "one thought, self-reliance" (*Journals* 8. 575), and it is this Stoicism which he calls for in his own time. The various elements which in "The Man of Letters" Emerson invokes in the scholar of today result in a picture of a Stoic man (*CW* 10. 250–251):

So let his habits be formed, and all his economies heroic; no spoiled child, no drone, no epicure, but a stoic, formidable, athletic, knowing how to be poor, loving labor, and not flogging his youthful wit with tobacco and wine; treasuring his youth. I wish the youth to be an armed and complete man; no helpless angel to be slapped in the face, but a man dipped in the Styx of human experience, and made invulnerable so, — self-helping. A redeeming trait of the Sophists of Athens, Hippias and Gorgias, is that they made their own clothes and shoes.

In "The Scholar," on a similar theme, he complains that we lack those "iron personalities, such as in Greece and Italy and once in England were formed to strike fear into kings and draw the eager service of thousands." Stoic calm and serenity are extoled in "Aristocracy." The superior man is one who can endure all trouble and adversity, "indeed on whom events make little or no impression, and who can face death with firmness." If we did not know this to be Emerson, we would take it to be Marcus Aurelius speaking. The "gentleman" described in "Manners" is really the classical hero in another guise. This is also clear from the examples which he gives (*CW* 3. 125) — Saladin, Sapor, the Cid, Julius Caesar, Scipio, Alexander, Pericles. "He is good company for pirates," Emerson says of this gentleman and it is certain that this is a reference to the capture of Julius Caesar by the pirates and his calmness and firmness when in their hands, for Emerson uses the Plutarchan story several times as an example of heroic "reserve of power." This term itself has a Stoic ring; such a man is the same to all men, never reaching the limit of his endurance and ability; he is a "supreme commander over all his affections and passions."

For his examples of heroism, then, Emerson constantly turns to the Greeks and Romans, repeatedly using the same names — Phocion, Timoleon, Epaminondas, the Spartans, among the Greeks; Fabius, Julius Caesar, and the real Stoic Cato among the Romans. Emerson's self-reliance has strong Stoic tinges in his emphasis on equanimity, ability to suffer as well as to act, control of the passions and emotions, self-denial and self-sacrifice. In quotations from the Plutarchan heroes it is often the Stoic or Stoic-sounding aphorisms which Emerson singles out. He is quite well aware of the difference between the more abstract and philosophical Greek Stoicism and the practical Stoicism of the Romans, but it is the latter which he finds more congenial to his own temperament and of greater value for his own generation. If, in spite of this predilection, the examples of this practical Stoicism, this self-reliance, whom he mentions are more often Greeks than Romans — Demosthenes, Pericles, Timoleon, Phocion rather than Scipio, Cato, or Cicero — this does not indicate dissent from Plutarch's view, for Plutarch, himself a Greek, displays a greater patriotic liking for the Greek heroes than for the Romans and at yet the same time, as we have mentioned before, gives his Greek heroes features and traits which are those of Roman practical Stoicism. In the *Lives* Cato is placed next to Phocion and the two are so compared that Phocion is given a Stoic coloring; he becomes another Cato, simple and austere. His honor is incorruptible, he never succumbs to the lure of popularity and can act in the face of adverse public opinion. At the same time he is a great military leader and like Cato goes to martyrdom for his principles. Other Greeks, whose names were familiar to Emerson and his generation, such as Timoleon and Pericles, are portrayed by Plutarch in much the same light.[39]

Emerson would be the first to admit that his hero worship and self-reliance are not new, that his heroes are the soldier heroes of Plutarch. He never outgrows his youthful liking for the brave soldier, nor could he do so, for this type of hero worship was constantly reinforced by his reading of his predecessors who like him felt the greatest admiration for Plutarch and his Greeks and Romans. Emerson, Montaigne, and Plutarch all admire the same type of great man; a single heroic type emerges from the descriptions given by each of the three. He is humble, reasonable, simple, self-reliant, self-denying, devoted to principle. All these qualities make him in Emerson's time (and in our own) a "Stoic" hero.

V

THE PLUTARCHAN PHILOSOPHY

[Plutarch] has a just instinct of the presence of a master, and prefers to sit as a scholar with Plato, than as a disputant. . . . He is an eclectic in such sense as Montaigne was, — willing to be an expectant, not a dogmatist.

"Plutarch"

Iᴛ is manifestly impossible to select out of all the many influences which lie behind American Transcendentalism any one author and to say that here is the chief source of transcendental idealism. A great variety of definitions of Transcendentalism have been given and many sources have been listed and examined. These source studies seldom make adequate reference to the part played by renewed reading in Plutarch and the Roman Stoics; but one participant in the movement saw at least some of their significance. William Henry Channing says [1] that Transcendentalism was in part:

a reaction against Puritan Orthodoxy; in part, an effect of renewed study of the ancients, or Oriental Pantheists, of Plato and the Alexandrians, of Plutarch's *Morals*, Seneca and Epictetus; in part, the natural product of the culture of the place and time. On the somewhat stunted stock of Unitarianism — whose characteristic dogma was trust in individual reason as correlative to Supreme Wisdom — had been grafted German Idealism, as taught by masters of most various schools — by Kant and Jacobi, Fichte and Novalis, Schelling and Hegel, Schleiermacher and De Wette, by Madame de Staël, Cousin, Coleridge, and Carlyle; and the result was a vague yet exalting conception of the godlike nature of the human spirit.

It is equally difficult to separate out the influences which operated on Emerson, the chief exponent of Transcendentalism, from those which affected other members of the group; Emerson's eclecticism, the same thing which he admired in Plutarch, must always be kept in mind; others tended to follow one leader in America or in Germany, but Emerson, while widely acquainted with contemporary ways of thought in his country and Europe, "assimilated all foreign ideas into the special ways of his own expression." [2] It is the working of this process of assimilation in Emerson which makes the tracing of his sources so difficult and at the same time so interesting. Much progress in this area has been made in the last few years; almost all of the sources mentioned by Channing have been studied in connection with Emerson except that of Plutarch and the Stoics; it now appears that Coleridge and Carlyle were important as agents in bringing German philosophy to the attention of Emerson and other New Englanders; at the same time the debt of Emerson to the Germans has been to some extent discounted — it has been demonstrated by René Wellek that "Emerson was looking among the Germans for support for his own faith," a faith which was already deeply rooted in his own mind and spiritual ancestry; [3] and Perry Miller has reminded us that Transcendentalism in the sense of mysticism and a tendency toward pantheism is evident in some of the strains of Puritanism in seventeenth-century New England. [4] Stephen Whicher's thorough study of the development of Emerson's thought between 1837 and 1840, the period when most of his ideas took firmer shape, shows how Emerson arrives at an "acquiescence" or acceptance in his attitude towards fate and destiny. It is an attitude very close to that of the Stoics and there are Stoic elements, of the Plutarchan type, in his writing of the period before he reached this position; the resigned acquiescence may well be the result of, among manifold influences which play on him, an increased "affinity" for Stoicism, an often unconscious falling into the

ways of Stoic thought.[5] His acquaintance with the loose Stoicism of
Plutarch, and a lesser acquaintance with the Stoic cosmology and
theology may well have helped him to achieve this optimistic acquiescence with the laws of nature and of the universe.

This Plutarchan and Stoic element in Emerson's thinking is
generally overlooked; when Emerson expresses admiration for
Stoicism it is usually dismissed as rhetoric or identified with Puritanism; the greater part of his debt is usually said to be to Platonism
and Neoplatonism, with the Eastern strain in the latter accounting
for at least some of the kinship between Emerson and Persian
writers; Carpenter and others have pointed out that Emerson's
Plato is a "composite, mystical Plato," a mixture of Plato and the
Neoplatonists. Although it would certainly be an exaggeration to say
that "the statement of any important conclusion will be found to
have a Platonic source, either in the canon of Plato's own work or in
the Neoplatonists,"[6] Emerson himself encourages that view by saying that Transcendentalism is idealism, that is, Platonism. For the
basic doctrines of Platonism, Emerson could go to the fountainhead,
Plato himself, for he read Plato both in the Greek and in translation. It is doubtful whether he does this often, however, for idealism was strong in the first half of the nineteenth century and he
could find Platonism in philosophers and writers such as Coleridge,
Kant, Goethe, Berkeley, and Swedenborg, and Neoplatonism in the
Cambridge Platonists like Cudworth, where he first met direct
quotations from Proclus, Plotinus, and Iamblichus.[7] But we must
also take into account in Emerson's thought, besides the Platonists
and Neoplatonists, other classical philosophers, especially the Stoics
and those of the pre-Socratics who anticipated Stoicism. Here as in
many other respects Emerson's relation with Plutarch was particularly close. He found in him a kindred spirit in that he was fundamentally a Platonist; then too they had another philosophical source
in common, for Plutarch supplements the Platonic tradition by
drawing upon the Stoics for many special aspects of his thought;
and Emerson felt much sympathy in attitude and outlook toward

this combination. He admires Plutarch's selection of certain forms of Stoicism, expressing his admiration in terms which apply just as aptly to himself (*CW* 10. 308–309): "'T is a temperance, not an eclecticism, which makes him adverse to the severe Stoic, or the Gymnosophist, or Diogenes, or any other extremist. That vice of theirs shall not hinder him from citing any good word they chance to drop." Again Plutarch was a moralist who wrote moral essays of the Stoic type and with this moral and Stoic bias Emerson could agree wholeheartedly. He commends Plutarch, saying that he "is not a metaphysician," he is not the founder of any sect or community. Like Plutarch, Emerson usually assumes or takes for granted the Platonic metaphysical basis on which an ethical system must rest and he devotes the greater part of his attention to the same practical problems which concerned the Stoics. These are connected with the question, "how are the Platonic ethical standards to be applied and used in all the various aspects of everyday living?" It is in the pragmatic side of his thinking, his interest in morality, that Emerson most closely approaches Plutarch.[8]

We have seen that Emerson could obtain his Platonism from a great variety of sources and that Plutarch was by no means his chief source here; but the situation is far different in regard to the pre-Socratic philosophers. Plutarch is Emerson's chief source for his acquaintance with the pre-Socratics and there is strong evidence that for a number of "opinions" of these earlier Greek philosophers Emerson found a convenient summary in the work in the Plutarchan corpus entitled "Concerning Those Opinions of Nature wherein the Philosophers Delighted." [9] Several of these pre-Socratics, notably Heraclitus, exerted a marked influence upon Emerson in idea and language and here Plutarch was probably the intermediary. Emerson's acquaintance with Plutarch in this connection, however, was probably not direct at first.

In 1830 Emerson read for the first time Baron Gérando's *Histoire Comparée des Systèmes de Philosophie*.[10] Gérando's outline of Greek pre-Socratic philosophy relied heavily on writers who had listed the opinions of the philosophers on various topics, especially on Plutarch's "Concerning Those Opinions of Nature wherein the Philosophers Delighted" and on Diogenes Laertius' *Lives of the Philosophers*. Emerson had probably read some of the essays of the *Moralia* before 1830 but it is likely that he first became acquainted with Plutarch's listing of the opinions of the pre-Socratics through Gérando and that as a result of this reading he turned later to Plutarch as one of Gérando's sources. It is significant that whenever Emerson quotes one of the opinions of a pre-Socratic it is a brief opinion and so we can safely conclude that his acquaintance with the Greek philosophers before Plato largely consisted of tags of this kind, with Gérando sometimes serving as the intermediary. In *Journals* 2. 336–345, he notes a number of passages on the Greek philosophers and their opinions. For example, on Thales he writes: "Yet doth it appear that, over all this matter, he set a universal cause, and Diogenes Laertius and Plutarch give these three maxims to him; *God is the oldest, for he was not made. The world is most perfect, for it is the work of God. No action, no thought even is hid from God."* Emerson is here, from the reference to Diogenes on, translating from Gérando.

When Emerson begins to read Gérando he is interested in his technique as well as in his sources. He remarks in his journal: "I begin the *Histoire Comparée des Systèmes de Philosophie par M. de Gérando*. This leads me in the outset back to Bacon (*De Augmentis Scientiae*)." He goes on to observe that Gérando's arrangement of philosophical concepts follows that of Bacon and that Plutarch's method — of listing the topics and then giving the opinion of each philosopher on that topic — has shortcomings; this does not necessarily indicate that Emerson has now a close acquaintance with Plutarch's collection of the opinions of the philosophers, for he is relying on Bacon [11] and says: "But he [Bacon] expressly warns that it should 'be done distinctly and severally, the philosophies of every one throughout by themselves, and not by titles packed and faggotted up together as hath been done by Plutarch'." It seems very likely that his reading of Gérando's and Bacon's references to Plutarch set Emerson to read Plutarch, as Gérando sent him to Bacon. Emerson's copy of the *Moralia* is much marked and annotated in this part of the work and he probably turned to Plutarch's account of ancient philosophy at this time. From then on, his references to the pre-Socratics are usually based on Plutarch.

The characteristic of Plutarch's collection of the opinions of the ancient philosophers which specially attracted Emerson is the modernity of the ideas. He writes in *Journals* 8. 127–128:

> Every great fact in natural science has been divined by the presentiment of somebody. When I looked into Plutarch's *Placita Philosophorum* the other day, it was easy to see that Spinoza, Laplace, Schelling, and Oken, and Plato are pre-existent; that these old men, in the beginning of science, as we are apt to say, had little to learn from all our accumulation of facts.
>
> *Thales, Anaximenes,* Air is the soul and source of things. *Empedocles, Pythagoras,* made the first discovery of the obliquity of the ecliptic, but one *Oenopides* of Chios challenges to himself the invention of it. *Aristarchus* "places the sun among the fixed stars; that the Earth is moved about the Sun by its inclination and vergency towards it, intercepts its light, and shadows its orb." What could Copernicus add? *Thales,* that the moon borrows all its light from the sun; that the earth is globular; the moon's eclipse is perfectly known. *Metrodorus,* infinite worlds in infinite space.

The second paragraph of this passage, which was summarized later in "Fate," relies heavily on Plutarch's collection [12] and Emerson had already in "Literary Ethics" mentioned his discovery that the most recent philosophers like Fichte or Kant were anticipated by "the earliest enquirers" such as Parmenides, Heraclitus, and Xenophanes, whom he knew from Plutarch.

Some of these *placita* appear from time to time in Emerson and sometimes we can see how his use of a favorite one develops. In *Journals* 7. 357 he writes: "In Plutarch's *Placita Philosophorum*, I remember some one found the soul in the air circulating, respired and expired by all alike." He is attracted by the figure of speech and puts it to work: "Yes, Wisdom is in the air, and good health gets it all." In "Country Life" in 1858 he talks of the pleasure of the open air after much confinement to the house (*CW* 12. 140–141); this time he has identified the "some one" of the journals as Anaximenes:

> The power of the air was the first explanation offered by the early philosophers of the mutual understanding that men have. "The air," said Anaximenes, "is the soul, and the essence of life. By breathing it, we become intelligent, and, because we breathe the same air, understand one another." Plutarch thought it contained the knowledge of the future. "If it be true that souls are naturally endowed with the faculty of prediction, and that the chief source that excites that faculty is a certain temperature of air and winds," etc. Even Lord Bacon said, "The Stars inject their imagination or influence into the air."

Emerson has found this reference to Anaximenes in "Concerning those Opinions of Nature . . ." and that he is thinking of Plutarch is indicated by the presence of his name in the paragraph. The dictum of Plutarch on the soul's power of divination is also apparently from Anaximenes; this too is a favorite of Emerson; he copied it into his journals in 1839 (5. 287) and used it in "Inspiration" and in his essay on Plutarch. We may conjecture that the reason for Emerson's interest in Anaximenes' elemental form of pantheism, or at least a theory which stresses the unity of mankind, is that it is a primitive physical theory which has in it the seeds of Stoic monism and of his own "Over-Soul." There is a reminiscence of it in another essay: the conclusion of "The Method of Nature," like the concluding paragraphs of a number of his lectures and essays, has an upward sweep toward the ideal world; but the Stoic echo is strong also and perhaps Anaximenes' theory is in Emerson's mind when he says that the soul "circulates" through the universe, penetrating everything.

When we come to Plato, Emerson very occasionally found in Plutarch a brief statement of a Platonic dogma, a quotable tag of Platonism which attracted him as much by its aphoristic language as by the thought itself. Twice in his journals (7. 92, 10. 338) he noticed the passage in the "Symposiacs" (*Moralia* 3. 402–406) on the Platonic statement "that God geometrizes." In the second journal entry he characteristically went back to the familiar copy of the "Several Hands" translation although the new version was now available. But this aphorism was also noted because its concept of God fitted in with Emerson's own — that God is eternal — and with the comparison of God to a circle "whose centre was everywhere and its circumference nowhere"; at the same time it conveyed in the form of an aphorism the Emersonian belief, expressed repeatedly, that there are laws of nature and hence laws of morals which "give to moral nature an aspect of mathematical science" (*Journals* 3. 434).[13] For another Platonic apothegm in Plutarch he read and compared the original translation with Goodwin's revised version and wrote in *Journals* 10. 339: "Plato says that Time had its original from an intelligence — PLUTARCH, *Morals*, vol. iii, p. 158."

Plutarch's own philosophical "opinions" (to use Plutarch's term in the "Several Hands" translation), as distinct from those of Plato quoted by Plutarch, are given very seldom by Emerson. In "The Scholar," for example (*CW* 10. 280ff.), Emerson upheld the world of the intellect against the material tendencies of modern America, declaring that the modern world is hostile to what he calls "the morbid intellectual tendency" in youth and that the demand of America is for practical knowledge and utility. We must cheerfully uphold, Emerson said, what we believe in; if we believe that intellect is superior to material things, we must say so courageously. He recalled that Plotinus decried the world of the senses and Plutarch said that "matter is privation." [14] What he did not say is that Plutarch's remark is originally Platonic and he used it in "The Scholar" because he himself agreed heartily with this Platonic dictum, even if his own version would probably not have taken such a sweeping form. The passage is also interesting because it is the only passage in Emerson's writing where he puts Plutarch and Plotinus together; by doing this he seems to acknowledge Plutarch's connection with the Neoplatonists to whom he himself owed so much.

ii

We have shown that Emerson received his knowledge of the theories of the Greek pre-Socratics, occasionally of Plato, from Plutarch, and these theories, usually in the brief form which Plutarch used, appear and reappear in journals and essays. They were noted usually as instances of the modernity of the oldest concepts. But two of these theories seem to have had a special attraction for and exerted a special influence upon him and it is significant that they are both ideas which were basic to Stoicism, theories which formed the foundation on which the Stoics laid their own philosophic system. In the same part of the journals in which he made his notes from Gérando he for the first time (also probably from Gérando) noted (2. 340) what later became one of his favorite apothegms — that the Pythagoreans first called the world *kosmos*, which Emerson, adopting one of the two terms which the "Several Hands" had used to translate the Greek word, called "beauty." This remark, attributed to "the Greeks," reappears at the beginning of the third chapter of "Nature," in "Works and Days," and in "Michael Angelo" and comes originally from Plutarch, *Moralia* 3. 132: "Pythagoras was the first philosopher that gave the name of *kosmos* to the world, from the order and beauty of it." Although he seems to have met the apothegm first in Gérando, he soon read it in Plutarch and many years later he copied it into his journal "ST," this time in Goodwin's translation. Such a progression, from a secondary source to Plutarch himself, is typical of Emerson.

Of all the instances of borrowing from Plutarch's "Concerning those Opinions of Nature . . ." this is the most interesting, and it is significant that Emerson used it often. A repetition of this remark is as close as we ever find Emerson coming to the problem of cosmology; he seems to have been more attracted to this Pythagorean concept than to the cosmology of Plato's *Timaeus* which did not interest him. Modern science was putting the ancient cosmographers like Plato out of date, but this Pythagorean concept of an orderly universe working according to rules was still modern. It is one of the many instances in which, as Emerson said, the ancient philosophers anticipated the most modern philosophic and scientific thought. Thus Emerson found the Pythagorean *kosmos* still pertinent and descriptive; the remark appears in his own writings almost like the text of a sermon. Certainly it fitted in with the Emersonian conception of the world, with his idea that nature is one and orderly (for *kosmos* means "orderly arrangement"), working consistently and according to a law — the law of nature. From whatever source or sources, Platonic or Oriental, Emerson drew his monism, or as his detractors called it, his pantheism, he found a neat expression of it here in one of the earliest Greek philosophers. The way in which he uses this expression in "Nature" also confirms what he himself says, that he likes to use a remark from one of the ancient writers whom he read, to start a train of thought; here the sentence from Pythagoras gives the key idea which he develops in the course of the chapter, that "a nobler want of man is served by nature, namely, the love of Beauty" (*CW* 1. 15). This theory of the orderly nature of the universe, expressed by Pythagoras, is centuries later taken up and developed by the Stoics and one of the important Stoic arguments for the divinity of the universe is based on the perception of the orderly arrangement of the elements in it. Here again, we may perhaps say, Emerson's affinity for the Stoic philosophy appears.

Except for his liking for the Pythagorean term *kosmos*, beauty and order, Emerson does not show much interest in Pythagoras. He could feel little sympathy with his political philosophy and magical aspects. Even so he was acquainted with the Pythagorean emphasis on the power of numbers, and especially the number five. A line in the poem "Woodnotes" (*CW* 9. 43–44) seems to refer to this:

Knowledge this man prizes best
Seems fantastic to the rest . . .
Why Nature loves the number five.

In "Why the Oracles Cease" Plutarch says, "nature divideth many
things by this number" and the essay "Of the Word EI at Delphi"
has something to say on the magic power of the number five and
of the reason for Pythagoras' singling out this number for special
mention. Emerson also refers several times in terms of approval
to Pythagoras' advocacy of "solitude" or "silence" for the student
and the philosopher; he begins his short paper "Prayers" with a
remark of Plutarch, "Pythagoras said that the time when men are
honestest is when they present themselves before the gods." [15]

But while Emerson knew the pre-Socratics through Plutarch and
seems specially drawn to the Pythagorean *kosmos*, there is another
philosopher from whom he quotes much more often and whose ideas
seem to recur constantly throughout his writings. This is Heraclitus,
the philosopher of flux and change. There is a reference to him in
"Illusions"; "The Method of Nature" quotes his familiar apothegm,
"You cannot bathe twice in the same river"; in "Intellect" Emerson
remarks that "Heraclitus looked upon the affections as dense and
colored mists." In "English Traits" and in "Manners" Emerson
shows that he is attracted by Heraclitus' expression "dry light." [16]
The later lecture on "Character" (1865) and the Harvard Commemoration Speech quote other familiar apothegms. In "Demonology"
we meet Heraclitus' remark, "There is one world common to all
who are awake, but each sleeper betakes himself to one of his
own," a passage from Plutarch's "Of Superstition." In the essay
on Plutarch we read. "Do you not observe, some one will say,
what a grace there is in Sappho's measures, and how they delight
and tickle the ears and fancies of the hearers? Whereas the Sibyl,
with her frantic grimaces, uttering sentences altogether thoughtful
and serious, neither focused nor perfumed, continues her voice
a thousand years through the favor of the Divinity that speaks
within her." [17] This is a direct quotation from *Moralia* 3. 74 and

there the sentence on the Sibyl turns out to be a quotation from Heraclitus. Again at the end of the Plutarch essay Emerson quotes from *Moralia* 2. 477: "Were there not a sun, we might, for all the other stars, pass our days in the Reverend Dark, as Heraclitus calls it." In many of his journals and notebooks the Greek phrase *hoi reontes* occurs, sometimes merely scrawled in the margin; it is the term for the "flowing philosophers," the followers of Heraclitus who believed that the universe is constantly in flux, comparable to a stream ever flowing onward; and Heraclitus' doctrine *panta rei*, "all things flow," is mentioned in "Quotation and Originality." [18] From Gérando in 1830 Emerson summarizes Heraclitus' doctrine in *Journals* 2. 344: "[Wisdom] consisted in discovering the law which governs all things. All nature is governed by constant laws. The phenomena themselves, which appear discordant, concur in the harmony of the whole. . . . Meanwhile all change. Attraction, Repulsion." Plutarch quotes a number of aphorisms, like the one on the Sibyl, and includes philosophic opinions of Heraclitus. Only in the passages in the "Consolation to Apollonius" (*Moralia* 1. 308–309) and in "Of the Word EI at Delphi" does he devote a little more space to Heraclitus. In the first of these he summarizes the philosophy of flux:

For, as Heraclitus saith, it is the same thing to be dead and alive, asleep and awake, a young man and decrepit; for these alternately are changed one into another. For as a potter can form the shape of an animal out of his clay and then as easily deface it, and can repeat this backwards and forwards as often as he pleaseth, so Nature too out of the same materials fashioned first our grandfathers, next our fathers, then us, and in process of time will engender others, and again others upon these. For as the flood of our generation glides on without any intermission and will never stop, so in the other direction the stream of our corruption flows eternally on. . . .

Emerson's concept of the illusory, flowing nature of the world and of experience has also sometimes been attributed to Oriental influences. Nevertheless, we can clearly see that he is well aware of

Heraclitus' doctrine of flux, directly in Plutarch or indirectly through Gérando or some similar work. The same motif appears in "Nature": "Who looks upon a river in a meditative hour and is not reminded of the flux of all things?" In "The Poet" life is "the flowing or metamorphosis," and in the essay on Swedenborg in *Representative Men* the "flowing of nature" is illustrated by the story of Amasis which is taken from Plutarch; in "Montaigne" nature or life is "the flowing power which remains itself in all changes." In "Fate," matter becomes fluid on the approach of mind "and the power to flux it is the measure of mind." Emerson believes that beauty too is flowing, and that motion provides better symmetry than motionless form does; in "Beauty" there is a reference to Plato's "all-dissolving Unity." In "Farming" Emerson says, "all things are flowing, even those that seem immovable," and here he adds another figure to illustrate a different facet of the same idea; speaking of the aspect of decay in nature, he employs the simile of combustion which goes on continually and which sounds rather like the Stoic recurrent conflagration. In the introductory essay in "Poetry and Imagination" Emerson returns to the same idea that nature is always changing, "always passing into something else, streaming into something higher." "Thin or solid, everything is in flight" (*CW* 8. 5); and again, "The nature of things is flowing, a metamorphosis" (*CW* 8. 71). In "Woodnotes" he elaborates:

> The rushing metamorphosis,
> Dissolving all that fixture is,
> Melts things that be to things that seem,
> And solid nature to a dream.

In the same poem Emerson employs the figures of both water and fire together:

> Onward and on, the eternal Pan,
> Who layeth the world's incessant plan,
> Halteth never in one shape,
> But forever doth escape,

> Like wave or flame, into new forms,
> Of gem, and air, of plants, and worms.

In "The Natural History of Intellect," memory is the only thing that "abides in the flowing." Strauch thinks that there is a connection between "the idea of a flowing stream prefigured in the pouring of the deluge" in the poem "Song of Nature" and a passage in Plutarch's "Why the Oracles Cease to Give Answers" and that another reference to the flowing of water in "Uriel," which is in the manuscript associated with the "Song of Nature," may also come from a reading of Plutarch. But one cannot be dogmatic in matters of this kind, for the poems which contain this and similar metaphors draw upon much varied reading, as diverse as Mary Moody Emerson and a textbook on agricultural chemistry; "the whole," says Strauch, "suggesting a freely flowing association of ideas in Emerson's characteristic mode of random, spontaneous creation." [19] The only point to be made here is that the Heraclitean flux is especially attractive to Emerson, and the modern concept of evolution only serves to reinforce its influence upon him; it could be found in many sources contemporary as well as ancient, and it appears quite definitely in the favorite Plutarch and in a favorite essay of Plutarch's *Moralia*.

But, as Emerson observed in his note on Heraclitus in Gérando's work, even in Heraclitus the flux and metamorphosis, the constant diversity and impermanence, is accompanied by its opposite, an underlying unity and permanence,[20] akin to the Pythagorean *kosmos*, and indeed perhaps a development from it. This dualism of contraries in Heraclitus and the unique combination of unity and diversity, constant change as well as constant permanence, evidently impressed the Stoics as being logical and consistent, for they took over Heraclitus' flux and unity and developed them into, or superimposed on them, a cyclic theory. It is also a dualism which is attractive to Emerson, striving to reconcile, as Heraclitus did, unity with diversity, monism with dualism. This combination of opposites is quite evident in and basic to "The Method of Nature":

"The wholeness we admire in the order of the world is the result of infinite distribution. Its smoothness is the smoothness of the pitch of the cataract. Its permanence is a perpetual inchoation. . . . If anything could stand still, it would be crushed and dissipated by the torrent it resisted. . . ." And I do not think one would be far wrong in suggesting that in "the order of the world" we have another reference to the Pythagorean *kosmos*. All through this essay, so basic to Emerson's concept of nature, runs the Heraclitean flux — Emerson calls it "ecstasy" — which still has the completeness and unity of a circle; it is "to be represented by a circular movement," or it is "tendency" or "rapid metamorphosis." More often it is the diversity and the change which Emerson stresses; all the ends of man's life are "momentary," but the same figure of motion is used to describe the unified relation of the universal and the particular, of God or nature and man: man's greatness consists in his being "the channel through which heaven flows to earth"; we must be "vessels filled with the divine overflowings." In its greatest moments the human race has been "God rushing into multiform benefit." Emerson says the same thing and uses the same Heraclitean metaphor to express unity in diversity in "Self-Reliance": "Society is a wave. The wave moves onward, but the water of which it is composed does not. The same particle does not rise from the valley to the ridge. Its unity is only phenomenal. The persons who make up a nation to-day, next year die, and their experience dies with them." When the young Emerson says that he has something of Heraclitus in him, he is closer to the truth than he realizes.

We have seen that the Stoics added a cyclic theory to Heraclitus' flux and permanence — the periodic conflagration of the universe is followed by a reconstruction. It is probably not much more than a coincidence (though it again may show Emerson's "affinity" for Stoicism) that he too sometimes adapts Heraclitus in the direction in which the Stoics also did, shifting Heraclitus' flux to alternation (*CW* 9. 315):

Giddy with motion Nature reels,
Sun, moon, man undulate and stream,
The mountains flow, the solids seem,
Change acts, reacts; back, forward hurled,
And pause were palsy to the world.

Viewed in this aspect, the world is one of illusion and constant change. He introduced his essay "Illusions" with a curious and turbulent poem which embodied the essence of that belief:

Flow, flow the waves hated,
Accursed, adored,
The waves of mutation:
No anchorage is.
Sleep is not, death is not;
Who seem to die live . . .

When thou dost return
On the wave's circulation,
Beholding the shimmer,
The wild dissipation,
And, out of endeavor
To change and to flow,
The gas become solid,
And phantoms and nothings
Return to be things,
And endless imbroglio
Is law and the world . . .

Here the repeated figure is the typical Heraclitean one of the wave which flows constantly; and the identity of sleep and death and the negation of both is Heraclitean and comes without doubt from Plutarch; perhaps from "Of the Word EI at Delphi" where the Platonic and Heraclitean concept of illusion is treated at some length. The passage is a long one but Emerson had a double opportunity to meet these remarks of Plutarch since his favorite Montaigne quoted them, with some alterations and omissions, at the end of the "Apology for Raimond Sebond." [21] Indeed the motto poem seems to be Emerson's summary of the following passage from Plutarch's "Of the Word EI at Delphi" (*Moralia* 4. 494–459):

For we cannot, as Heraclitus says, step twice into the same river, or twice find any perishable substance in the same state; but by the suddenness and swiftness of the change, it disperses and again gathers together, comes and goes. Whence what is generated of it reaches not to the perfection of being, because the generation never ceases nor is at an end; but always changing, of seed it makes an embryo, next an infant, then a child, then a stripling, after that a young man, then a full-grown man, an elderly man, and lastly, a decrepit old man, corrupting the former generations and statures by the latter. But we ridiculously fear one death, having already so often died and still dying. For not only, as Heraclitus said, is the death of fire the generation of air, and the death of air the generation of water; but you may see this more plainly in men themselves; for the full-grown man perishes when the old man comes, as the youth terminated in the full-grown man, the child in the youth, the infant in the child. So yesterday died in to-day, and to-day dies in tomorrow; so that none remains nor is one, but we are generated many, according as matter glides and turns about one phantasm and common mould. For how do we, if we remain the same, delight now in other things than we delighted in before? How do we love, hate, admire, and contemn things contrary to the former? How do we use other words and other passions, not having the same form, figure, or understanding? For neither is it probable we should be thus differently affected without change, neither is he who changes the same. And if he is not the same, neither is he at all; but changing from the same, he changes also his being, being made one from another. But the sense is deceived through the ignorance of being, supposing that to be which appears.

What then is it that has really a being? That which is eternal, unbegotten, and incorruptible, to which no time brings a change. For time is a certain movable thing appearing in connection with fleeting matter, always flowing and unstable, like a leaky vessel full of corruption and generation; . . . Now if the same thing befalls Nature, which is measured by time, as does the time which measures it, there is nothing in it permanent or subsistent, but all things are either breeding or dying, according to their commixture with time. . . .

But God, we must say, *is*, and he is not in any time, but in eternity, which is immovable without time, and free from inclination, in which there is nothing first, or last, or newer; but being one, it has filled its eternal duration with one only "now"; and that only *is* which is really according to this, of which it cannot be said, that it either was or shall be, or that it begins or shall end.

This Heraclitean passage of Plutarch, translated in Montaigne, and showing a kinship with Emerson's own thinking, can hardly have escaped his attention. His awareness of the illusory nature of experience is obvious to every reader of Emerson. It is outlined, with a personal feeling unmatched elsewhere, in "Experience," it is less personal but is still an attitude which all men face at some time or another in "Montaigne," and it is described in greater detail but with a greater detachment and impersonality in "Illusions." Stephen Whicher has shown how these essays fit into the story of Emerson's own developing thoughts on experience and why the picture of illusion made its impact felt on him.[22] For our purposes the interest is in observing that this "doctrine of the Illusionists" is still that of Heraclitus, even if Emerson found it restated in some of the Oriental thinkers; it is still more vital, since it is confirmed by the ancients of the Eastern world as well as of the West.

"Experience" begins with a reference to the classical daemon — the Genius at our birth has mixed the cup of forgetfulness too strongly, so that a sleepy lethargy trails us all through life; "all things swim and glitter" and Emerson speaks of "the evanescence and lubricity of all objects." "Dream delivers us to dream." We are in constant motion: "gladly would we anchor, but the anchorage is quicksand." "Life itself is a bubble and a skepticism, and a sleep within a sleep." Seven "lords of life" are described — illusion, temperament, succession, surface, surprise, reality, subjectiveness. One sentence sounds genuinely Stoic and Heraclitean. Emerson reminds us that the ancients exalted chance into a divinity, "but that is to stay too long at the spark, which glitters truly at one point, but the universe is warm with the latency of the same fire." To one acquainted with ancient philosophical schools, this sounds like a rejection by Emerson of the Epicurean "chance" and the

acceptance of the Stoic "fire." It may well be only an artistic metaphor here, but knowing Emerson's view of fate, it is tempting to
conclude that this also is the fate which Plutarch believes in; what
appears to be chance from one point of view is in reality governed
by the all-inclusive providence or necessity, identical with the Stoic
vital substance, fire. Perhaps it is in the section on the flux in
temperament that Emerson sounds most Heraclitean. Life is a
"flux of moods"; being is only a "vast-flowing vigor." But still
under all that is transitory and flowing is the Heraclitean unity;
"Every day, every act betrays the ill-concealed deity"; "yet is the
God the native of these bleak rocks." This God is in us, and the
moral taught by illusion is that of self-trust.

In "Montaigne" the two extremes of flux and stability, of difference and identity, are described as the doctrines of "the material-
ist" and "the abstractionist," and the skeptic like Montaigne occupies
the middle ground. He is self-reliant and adaptable and here the
metaphor of flux is transferred to another area. "The philosophy
we want is one of fluxions and mobility. The Spartan and Stoic
schemes are too stark and stiff for our occasion." On the other hand,
non-resistance is "too thin and aerial. . . . We want a ship in these
billows we inhabit." Later he says that the sceptic's questioning
of established custom is a "stage in the growth of every superior
mind, and is the evidence of its perception of the flowing power
which remains itself in all changes." Here again Emerson shows
his awareness of both poles of Heraclitus' thought, of flux and
permanence. He ends the essay with his answer to the "illusionists"
— the permanent element is the moral sentiment: "This is the
drop which balances the sea," this is "the permanent in the mutable
and fleeting."

"Illusions" shows additional dependence on Heraclitus and his
theory, as transmitted by Plutarch. Since we live among hallucina-
tions, says Emerson, life is largely subjective and does not exist
apart from the subject who beholds it. It is a mask, a riddle. We
drop the mask and solve the riddle only by ascent from "beauty" to

"Beauty" on the Platonic ladder. Science, he continues, is the search for identity amid the multiplicity and Heraclitus and Xenophanes were the earliest thinkers who wrestled with this problem (*CW* 6. 324). He here no doubt recalls the stress on the unreliability of the phenomena of the senses found in Xenophanes and especially in Heraclitus and he has read their statements in Gérando who used Plutarch.[23] Certainly the theme of metamorphosis or perpetual change is the same in both Plutarch and Emerson. Both follow this Stoic changeableness into human nature; Plutarch, in the passage quoted above from "Of the Word EI at Delphi," puts the problem in a question: "For how do we, if we remain the same, delight now in other things than we delighted in before? How do we love, hate, admire, and contemn things contrary to the former?" Emerson puts the same question in different language: "How can we penetrate the law of our shifting moods and suscepti- bility? Yet they differ as all and nothing."

Both mention the "illusion of time" which is broken up into past, present, and future, when in reality all time is a unity. Emerson says (*CW* 6. 319): "There is the illusion of time, which is very deep; who has disposed of it? — or come to the conviction that what seems the *succession* of thought is only the distribution of wholes into causal series?" And Plutarch writes (*Moralia* 4. 495): "For time is a certain movable thing appearing in connection with fleeting matter, always flowing and unstable, like a leaky vessel full of corruption and generation." Emerson adds the figure of a dream: "If life seem a succession of dreams, yet poetic justice is done in dreams also. The visions of good men are good; it is the undisciplined will that is whipped with bad thoughts and bad fortunes." This may be Emerson's version of Plutarch's idea that dreams indicate character, which appears in "Of Man's Progress in Virtue" (*Moralia* 2. 469).

It is interesting to observe how Plutarch, Emerson, and Montaigne conclude their similar treatment of the same topic — the change- able nature of the human character. For Plutarch the Platonist the only really eternal being which has neither beginning nor end is God, and on this rational note he concludes "Of the Word EI at Delphi." Montaigne at the end of the "Apology for Raimond Sebond," after his long quotation from this essay of Plutarch, quotes the Stoic ideal of Seneca, only to reject it as invalid:

To this religious conclusion of a pagan [Plutarch] I shall only add this testimony of one of the same condition [Seneca], . . . "What a vile and abject thing," says he, "is man, if he do not raise himself above humanity?" 'Tis a good word, and a profitable desire, but withal absurd; for to make the handle bigger than the hand, and the cubit longer than the arm, and to hope to stride further than our legs can reach, is both impossible and monstrous; or that man should rise above himself and humanity; for he cannot see but with his eyes, nor seize but with his power. He shall be exalted, if God will lend him His extraordinary hand; he shall exalt himself, by abandoning and renouncing his own proper means, and by suffering himself to be rais'd and elevated by means purely coelestial, it belongs to our Christian faith, and not to the Stoical vertue, to pretend to that divine and miraculous Metamorphosis.

So far Emerson in "Illusions" seems to follow Plutarch (perhaps in Montaigne) fairly closely, but Montaigne's Christian conclusion does not attract him, nor does the coldly philosophical language of Plutarch's conclusion. However, for Emerson there is, as for Plutarch, something permanent behind the veil of illusion (*CW* 6. 325), something divine, whether it be called "God" or "the gods" or "Nature" or "the law of nature":

There is no chance and no anarchy in the universe. All is system and gradation. Every god is there sitting in his sphere. The young mortal enters the hall of the firmament; there he is alone with them alone, they pouring on him benedictions and gifts, and beckoning him up to their thrones. On the instant, and incessantly, fall snow-storms of illusions. . . . Every moment new changes and new showers of deceptions to baffle and distract him. And when, by and by, for an instant, the air clears and the cloud lifts a little, there are the gods still sitting around him on their thrones, — they alone with him alone.[24]

Emerson here seems drawn more to Seneca's Stoicism which

Montaigne rejects. "What a vile and abject thing is man!" says Seneca, and Emerson's youth too "fancies himself poor, orphaned, insignificant." In spite of Montaigne, Emerson's answer to the complaint of man is that of Seneca the Stoic — Endure, knowing that beneath all the illusion, there is permanent and immutable law, the law of Nature. In this famous ending of "Illusions," highly praised by Carlyle and described by Professor Carpenter as marking "the climax of Emerson's writing," there is an amalgam of a number of sources. There is the well-known "flight of the alone to the alone" of Plotinus, there is the debt to Plato's *Phaedo*, and there are the references to Oriental thought which precede the final paragraph. Heraclitus and Stoicism also find a place among those from all schools of thought who not only observed the illusion but also perceived the permanence behind it. And if Heraclitus' flux is in the background of "Illusions," so also is Heraclitus' identity or unity. Suddenly on rare occasions the law which rules the flowing is revealed. Emerson does not adopt only one of the Heraclitean elements, the changing, illusory one; he takes up both and, as always, retains a basic duality, that of the changing and the permanent, the many and the one.

Elsewhere both Plutarch and Emerson in several passages discuss the shifting and transitory element in human nature from the psychological or moral point of view. For Emerson "the law of our shifting moods and susceptibility" confirms the theory of Heraclitus, when we look at the rapid change from one mood to another. Thus the answer to the question "Is human nature wholly good or bad?" must be that man is a mixture of good and bad, and that each struggles for predominance over the other in a constant process of action and reaction. Emerson puts this in the form of a Platonic or Plutarchan myth at the end of "Manners" (*CW* 3. 155):

"I overheard Jove, one day," said Silenus, "talking of destroying the earth; he said it had failed; they were all rogues and vixens, who went from bad to worse, as fast as the days succeeded each other. Minerva said she hoped not; they were only ridiculous little creatures, with this odd circumstance, that they had a blur, or indeterminate aspect, seen far or seen near; if you called them bad, they would appear so; if you called them good, they would appear so; and there was no one person or action among them which would not puzzle her owl, much more all Olympus, to know whether it was fundamentally bad or good."

I believe with Harrison that this fable is likely a presentation in dialogue form of an idea which Emerson had noticed in Plutarch's "Of Isis and Osiris" (*Moralia* 4. 105–106) and which he had marked in his own copy.[25] Plutarch said:

For the harmony of the world is (according to Heraclitus) like that of a bow or a harp, alternately tightened and relaxed; and according to Euripides,

>Nor good nor bad here's to be found apart;
>But both immixed in one, for greater art.

And therefore this most ancient opinion hath been handed down from the theologists and law-givers to the poets and philosophers, it having an original fathered upon none, but having gained a persuasion both strong and indelible, and being everywhere professed and received by barbarians as well as Grecians, . . . that the world is neither hurried about by wild chance without intelligence, discourse, and direction, nor yet that there is but one reason, which as it were with a rudder or with gentle and easy reins directs it and holds it in; but that on the contrary, there are in it several differing things, and those made up of bad as well as good; or rather (to speak more plainly) that Nature produces nothing here but what is mixed and tempered.

It is probable that Emerson derived his topic for the conclusion of "Manners" from this passage which connects Heraclitean change with the mixture of good and evil in mankind; though here again Montaigne's essay on this theme, "That We Taste Nothing Pure," may have served as an intermediary.

The concept of "compensation" is equally basic in Emerson's thought and there can be no doubt that it is a development of his combination of monism and dualism, of permanence and flux; the circle figure or the operation of the magnet help to describe its operation, but it is a natural law of the universe and man, the law of polarity which works in every sphere of thought and activity. Emerson's development of it and his extension of it from a law of the cosmos to a law operating also in man the microcosm is original and characteristic. But still the fundamental concept of alternation and compensation in a more simple sense of the term is very old, and again classical. In the form of a cyclic theory, it is a feature of Stoic cosmology and very probably derived from the theory of Heraclitus which, as we have seen, Emerson summarized from Gérando as "Attraction, Repulsion." He acknowledges that this concept is classical; in "Compensation" he applies it to moral law and shows that he is aware that it is the basis of Greek tragedy; he gives it its classical term, nemesis; he quotes Heraclitus (from *Moralia* 3. 26) to explain what the term means (*CW* 2. 107): "This is that ancient doctrine of Nemesis, who keeps watch in the universe and lets no offence go unchastised. The Furies, they said, are attendants on justice, and if the sun in heaven should trangress his path they would punish him." In another passage on nemesis, in "The Sovereignty of Ethics," Emerson seems to recall in characteristic Emersonian language this same remark of Heraclitus (*CW* 10. 193): "Secret retributions are always restoring the level, when disturbed, of the Divine justice. It is impossible to tilt the beam. . . . Settles for evermore the ponderous equator to its line, and man and mote and star and sun must range with it, or be pulverized by the recoil." And in a number of his poems the classical term "nemesis" recurs.[26] In "Compensation" too Emerson gives a paragraph of proverbs which illustrate this theory of retribution and nemesis. One of these, "Bad counsel confounds the adviser," seems to be his own briefer version of Hesiod's

> Bad counsel, so the gods ordain,
> Is most of all the adviser's bane

which he had copied from the *Moralia* in his journal in 1837.

The same nemesis or alternation in the universe is behind the concept of self-reliance and is one of the arguments for independence; man, Emerson says in "Self-Reliance," must rely on his own powers since all else is changeable and transitory. Society "recedes as fast on one side as it gains on the other." It changes continually, gaining civilization, Christianity, wealth, science, but "for every thing that is given something is taken." It acquires new arts but loses "old instincts." The increase of wealth causes the decline of primitive health; man looks at his path and does not know the stars — he adopts the artificial and loses contact with nature. Finally, Christianity and its refinements cause the loss to us of energy and "some vigor of wild virtue." As if to confirm the Stoic tone of this phrase, Emerson mentions Stoicism (*CW* 2. 84–85): "For every Stoic was a Stoic; but in Christianity where is the Christian?"

The importance of the sense of the flux of things in Emerson's thought has been observed by Matthiessen and Whicher; the latter observes that it is reinforced by the new idea of evolution and that from one viewpoint it is the central core of Emerson's philosophy of nature.[27] But its connection with Emerson's Stoicism and its source in Heraclitus by way of Plutarch has apparently not received much comment. Matthiessen points out that in Emerson's mind "the prevailing thought of his century" was "its reassertion of the Heraclitean doctrine of the flowing"[28] and this remark serves as a timely reminder that we must not attribute every reference in Emerson to flux and flowing, to change and alternation, to his reading of Plutarch or Heraclitus. For this ancient doctrine, now rediscovered and given fresh emphasis, suits all the Transcendentalists very well, in Germany, in England, in America, and Heraclitus' "all things are in a state of flux" as well as his establishment of the principle of dualism spread their influence widely upon a variety of thinkers and writers. They influenced Spinoza, Schleiermacher, Herbert Spencer; they are part of the common, often unconscious, Stoicism of the age, and many readers of Seneca, Epictetus, and Marcus Aurelius echo the Heraclitean phrase though they show not the slightest acquaintance with Plutarch. It is perhaps strongest in Goethe, who expresses over and over again almost all the ideas of Heraclitus — flux and alternation, the harmony of opposites in the unity of nature, the concept of fire as the World-Soul, God as the symbol of the change process, His immanence and transcendence together in nature, the need for self-knowledge. In *Dichtung und Wahrheit* we are told that when he first read the Greek philosophers he had no liking for the pre-Socratics or Plato or Aristotle, but was strongly drawn to the Stoics like Epictetus; the Heraclitean side of this Stoicism is strong all through his changing thought; indeed in the history of thought Goethe is a veritable Heraclitus of change and diversity, and yet of a basic underlying unity. The same strain is, perhaps naturally, in Carlyle, when he speaks of the changes wrought by time, which is after all only an illusion; when he seems drawn to the Heraclitean theory of alternation; or when he adopts the Stoic terminology of "fear" and "desire," or when he speaks of Teufelsdrockh's "centre of indifference." This is part of Carlyle's debt to German Transcendentalism.

Heraclitean flux and change is almost a commonplace theme like the Stoicism with which it is connected historically as well as logically. In the case of Emerson, who knows his Plutarch, the Heraclitean element in German contemporary thought was certainly known to him and is part of the service of Coleridge and Carlyle in bringing German transcendental ideas to his attention. But in this instance too the classical element in the contemporary German philosophers probably served only to confirm in his own mind the validity of older concepts and ideas which he had met before and which he had examined, adapted, and transformed in his own mind. Once more he was struck by the way in which the ancients anticipated the most recent thought. Heraclitus in Emerson is also firmly based on his reading of Plutarch and to this extent is part of the classicism which he never abandons.

The chief Greek philosophers who anticipated Stoicism or rather those whose ideas were taken up, developed, and combined by the

Stoics are Pythagoras, Heraclitus, and Xenophanes. We have observed Emerson's acquaintance with the first two and he is also aware of some of the chief concepts of Xenophanes, the monist whose theory of the deity approached pantheism and to this extent foreshadowed Stoicism; for Emerson's "eternal ONE" is probably not unconnected with Xenophanes' "the One and the All" which indeed is referred to frequently in Emerson's writings. In "Nature" (*CW* 1. 43) it is to Xenophanes that Emerson appeals for witness as to the underlying identity of all in the diversity of nature, and as early as 1831 a poem which is curiously Stoic in tone contains a reminiscence of Xenophanes, even if it does not seem to have come to Emerson from Plutarch.[29] Here again Emerson could find the trend of his own thought supported and confirmed by one of the ancient thinkers and the thinker is again one of those who helped to shape or at least anticipated Stoicism.

iii

But Emerson's thoughts on determinism and on the relation between man and the universe are not finished with the introduction of flux, of an almost mechanical retribution or nemesis, or with the monism of Xenophanes. Transcendentalism, he says, is Platonism and there is a divine creator and a Providence which does not operate mechanically. Man too has a divine part, the soul, which is in communion with the divine source, or which is part of the divine whole. In Emerson, sometimes God the creator of nature is separated from nature (perhaps a reminiscence of the Platonic creator of the universe, the *demiurge*); more often God and man are united after the Stoic manner, as in "Nature": ". . . the currents of the Universal Being circulate through me; I am part or parcel of God." When Emerson wishes to express the unity of God and man he uses the term "Over-Soul," a concept which may arise from the emanation theory of the later Neoplatonists and which hence has something of Oriental mysticism about it, but which also owes something to Emerson's knowledge of the Greek pre-Socratics. This metaphysic of Emerson, complex, eclectic, and not always consistent, resembles that of Plutarch, who is also a Platonist in theology, whose universe is a duality. He emphasizes spirit above matter, and for him forms have more reality than material things. Plutarch's god is a living, personal deity, identified with "the Good," who created the world after the pattern of beauty. But Plutarch goes also to the Stoics for their immanent World-Soul, since for them the universe is God or Reason; among the attributes of Plutarch's deity are the Stoic ones of happiness, blessedness, and self-sufficiency. However, for Plutarch the stricter Platonist than Emerson, God and man are not identified in the Stoic fashion; man and nature are the work of God; and Plutarch's beliefs do not include the Neoplatonic or Emersonian mystical experience, the union with the Divine Being. He adopts the Greek concept of the daemon, a being half matter and half spirit, through which man can bridge the gap between himself and the divine and can receive divine inspiration and the power of prophecy and divination.

The chief difference between Plutarch's metaphysic and that of Emerson seems to stem from Plutarch's Platonism: his universe is god-centered; the human soul is the instrument of God and is not itself God. The universe of the Transcendentalists, on the other hand, is man-centered and Transcendentalism, including Emerson's individual variety of it, seems often to mean only "transcending the individual" and not "transcending mankind"; one of the later writers on Transcendentalism quoted a definition of Transcendentalism: "Pantheism is said to sink man and nature in God; Materialism to sink God and man in nature, and Transcendentalism to sink God and nature in man." [30] Bartol finds this definition both untrue and too narrow. The real Transcendentalist, he says, will not "sink" one element in another; all are one, and Emerson would sometimes make the same answer which the Stoics would give; to them, nothing can transcend mankind, since God is in all nature, including man. If Emerson sometimes tends to submerge God and nature in man, the reason is that his thoughts on the relation between man and God change, as Stephen Whicher shows; to adopt Whicher's apt image of a polarity or of several polarities in Emerson's thought, Emerson swings between the two poles of egoism and pantheism. From the belief that the Over-Soul is in the self, and nature an "exteriorization" of this "aboriginal Self," he arrives at the doctrine that the soul is within nature, with man as "her late, if supreme product." [31] The earlier Emerson is the egoist of "Self-Reliance," but his egoism is not atheistic, for God is in man. Coleridge, according to Whicher, provided the stimulus which turned Emerson to an examination of the doctrine that "a portion of the Deity lives in men" and it is unlikely that Emerson at this time realized that this is also a cardinal doctrine of Roman Stoicism; at this date, in the early thirties, the knowledge that the Stoics also believed in God in man would be no more than an interesting confirmation by pagans of the correctness of a more modern theory.

Yet always, along with this divine element in man, there exists the hard world of material things, of facts which had to be explained and lived with, so that we may even speak of Emerson's "monistic dualism or dualistic monism." [32] Plato might have solved the problem raised by this anomaly in human life, but as Whicher remarks, Emerson's closer acquaintance with the Platonists only came later. Plutarch's philosophy, with its mystical tinge which could provide the suprahuman anchor, and its practical bent which gave guidance for everyday life and ordinary human conduct, might have aided Emerson in his dilemma, but Plutarch the philosopher was at this stage not much more than a figure of literature, interesting and invigorating though he was. So far, the Plutarch of the *Lives* only seemed to increase man's self-reliance.

From this early egoism, with its unconscious Stoic background, Emerson gradually passed to another type of monism, more pantheistic and hence also more strongly Stoic in nature. By 1842 and "The Transcendentalist" Emerson could see that Transcendentalism or modern Platonic idealism had much in common with Stoicism: "this way of thinking, falling on Roman times, made Stoic philosophers." He is saying in effect that Platonism and Stoicism and nineteenth-century Transcendentalism are all ways of combating materialism, of linking man with God or nature or the ideal world.

Emerson's earlier Stoicism is orthodox Roman in its doctrine of God within man and it is also pantheism, since God is in all nature and nature includes man. Some of the Stoics used in defending themselves against the charge of pantheism an argument which Emerson later could have used when the same charge was made against him, but he would have regarded the argument as quibbling and evasion; the Stoics said that God is in the universe and hence in man but He is not evenly distributed throughout the universe. There is deity in all things but, said the Stoics, "as a man is called wise, being wise in mind, though he consists of mind and body; so the world is called God from its soul, though it consists of soul and body." [33] Only at a later stage in his thinking, after he had achieved a state of mind something like the Stoic equanimity, or to put it in another way, after his religion had been toned down so that it consisted of not much more than Stoic ethics,[34] did Emerson cautiously approach the Stoic solution to the problem of the relation of man, nature, and God. In the essay "Worship" in *The Conduct of Life* Emerson speaks of "God's delegating his divinity to every particle." This certainly sounds Stoic but the term "delegating" is perhaps carefully chosen; the particle is not itself God as the Stoics would have it. Emerson still shies away from a full acceptance of Stoicism; rather his solution is Platonic and Christian — and it is surprising that he has not adopted it before: "Man is the image of God." Still, he adds, "there is no flaw in either Epicureanism or Stoicism."

This Plutarchan blend of Platonism and Stoicism lies not far below the surface of much of Emerson's thought about man and God. It appears in his doctrine of fate, for to Emerson and the

Stoics, the unity of all nature provides, or itself is, a natural necessity.

To this unity which is "Necessity" Emerson also on occasion gives the name "Providence." In "New England Reformers" he does not use the term in the usual nineteenth-century fashion, as a pious synonym for "God," but in the classical sense of the time of the "Several Hands" translation, as the foreseeing and fore-ordaining power of God. Plutarch also uses "Providence" in this sense in "Concerning Such Whom God is Slow to Punish." Naturally, then, when Emerson outlines the views of the ancients on immortality, it is to Plutarch that he goes for a quotation which well fits his own ideas on the unity of nature, the unity between the human soul and God (*CW* 8. 330); Plutarch had said (*Moralia* 4. 170) in a Platonic vein, "Therefore, said I, there is one and the same reason to confirm the providence of God and the immortality of the soul; neither is it possible to admit the one, if you deny the other." Emerson says the same thing again in his own way, that God and the human soul are one and immortal.[35] But later in the same essay he seems to go even further in the direction of Stoicism (*CW* 8. 333): "The ground of hope is in the infinity of the world; which infinity reappears in every particle, the powers of all society in every individual, and of all mind in every mind." This sounds characteristically Emersonian with its undertone of *Representative Men* but it is also Plutarchan and Stoic; and we may add that it reached the Stoics originally from Emerson's favorite pre-Socratic, Heraclitus. For it was Heraclitus' doctrine of one substance in con-stant flowing mutation which first broke down the barrier between God and the world, between soul and body, and which paved the way for pantheism. For Plutarch, the Stoics, and Emerson, the divine providence or necessity extends its powers to every particle, and there are no exceptions to this natural necessity. The Stoics worked this out in detail and steadfastly affirmed that the separate atoms do not derive their activity from themselves, but from the living activity of the whole. Hence, for the Stoics, "God, Nature,

Reason, World-Soul, Germinal Reason, Law, Providence, Necessity, Destiny are but expressions of the different relations in which the one universe, the sum and whole of existence, stands to particular things and events within it." [36] This statement of Stoic doctrine could very well stand for Emerson's attitude. "The Over-Soul" expresses this idea: "as there is no screen or ceiling between our heads and the infinite heavens, so there is no bar or wall in the soul, where man, the effect, ceases, and God, the cause, begins." Life is described as "a flowing river, which, out of regions I see not, pours for a season its streams into me." Man lives in particles and within man is the soul of the whole, "the eternal ONE." To the Stoics the unifying force in God and man is Reason. Emerson too seems to use the term in the Stoic sense and uses it as an argument for self-reliance (*Journals* 3. 390): "Democracy, Freedom, has its root in the sacred truth that every man hath in him the divine Reason, or that, though few men since the creation of the world live according to the dictates of Reason, yet all men are created capable of so doing. To this truth we look when we say, Reverence thyself; Be true to thyself." God is described as "Highest Law" (*CW* 2. 270) and: "The soul in man . . . is not a faculty, but a light. . . . From within or from behind, a light shines through us upon things and makes us aware that we are nothing, but the light is all." This may have connection with Quaker sources, but still if here we were to substitute "fire" for "light" we should have a thoroughly Stoic sentence — for the Stoics, the soul of man is a spark of the divine fire.

Whicher has traced the development in Emerson's attitude to the problem of freedom and fate during the years when he was passing from Platonism to a kind of Stoicism, and Strauch has shown how Emerson between the writing of "The Tragic" (1839) and of "Fate" in *The Conduct of Life* (about 1853) philosophized the classical fate of Greek tragedy into a "cosmic limitation" which he calls "Necessity." [37] I am concerned here to show the points in which Emerson's thoughts on fate coincide with those of Plutarch and the

Stoics. For it is here that Emerson's religion, if we may so call it, approaches that of Plutarch more closely. In "The Tragic," Emerson shows that he cannot tolerate the concept of fate in Greek tragic drama, the belief in "a brute Fate or Destiny" which controls nature and events inexorably, completely indifferent to man and his wishes, "serving him if his wishes chance to lie in the same course, crushing him if his wishes lie contrary to it, and heedless whether it serves or crushes him." He describes fate as "whatever limits us" and calls the classical view, as Plutarch does, superstition. To this pessimistic view of the Greek tragedians, he opposes the more optimistic and more Stoic view of a "philosophical necessity," the law of nature, which subordinates the suffering individual to the good of all, and which gives man freedom by way of obedience. That this view of fate is Stoic is confirmed by echoes of Stoic terminology in Emerson; "The conversation of man," he says in "The Tragic," "is a mixture of regrets and apprehensions." This is exactly the state of affairs into which the Stoics endeavored to introduce their concept of the mean, and they would use exactly these terms. And Emerson himself advocates this mean when he says (CW 12. 411): "A man should not commit his tranquillity to things, but should keep as much as possible the reins in his own hands, rarely giving way to extreme emotion of joy or grief." He indicates that he is thinking of the Greeks here: "To this architectural stability of the human form, the Greek genius added an ideal beauty, without disturbing the seals of serenity; permitting no violence of mirth, or wrath, or suffering. This was true to human nature. . . . All that life demands of us . . . is an equilibrium. . . . We must walk as guests in nature; not impassioned, but cool and disengaged." The last sentence could have been written by any Stoic.

This Stoic concept of necessity which is the basis of Emerson's later acquiescence with the universe is, as Whicher points out, the polar opposite of the doctrine of self-reliance, but in a special sense it is still a form of self-reliance, a self-reliance which has a far wider and sounder basis than Emerson's earlier egoism. Emerson can still say, "rely on your own self," but the ground for confidence is now no longer the individual but the individual as being part of the whole, as the Stoics would put it, a part of the divine fire. Rely on your own nature, Emerson says, for — and he uses the old phrase of Heraclitus — character is destiny; or as he expressed it in an early sermon, "man is the architect of his fortunes." The use of Heraclitus' famous phrase is not Emersonian rhetoric, for this concept of fate is genuinely Heraclitean; it is Heraclitus' "Destiny" or the harmony of the universe, the controlling and regulating reason, and it has permeated much of Emerson's reading in philosophy — Gérando, Cudworth, Proclus, Plotinus, Plato.[38]

Whicher describes [39] this new kind of self-reliance as Emerson's "retreat to congenital Stoicism" which he adopted when hard pressed by the problems of freedom and fate, and it is certainly an integral and inseparable part of his philosophical training. It is also a fixed part of the Stoic element in his favorite Plutarch, the moderate Stoicism which pervades "Of the Tranquillity of the Mind" and in Plutarch it produces the same self-reliance; Plutarch says: "every man hath a storehouse of trouble and contentment in his own bosom; . . . the vessels which contain good and evil are not placed at Jupiter's threshold, but in the recesses of the mind." Here Plutarch like Emerson opposes to the classical view of Greek tragedy the milder, Stoic view; the same essay of Plutarch displays other Stoic elements — in his disregard for material prosperity, in the concept of moderation, especially in the passions, but he also has an optimism or a Stoic acquiescence akin to that of Emerson; he says for instance, "Therefore we ought not to vilify and depress our nature as if it could not get the ascendant over fortune" for (and Emerson borrowed this phrase from Plutarch) "every day is a festival to a good man." [40] If men would listen to reason, Plutarch thinks, "they might bear their present condition without fault-finding, remember the past with joy and gratitude, and live without fear or distrust, looking forward to the future with a joyful and lightsome hope." Plutarch's cheerful tone is Stoic, as its terminology shows, but it also sounds remarkably Emersonian.

But Emerson has much more to say about destiny and it is pertinent to note that he begins his volume *The Conduct of Life* with his essay on fate. Although Hindu influences on this essay are usually stressed, it contains ample evidence of his Platonism and Stoicism in the mixture which is characteristic of Plutarch. For Emerson as for Plato and the Stoics, fate is "the law of the world." "The Book of Nature is the book of fate," he declares. We might expect him to go on to say that man as a part of nature is governed by fate, that there is no self-determination open to man, that nature is inexorable. But this would be to forget the Emerson of "Self-Reliance," to forget the Transcendental opposition to Calvinism, the Calvinism by which "the broad ethics of Jesus were quickly narrowed to village theologies, which preach an election or favoritism" (*CW* 6. 6). Emerson believes that nature in its all-inclusive bounty also provides the ability to annul fate, that this ability is the function of intellect and power. "If Fate is so prevailing," he writes, "man is also a part of it and can confront fate with fate." Here there may well be another echo of Heraclitus, for whom mind pierced through the illusions of sense to the object itself, because like can only comprehend like and mind is kin in nature to reality. Within the monism here there is also an internal duality — that of mind and matter; it is, as we might expect, Platonic and it is evident in Plutarch. Emerson (at least at this point in his developing thought on fate) agrees, but again he goes farther than Plato in the direction of Stoicism. Mind combats all things, even destiny. In the first section of his own essay on "Fate" Plutarch outlines Plato's concept of fate as "a law ensuing on the nature of the universe" (*Moralia* 5. 294), for fate works according to the laws of causality, which can be determined by the mind. Emerson adopts the classical definition (*CW* 6. 31): "Fate then is a name for facts not yet passed under the fire of thought; for causes which are unpenetrated." Here the Stoic strain joins the Platonic in Emerson, for this is Stoic. Plutarch notes it in "Of Those Sentiments concerning Nature . . ." (*Moralia* 3. 131), and attributes it to Anaxagoras and the Stoics. Fate for the Stoics is the operation of the laws of nature; we call it fate, they said, because we cannot see the natural cause which lies behind the fateful event; it appears to operate at random and blindly. But always the law is there; at the end of the essay "Fate," Emerson thrice intones, "Let us build altars to the beautiful Necessity" which teaches that "Law rules throughout the universe." "Illusions" stressed the Heraclitean flux; he now turns to the other pole of Heraclitus' concept, the Pythagorean *kosmos*, the "beauty" and orderly nature of the universe, and in "Fate" arrives (as the Stoics did, building on the same foundations) at the doctrine of a philosophical necessity which evokes a feeling of confident acquiescence in the wise ordering of the world.

The essay "Art" elaborates this doctrine of fate as natural law. All departments of life express the identity of their law (*CW* 7. 37): "They are sublime when seen as emanations of a Necessity contradistinguished from the vulgar Fate by being instant and alive, and dissolving man as well as his works in its flowing beneficence." The term "flowing" incidentally reminds us of Heraclitus, but Emerson's essential point is that there is one law which governs all things; at certain times and to certain people it appears as "Necessity," the fate which is ordained by the law of the universe, but more usually it appears as a blind fate, divorced of any law or plan. Here he notices the classical dualism of providence or necessity on the one hand and chance or fate on the other, and points out that both are really the same thing, a "Law" which only appears different to different points of view. He could have met this classical distinction between fate and fortune in many passages in Greek literature, but his attitude towards fate in the essay of that title closely resembles Plutarch's essay "Of Fate"; from what we know of Emerson's way of working it is therefore likely that he read Plutarch's essay when preparing to write on the same theme. It is clear too that Plato, Plutarch, the Stoics, and Emerson had the same purpose — to show that one dualism of current thought is only an apparent one, that in reality all things are governed by natural law. Emerson uses Plutarch's classical phrase when he says, "fate is the daughter of necessity" and "comprehends all things." Fate or necessity thus includes fortune and chance. At the end of his essay Plutarch says that "the world is governed by nature," a concise expression of Emerson's doctrine also. For Emerson as well as for Plutarch fate, necessity, nature, law are one throughout the whole universe.

It is then to a certain extent Emerson's Stoic pantheism which furnishes him with a spirit of optimistic acquiescence in the operations of the universe. For Emerson and the Stoics the world is orderly, a *kosmos*, and man is a part of this orderly system; long before the Stoics, too, Plato had stated the same conclusion unhesitatingly. What appears to be fate is really an unseen cause; intellect by discerning the cause can annul fate and display the order.

<h2 style="text-align:center">i v</h2>

Plutarch was saved from complete subservience to Stoic fatalism by his Platonism and from time to time Emerson too shows interest in that particular doctrine of Plato which prevented Plutarch from becoming a complete Stoic. Fate in the time of Plutarch was real and the wise man of the Stoics was an ideal which was impossible to attain. But Plato had spoken of Socrates' "daemon" and this doctrine could be developed into something which could offset blind and arbitrary fate; Emerson too as we shall see was attracted to the idea that man's helpless acquiescence could be mitigated by clues given to us by demonology, but only when we interpret the term in a much wider sense than the ancients did.

According to Plato, Socrates had attached to him a "daemon" or "daimonion," an inner voice which spoke to him and stopped him when he was about to perform any action which would turn out to be to his own harm.[41] Plato's portrayal of the operation of this

spirit or vision was frequently studied, and the Stoics and Neoplatonists gave the daemons a prominent place as intermediaries
between God and man, developing the relationship in their own
way. Man could obtain hints of his destiny and of the future which
awaited him because the gods communicated through the daemons.
There came to be good and bad daemons, which treat men well or
badly. Good or bad fortune or luck is embodied in a good or bad
daemon, and eventually the daemon, since it was the cause of good
or bad fortune, was popularly confused with the fortune itself.

No ancient writer is more interested in demonology than Plutarch
is. He tackles the problem of the origin and nature of the daemons
in "Why the Oracles Cease to Give Answers" but arrives at no
solution; in "A Discourse concerning Socrates's Daemon" he stages
a discussion of this topic, and in "Of the Tranquillity of the Mind"
(*Moralia* 1. 158–159) he mentions the popular view that every
newborn child is attended by a guardian daemon or genius.

There are three passages in Emerson's writing which indicate
that he, too, is interested in the classical theory of the daemon. In
1842 he writes in a letter: "I suppose there are secret bands that
tie each man to his mark with a mighty force; first, of course, his
Daemon, a beautiful immortal figure, whom the ancients said,
though never visible to himself, sometimes appeared shining before
him to others. . . ." [42] In "Beauty" he says (*CW* 6. 287): "The
ancients believed that a genius or demon took possession at birth
of each mortal, to guide him; that these genii were sometimes
seen as a flame of fire immersed in the bodies which they governed:
on an evil man, resting on his head; in a good man, mixed with
his substance. They thought the same genius, at the death of its
ward, entered a new-born child, and they pretended to guess the
pilot by the sailing of the ship." In his lecture "Demonology" in
the series of 1839 entitled "Human Life" we read:

The ancients held that a Genius or good Daemon presided over every
man, leading him, whenever he suffered himself to be led, into good and
successful courses; that this Genius might even in some cases be pre-

ternaturally heard and seen: — when seen, appearing as a star immediately above the head and attached to the head of the person whom it
guided. If of an evil and vicious man, then was the Daemon so immersed
in his body that the light became dim as of a quenched star; if of a wise
and divine person, — the star was a pure splendor floating free over him
and illumining the way before him. But rarely seen by the eyes of man,
they rather waited to hear it as a voice, which at times became sensible
and commanding to the astonished ears of the individual, and even of
other men. . . .

The first two passages are simply shorter versions of the third,
which is obviously a version of Plutarch's description of the operation of the daemon in his "Discourse concerning Socrates's Daemon"
(*Moralia* 2. 409–410); Harrison long ago, without the longer lecture passage, noted the Plutarchan source of Emerson's demonology,[43] or at least of his picture of the connection between the
daemon and man; he noted that the last phrase of the passage
from "Beauty" — "they pretended to guess the pilot by the sailing
of the ship" — comes from another passage in the same essay of
Plutarch (*Moralia* 2. 399) and it is extracted by Emerson again
for his essay on Plutarch. Harrison points out also that while Emerson could have obtained an acquaintance with the classical theory
of the daemon from a number of other ancient authors, it is evident
that here at least he follows Plutarch. But Emerson goes further
and endeavors to explain the classical meaning of the term "daemon" for his contemporaries; he brings it up to date and gives it
a modern interpretation. Even today, he indicates in "Demonology,"
men may be controlled by some hidden force, either for good or bad.
They are not free, and the Greeks would say that they were influenced by their "daemon" or "genius." Emerson states however
that thought is the power which will free men who are beridden
by a daemon, just as intellect is able to annul fate. The Plutarchan
daemon appears elsewhere in Emerson. Harrison has also shown
that the three-fold division of the poem "Initial, Daemonic and
Celestial Love" is derived from Plato but that parts of the poem,
those referring to the "daemon" or "Genius," draw again on Plu-

tarch and that the references to the "Daemon" in another poem, "The World-Soul" and in the first paragraph of "Experience" are part of the same tradition which attracts Emerson by its poetical and picturesque character.

Here again however it would be very easy to overestimate the debt of Emerson to Plutarch on demonology. The whole of his age was interested in demonology and the term was familiar to his contemporaries — Sir Walter Scott's readers would at once know the meaning of his title *Tales of Demonology and Witchcraft* and also the meaning of the title of Emerson's essay "Demonology." Here he seems to give the current meaning of the term; it covers "dreams, omens, coincidences, luck, sortilege, magic and other experiences which shun rather than court enquiry." In this essay he indicates that it was Goethe who revived the term and made the concept vivid again and, we may add, Goethe is following the teachings of Hamann who had revived the study of Plutarch's portrayal of the daemon of Socrates. Emerson's interest in the classical demonology, then, a ruling spirit which takes control of an individual and, to use Goethe's words, "forms in the moral world, though not an antagonist, yet a transverse element," may well have come to him primarily from Goethe and only secondarily from Plutarch. But since we know that he read Plutarch on the daemons, it is of interest to see whether Emerson's demonology resembles that of Plutarch.

There are resemblances in viewpoint and in the explanation of what a daemon is, occasionally there are direct reminiscences which show that Emerson has not accepted Goethe completely or rather has gone to Plutarch for a classical explanation of a concept which was familiar in Emerson's own time. Plutarch adopts a modern attitude which suited Emerson well; it is an attitude which is moderate, which shows a proper respect for classical Greek religion and its attractive poetical concepts, to which he was strongly attached, and which at the same time does not exclude the Stoic emphasis on the operation of wholly natural causes.

There are in Plutarch's essay three explanations of the operation of Socrates' "daemon." The first is that it is the genuine manifestation of some supernatural being; the second, that it is not so, but rather Socrates' method of giving impressive weight to the powerful impulse of conscience or instinct.[44] A third explanation is suggested — that the daemon is simply Socrates' application of reason and probability to the multiple omens that are available to us; he noted the omens and also decided whether sense and likelihood were on the side of the event indicated by the omen. It is an explanation which relies completely on the reasoning powers of men. The daemon is nothing but a term for common sense. Plutarch himself inclines to this third view but expresses it in different terminology: "we . . . find out one another's conceptions by the voice; but the conceptions of the Daemons carry a light with them, and shine to those that are able to perceive them, so that there is no need of words. . . ." The character of the percipient enters in here with "those that are able to perceive them," for "the speeches of the Daemon, though indifferently applied to all, yet sound only to those who are of a quiet temper and sedate mind." The individual must also exert effort and when the soul has tried her strength and "endeavors to ascend," "the Deity permits her proper Genius to aid her." Here Plutarch finds a reasonable and moderate solution to the problem of demonology: daemons exist but their existence does not outlaw the chain of cause and effect. Oracular guidance is given to the soul which is properly attuned and which itself exerts effort.

In this essay Plutarch does not go so far as to say with Heraclitus that man's character is his own daemon; but he does make some progress toward breaking down the barrier between man and his daemon. For Plutarch there must be a harmony between the two; the daemon exhibits its power or brings divine power to the soul, but the soul must also play its part. In other words, the initiative is partly in man himself. When Emerson in "Beauty" introduces the idea that the daemon is partly in man himself he is not necessarily, as Harrison believes, importing into the Plutarchan concept of the daemon a Neoplatonic accretion, for it is clearly hinted at by Plutarch also.[45] For example, the unity of the daemonic and the human is quite explicit in another Plutarchan essay on the daemonic. This essay is the one entitled "Why the Oracles Cease to Give Answers." Here one particular power of the daemon — the prophetic power and the art of divination — is discussed. The question is, does divination come from the gods or does it have a physical or natural explanation? The physical explanation is summed up in the words of Ammonius, and a favorite Emersonian quotation, ". . . that souls are naturally endued with the faculty of prediction, and that the chief cause that excites this faculty and virtue is a certain temperature of air and winds." Neither Plutarch nor Ammonius himself commends this explanation and Plutarch takes over the conduct of the discussion, advancing the Platonic explanation of demonology, or rather applying the Platonic explanation of all causality to the operations of the diviner or oracle. All things working according to reason are the work of God, but this belief does not detract from the part played by the material or human instrument, just as the creative function of the artist does not detract from that of his medium in the production of a work of art. The early poets attributed all to God; the natural philosophers attributed all to matter. Plato, says Plutarch, combined the two opposing views into a convincing dualism (*Moralia* 4. 59): "For we do not deprive divination either of God or of reason; seeing we allow it for its subject the soul of man, and for its instrument an enthusiastic exhalation." For the sun and the earth, matter, are also considered to be gods and the daemons are only the moderators or controllers of the intensity of the activity of divination. The imaginative part of the soul and the exhalations from the atmosphere work in harmony and, when they operate in the correct proportions, "enthusiasm" or the power of divination displays itself.

There is evidence that Emerson was well acquainted with this essay of Plutarch. In "Inspiration" he discusses poetic inspiration and follows Plato in emphasizing the part played by the daemonic element, i.e., the inspiration which is beyond the power of the artist, which Plato called "divine madness." But like Plutarch, Emerson goes on to point out that this is not the whole story; there must be "mind" and "sight" as well as "soul." The human element also plays its part in demonology. He lists eight sources of inspiration. They are health, letter-writing, rest, will power, atmosphere, solitary communication with nature, conversation, and new poetry. These topics indicate that he is dealing with poetic inspiration but when he comes to the fifth source, "atmosphere," he shows his acquaintance with "Why the Oracles Cease to Give Answers" by quoting from it the naturalistic explanation of divination stated by Ammonius — that the atmosphere excites the natural ability of the soul to predict the future.[46]

To return to "Demonology," Emerson's explanation of inspiration or demonology is precisely the Platonic-Plutarchan one. For both, nature and the supernatural are not mutually exclusive; or, from another point of view, they do not believe in "supernatural" activity. Emerson puts it briefly and Platonically: "the whole world is an omen and sign. Why look so wistfully in a corner? Man is the image of God"; or in the motto for the essay "Fate":

> For the prevision is allied
> Unto the thing so signified;
> Or say, the foresight that awaits
> Is the same Genius that creates.

Again too, in spite of Plutarch's criticism of the Stoics on divination, we find Plutarch and Emerson both adopting a viewpoint which, probably without their awareness of the fact, is characteristically Stoic. For the Stoic Epictetus says: "What need have I to consult the viscera of victims and the flight of birds, and why do I submit when [the diviner or soothsayer] says 'it is for your interest'? Have I not within me a diviner?" That this "diviner" is, according to the Stoics, to be identified with reason, is shown clearly in a passage of the Stoic emperor, Marcus Aurelius: "A man lives with the gods if he always presents to their view a soul that is satisfied with what they give him, and that does the will of the genius [daemon] given him by Zeus, as a particle of his own Being, to be his protector and governor. This genius consists in the Mind and Reason of each of us." [47] Here the Stoic pantheism is evident — the inmost part of man is a particle of the divine and it consists of reason. Hence man and God are one, joined (along with nature) in a single ordered world, the *kosmos*. This explanation of destiny suits Emerson admirably, for it preserves free will and self-reliance. It is deterministic, but the determinism is that of man's own nature, which is itself divine, not that of an outside element, alien to and oblivious to man. He could agree on this point as on several others with Heraclitus that "man's character is his daemon." Emerson says the same thing again in "Demonology"; when he speaks of the many facts which are to be used by man as signs, we recall Plutarch in the passage from the essay on the daemon of Socrates (quoted above) on the manifold evidence available for the human mind to work on; Emerson says: "The soul contains in itself the event that shall presently befall it, for the event is only the actualizing of its thoughts. . . . Every man goes through the world attended with innumerable facts prefiguring (yes, distinctly announcing) his fate, if only eyes of sufficient heed and illumination were fastened on the sign." To put it succinctly, all action is the result of traits of character. For Emerson as for Plutarch, what appears to be luck or the work of some daemon is often skill, in that it arises from within man, in man's divine nature; there is no blind, external force like the common concept of "lucky." Emerson supports this by a quotation from Euripides in Plutarch (*Moralia*, 4. 50), to the effect that the best prophet is not he whose guess turns out to be correct but he who uses his mind and reasoning powers with the help of his knowledge of what is probable, before making his conjecture.

There is, Emerson thinks, something of value in "demonology," for it implies a recognition of the spiritual world, the world of the

Over-Soul; in addition demonology requires the attunement of the individual soul so that it is able to read the signs. As he says in "Worship," "miracles come to the miraculous." Emerson does not share in Plutarch's omens, which are those of classical superstition; rather he fits his demonology into his theory of nature — all nature is one tremendous sign and signal to those who can read it aright.

v

Emerson appears to have taken from Plutarch another, minor, aspect of demonology connected with enthusiasm, dreams, drunkenness, and kindred subjects. In "The Over-Soul" he notices the tendency to enthusiasm in religion, and in the last paragraph of "Circles" he says that "nothing was ever achieved without enthusiasm." He seems to use the term "enthusiasm" here in the Greek sense of "inspired madness" and writes at the end of this essay that "dreams and drunkenness . . . are the semblance and counterfeit of this oracular genius." The idea that dreams and drunkenness have some kinship with the daemonic, that the daemon communicates with the individual by means of dreams, that he is no longer in control of himself and hence that dreams resemble drunkenness, is common in Greek thought and is mentioned several times by Plutarch.[48] Emerson devotes some attention in "Demonology" to the problem of the meaning of dreams and the question whether they convey any deeper meaning, whether they are an aspect of the demonological, and he quotes from Plutarch's "Of Superstition" an apothegm of Heraclitus on dreams; but he also shows by a quotation that Goethe felt there may be some connection between dreams and fate and Emerson may here be following Goethe as much as he follows Plutarch.

Like Plutarch and Goethe, Emerson in "Demonology" believes that dreams have some connection with character and some correspondence with fact; they have "a poetic integrity and truth." He elaborates this in a casual, vivid, personal way and adds that the same thing may be applied to all "omens and coincidences." He feels that what is popularly called demonology is actually a reasoning from character; it is a perfectly logical process. Plutarch says very much the same thing in *Moralia* 2. 389, while in another essay, "Of Man's Progress in Virtue," he repeats this and indicates by reference to and quotations from Zeno and Plato that he here follows the Stoic and Platonic tradition. Dreams, Plutarch thinks, are a guide to character, in that pleasant dreams indicate the beginning of a progress to goodness, while bad dreams indicate a relaxation in the fight toward goodness so that the soul is off its guard and opened to the assault of the passions. For Emerson too dreams have a prophetic element and he turns to three quotations in illustration; the first two are Plutarchan (*CW* 10. 13–14), and when Emerson mentions individuals who are "attended by a good fortune which makes them desirable associates in any enterprise of uncertain success" he may well be thinking of "Sulla the Fortunate" or Demosthenes with "Good Fortune" on his shield (Emerson had noted this in his journals) or of his favorite Plutarchan hero Timoleon, attended by signs of divine favor.

Then Emerson points out (*CW* 10. 16) that, in the common view, the usual agents of demonology are selective; fairies, angels, and saints single out special individuals for their favor. He indicates clearly that this favoritism is contrary to our concept of religion and contrary to scientific knowledge. Plutarch is not quite so outspoken. He seems to adhere to the popular belief, that Fortune has a tendency to select individuals, but he suggests that these individuals are not chosen at random; they have special mental powers, special abilities (*Moralia* 2. 413–14). Emerson's idea that belief in demonology and magic runs contrary to science and religion is also found in Plutarch, who says in "A Discourse concerning Socrates's Daemon" (*Moralia* 2. 387): ". . . these pretences seem not only unbecoming philosophy, but quite opposite to all those fine promises she makes. For having promised to teach us by reason what is good and profitable, falling back again to the Gods as the principle of all our actions, she seems to despise reason, and disgrace that demonstration which is her peculiar glory; and she relies on dreams and visions, in which the worst of men are oftentimes as happy as the best." Emerson thus seems to have obtained the key for his section on dreams in "Demonology" from Plutarch but to have developed it in his own way, confirming it by a long quotation from Goethe.

There are in "Demonology" two "lustres" which, it has not been noticed before, come from another essay by Plutarch which has to do with oracles and divination. At the end of "Wherefore the Pythian Priestess Ceases to Deliver Her Oracles in Verse" Plutarch says:

But although there were some formerly who blamed the ambiguity and obscurity of the oracle, and others who at this day find fault with its modern plainness and perspicuity, yet are they both alike unjust and foolish in their passion; for, *like children better pleased with the sight of rainbows, comets, and those halos that encircle the sun and moon, than to see the sun and moon themselves* in their splendor, they are taken with riddles, abstruse words, and figurative speeches, which are but the reflections of oracular divination to the apprehension of our mortal understanding.

Plutarch indicates that to pay attention to the manner of the oracle's expression, to commend it or to find fault with it, is to concentrate on the superficial and external element in the oracle. The real oracles are still available to us but in different forms. Emerson says the same thing; like Plutarch he attacks "superstition" and denies that it has anything to do with religion. He recalls Plutarch and indicts the ancient forms of superstition (*CW* 10. 23), "coincidences, dreams, animal magnetism, omens, sacred lots" and then turns to current superstitions. He is specially annoyed by the current popular fad of mesmerism, and borrows Plutarch's figure of those attracted by the halos, the rainbow, and the sun; and he employs it for the same object: "Mesmerism is high life below stairs; Momus playing Jove in the kitchens of Olympus. 'T is a low curiosity or lust of structure, and is separated by celestial diameters from the love of spiritual truths. It is wholly a false view to couple these things in any manner with the religious nature and sentiment, and a most dangerous superstition to raise them to the lofty place of motives and sanctions. *This is to prefer halos and rainbows to the sun and moon.*"[49] Here is the old Plutarchan distinction between religion and superstition, and Emerson, like a true classicist, finds Plutarch perfectly applicable to the present age. To Plutarch the riddle and abstruse words, all the machinery of the oracle, are but "the reflections of oracular divination" and for Emerson mesmerism and all the other fads are still superstition, but they disclose the "inextinguishableness of wonder in man" and indicate the conviction that behind all of them is "a vast and potent and living Nature" which cannot be explained. He sums it up as Plutarch might well do, "Demonology is the shadow of theology."

The second Plutarchan lustre occurs in the final paragraph of "Demonology." Emerson concludes: "The whole world is an omen and a sign. Why look so wistfully in a corner? Man is the Image of God. Why run after a ghost or a dream? The voice of divination resounds everywhere and runs to waste unheard, unregarded, as the mountains echo with the bleatings of cattle." There can be no doubt, I think, that Emerson has yet another of Plutarch's essays on demonology, "Why the Oracles Cease to Give Answers," before him; Plutarch says (*Moralia* 4. 12–13) that the reason for the cessation of the oracles in Boeotia is simply that the population has moved away or has died out; only a few oracular shrines are left because the people who dwell in Boeotia are few: "So that we should think it strange, if the God should suffer the prophetical divination to be spilt and run to waste like water, or everywhere to resound, as in solitary fields we hear the rocks echoing the voices of shepherds and bleating cattle." The content and purpose of Plutarch's remark is not the same as that of Emerson, but Emerson has noticed and approved the two pictures, water running to waste and cattle lowing in deserted places, and has adopted them as his own. This is nothing more than an attractive lustre, but together with the former lustre it indicates that Emerson has looked at all Plutarch's essays which deal with divination and the oracular. From Plutarch he adopts as still valid the concept that there are ways of getting into tune with the infinite; the oracles are not silent, only one must be sure to consult the real oracles, not the vivid outward occurrences which are in reality not more than that; no oracle is allowed to be wasted to no effect. Emerson and Plutarch agree that there are oracles everywhere. As the Stoics said, the whole universe is a unity, is nature and God. And as Plato said, the whole physical world is a sign of the daemonic, of the spiritual world.

There is proof then that Emerson knew all of Plutarch's essays which deal with oracles and divination; he quotes from them all, including "Of Superstition." In this last essay Plutarch attacks scepticism in religion and, as we shall see, his views again coincide with those of Emerson.[50] Thus there is a similarity in thought between Plutarch and Emerson when they discuss religion, atheism, and scepticism. But the chief similarity is one of tone and attitude. Both adopt a reasonable, sensible, moderate view. They do not, except in this instance, attack the same things, however, since the circumstances of nineteenth-century America are not the same as those of second-century Greece. The beginning of Emerson's essay on worship shows that he has been charged with materialism and fatalism; hence he wishes to show that man has a great part toward winning his own victory and he denies his own atheism or materialism by attacking it in his own time. The objects of Plutarch's hatred are superstition (which is for him a kind of determinism) and atheism, another aspect of superstition, and not its opposite. Both Emerson and Plutarch arrive at a philosophy of independence and moderation; for Plutarch fortune and work and for Emerson Divine Providence and work constitute the ideal partnership. In other terms, both advocate self-reliance; again and again Emerson and Plutarch coincide in their Stoic aspects. Either could have said: "The ignorant man's position and character is this: he never looks to himself for benefit or harm, but to the world outside him. The philosopher's position and character is that he always looks to himself for benefit and harm." But the man who did say it was the Stoic slave Epictetus.[51]

v i

There is another aspect of Emerson's thought, a minor one perhaps, in which it seems to me not only his classicism and his Platonism but also his Plutarchan type of Platonism make a brief appearance. Emerson's readers and critics in his own time often spoke of his idealism and lack of practical, down-to-earth philosophy. He is, they felt, up in the clouds, following Plato. But Emerson himself and the Transcendentalists were well aware that Greek philosophy and above all Plato judiciously blended the divine and the human, the "real" and the ideal. It was precisely for this reason that idealism seemed so adequate a philosophy for the modern age. It gave proper proportion to the mundane and the heavenly, the practical and the contemplative, the sense and the "Over-Soul." But still the critics' objections have to be answered, the philosopher must show that he takes into account the real world and practical concerns. As with Plato, he must return from time to time to the cave from his lofty world of forms. So Emerson, after the Platonic, upward-moving essays on love and friendship comes down to earth with his essay "Prudence" and he says at the beginning of it: ". . . it would be hardly honest in me not to balance these fine lyric words of Love and Friendship with words of coarser sound, and while my debt to my senses is real and constant, not to own it in passing." Prudence, then, to Emerson, deals with the world of the senses and his basic dualism is at once made clear. The world of the senses is a lower, coarser world and he begins by indicating that prudence deals with economy, with money and the practical concerns of everyday life. But even so it must not be divorced entirely from the higher world, it is still "the outmost action of the inward life." It is "God taking thought for oxen." He protests against the usual detachment of the material from the immaterial (*CW* 2. 222): "The world of the senses is a world of shows; it does not exist for itself, but has a symbolic character; and a true prudence or law of shows recognizes the co-presence of other laws and knows that its own office is subaltern; . . . Prudence is false when detached. It is legitimate when it is the Natural History of the soul incarnate; when it unfolds the beauty of laws within the narrow scope of the senses." Emerson distinguishes between a "base" or "spurious" prudence which deals only with the world of the senses, making the senses final, and the true prudence which "limits this sensualism by admitting the knowledge of an internal or real world." Real prudence is valuable. It is not philosophic or introspective. It takes the laws of the world as they are "and keeps these laws that it may enjoy their proper good." Any neglect of prudence is punished; there is such a thing as truth to the senses, or what Emerson calls "perpendicularity" and this must be observed and retained. It is the lack of this perpendicularity and of ideal goals or standards which makes us content with less than the best, and since we lack the best we call beautiful or clever that which has really little beauty or genius about it. In the same way we excuse great errors by calling them trivial. Here the Stoic tone, never far away, comes in. Scholars, Emerson says, are notoriously imprudent in practical affairs. They should be Stoic, accept the "pains and mortifications" which come to them, for they are sent by nature. The scholar must follow nature's counsels, live simply and frugally, controlling expenditure, practising prudence. But the Heraclitean flux is also here — Americans are on the edge of this prudence. Commodities cannot deteriorate provided they pass swiftly from one to another — "In skating over thin ice our safety is in our speed." Emerson advocates for America a higher prudence and it is a Stoic one — self-reliance and independence may enable a solitary individual still to make a mark upon the world. But the virtues are all one and the good man will also be wise, the single-hearted will also be "politic"; in his relations with others he will show the courage which comes from self-reliance. Thus, Emerson concludes, "all the virtues range themselves on the side of prudence, or the art of securing a present well-being." His "words of a coarser sound" are not so very coarse after all. Finally, prudence is linked with love and friendship also, indeed with all the virtues, and throughout the essay we have been continually reminded that real prudence is not completely on the level of the senses but is linked always with the inner life.

"Prudence" belongs to Emerson's most Plutarchan period, 1837–38, when he was reading through the *Moralia*, or at least when more evidence than usual of a reading of Plutarch appears in the *Journals*. We should indeed expect Plutarch to take the same sort of reasonable view of "prudence" and practical affairs that Emerson does since they are akin in so many other aspects and share a Platonic view of life. Plutarch does discuss prudence under the term "moral virtue." This "moral virtue" is not the absolute virtue but is the Platonic secondary virtue, or virtue of the *mores*, concerned with action and the passions rather than with the contemplative life. The first sentence of the essay "Of Moral Virtue" (*Moralia* 3. 461) tells us this: "My design in this essay is to treat of that virtue which is called and accounted moral, and is chiefly distinguished from the contemplative, in its having for the matter thereof the passions of the mind, and for its form, right reason." Moral virtue, Plutarch says, is not "a kind of insensibility, or total freedom from passions" but is an ordering and control of the passions and it is brought about by the exercise of "wisdom and prudence." He defines prudence more fully: "Prudence consists in a certain application and relation of the contemplative faculties of the soul to those which are practical, for the government of the sensual and irrational part, according to reason. To which purpose prudence has often the need of Fortune." It is further identified with "practical reason," working according to nature, and it corrects the excesses and defects of passion "by reducing them to a true mediocrity." I do not claim that Emerson borrows Plutarch's definition of prudence but merely observe that both are Platonic in the division of virtue into a higher and a lower and in the Stoicism which both present as a characteristic of true prudence. Emerson's classical bias and his moderate Platonism, toned down and made practical by Stoicism, is again evident here. This Stoic moderation can be seen clearly in both and in a way which is indicative of the liberal temper of both Emerson and Plutarch. Plutarch is eager to emphasize that prudence does not mean negation of the senses or denial of their significance — he is too much of a practical moralist for that and must always keep in touch with and give due value to the world of the senses. Emerson on the other hand will not have his audience mistake his real prudence for current materialism and "sensuality." His idealism is always present; he feels that America would be likely to misunderstand the term "prudence" and to take it as license for still greater emphasis on material well-being.

Towards the end of "Prudence" Emerson takes up another theme which is classical, Stoic, and Plutarchan. "The prudence which secures an outward well-being is not to be studied by one set of men; whilst heroism and holiness are studied by another, but they are reconcilable." He comes back to this theme — the unity of all the virtues — in the last paragraph. "All the virtues range themselves on the side of prudence" and "I do not know if all matter will be found to be made of one element, as oxygen or hydrogen, at last, but the world of manners and actions is wrought of one stuff, and begin where we will, we are pretty sure in a short space to be mumbling our ten commandments." This emphasis on the unity of the virtues is characteristically Emersonian, for all objects and all qualities are part of the eternal One. "There is," Emerson says in "The Method of Nature," "no revolt in all the kingdoms from the commonweal; no detachment of an individual." It appears also in "The Over-Soul." All the virtues are connected; the progress of the soul therefore cannot be represented by a straight line. "The growths of genius are of a certain total character" which do not advance the individual first over one man and then over another, but which grow, impelled by a divine impulse, so that the soul eventually "comes out into eternity" (*CW* 2. 275): "It converses with truths that have always been spoken in the world, and becomes conscious of a closer sympathy with Zeno and Arrian than with persons in the house. . . . The simple rise as by specific levity not into a particular virtue, but into the region of all the virtues. They are in the spirit which contains them all. . . . To the well-born child all the virtues are natural, and not painfully acquired." This is an old Stoic theme and Emerson's predilection for Stoicism reappears here. That he is aware that it is Stoic is indicated by his mention of Zeno and Arrian, two of the chief teachers of the Stoic school. But while Arrian collected the sayings of the Stoic slave Epictetus, he is better known as the biographer of Alexander and it is in Plutarch's "Of the Fortune or Virtue of Alexander" that we find this dogma set down (*Moralia* 1. 488):

Not that I . . . go about to distinguish between the several acts of Alexander, and to ascribe this to fortitude, that to humanity, another to temperance; but I take every act to be an act of all the virtues mixed together. This is conformable to that Stoic sentence, "What a wise man does he does by the impulse of all the virtues together; only one particular virtue seems to head every action, and calling the rest to her assistance drives on to the end proposed."

The theme here — the unity of the virtues — is the same in Plutarch and in Emerson. Both refer to it as a Stoic tenet and when we add that Emerson knew both Plutarchan essays on Alexander, we can at least conjecture that he recalled this paragraph of Plutarch in writing "The Over-Soul."

In this instance and in numerous other passages mentioned in this chapter Emerson's interest in the Stoic side of Plutarch appears. Indeed Emerson quite often speaks like one of the later Stoics, like the Roman Seneca or like the Greek Epictetus of the Roman Empire. In the last passage the name of Zeno the founder of the

Stoic school is mentioned and the reference to Arrian indicates that he is thinking of Epictetus. Like the Stoics, he is early attracted by Heraclitus, "the flowing philosopher," and he ends "Illusions" on a Stoic note, perhaps deliberately approving a Senecan attitude which he found was rejected by Montaigne. He likes the term *kosmos* for the orderly universe and one of the Stoic arguments for the divinity of the universe was based on the perception of the orderly arrangement of the elements in it. He seems very well acquainted with the classical "demonology" which was a prominent element in the Stoic theology, but he rejects the supernatural operation of the daemons on the same grounds and for the same reasons as the Stoics, like Epictetus for example, did. He rejects the old Greek determinism and fatalism. The Roman Stoics, those contemporary with Plutarch, also admitted a very great degree of free will and emphasized self-sufficiency, for man not only relies on God, he *is* God. Later on, Emerson often adopts in regard to ethical or theological problems the moderate view of the late Stoics and of Plutarch. His definition of chance as an unknown cause is characteristically Stoic; his identification of the individual and nature approaches Stoic pantheism but seems to be carefully modified, as it was for Plutarch, by the Platonic dualism. In ethics and human conduct he advocates like a Stoic the life according to nature and the middle road. He finds fault with the superficial attitude of America to the harshness of fate. Great nations have not been "boasters and buffoons" but "perceivers of the terror of life, and have manned themselves to face it" (*CW* 6. 5). The Spartans are mentioned as an example of this brave and fearless attitude, but this is what is often even today called Stoicism.

vii

It might be objected that Emerson in philosophy and religion owes more to Stoicism than to Plutarch, whose anti-Stoic bias is well known. We must remark again, therefore, that Plutarch's antagonism is confined to the logical technicalities of Stoicism and to a few of its larger concepts, such as that of the ideally wise man as a goal which can be attained by mortals. But in his attitude to life in general, we can see clearly the simple Stoic doctrine of the unity of man, nature, and God. Plutarch commends life according to nature, emphasizes contentment and endurance. He is not, and would never permit himself to be called a Stoic in the strict sense of the term, but the Platonism modified by an eclectic tendency, which makes a combination characteristic of Plutarch, is often very close to contemporary Stoicism and in a number of aspects cannot easily be distinguished from it. There are in the ancient world many who adopt Stoicism unconsciously. They are not aware that they are Stoics, and those who adopted it entirely and ready-made as a philosophical system are few. Rather there is a native Stoicism in man which is what Bonamy Dobree [52] has called "a public theme" and as such has exerted a widespread influence at many different times and in many different literatures. So in English literature and thought we can often find ideas which may be called "Stoic" because they echo Seneca or Epictetus or Marcus Aurelius. But besides these more obvious sources or parallels, which come to mind at once because they are the great representatives of the Stoicism of the Roman Empire, there is also Plutarch, less obvious because of his profession to be anti-Stoic. Emerson is not outside the great stream of Stoicism in English literature. It is only less noticeable in him because he does not refer often to the great Stoics. But he knew his Plutarch fairly thoroughly and when he speaks like a Stoic moralist he may well be echoing some idea which has attracted his attention in Plutarch's moral essays. Using the loose sense of the term, the sense familiar to all readers of English for centuries, he is as much of a Stoic as Plutarch is, and no more.

VI

BUILDING ON PLUTARCHAN THEMES

It should be easy to say what I have always felt, that Stanley's Lives of the Philosophers, *or* Marcus Antoninus, *are agreeable and suggestive books to me, whilst St. Paul and St. John are not, and I should never think of taking up these to start me on my task, as I have often used Plato or Plutarch.*

Journals

Emerson says that every writer "builds on his predecessors" and his own favorite method of using his predecessors he describes as "reading for lustres." [1] It is for these lustres especially that he reads Plutarch, looking for anecdote or apothegm, an impressive symbol or a vivid figure which could be used again, incorporated into an essay either in the same context or in one totally different from that in which Plutarch had used it.

But an author like Plutarch is also "spermatic"; he often starts a train of thought in the reader and Emerson says that he himself used Plutarch when he contemplated beginning a moral essay. There are several essays which give the appearance of having been begun in this way, though quite often only the title and the topic have been borrowed. But also, in several instances while treating a topic handled by Plutarch and other moral essayists, he adopts much the same treatment and theme, and in one essay, "Love," he follows Plutarch's essay of the same title fairly closely, adopting similar subtopics and a similar viewpoint. He discards what does not appeal to him and from time to time elaborates a theme in his own way, but even when he does this, the treatment does not usually turn out to be original. His ideas on love are the classical ones of the moral essay and can be found in other essays of Plutarch besides the one on love. Emerson's sense of affinity and kinship with Plutarch which comes from their common Platonism and Stoicism prompts him to adopt the same attitude, and to elaborate Plutarchan themes. If Emerson consulted his predecessors among the moral essayists, he must have found Bacon's "Of Love" too brief, Montaigne's treatment of the subject in "On Some Verses of Virgil," if thorough, too free and unconventional; only Plutarch's attitude to and treatment of love seems to be adapted to Emerson's own mind.

The essay "Love" is identical with the fourth lecture in a course entitled "Human Life" which Emerson gave in Boston in 1838–39; thus he wrote the essay probably fairly soon after a period when he had been reading the *Moralia* and had made the journal notes on it in 1837. This essay and the one on friendship which follows it in *Essays: First Series* have puzzled some of Emerson's critics. Firkins long ago found "Love" distasteful and annoying; he is especially troubled by the rhapsodical "Venetian" treatment of the topic, while at the same time conceding the attractiveness of several vignettes in the essay — of the love of mankind for a lover, of the schoolgirls. He concludes: "On the whole, the essay on 'Love' is too full of alternating exhilarations and disappointments to rank among satisfying products; but as a unique document in the Emerson *dossier* its significance is undeniable." [2] This is fair enough; anyone who has read "Nature" and the essays which precede "Love" in *Essays: First Series* is conscious of a feeling of disquiet and uncertainty when he reads "Love." This is not the treatment which we had been led to expect. We should rather expect Emerson to treat love in general terms as the quality, almost synonymous with his "affinity," which makes the individual perceive his unity with other individuals and with the universe and if we were looking for a source we should expect to find Plato his mainstay. It is true that the Platonic view of love is fundamental to the last part of the essay and it is remotely in the background of the first part also, but still the difficulty remains and while Emerson's rhapsodic description of the effect of love on the individual is attractive its very attractiveness is un-Emersonian.

To put the problem in another way, where is Emerson's Stoicism in this essay? There is no Stoic restraint, no reference to the happy mean; indeed this enthusiastic view of love is not Stoic at all. The difficulty of the "uniqueness" of this essay is largely resolved when we compare Emerson's essay and his treatment of love there with the corresponding essay in Plutarch's *Moralia*. Emerson is merely following Plato indirectly, through Plutarch, and following his source more closely than usual in this essay. The topics are often rearranged in order and elaborated or compressed in Emerson, but most of them can be found in Plutarch. The absence of Stoic restraint in Emerson here may well be occasioned by the fact that it is not present at all in Plutarch's essay on love. If Emerson had read another Plutarchan essay, "Of Brotherly love," in conjunction with this one "Of Love," the erotic emphasis would have been modified and we would have been given some doctrines which might much more closely approximate Stoic restraint. But Plutarch's essay on love resembles a rhetorical exercise on the power of love over mankind; it has some of the Platonic enthusiasm of the *Symposium* and the Platonic dialogue form is more evident here than in other essays in the collection; again imitating some of the Platonic dialogues, a particular situation and a particular love affair are made the origin of the discussion and we have at the outset a romantic setting—a rich and noble widow is in love with a handsome young man. Is this affair between two people of disparate age to be approved? Here is the Platonic question, the topic which starts the dialogue which then roams over many aspects of love and its effects in a conventional classical essay.

Emerson's enthusiastic note at the beginning is simply Platonic and Plutarchan — that love is a "divine rage and enthusiasm" which "seizes on a man at one period." Later it is called a "celestial rapture" which "seizes" the young. This theory of love as a divine madness is given much attention also in Plutarch's essay and as we shall see Emerson borrows a vivid lustre from a paragraph in Plutarch which describes its operation. Love to Plutarch is "a certain madness" or "a kind of fury, partaking something of divine inspiration." Plutarch describes various forms of this fury but returns to "that erotic fury that possesses lovely youths and chaste women, yet a hot and vehement transport." Emerson borrows one of Plutarch's terms, for Plutarch calls love a "celestial rapture of the mind."

Emerson's second paragraph rather curiously, and in graceful and elaborate language, raises the question whether love is only for the young. Emerson challenges this contention; love changes its nature with age but it is not only for the young: in fact "it matters not . . . whether we attempt to describe the passion at twenty, thirty, or at eighty years." It would almost seem that Emerson is here refuting the argument that love is for the young only, which occurs several times in Plutarch's essay — the romantic story which introduces the dialogue raises this point and Plutarch quotes Hesiod in support of marriage by the age of thirty.

Even the metaphor Emerson employs — that love is a fire — is a very old and familiar one. It is not missing in Plutarch: love is "a flame," "its raging heat" can be extinguished by reason and maturity, so that only "a warm and glowing heat in the soul" is left. Emerson borrowed from the paragraph which uses these terms another lustre; there can be no doubt that he read the entire paragraph and noticed how Plutarch elaborated the metaphor with details. Emerson himself does the same thing in his own way; while for Plutarch love is a fire whose raging heat can be extinguished by reason, leaving only a warm glow, Emerson employs the figure differently — love is a fire kindled in the hearts of two, which then glows and enlarges until it lights up the whole world. This turn of phrase suits Emerson better because it tends to universalize love instead of making it (as Plutarch did and as Emerson does for part of the essay) the feeling of one individual for another. He continues — and perhaps he is thinking of Plutarch's romantic love story again — "How we glow over these novels of passion, when the story is told with any spark of truth and nature!" Emerson thus continues the theme of love as a fire in a subtle but forceful way.

Still another theme in Emerson is conventional, classical, and Plutarchan. Love is "the dawn of civility and grace in the coarse and rustic"; the "rude village boy" is changed by love and he describes in pleasant terms the first timid actions which mark the birth of love in a boy or girl. This is a familiar theme in many classical authors besides Plutarch, but in a rhetorical conventional essay of this type, Plutarch naturally elaborates this topic — the changes wrought in an individual by love — at greater length than usual. Emerson is much more attractive than Plutarch here and paints a delightful picture of the effect of this change created by love in the attitudes and actions of the boys and girls of a New England village. The picture owes its success, I think, to the fact that here he abandons his classical authority and, instead of consulting a book, looks about at Concord and its people. But after a few more personal paragraphs he seems to return to Plutarch again and Plutarch's description of the changes wrought by love. Emerson writes (*CW* 2. 174–176):

But here is a strange fact; it may seem to many men, in revising their experience, that they have no fairer page in their life's book than the delicious memory of some passages wherein affection contrived to give a witchcraft, surpassing the deep attraction of its own truth, to a parcel of accidental and trivial circumstances. In looking backward they may find that several things which were not the charm have more reality to this groping memory than the charm itself which embalmed them. But be our experience in particulars what it may, no man ever forgot the visitations of that power to his heart and brain, which created all things anew; which was the dawn in him of music, poetry and art; which made the face of nature radiant with purple light, the morning and the night varied enchantments; when a single tone of one voice could make the heart bound, and the most trivial circumstance associated with one form is put in the amber of memory; when he became all eye when one was present, and all memory when one was gone; when the youth becomes a watcher of windows and studious of a glove, a veil, a ribbon, or the wheels of a carriage; when no place is too solitary and none too silent for him who has richer company and sweeter conversation in his new thoughts than any old friends, though best and purest, can give him; for the figures, the motions, the words of the beloved object are not, like other images, written in water, but, as Plutarch said, "enamelled in fire," and make the study of midnight: —

> "Thou art not gone being gone, where'er thou art,
> Thou leav'st in him thy watchful eyes, in him thy loving heart."

In the noon and the afternoon of life we still throb at the recollection of days when happiness was not happy enough, but must be drugged with the relish of pain and fear; for he touched the secret of the matter who said of love, —
"All other pleasures are not worth its pains:"
and when the day was not long enough, but the night too must be consumed in keen recollections; when the head boiled all night on the pillow with the generous deed it resolved on; when the moonlight was a pleasing fever and the stars were letters and the flowers ciphers and the air was coined into song; when all business seemed an impertinence, and all the men and women running to and fro in the streets, mere pictures.

So many little details in this resemble Plutarch that I must quote him at some length (*Moralia* 4. 280–281):

Whereas the fury of love, wherever it seizes either man or woman, sets them in a flame; no music, no appeasing incantations, no changes of place are able to quench or put a stop to it; but being in presence, they love; being absent, they desire; by day they prosecute their importunate visits; by night they serenade at the windows; sober, they are continually calling upon their loves; and when they are fuddled, are always teasing the company with their love songs and madrigals. Neither, as one was pleased to say, are poetical fancies, by reason of their lively expressions, rightly called waking dreams; but the dialogues of persons enamored,

discoursing with their absent loves, and dallying, embracing, and expostulating with them as if they were present, much rather deserve this
name. For the sight seems to delineate other fancies in the water, that
quickly glide away and slip out of the mind; whereas the imaginations
of lovers, being as it were enamelled by fire, leave the images of things
imprinted in the memory, moving, living, speaking, and remaining for
a long time. So that Cato the Roman was wont to say, that the soul of a
lover dwelt in the soul of the person beloved, for that there is settled and
fixed in the one the form, shape, manners, conversation and actions of
the other; by which being led, the lover quickly dispatches a long
journey . . . and he is carried from love to friendship, as it were with
wind and tide, the God of Love assisting his passion.

Both Emerson and Plutarch mention the vividness imparted to
memories by love; Emerson takes directly from Plutarch the phrase
"enamelled in fire," indeed the whole of the above passage of
Emerson seems to be a revision of Plutarch; the theme is the same
— love imprints on the memory the image of the loved one; Emerson elaborates it by recalling the manner in which love recreates
trivial incidents which had but minor significance at the time they
occurred. From Plutarch he takes the picture of the lover who
becomes "a watcher of windows"; Plutarch's "being in presence,
they love; being absent, they desire; by day," etc. is elaborated in
Emerson: "when he became all eye when one was present, and
all memory when one was gone; when the youth becomes a
watcher of windows and studious of a glove, a veil, a ribbon, or the
wheels of a carriage." For Plutarch, music has no charm to allevi-
ate the pain of love, yet when they have been in convivial company
the lovers "tease the company with their love songs and madrigals";
Emerson too mentions music, but it is only to recall another idea
of Plutarch, that love is the birth of music and art in the lover; the
picture of the drinking revellers does not appeal to Emerson. For
both, other fancies are delineated in water (Emerson says "written
in water"). Emerson's triad "figures, motions, words" is his version
of Plutarch's "moving, living, speaking." To match Plutarch's familiar expression of Cato, Emerson has with great ingenuity re-

called Donne's couplet which is simply a poetical rendering of Cato's famous sentence.

The same theme is elaborated later on in the essay and here again some of the subtopics occur in Plutarch, though Emerson chooses to emphasize the changed aspect of nature to the eye of the lover rather than the change which Plutarch finds in the lover himself. But still Emerson's amusing picture of the frenzied lover, "Behold there in the woods the fine madman!" resembles, even if it is more poetically described, a similar picture in Plutarch of the lovers "discoursing with their absent loves, and dallying, embracing, and expostulating with them as if they were present." The thought that love inspires poetry is also Plutarchan, but Emerson touches on this much more briefly than Plutarch. It is worth noting that he had a double opportunity to come upon this topic as he leafed through his copy of the *Moralia*, for the theme constitutes a question in the first book of "Symposiacs," which Emerson liked, and much of the same material seems to make its appearance a second time in Plutarch. In "Of Love" Plutarch elaborates the more general theme, the changes wrought by love, at some length, and this turns into a discussion of the idea that love is a god. Emerson omits this; however, his figure, that beauty is "welcome as the sun wherever it chooses to shine" (*CW* 2. 178) may be an unconscious echo of Plutarch's lengthy comparison of love to the sun.

Still another theme in Emerson is classical — that love is a mixture of pleasure and pain. This is pretty much of a commonplace by the time of Plutarch and can be found in a number of passages; he speaks of love's "pleasing pain" and of "the bittersweet of love," but Emerson transforms his conventional remark with a vivid picture, starred with bright metaphors and references to moonlight, stars, and flowers, of the lover's restlessness.

There is at least one lustre which Emerson derives from Plutarch. "The ancients called beauty the flowering of virtue," he says. And Plutarch says in his essay on love, "But some say that beauty

is the flower of virtue."[3] Plutarch continues: "Will they then
affirm, that the female sex never blossoms nor makes any show of
tendency to virtue? It were absurd to think so. Therefore was
Aeschylus in the right when he said, that he could never mistake
the fire in the eye of a young woman who had once known a man."
This is too gross for Emerson and his readers, and in effect he
challenges Aeschylus (*CW* 2. 179):

Who can analyse the nameless charm which glances from one and
another face and form? We are touched with emotions of tenderness and
complacency, but we cannot find whereat this dainty emotion, this
wandering gleam, points. It is destroyed for the imagination by any
attempt to refer it to organization. Nor does it point to any relations of
friendship or love known and described in society, but, as it seems to me,
to a quite other and unattainable sphere, to relations of transcendent
delicacy and sweetness, to what roses and violets hint and foreshow.
We cannot approach beauty. Its nature is like opaline doves'-neck lustres,
hovering and evanescent.

Aeschylus' remark mentions something which cannot even be
"described in society"; let us have rather "transcendent delicacy"
and Emerson finishes off with violets and roses and doves.

Then he outlines (*CW* 2. 181) the Platonic theory of love as in
the *Phaedrus* and the *Symposium* — the soul of man is placed into
matter and wanders in the world looking for its own real, heavenly
world of forms. But it is blinded by the sun and cannot see beyond
this world and matter. God therefore sends physical beauty in
youth before its eyes, to aid the soul in its recollection of ideal
beauty. Joy in physical beauty is created by recollections of ideal
beauty which the soul of the man sees in the maiden. It has been
pointed out by Harrison that this paragraph of Platonism is an
abstract of a paragraph in Plutarch (*Moralia* 4. 294–295). Emerson's son was probably unaware of his father's close use of Plutarch,
but he does remark in his notes to this passage that a single sentence
recalls a similar one in Plutarch.[4]

The next paragraph in Emerson (*CW* 2. 181–183) continues, as

Harrison observed, to follow this Plutarchan-Platonic train of thought — contentment with physical beauty brings only sorrow, but the soul passes from loving physical beauty to loving beauty of character. Love is purified and can ascend to love of good qualities and beauty in all human beings and hence to "the highest beauty, to the love and knowledge of the Divinity, by steps on this ladder of created souls," and one sentence contains several phrases which are borrowed verbatim from Plutarch.[5] The last part of Emerson's paragraph, however, which includes the above quotation, reminds the reader more immediately of part of Diotima's speech in Plato's *Symposium*, where the ascent of love from the material to the ideal realm is described. The last part of Plutarch's paragraph resembles rather Plato's other dialogue on love, the *Phaedrus* (247C–248D). Both Emerson and Plutarch are following a Platonic train of thought; Plutarch ends, "But these are points too high for the discourse which we have proposed to ourselves." Emerson is ready, however, for the Platonic heights and the higher flight into the ideal realm and so he goes on to outline the Platonic theory of celestial love. Emerson begins his next paragraph (*CW* 2. 183): "Somewhat like this have the truly wise told us of love in all ages. The doctrine is not old, nor is it new. If Plato, Plutarch and Apuleius taught it, so have Petrarch, Angelo and Milton." There, almost hidden in the list of names, like many another list of names in Emerson's writing which does not convey much, is the name of one of his chief sources throughout the essay "Love." Nor is Emerson quite finished with Plutarch, though the reminiscences from this point to the end of the essay are much slighter. Both Emerson and Plutarch turn to married love and to the part of the woman: Emerson mentions it briefly in the next sentence; he thinks that marriage is too often referred to in terms of "prudence" that is, in material terms, or economic terms. This "sensualism" or materialism has influenced the education of young women, so that marriage is often regarded by them as housekeeping, as a practical, material affair. So, too, woman in marriage, with perhaps an undue emphasis on "sensualism" of a different kind which would only be distasteful to Emerson, is Plutarch's topic for one and one half pages (304–306). Emerson then, after two sentences on the theme, returns to a long paragraph on the beauty of love, the text of which is the sentence (p. 184), "Thus even love, which is the deification of persons, must become more impersonal every day." It is written more poetically, spontaneously, and naturally than are the paragraphs in which Emerson echoes Plutarch. Whenever Emerson follows his source too closely he acquires the stiff, hieratic tone which make his words sound like a translation, like the translation which he is following too closely for the good of his style. When he can get back to nature and can rhapsodize, when fact and statement are abandoned, Emerson becomes himself again.

The parallelism in theme continues. Love is not perfect and lovers have their quarrels. To Emerson these failures in harmony arise in the disparity between the ideal love that the lover seeks and the qualities that actually appear in the beloved; but after all, the underlying ideal beauty and virtue will draw them together again. This is much more Platonic and more lofty in tone than Plutarch, who looks upon quarrels as simple, natural "effervescences" of two different liquids mixed together; they settle down after a time. This is an attitude which could never attract Emerson; he adopts the Platonic solution; but still for both, love is a purification and both express admiration for the love which as Emerson says binds a man and woman "shut up in one house to spend in the nuptial society forty or fifty years." Emerson ends the essay on a Platonic note, and virtue, as always in the Platonist, comes in; he begins his final paragraph: "Thus we are put in training for a love which knows not sex, nor person, nor partiality, but which seeks virtue and wisdom everywhere, to the end of increasing virtue and wisdom. We are by nature observers, and thereby learners. That is our permanent state. But we are often made to feel that our affections are but tents of a night." The first sentence recalls that with which Plutarch, after the preliminaries and stage setting, began his discourse (*Moralia* 4. 258): "For love that is bred in a young and truly generous heart, by means of friendship, terminates in virtue," and Emerson's final words in the metaphor "tents of a night" recall a sentence of Plutarch (*Moralia* 4. 307) which Emerson seems to have noticed in a section which, because of its reference to pederasty, was otherwise unacceptable: ". . . and the lovers themselves are like the wandering Scythians, who, having spent their spring in flowery and verdant pastures, presently dislodge from thence, as out of an enemy's country." Except for the story of Sabinus and Empone, the story of a long and faithful love of a wife for her husband, Plutarch is at the end of his essay "Of Love." Emerson instead ends his essay on a Platonic note. Indeed the essay is Platonic throughout; as Rusk says, "Love" was "one of the most pleasing and was the most Platonic of all the writings of Emerson, lover of Plato. The *Phaedrus* and the *Symposium*, whose exotic homosexual elements were conveniently ignored, together accounted for essential parts of this essay." [6] But the Platonism seldom comes directly from Plato; rather it is that of Plutarch, another lover of Plato, and Emerson's essay stands out from all the rest of his writing in the way in which Plutarch is followed. Almost all his themes here are Plutarchan and almost all of them come from a reading of one essay of Plutarch.

We may properly speculate on the reason for this close following of Plutarch's steps in this particular essay and on this particular theme. Granted that Emerson's view of love would naturally tend to be the Platonic one, why did he not consult Plato directly and show himself an outright Platonist? This essay was part of a course of lectures, and especially for such a popular course and a presumably ordinary audience the flight to the Platonic world must not be too high, or if it must be high it must return to the ground from time to time if it is to have any appeal at all. If Emerson was to fortify the conscience and give hope and understanding to the ordinary American he must not lead him out of his depths by over-abstraction. Emerson's professed Stoicism was more than mere rhetoric; the Stoics dealt with ethics and manners in such a way that they appealed to the ordinary man, or at least to the practical man who wanted more in his philosophy than Platonic abstractions and lofty ideals. And if there was little Stoicism in Plutarch's treatment of love, he was Stoic in his emphasis on the practical, in his remaining on the human level and only occasionally resorting to Platonism and the higher world. Plutarch was popular because he was readable and I have no doubt that Emerson was well aware of this and felt that in "Of Love" he would find a judicious blending of the abstract and the real, a blending which met a genuine response in his own nature, shifting between the material and the spiritual, the one and the many. So as he looked through the Plutarch essay he saw that the topics were still applicable and modern, and that even Plutarch's attitude towards love might be adapted for today; the language would not do, of course, and the pictures must be changed and moved from a Greek background to an American setting.

This modernization of the setting and background, the intrusion of simple, New England words and expressions, is not merely the superficial dressing up of an abstract topic. It is basic to Emerson's conception of the function of the lecturer in America. The lectures are not mere entertainment. Emerson knows well that the lyceums are "a college for the young rustic" and that as a professional lecturer he had a specific and important task. The sermons of the time, he complains to Carlyle, display a deep gulf between the faith and belief of the minister and of his audience; the very fact that the preacher speaks from a pulpit results in beliefs being attributed to him which he need not necessarily hold.[7] The lyceum platform, on the other hand, gives the lecturer freedom to say what he wants, without shackle or impediment. The very fact that Emerson contrasts the lecture and the sermon in this way, stating that the lyceum is a better instrument for instruction than the pulpit, shows that in his mind the functions of the two occupations, lecturer and preacher, are similar. The lecturer must instruct and edify, must improve and raise the intellectual and spiritual level of his hearers. Emerson's stress on the significance of quotation and his many references to books are also part of his sense of the mission of the lecturer. He wants to widen the intellectual horizon of America, and to turn its eyes away from the trivial and transient things of the present place and time to the great intellectual and moral truths and to the writers and thinkers who uttered them. But this can only be done by starting with the familiar and the near as a point of departure and by returning to it from time to time. Much of Emerson's success as a lecturer must be attributed to this careful pedagogical technique and Lowell points out that it was this aspect of his "practicality" which made him the most popular lecturer in America.[8] His secret is that "he out-Yankees us all," his "range includes us all"; while giving "ravishing glimpses of an ideal under the dry husk of our New England," at the same time "his mysticism gives us a counterpoise to our super-practicality." Theodore Parker wrote of Emerson that he "illustrates his high thought by common things out of our plain New England life." He treats of "John and Jane, not Coriolanus and Persephone";[9] thus in "Love" we have the New England background which occasionally shows through and which is almost the only element which prevents us from realizing the classicism and the conventional nature of the treatment.

It is the Plutarchan contribution which makes this essay seem different from most of the others; and Emerson never did this again; in no other essay does he appear to follow a predecessor as closely as he keeps to Plutarch here.

Several other topics to which Emerson devotes essays had also been taken up by the great moral essayists whom he read and occasionally a quotation from Plutarch or Montaigne on the same theme gives a clue to his reading of them. More often the similarity is one of general ideas which does not indicate a direct borrowing but rather shows that he is content to treat the same aspects of a topic as the moral essayists of the past; but of course he does not limit himself to these aspects; except for the essay on love, he always employs his own points of view and often novel ideas but still retains a few of the old conventional remarks alongside what is contributed by his own ingenuity. I do not mean for a moment to imply that Emerson simply takes the themes out of a predecessor; they would occur to almost anyone and they have become conventional because they are so true and relevant that anyone writing on the topic must almost inevitably have them in his mind. Only a very original writer who deliberately decided to say something which had not been said before would avoid them, and a topic so fundamental as love, for instance, can scarcely provide a single general remark which has not been said before; the only original element which may be contributed by anyone is an originality in illustration or in language and style.

Friendship was another favorite topic of the moral essayists and the Stoics laid great stress on friendship and the value of friends. Plutarch has three essays in the *Moralia* which deal with various aspects of friendship; Montaigne and Bacon both wrote of friendship and none of them could raise topics which had not been raised already by the Stoics or by Cicero's *De Amicitia*, which leans on Stoic ideas. We now know something of Emerson's general debt to Montaigne and Bacon, both of whom indicate by quotation and apothegm that they knew Plutarch's essays on friendship. In writing "Old Age" Emerson tells us that he has reread Cicero's *De Senectute* when he thought of writing on the same theme, but in the case of the essay, "Friendship" there is no indication that he has gone back to Montaigne, Bacon, Plutarch, or Cicero. A number of the subtopics in his essay on friendship are similar to those of his predecessors, but these can quite well be purely accidental or merely another indication of his inborn affinity for the classical moralists, especially the Stoics. He does not, as far as I can determine, use a single lustre which can be traced to one of these essays on friendship. He is writing in a style far different from that which he used when he put pen to paper for "Love"; he is away from his

books and speaks more genuinely for himself. It has been pointed
out fairly recently that this essay is evoked by the charge made by
two of Emerson's own friends that he is cool and aloof to friendship;
that this essay is his self-defence.[10] As Rusk observes, "one so widely
acquainted with authors must have heard faint echoes of many
familiar voices as he wrote, voices at least as distant in antiquity as
Aristotle's, but he had his private resources." [11] We now know that
parts of the essay are taken from the journals and that there they
had specific references to particular individuals; the anonymous
"friends" mentioned in the essay can now be named and we can
appreciate the real warmth which underlies the superficial coldness. For there certainly is a chilly atmosphere about the essay; the
warmth of tone and the high value set on friendship, the enthusiastic language, are certainly present but still the tone sounds impersonal. If we did not know that individuals were referred to
and that Emerson is really talking about his own type of friendship and his own friends, we should be suspicious of the very
indefiniteness and anonymity of the term "friends" or "my friends,"
and should take the use of the first person singular as merely a
rhetorical device to add sharpness and vividness. This element is
certainly contributed by Emerson's own native reserve, his liking
for his own company and his tendency towards introspection, by
the fact that as many of his friends are long-dead authors as living
people round about him, but also there is in his attitude to friendship, as Sherman Paul has pointed out, an inability to express his
feeling for his friends except intellectually; "He was cold at the
surface where human beings touched, but warm at the core where
ideas had their being." [12] Surely it is strange in an essay on friendship to find not a single individual, living or dead, named. Perhaps
the reason is that, as Emerson says here, he finds "very little written
directly to the heart of this matter in books." He then gives one
quotation, and it is from Montaigne, but the anonymity is still
preserved. Montaigne is called "my author." Even if the coldness
is only superficial and a formal one, it is still present and it is in-

creased by the extraordinary absence of lustres of any kind; the first person singular occurs often enough, but along with it are many abstract ideas and generalities on friendship.

These generalities are usually sharpened and brightened by concrete figures and pictures; Emerson prefers the company of "ploughboys and tin-peddlers" to "frivolous display" and curricles and taverns. Or in recommending standing away from friends, "give those merits room," he demands, "Are you the friend of your friend's buttons or of his thought?" But except for a few phrases like these, the essay gives the impression of a moral essay of a Stoic type.

Friendship, according to Emerson in this essay, is a severe and exacting relation which requires such high qualities that friendship can only rarely subsist. He admits, "I embrace solitude," but adds that he welcomes friends, friends of this high quality, so high that they are "a semblance of myself" or better still really a part of himself, so much so that they do not constitute a separate being but are at one with him. Here the stress on the complete union of friend with friend is that of Montaigne. The two qualities which bring this unanimity about are truth or sincerity and tenderness and Emerson puts on both these qualities the same exacting, rigorous meaning. Every man alone and by himself is sincere and the sincerity required in a friend must approximate this ultimate sincerity of the man alone. Tenderness is love and this too is a rare quality, for the object of friendship is "a commerce the most strict and homely that can be joined; more strict than any of which we have experience." Again and again the exacting nature of friendship is stressed — it is made of "the tough fibre of the human heart" and requires "the tough husk" of "bashfulness and apathy"; it must be treated with "the roughest courage" and must be good for "rough roads and hard fare, shipwreck, poverty and persecution." It is a simple relation and a friend must adopt "a manly furtherance or at least a manly resistance" instead of a weak compliance to his friend's wishes; friendship "demands a religious treatment" and reverence must be present in large degree; it is bought only by a long probation; its laws are "holy." It is not a matter of "childish luxury" but of "austerest worth"; it is a contest like the Olympic games of ancient Greece, where "Time, Want, Danger are in the lists."

Emerson thus defends himself against the charge of coldness and formality by first admitting that he embraces solitude and then by affirming in warm and enthusiastic tones that he values his friends but that he sets such an exacting requirement on his concept of friendship that real friends are rare. Implicit throughout, and only explicit once or twice, is the feeling, arising out of Emerson's natural reserve, perhaps in his Puritan ancestry, that he cannot be demonstrative, that if he feels deep friendship for anyone he cannot say so; friends are too close to permit even the civility of the affirmation of friendship, for such civilities by their very existence create formality and diminish the friendship itself. But besides this Puritan reticence or "bashfulness" the Stoic attitude to friendship is also clearly present in the rigorous terms which he uses to describe what he means by friendship. Indeed Emerson's concept of friendship is very much the Stoic one; to show that I am not reading Stoicism into Emerson which is not there, here is a picture of the doctrine of friendship of the Roman Stoics:

The young should train themselves alternately to bear solitude and to profit by society: since the wise man is never dependent on his friends, though none can take better advantage of them. In living alone a man follows the example of the deity, and comes to know his own heart. . . . The right choice of friends calls for true wisdom; for the soul cannot but be soiled by bad company. The only true friendship is based on the mutual attraction of good folk; therefore the wise are friends one to another even whilst they are unacquainted. It is well to consider much before choosing a friend, but afterwards to give him implicit trust; for a true friend is a second self. Such friendship can only arise from the desire to love and be loved; those who seek friends for their own advantage, will be abandoned by them in the day of trial. In the companionship of well-chosen friends there grows up the "common sense," which is an

instinctive contact with humanity as a whole, making each man a partner
in the thoughts and needs of all around him.[13]

This summary of Stoic friendship seems to me almost completely
identical with that of Emerson. His reticence is Stoic and his high
demands of friendship have a Stoic ring; his friendship rests, he
says, on a basis of "virtue": "By oldest right, by the divine affinity of
virtue with itself, I find them, or rather not I, but the Deity in me
and in them . . ." In Stoic terms, Emerson says that his relation to
his friends is that of "simple affinity." The Stoic alternation is present
too; Emerson speaks of "the ebb and flow of love"; we idealize our
friends when we have met them for the first time; they turn out
to be less than ideal, in fact very human. In that very process
they become less our friends, for "the law of nature is alternation
for evermore" and "the soul environs itself with friends that it
may enter into a grander self-acquaintance or solitude." He stresses,
like the Stoics, the need for friendships to ripen slowly and the
danger of snatching at too quick a benefit. We must not be betrayed
into "rash and foolish alliances" with "cheap" people.

Granting this Stoic background in Emerson's friendship, it is
almost inevitable that some of his general statements should be
traditional and also Plutarchan. If we can find parallels in topic
among Emerson, Plutarch, and Cicero it may be possible to indicate one cause of the superficial coldness of his tone.

Emerson's connection between friendship and virtue is one of the
key ideas of Plutarch's "Of Large Acquaintance" and it is also a
fundamental concept of Cicero's *De Amicitia*. Again for Emerson
there is a close connection between friendship and love; he calls
his friends "lovers" and tends to make love and friendship synonymous; but it was Cicero who pointed out that the Latin terms for
love and friendship are cognates and for both Cicero and Montaigne
love and friendship are closely akin. Emerson may well be thinking of one of these when he writes that "in poetry and in common
speech the emotions of benevolence and complacency which are

felt towards others" are compared to the effects of fire, for Cicero for instance uses the comparison, although for a different purpose, to emphasize love's universality rather than its evanescence. Plutarch devotes an entire essay to the theme that man requires too many friends and that he changes friendships too quickly. Cicero also mentions this and Emerson writes in the same strain; in his apparent feeling that the ultimate aim of friendship is the ability to do without friends altogether he is, as we have seen, a Stoic and is thinking of the Stoic self-reliance. Bacon said something similar at the beginning of "Of Friendship" and Cicero had attacked this Stoic view.

Friendship, Emerson says, consists in harmony of mood, and true friendship must ripen slowly; he repeats this in "Behaviour." Plutarch mentions the first point in several passages and agrees with Emerson and Cicero that friends must be carefully selected; he writes, for instance, in "How to Know a Flatterer from a Friend" (*Moralia* 2. 102), paraphrasing Sophocles, "we should rather try our friend, as we do our money, whether or not he be passable and current, before we need him." Again (*Moralia* 1. 468), "what is cheap and with ease obtained is below our notice," and Emerson uses the same term "cheap" of friendships which are easily acquired.

Cicero, Plutarch, Emerson tell us that friendship must be able to endure prosperity as well as adversity. It requires courage, and Emerson elaborates this a little in finer language — a friend is a hero who enters a contest like the Olympic games. Like Plutarch and Cicero, in the earlier part of the essay on friendship he stresses identity or at least close similarity between the natures and interests of friends as essential to real friendship. Later on he shifts his ground slightly and thinks that "friendship requires that rare mean betwixt likeness and unlikeness." Emerson does not want "a mush of concession" but a "manly resistance"; in effect he contrasts what the simpler language of the ancients called "a friend" and "a flatterer." Cicero says that flattery is fatal to friendship and Plutarch devotes a whole essay to "How to Know a Flatterer from a Friend."

This mean between antagonism and compliance Emerson calls "reverence;" the term itself is classical, and is used by Cicero (*verebuntur, verecundia*). The relation between friends should not become too personal.[14] Indeed according to Emerson friends are no more useful than enemies; he says, "Let him be to thee for ever a sort of beautiful enemy, untamable, devoutly revered, and not a trivial conveniency to be soon outgrown and cast aside." Plutarch quotes the same idea from Diogenes (*Moralia* 2. 155–156) and Cicero quotes a familiar apothegm of Cato to the same intent. Emerson's remark may possibly be his own expression of one or other of these similar apothegms.

Emerson mentions two elements that go to the composition of friendship — truth or sincerity and "tenderness"; a third is implicit throughout the essay — virtue. Here again we meet familiar themes. For example, Plutarch in "Of Large Acquaintance" names "three requisites to a true friendship": virtue, familiarity, advantage (by this last he means what we would call "material benefits"). Two of these are in Emerson also, for his "truth" or "sincerity" is Plutarch's "familiarity." Emerson narrows down Plutarch's term to pleasure in conversation, indicating that you must know your friend so well that he can speak frankly to you even to the point of finding fault with and chastising you. He devotes the final part of the essay to this aspect of friendship. Plutarch defines the third requisite, advantage, by saying, "upon occasion he must be useful to us in our concerns." Conversely, Cicero had specifically opposed those who affirm "that friendships should be sought for the sake of defence and assistance, and not from motives of goodwill and affection" and thoroughly ridicules this mercenary version of friendship. Perhaps Emerson is following Cicero when he writes: "We chide the citizen because he makes love a commodity. It is an exchange of gifts, of useful loans; it is good neighborhood; it watches with the sick; it holds the pall at the funeral; and quite loses sight of the delicacies and nobility of the relation." Certainly Plutarch's view that friends are useful, even if he puts it last in the list of the elements of friendship, does not fit in with Emerson's poetical, metaphysical, unworldly concept of friendship as something noble and good rather than useful.[15]

Thus Emerson seems at least to refer to two of the three conventional aspects of friendship. But his second quality, tenderness, is his own. Indeed, he says that he finds little written in books on this subject; it is too personal and loses its vitality when put into formal expression. He seems to introduce it for the express purpose of replacing the element "advantage" which he refuses to admit to friendship. One gets the impression that he has made this modification in the conventional list with the specific purpose of showing that he is not cold towards friendship, for friendship — "when a man becomes dear to me" — is equated with love and a genuine warmth infuses the passage, a warmth greater than any bookish source could produce.

In one aspect of his treatment of friendship, Emerson may well follow Plutarch rather than the conventional essays of Cicero, Montaigne, and Bacon. In "Love" he had treated love as the love of two, a man and a woman. We might expect Emerson to widen out and to generalize his concept of friendship and he does this when he describes the metaphysical basis of friendship, but in general throughout the essay he assumes that friendship is the relation between two people. In his fourth paragraph he says, "what [is] so delicious as a just and firm encounter of two, in a thought, in a feeling?" Again friendship is "alliance with my brother's soul"; he is "my friend" and "no two men but being left alone with each other enter into simpler relations. Yet it is affinity which determine *which* two shall converse." However, later on he modifies his attitude and would have "a circle of godlike men and women variously related to each other and between whom subsists a lofty intelligence," and in "Society and Solitude" he repeats this. The number of one's friends is not significant, rather it is the "readiness of sympathy" which is important. He may quite well be thinking of Plutarch in both these passages, for Plutarch's essay "Of

Large Acquaintance" treats of the folly of having many friends rather than a few; at the beginning, after the introduction and after mentioning several famous pairs of friends in history and mythology, Plutarch elaborates on the commonplace that a friend is another self. Here Emerson agrees with Plutarch and the moralists on friendship but goes farther in the Stoic direction, towards the concept that friendship is but a second best to solitude; he adds at once that for conversation two is the ideal number of participants and that the presence of a third impairs good conversation. Plutarch similarly stresses conversation and the need for two and not more than two participants in "Of Large Acquaintance" and his view is that of Emerson, that conversation is one of the chief goals, if not the chief goal, of friendship. Emerson expands in characteristic style Plutarch's proverb "a friend is another self": "A friend therefore is a sort of paradox in nature. I who alone am, I who see nothing in nature whose existence I can affirm with equal evidence to my own, behold now the semblance of my being, in all its height, variety and curiosity, reiterated in a foreign form; so that a friend may well be reckoned the masterpiece of nature." There may possibly be a single verbal reminiscence of Plutarch in Emerson; this is in the remark (197): "I cannot deny it, O friend, that the vast shadow of the Phenomenal include thee also in its pied and painted immensity, — thee also, compared with whom all else is shadow." And towards the end of the essay Emerson speaks of "those rare pilgrims whereof only one or two wander in nature at once, and before whom the vulgar great show as spectres and shadows merely." In the first quotation the repetition of the word "shadow" is an Emersonian rhetorical device, but Emerson may have recalled Plutarch, near the beginning of "Of Large Acquaintance" (*Moralia* I. 464): "However, we cannot but extol the sense of that young man in Menander the poet, who said that he counted every man wonderfully honest and happy who had found even the shadow of a friend." Plutarch used the Menander quotation again in "Of Brotherly Love"; Montaigne used it in his essay "Of Friendship" and we know that it attracted Emerson, for he quoted it from Plutarch in his journals in 1837 [16] and used it in "Domestic Life."

Emerson ends his essay on friendship on a lofty Platonic note, and leaves Plutarch far behind. The latter ends rather flatly with a long discussion on the means of chastising and rebuking a friend. Plutarch is always a moralist and a preacher; everything for him, as for Cicero on this topic, is a means of inculcating virtue; if Emerson is likewise often conscious of "virtue" or "the moral sentiment," in this essay at least, since he is defending himself against the charge of coldness, he adopts a classical eulogy of friendship and avoids preaching by employing a poetic treatment.

The similarity between Emerson and Plutarch is confined to one of topic. He has probably looked into Plutarch, Montaigne, and Bacon, and perhaps Cicero, but they are not of much help to him on this occasion. He goes on his own way but whether he wishes it or not, the same subtopics keep coming to his mind when he writes on friendship.

Conversation and friendship are closely connected and conversation was referred to in "Friendship." Emerson's essay "Clubs" delivered as a lecture in 1859 and partly reused in another, "Table-Talk" in 1864, contains material used before in the several essays on manners and also in "Friendship." Again, conversation is limited to two who are friends; a friend is another self, "this wise and genial counterpart." He uses an apothegm of Isocrates which is twice in Plutarch [17] and a reference to the seven sages may come to his memory from Plutarch's "Banquet of the Seven Wise Men." Here and again in "Social Aims" he urges that conversation must not exclude any person or any topic; Plutarch says the same thing at least twice in his essays on conversation. "A scholar," Emerson says (*CW* 7. 246), "does not wish to be always pumping his brains; he wants gossips" and he thinks that the best conversation comes from manufacturers, merchants, and shipmasters, who discuss their travels and their own craft. Plutarch too mentions travelers and sailors in the same connection (*Moralia* 3. 231). As if to confirm our conjecture that Plutarch comes to Emerson's mind, he mentions him — at such banquets of convivial spirits the conversation is more important than the meal itself: "The hospitalities of clubs are easily exaggerated. No doubt the suppers of wits and philosophers acquire much lustre by time and renown. Plutarch, Xenophon and Plato, who have celebrated each a banquet of their set, have given us next to no data of the viands; and it is to be believed that an indifferent tavern dinner in such society was more relished by the *convives* than a much better one in worse company." [18] I think that here Emerson may well have read the introduction to Plutarch's sixth book of the "Symposiacs." Plutarch says:

But if things pertaining to the body had afforded any pleasure, Xenophon and Plato should have left us an account not of the discourse, but of the great variety of dishes, sauces, and other costly compositions that were prepared in the houses of Callias and Agatho. Yet there is not the least mention made of any such things, . . . but whatever things were treated of and learnedly discussed by their guests were left upon record and transmitted to posterity as precedents, not only for discoursing at table, but also for remembering the things that were handled at such meetings. [19]

"Clubs," "Behavior," the two essays on "Manners" and that on "Social Aims" all pay due attention to the art of conversation and the conventional subtopics appear once more. All of them are at least referred to and occasionally expanded by Plutarch. The "frivolous man," the "contradictors," the "over bold" are dramatically portrayed by Emerson; Plutarch calls them "triflers" and "babblers." Both agree that sickness or calamities should not be mentioned. Emerson takes the viewpoint of the speaker and employs a didactic tone; Plutarch has a more cynical view of conversation and takes the viewpoint of the audience, instructing his readers how to get most value from a speaker and at the same time give him pleasure. Both agree that conversation must be serious, not trivial or frivolous; it must not be monopolized by a single individual and must concern itself with topics worth discussing, topics on which men are likely to have interesting opinions.

Both castigate the garrulous man. Emerson advocates self-command in manners — laughter must be kept under strict control, while in "The Comic" he is still more severe: "reason does not joke and men of reason do not." In "Social Aims" Emerson characterizes "swainish, morose people" and in "Of Hearing" Plutarch similarly describes "the morose and rigid hearer." Plutarch dislikes contention and wrangling in conversation; Emerson on the other hand is rather fond of the figure of a "contest" in conversation; all things are its weapons, but he adds (*CW* 8. 95–96) that we must not always fight for victory; conversation is not always a battle to the death.

But if Emerson does not care for joking he still appreciates wit, which "makes its own welcome, and levels all distinctions." This is mentioned in "The Comic" and he recalls Plutarch at this point and will go as far as his favorite Greek moralist goes: "Plutarch happily expresses the value of the jest as a legitimate weapon of the philosopher." Emerson then gives a long quotation from "The Symposiacs" (the longest anywhere in his writing) which he had copied into his journal in 1837;[20] Plutarch's moderate view and statement of the value of wit appealed to Emerson; it is a moderation of the sort which he liked. Plutarch is calm and serene and genial, and as he himself says at the end of "Concerning the Cure of Anger": ". . . this courteous, gentle, and kindly disposition and behavior is not so acceptable, so pleasing, and so delightful to any of those with whom we converse, as it is to those that have it." Emerson was struck by this passage, with its concept that good nature is pleasant to both parties; he noted this in his journals and used it in his essay on Plutarch. When we are discussing wit and humor it is worth observing Plutarch's admonition that wit should only be at one's own expense, for it is curious to find Emerson's son remarking that his father's wit was more often of this kind.[21]

Apparently another classical topic in connection with conversation is the idea that the host who wishes to aid good conversation must pay attention to the seating arrangement of his guests; Plutarch devotes a "question" in the "Symposiacs" to this subject (*Moralia* 3. 215–216). He would seat his guests carefully, a good talker next to a good listener, a good-natured man next to a morose man and so on; and farther on in this "question," beginning with a sentence which Emerson had noted in his journals (4. 286), Plutarch says:

It is a common saying, that a voyage near the land and a walk near the sea are the best recreation. Thus our steward should place seriousness and gravity next jollity and humor; that, when they are merry, they should be on the very borders of gravity itself, and when grave and serious, they might be refreshed as sea-sick persons, having an easy and short prospect to the mirth and jollity on the shore. For mirth may be exceedingly useful, and make our grave discourses smooth and pleasant. . . .

Emerson's advice on this topic in "The Comic" and in "Society and Solitude" (*CW* 7. 14) is exactly the same: "The peace of society and the decorum of tables seem to require that next to a notable wit should always be posted a phlegmatic bolt-upright man . . ." We know too that he was acquainted with this essay of Plutarch and with the topic of the seating of guests, for in 1836 he made several journal notes from it on the arrangement of the gods at their banquets.[22]

Emerson's discussion of manners may be summed up in the terms "restraint" or "moderation." While some of the features of the gentleman portrayed in Emerson's various remarks on manners make us think here of the Victorian gentleman or of Emerson's Puritan strain and his tempermental reserve and aloofness, much of his idea of manners recalls classical Stoicism with its emphasis on calmness, moderation, and avoidance of exaggeration. He commends (*CW* 6. 182) "a calm and resolute bearing, a polished speech, an embellishment of trifles, and the art of hiding all uncomfortable feeling." These, Emerson says, are the manners of a royal court; but they are also the qualities of Plutarch's Stoic heroes and they are those which Plutarch enjoins in the *Moralia*. Emerson's Stoic gentleman reminds us of the cultivated gentleman of later Greece, the individual so completely portrayed by Plutarch; he is the cultivated young man to whom Plutarch addresses his precepts in "Of Garrulity," in "How to Know a Flatterer from a Friend," in "How a Young Man Ought to Hear Poems," and in many questions of the "Symposiacs" or "Banquet Topics." The features which go to make up the civilized man, the "gentleman" do not change greatly throughout the centuries and perhaps the resemblances between Emerson and Plutarch are not surprising. Emerson repeatedly says that it is this which attracts him to Plutarch and the other writers on morals; the ethical standards of conduct which they set up are always valid and hence he can quote Plutarch, for example, on the value of the jest in philosophy, for he feels that these remarks are equally applicable today. It may well be that Emerson quite unconsciously sounds like his master moralist but it is more than likely that as he had observed Plutarch's quotable anecdotes and attractive language, so also he had noticed his attention to Stoic manners.[23]

iii

Education has always been a favorite topic of the moral essayist. Plutarch has a long essay, the "Discourse on the Training of Children"; Montaigne wrote one of his longest essays on the same topic, an essay which includes much classical material and a fine tribute to Plutarch. Bacon has a short work, "Of Customs and Education." And Emerson has his own essay, originally an address, entitled "Education." Again several themes occur in both Emerson and Plutarch but this is likely accidental. Plutarch's essay depends on the three classical parts of learning, which he calls nature, reason, and use. Emerson reduces them to two which he calls "genius" or "enthusiasm" and "drill." These are the first and last of Plutarch's triad but the central one, reason, is also implicit all through Emerson's remarks. Both essays conclude in the classical style, emphasizing the value of teaching by one's own example. Both remark that the sensual element requires control; both advocate the proper use of solitude which Plutarch calls "contemplation"; both distinguish in the method of teaching between corporal punishment and what Emerson calls "the methods of love." Both think the main part of education is the training of the moral nature. Of books Plutarch merely suggests "the writings of the ancient authors" and Emerson adds that the modern novel, which teaches self-trust, should not be spurned. He advocates patience in the teacher: "Respect the child. Be not too much his parent. Trespass not on his solitude" and Plutarch in somewhat similar vein criticizes those parents who are eager to advance their children too quickly: "we ought therefore to give children some time to take breath from their constant labours."

Emerson's views on education are similar to those of Plutarch; perhaps because the current educational principles of their own ages, though almost two thousand years apart in time, are surprisingly similar, and both Plutarch and Emerson are a little ahead of their own times, somewhat more liberal than most of their contemporaries. Again the topics and emphases are Stoic, for the Stoics stress the value of relaxation, the evils of corporal punishment; moderation in all things is the rule; the dominant Stoic precept is that all education aims at moral growth, and throughout the essay Emerson calls for manliness, heroism, self-reliance. Again Emerson may be completely original in his thoughts on education but he cannot help his resemblance to the Stoic theory of the training of children.

Finally, another topic received the attention of all the moral essayists whom Emerson read. This is the subject of old age. Plutarch wrote "Whether an Aged Man Ought to Meddle in State Affairs," Montaigne wrote "Of Age," and Bacon "Of Youth and Age"; Emerson also attempted the topic in his essay "Old Age." The whole line of moral essayists treat in various ways and with varying emphases the theme that had been introduced before even the first of them lived, for before Plutarch, Cicero had written

the *De Senectute* which is so comprehensive and which had such
a high reputation that their own essays appear inevitably to be
restatements of Cicero. In the case of Emerson's essay it is doubtful whether he borrows from Plutarch, for he begins by saying
frankly that he has been led to write down his thoughts on this
topic by rereading Cicero. But Cicero did not exhaust the topic;
rather he "invited the attempt to add traits to the picture from
our broader modern life." Any similarity therefore which we can
find between Plutarch and Emerson on old age is probably to be
explained by the familiarity of both with Cicero's *De Senectute*.
Plutarch's thesis is that old men can still serve the state and that
retirement in old age is lazy and selfish; the old cannot be expected
to battle in the political arena but there is still work of value, honor,
and dignity which they can do; they can guide, instruct, and assist
their juniors who are actively engaged in public affairs. Emerson's
thesis is not very different. He mentions, however, the illusions of
wisdom which old age and a reverend aspect can provide, but his
remaining topics are those of the classical moral essay: the old
have experience behind them; the councils of the ancient world
were composed of old men; while young men have accomplished
great things, the old also have been generals or artists or statesmen
at an advanced age. Most of the topics are commonplaces and
must be noted here only as parallels, to indicate the identity of outlook between Emerson and Plutarch which is so often noticeable.
Emerson says that the essence of old age is intellect; the old can
instruct the young out of their experience. Plutarch says the same
thing repeatedly. To Emerson's mind, "youth is everywhere in
place," and Plutarch quotes Homer: "For all things perhaps, as
Homer says, equally become a young man." [24]

In Emerson's thinking, age requires suitable surroundings: "Age
is comely in coaches, in churches, in chairs of state and ceremony,
in council-chambers, in courts of justice and historical societies.
Age is becoming in the country." Age is not in place, he says, in
the noisy and busy city, and the aged there show dejection and a

feeling of injury. Plutarch treats the same theme from a negative viewpoint — an old man should not be engaged in heavy and hurried business, in servile and trivial occupations; the same topic is mentioned in several other brief passages in Plutarch's essay on old age, and both Emerson and Plutarch name the standard classical exemplar of great age — Tithonus. Both mention another similar argument — that there are some contributions that only old age can make or can best make. Emerson goes to the legislatures of the ancient world for an example: "But in all governments, the councils of power were held by the old; and patricians or *patres*, senate or *senes*, *seigneurs* or seniors, *gerousia*, the senate of Sparta, the presbytery of the Church, and the like, all signify simply old men." This illustration from etymology is also in Plutarch [25] and the Spartan *gerousia* and the Roman senate are there. Emerson has added the Roman patricians and the French seigneurs and has brought Plutarch's list up to date by adding the reference to "presbytery." To match Plutarch's list of Greeks and Romans who contributed to the welfare of their respective communities in their old age, Emerson has his own list; only two names in it are from the Greek and Roman world; like Plutarch, Emerson mentions Socrates and also refers to another of his favorite Plutarchan heroes, Archimedes, "holding Syracuse against the Romans by his wit, and himself better than all their nation." In the last phrase he seems remotely to echo Plutarch in the familiar life of Marcellus: "And, doubtless, the rest of the Syracusans were but the body of Archimedes' designs, one soul moving and governing all."

After his list of great men who made contributions to the world at an advanced age, Emerson seems to follow Cicero in listing the benefits of old age. He touches on freedom from sexual passion, a topic which Plutarch also mentions briefly. His second benefit is that in old age "a success more or less signifies nothing"; that is the freedom from ambition and envy, qualities which Plutarch also considers most unbecoming in the old.

In the case of the topics of old age, education, conversation, and friendship, Emerson thinks along the same lines as Plutarch and except for an occasional lustre drawn from Plutarch there is little indication of direct borrowing. Most of the similarities are commonplaces and many of them probably were such when Plutarch was writing. Emerson's use of them again indicates that when he takes up a conventional theme of the moral essayists his treatment is also often classical and conventional.

VII

READING PLUTARCH FOR "LUSTRES"

*I find the most pleasure in reading a book in a manner least
flattering to the author. I read Proclus, and sometimes Plato,
as I might read a dictionary, for a mechanical help to the
fancy and the imagination. I read for the lustres, as if one
should use a fine picture in a chromatic experiment, for its
rich colors. . . . It is a greater joy to see the author's author,
than himself.*

"Nominalist and Realist"

An eminent English critic says of Emerson, "Of aphorism and
apophthegm he is one of the greatest masters in literature; the equal,
I think, of Seneca." He adds: "His works, take them where you
will, are a storehouse, singularly rich, of great sayings and great
actions picked from all parts of history" and he goes on to point out
that Emerson's favorite Plutarch gives the reader the same kind
of pleasure to a lesser degree.[1] Emerson of course has much to say
on the question of the quotation and borrowing of sayings and
anecdotes from other writers. "In a large sense, one would say there
is no pure originality. All minds quote."[2] Modern philosophical
ideas, he points out, are often borrowed from, or at least anticipated
by, ancient thinkers; Christian dogma and much of what passes
for the latest thought is in Plato or the pre-Socratics; "Whoso knows
Plutarch, Lucian, Rabelais, Montaigne and Bayle will have a key
to many supposed originalities."[3] No writer is original; everyone
"builds on his predecessors," borrowing consciously or unconsciously

not only the great ideas of philosophy but also anecdotes and illustrations which still seem fresh and vivid, which lose none of their vigor from being used again. Indeed it is this interest in quotation from, and references to, one's predecessors which makes a great writer "representative" in Emerson's eyes. Plato is, naturally enough, the first of the "representative men" to whom Emerson devotes an essay. He is representative in the double sense that he finds his ideas everywhere and that the great since his time have been constantly in his debt; Plato appears to plagiarize (*CW* 4. 42), "But the inventor only knows how to borrow; and society is glad to forget the innumerable laborers who ministered to this architect, and reserves all its gratitude for him. When we are praising Plato, it seems we are praising quotations from Solon and Sophron and Philolaus." "Every book is a quotation" and Plato sums up the cumulative thought of his time.

If Emerson felt it necessary to defend his own extensive borrowing from the books which he read, this would be his defence. While he mines his quotations with the untiring vigor of the Plutarchan hero, he reflects that Plato did the same and so does every great thinker. Thus when he defends Shakespeare's borrowing in *Representative Men* he is also justifying his own practice: "He steals by this apology, — that what he takes has no worth where he finds it and the greatest where he leaves it. . . . Thought is the property of him who can entertain it and of him who can adequately place it." In his essay on Plutarch, Emerson states that much of Plutarch's usefulness for him consists in the "sentences" in prose or verse from other writers, many of whose works are otherwise lost; many of these "embalmed fragments" have become the "proverbs of mankind." Emerson is charmed away, he admits, from the solid substance of Plutarch's thought by the poetic charm of the lustres. There are times when he loses interest in the thought and "raffles the pages of Plutarch" for sidelights which are vivid and which live in the memory.

It is curious to see that in one of the passages in which Emerson states his idea that every writer borrows from another, he himself borrows a phrase from Plutarch; in the first paragraph of "Shakspeare" he writes: "Great men are more distinguished by range and extent than by originality. If we require the originality which consists in weaving, like a spider, their web from their own bowels; in finding clay and making bricks and building the house; no great men are original." The expression, "weaving, like a spider, the web from their own bowels" strikes the reader, as it must have struck Emerson, by its vividness and earthiness. Plutarch had used it for the same purpose, to describe literary originality in "Of Isis and Osiris" (*Moralia* 4. 82); he speaks of "those foppish tales and vain fictions which poets and story-tellers are wont, like spiders, to spin out of their own bowels, without any substantial ground or foundation for them, and then weave and wire-draw them out at their own pleasures. . . ." This vigorous and "vulgar" expression, which sounds so typically Emersonian, came from the "Several Hands" translation of the *Moralia*.[4]

Emerson a number of times expresses the idea that the quotation of an anecdote or an aphorism or even of a striking metaphor or analogy (for his term "lustre" would include all of these) heightens and sharpens a prosaic narrative or exposition. In historical writing, he feels, anecdote and aphorism have a special value, for history consists of the lives of individuals and anecdote and epigrammatic remark portray the heroic individual much more adequately than the dry facts of biography and history. Not only do they make history readable and lively but they give a true picture of character. They sum up briefly the whole personality and illumine the nature of the man by concentrating the light on one feature; the aphorism discloses multiple meanings in its simple language. But it is also "prospective" in that it looks forward to future times, bringing home the pertinence of this particular hero to the reader today, making the life of an individual long since dead still relevant to us and capable of exerting a moral force on us. Thus he says in "Intellect" (*CW* 2. 332): "The immortality of man is as legitimately preached from the intellections as from the moral volitions. Every intellection is mainly prospective. Its present value is its least. Inspect what delights you in Plutarch, in Shakspeare, in Cervantes. Each truth that a writer acquires is a lantern which he turns full on what facts and thoughts lay already in his mind, and behold, all the mats and rubbish which had littered his garret become precious." Plutarch, he says, the biographer who employs aphorism and anecdote to a greater degree than any other ancient writer, is read, and rightly, to the neglect of more careful historians. In this paragraph again Emerson may well be resorting to Plutarch for a lustre, the figure of the lantern, for this paragraph contains a reference to Plutarch and in 1834 Emerson read Plutarch's "Lives of the Ten Attic Orators" and copied several extracts into his journals (*Journals* 3. 386). The longest extract begins, "The dear old Plutarch assures me that the lamp of Demosthenes never went out." He is evidently reading *Moralia* 5. 53: "They say of him [Demosthenes] that he never put out his lamp — that is, never ceased polishing his orations — until he was fifty years old." The metaphor of the lamp, I suggest, attracted Emerson and he noted it in his journals and recalled it later, characteristically employing it for a different purpose and with a changed meaning.

But if history is biography, biography is also autobiography; the most illuminating anecdotes come from a source very close to the hero, perhaps from the hero himself. They show the real man among his closest friends, not the man whom the world sees. Plutarch himself observed this and in his journals for 1832 (2. 454–455) Emerson quotes from the life of Pericles:

Write a sermon upon a house-hero, upon the hero to his *valet-de-chambre*; the ugly face that obstinate association of true words and good acts has made beautiful.

"Real virtue is most loved where it is most nearly seen, and no respect which it commands from strangers can equal the never ceasing admiration it excites in the daily intercourse of domestic life."

The books which give us such sidelights or lustres are many and

Emerson places Plutarch first in the list of writers who evoke "inspiration," that is, provide an idea which starts a chain of thought in the reader's mind. Curiously enough, Montaigne is specifically excluded from the list (*CW* 8. 295):

> You shall not read newspapers, nor politics, nor novels, nor Montaigne, nor the newest French book. You may read Plutarch, Plato, Plotinus, Hindoo mythology and ethics. You may read Chaucer, Shakspeare, Ben Jonson, Milton, — and Milton's prose as his verse; read Collins and Gray; read Hafiz and the Trouveurs; nay, Welsh and British mythology of Arthur, and (in your ear) Ossian; fact-books, which all geniuses prize as raw material, and as antidote to verbiage and false poetry.

Carlyle's study of Frederick the Great is valuable because it is another fact book, "a book holding so many memorable and heroic facts, working directly on practice; with new heroes, things unvoiced before — the German Plutarch . . ." (*CW* 12. 298). Plutarch is frank in giving "things, not words"; it is for these that Emerson reads — for "sentences" in the classical sense of the term, for a quotable or gnomic expression, for a proverb or a symbol in sharp language which can be extracted from its source and used again and again. It retains its freshness and vigor in other circumstances, in another context (*Journals* 7. 92–93): "I think the Platonists may be read for sentences, though the reader fail to grasp the argument of the paragraph or chapter. He may yet obtain gleams and glimpses of a more excellent illumination from their genius, outvaluing the most distinct information he owes to other books." Among the "Platonists" whom he reads in this way he would certainly include Plutarch, even if he is not specifically mentioned here; Plutarch too he describes as "an encyclopaedia of Greek and Roman antiquity"; "a repertory for those who want the story without searching for it at first hand, — a compend of all accepted traditions" and Emerson reminds us that Henry IV of France found in Plutarch "many good suggestions and maxims for my conduct and the government of my affairs."

Thus Emerson's method of using Plutarch is no new one; it is at least as old as the Renaissance collections of maxims and aphorisms. At one time Emerson thinks seriously of composing a collection of "facts," of anecdotes and maxims in the style of the Renaissance. As early as 1820 he dedicates a page of his *Journal* (1. 22–23) to "the down-putting of sentences quoted or original, which regard Greece, historical, poetical and critical"; and in 1828 (*Letters* 1. 255) he writes to his brother (and the reference to Marcellus is surely to the biography by Plutarch): "Have you looked at Marcellus' life that we talked of? I fancy when our school keeping epoch (which answers to the age of brass in univ. hist.) comes to an end we could make up 'a Schoolmaster' among us that should beat Ascham's to consist of plans of government, cunning fetches of dignity & discipline, bon mots, stories, & so forth." This is casually written and the connection between the question and what follows it is not clear, but here Emerson seems to state for the first time what he finds valuable in the Plutarch of the *Lives*. "Cunning fetches of dignity and discipline" seems to refer to Plutarch's anecdotes of the heroes and probably specifically to those about Archimedes in the life of Marcellus which are always special favorites of Emerson; dignity and discipline are the heroic qualities, what Emerson later calls "the reserve of power" in the hero, the "self-discipline," the "Stoicism" which he always manages to find in the men of Plutarch; the "bon mots and stories" too constitute one of the chief reasons for his reading of Plutarch and here again those of Archimedes in the life of Marcellus are among his favorites. He thinks again of such a collection in 1835–36 and is now specially interested in "moral sentences"; in the lecture "Ethical Writers" he speaks of the special capacity of the English mind for ethical truth. This is evident most clearly in the King James version of the Bible and it explains the "fragrant piety" of English devotional writers. He singles out a number of ethical writers — Bacon, Spenser, Sidney, Hooker, John Smith, Henry More, Jeremy Taylor, Archbishop Leighton, Harrington, Algernon Sidney, Milton, Donne, Browne, Bunyan, and Clarendon. Locke, Addison, and Samuel Johnson of the next century are paid special tributes for their ethical insights. Emerson adds: "I am persuaded that a selection might be made of moral sentences from English literature from the works of Bacon, Shakspear, Milton, Taylor, from Sir T[homas] Browne, Barrow, South, Johnson, and Burke that should vie with that which any language has to offer, quicken the pulse of a virtuous ambition and inspire [in] men the feeling of perpetual youth; for as these truths concerned are immutable, so our apprehension of them is the certificate of man's immortality." [5] Such books as these are "vocabularies" or "dictionaries." They form the seed from which may be developed a thought or an entire essay. Emerson thus quickly finds what he is looking for in the author he reads; often he is not concerned with the main argument, but his eye is trained to catch some well turned *mot*. In this characteristic Emerson follows, perhaps unconsciously, his predecessors in the essay, Bacon, Montaigne, and Plutarch. Then too he reads the sermons of the seventeenth-century divines and, as we have seen, many of them also used quotable anecdotes and attractive expressions drawn from many classical writers. Emerson the young preacher seems to have followed their example in his sermons which, like those of his favorite, Jeremy Taylor, contain many quotations, not confined to the Bible but drawn from a great variety of writers pagan as well as Christian.[6]

Facts are not merely facts; they are symbols also of something else; this is the chief concept of "The Poet" and in the very first paragraph of that essay we see the name of Plutarch: ". . . the highest minds of the world have never ceased to explore the double meaning, or shall I say the quadruple or the centuple or much more manifold meaning, of every sensuous fact; Orpheus, Empedocles, Heraclitus, Plato, Plutarch, Dante, Swedenborg, and the masters of sculpture, picture and poetry." Emerson here seems to include Plutarch in the number of those who see not only the sense meaning, the primary meaning underlying a fact, but also a symbolic meaning. He may be thinking of the two layers of meaning which Plutarch attributes to the sentences of Pythagoras, or the way in which Plutarch gives a natural as well as a mythological or symbolic significance to the story of Isis and Osiris; for in "History" he probably recalls "Of Isis and Osiris" when he writes (*CW* 2. 14): "In man we still trace the remains or hints of all that we esteem badges of servitude in the lower races; yet in him they enhance his nobleness and grace; as Io, in Aeschylus, transformed to a cow, offends the imagination; but how changed when as Isis in Egypt she meets Osiris-Jove, a beautiful woman with nothing of the metamorphosis left but the lunar horns as the splendid ornament of her brows!" Emerson probably is aware of the identification of Isis with the moon from Plutarch and in an undated note for a lecture he observes the meaning which is behind the myth. Fable and myth delight him when he contemplates the lack of the mythological and fabulous in his own time; myth removes us from the surrounding contemporary dullness. And, reading mythology itself, Emerson goes behind the purely physical and narrative element to its "occult spiritual essence." Plutarch is his model here, rationalizing fables, to bring out the essential truth.[7]

This is what the poet is to Emerson — a seer who can understand the manifold meanings of a fact or experience and who can give expression to them. In the first paragraph of "Poetry and Imagination" we find the name of Aesop given as an example of "common sense" and later as an example of real poetry. At first sight, the name seems to have been set down without any care, and appears to be merely another name in Emerson's mind; but in *English Traits*, "Aesop and Montaigne, Cervantes and Saadi" are "men of the world" and in "The Poet," Aesop's cataloguing of human relations "through the masquerade of birds and beasts" intimates to man "the immortality of our essence." Aesop then is mentioned with a purpose; he deals with common, everyday truths in the form of symbols and this is what Emerson calls "common sense"; his ingenious fables, all that constitutes a fable, make his writing poetry. Emerson may have observed that both Montaigne and his master Plutarch set a high value on Aesop; Plutarch says in "How a Young Man Ought to Hear Poems" that when Socrates tried to write poetry, he "made choice of Esop's fables to turn into verse; as judging nothing to be true poetry that had in it nothing of falsehood." Plutarch and Emerson are in agreement again — that Aesop's fables, for example, have the essence of true poetry. But further, the poets are regarded as inspired; they are, to use one of Emerson's terms, "oracular"; words are instruments of a higher meaning. So he writes: "Plutarchiana this morn. Verses and words served as hampers and baskets to convey the oracle's answers from place to place. . . . Then was it that History alighted from versifying, as it were from riding in chariots, and on foot distinguished truth from fable. He speaks of the lovers of omens, etc., as preferring rainbows and haloes to the sun and moon." This is all Plutarch, from "Why the Pythian Priestess Ceases Her Oracles in Verse" [8] and it appeals to Emerson's liking for the oracular; the vivid figures used here impress him also and it must be from this passage that he adopts a figure in "The Poet" when he says, "language is a vehicle, like ferries and horses"; he has noticed the simile but has made his own change in the terms; and the second figure, of rainbows and haloes, was incorporated in his essay "Demonology."

i i

Emerson repeatedly indicates that one of the elements which he specially values in such writers as Plutarch is their use of quotations from the poets, treasured not only because many of these fragments would otherwise have been lost, but because of the vivid symbols and expressions which they employ, because of the "oracle" preserved in them. In "Quotation and Originality," adapting a passage from the 1835 lecture on Chaucer, he comments on this use of poetical quotations by the ancient writers:

Originals never lose their value. There is always in them a style and weight of speech, which the immanence of the oracle bestowed, and which cannot be counterfeited. Hence the permanence of the high poets.

Plato, Cicero and Plutarch cite the poets in the manner in which Scripture is quoted in our churches. A phrase or a single word is adduced, with honoring emphasis, from Pindar, Hesiod or Euripides, as precluding all argument, because thus they had said: importing that the bard spoke not his own, but the words of some god.

He returns to this in *Journals* 4. 267: "I am struck with the splendor of the sentences I meet in books, especially in Plutarch, taken from Pindar, Plato and Heraclitus, these three. It was Menander who said, 'Whom the gods love die young'." Here Emerson includes the aphorisms of prose writers as well as the poets and takes pleasure in identifying the source of a familiar aphorism.

One of the subordinate charms of writers of anecdotes and aphorisms like Plutarch is that in them we find anecdotes which have long since become proverbial; in "Old Age" Emerson elaborates this at length, saying that this is one of the pleasures of old age — expressions and stories remain in the memory for many years, their source forgotten or never known. Reading and the course of time bring them to light again and the name of the forgotten author is recovered; or better still, the isolated thought of a writer "is suddenly matched in our mind by its twin, by its sequence, or next related analogy" so that this story or expression radiates light and its deeper meaning is beheld for the first time. Emerson must have felt his kinship with Plutarch when he read in "Of the Tranquillity of the Mind": "The prudent man retrieves things that were lost out of their oblivion, by strength of recollection renders them perspicuous, and enjoys them as if they were present." Sometimes we can watch Emerson himself doing just this, identifying in Plutarch the origin of a familiar anecdote; for example in *Journals* 10. 320 he notes that the anecdote of Alexander weeping that there were no more worlds to conquer is given correctly by Plutarch (*Moralia* 1. 140); in the same volume of the journals he notes that Plutarch in "Concerning Such Whom God Is Slow to Punish" quoted the old proverb about the mills of God. Again, even in Plutarch's time there was a longing for the good old days;

in *Journals* 3. 544 he paraphrases a passage in Plutarch's "Laconic Apothegms": "' The fading virtues of later times were a cause of grief to his father, Archidamus, who again had listened to the same regrets from his own venerable sire,' said Agis." He notes that the story of Rip Van Winkle is already told by Plutarch of one Epimenides and in a notebook under the heading "Quotation and Originality" he observes the ancestry of the tall tale about the speaker whose words in a cold climate froze in his mouth and then became audible next spring; he notices that it comes from Plato by way of Plutarch to *Hudibras* and Baron Munchausen.

Occasionally we can find an apothegm given by Emerson which, he has not observed, is much older than supposed. In *Representative Men* he quotes an aphorism of Napoleon, "You must not fight too often with one enemy, or you will teach him all your art of war." This is a variant of a saying of Lycurgus, in Plutarch's *Lives*.

Another paragraph in "Quotation and Originality" speaks of the doubtful paternity of many proverbs. Emerson finds the original of Rabelais' dying words, "I am going to see the great Perhaps," in the "IF" inscribed on the portal of the temple of Apollo at Delphi, and he probably thinks of the essay of that title in the *Moralia*. I think that in another instance we can see how Emerson changes and adapts an old "lustre," giving it greater sharpness; he was probably well aware of the origin of the aphorism which he gives in "The Sovereignty of Ethics," for he notes that it is attributed to many: "'T is a sort of proverbial dying speech of scholars (at least it is attributed to many) that which Anthony Wood reports of Nathaniel Carpenter, an Oxford Fellow. 'It did repent him,' he said, 'that he had formerly so much courted the maid instead of the mistress' (meaning philosophy and mathematics to the neglect of divinity)." One of the ancient sources of this is in Plutarch's "Of the Training of Children," where it is attributed to Bias, one of the Seven Sages. But there may be another source; Emerson is very fond of the story of Archimedes and his concentration on his studies even during the siege of Syracuse; in a lecture on "Greatness" in 1868 he quotes Plutarch's life of *Marcellus* indirectly, from Thomas Taylor's *Proclus*: "'Archimedes,' Plutarch tells us, 'considered every art connected with the common purposes of life ignoble and illiberal; and those things alone to be objects of his ambition with which the beautiful and the excellent were present, unmingled with the necessary'." And he uses this passage again, along with the story of Archimedes' death, in "The Celebration of Intellect." Emerson then is aware of the statement of Plutarch that Archimedes was not interested in the utility of scientific study; he also probably knows the aphorism of Bias, from Anthony Wood or from Plutarch. It would be characteristically Emersonian to sharpen and make concise the statement about Archimedes by use of the apothegm of Bias; this is done in a journal entry of 1832 (2. 536): "'Teach me,' said the young Syracusan to Archimedes, 'the divine art by which you have saved your country.' 'Divine, do you call it?' said Archimedes. 'It is indeed divine, but so it was before it saved the city. He that woos the goddess, must forget the woman'." It would be like Emerson to turn the general statement into an anecdote which contains an epigram; to elevate the terms from "mistress" and "maid" to "goddess" and "woman." The final epigram is obscure and it can really only be explained by saying that Emerson refers to the Plutarchan statement about the concentration of Archimedes on scientific problems which have no connection with practical affairs.

In the journals of August 19, 1837 (4. 284–286), Emerson indicates that he is reading the *Moralia* fairly extensively, looking for apothegms and interesting quotations from the poets. He copies a number down; the published journals give only a few but they are of interest because they show very well what sort of thing Emerson looked for in the *Moralia*; I have therefore transcribed the entire list from journal "C." All the quotations come from the "Several Hands" translation:

1.   Man serried close to man in dangerous field
         While morions morions touched, & shield to shield.

2. the glory at Marathon, the honor gained over the Carymedontes
and the Dianium,
    — Where the Athenian youth
    the famed foundations of their freedom laid.

3. Hesiod says
    "Bad Counsel, so the gods ordain,
    Is most of all the advisers' bane."

4. The Delphian oracle said to Corax the Naxian:
    It sounds profane impiety
    To teach that human souls e'er die.

5. They should have left every one in those sentiments which they
had from the laws and custom concerning the Divinity,
    Since neither now nor yesterday began
    These thoughts, that have been ever, nor yet can
    A man be found who their first entrance knew.

6.   Dost thou behold the vast and azure sky
    How in its liquid arms the earth doth lie?

7. Truth being the greatest good that man can receive and the
goodliest blessing that God can give.

8. There is no greater benefit that men can enjoy from God than
by imitation and pursuit of those perfections & that sanctity
which is in him, to be excited to the study of virtue.

9. Nature sent us out free and loose, we bind and straiten and pin
up ourselves in houses, and reduce ourselves into a scant and
little room.

10.   Not on the store of sprightly wine,
    Nor plenty of delicious meats,
    Though generous Nature should design
    To court us with perpetual treats,
    'Tis not on these we for content depend
    So much as on the shadow of a friend.

11.   Stern Jove has in some angry mood
    Bereft us of his solitude.

12.   Unvanquished love! whatever else deceives
    Our trust, 'tis this our very selves outlives.

13. Plato will have a man to be a heavenly tree growing with his
root, which is the head, upward.

14. Men cannot exercise their rhetoric unless they speak but may
their philosophy whilst they are silent or jest merrily; for 'tis
not only as Plato says, the highest degree of injustice not to be

just and yet seem so; but the top of wisdom is to philosophize yet not appear to do it, and in mirth to do the same with those that are serious and seem in earnest; for, as in Euripides, the Bacchae, though unprovided of iron weapons and unarmed, wounded their invaders with their boughs, thus the very jests and merry talk of true philosophers move those that are not altogether insensible. . . .

15. And if the greater part consists of such who can better endure the noise of any bird fiddlestring or piece of wood than the voice of a philosopher, —

> The Isthmian garland will I sell as cheap
> As common wreaths of parsley may be sold.

16. Evenus said that Fire was the sweetest of all sauces in the world.

17. It is an expression of Pindar, that we tread the dark bottom of hell with necessities as hard as iron.

18. After a festival you may see 'the dirt of wine.'

19. To reap corn with slings.

20. The sea was the tear of Saturn.

21. A walk near the sea and sail near the shore was best.

This comprehensive list of lustres from Plutarch indicates the sort of thing Emerson looked for. He seems to have been especially attracted by quotations from the Greek poets, probably not only for the compression and epigrammatic quality, but also for the attractive language of the seventeenth-century translation which he always admired. Again, as Emerson says in "Inspiration" — "Words used in a new sense and figuratively, dart a delightful lustre; and *every* word admits a new use, and hints ulterior meanings." The language has the economy, the sharp juxtaposition of striking words, the vivid and unusual metaphor (like that of "liquid arms" in no. 6) which seem to have caught Emerson's eye and which he cultivated in his own poetry. The prose passages which he noted down also have some of these same qualities; these prose lustres, in addition to the attractive language, have the merit of surprise and paradox; perhaps no. 14 is an instance; there is novelty in the idea that philosophy can appear and operate through silence; the parallel from Plato is ingenious, and there is this same ingenuity, and at the same time the classical Greek vigor and picturesqueness, in the lines from Euripides' *Bacchae*. The lustres which come at the end of the list are all bright metaphors and almost all of them reappeared subsequently in essays, lectures, or journals.[9] No. 17 from Pindar was a special favorite, from *Moralia* 1. 303. It did not matter that the vivid expression "tread the dark bottom of hell with necessities as hard as iron" was an invention of the seventeenth-century translator and was removed in the revised version; Emerson liked the poetry in the expression and it was treated by him as if it were genuinely Plutarchan. He used it in the lecture on George Fox and, with Pindar's name, in "The Progress of Culture" and there can be no doubt that it is quoted again in "New England Reformers" where Emerson says of energetic great men, "they would know the worst and tread the floors of hell," while in *Representative Men* "tread the floors of the Pit" is surely the same phrase of Pindar; another Pindaric quotation from Plutarch appears several times in Emerson.[10] The last of the lustres listed above has another quality which Emerson would probably describe as "oracular." It says a great deal in simple terms and can be applied in a number of ways; the number of interpretations which could be placed on it is manifold.

Emerson makes use of other quotations from poetry in Plutarch. He mentions Hesiod as one of the poets quoted by Plutarch and other "ancient writers" and in "Gifts" he takes from Plutarch (*Moralia* 2. 63) a couplet of Hesiod. Euripides is a favorite of Plutarch and Emerson twice noticed lines quoted by Plutarch. In 1841 (*Journals* 6. 137) he copies from the *Moralia* 2. 181:

> "And cakes by female hands wrought artfully,
> Well steep'd in the liquid of the gold-wing'd bee."

The elaborate periphrasis for "honey" probably interests him. Another Euripidean quotation from Plutarch appears in *Representative Men* (*CW* 4. 138). Emerson gives it as:

> "Goodness and being in the gods are one;
> He who imputes ill to them makes them none."

Emerson found this in *Moralia* 2. 56.[11] In *Journals* 7. 513–514 he
puts together several passages from Plutarch on the mathematics of
the ancient world, and includes a Greek couplet on Pythagoras:

> "When the famed lines Pythagoras devised
> For which a hecatomb he sacrificed."

Emerson notes this couplet in his journals again in 1865 (10. 103)
and says that the university undergraduate should know it and also
"Archimedes' *Eureka*." Both these expressions are in *Moralia* 2. 174.

iii

But not only poetry has the strength of poetic truth and the
charm of vivid expression. Moral anecdotes have an oracular character and convey eternal truths. In *Journals* 4. 154 he returns to the
oracular element in Plutarch. He speaks of the *"cyclus* of orphic
words" which he finds in Bacon, in Cudworth, in Plutarch and
Plato: "They do touch the intellect and cause a gush of emotion
which we call the moral sublime." Anecdote and aphorism are
here as valuable as poetry and the *Lives* contain as many "lustres"
of this kind as the *Moralia*. For example, in 1841 Emerson makes
in journal "H" a selection of notes on his reading of the *Lives* at
that time:

The killing of brothers, Plutarch thinks a postulate in royal geometry.
Protogenes lived on lupines whilst he painted the history of Ialysus
that his judgment might not be clouded . . . . A Lacedaemonian youth
resembled the great Hector exactly. This young man, Myrsilus informs
us, was crushed to death by the multitude who came to see him as soon
as that resemblance became public. The wrestlers used to break up the
ground with the mattock by way of exercise to improve their strength.
The Sicyonians who buried no body within their walls sent to Delphi
to inquire where they should bury Aratus and had this answer:

> What holy rites for liberty restored
> Sicyon shall pay to her departed lord
> She asks: who grudge him a resting place
> Of earth and skies and seas is the disgrace.[12]

In the margin Emerson gives clues as to where he found these remarks — they came from Langhorne's translation of the life of Demetrius, from a note by Langhorne in the same biography, and from the life of Aratus; at least two of the quotations are used verbatim. A notebook of Emerson's labeled "Morals" contains more of the sort of thing for which he relishes Plutarch; inside the front cover he quotes from Plutarch, *Moralia* 2. 92, the words attributed to Thespis and he notes from Moralia 4. 59: " 'Jove, the beginning, middle, source of all'." There is a passage on courage which refers to a remark of Plutarch; this whole note was incorporated into the essay "Courage"; under the heading "Immortality" he notes two passages from Plutarch on this theme, referring to Goodwin's translation. Finally, Emerson quotes a passage on the language of the Sibyl which he finds in "Why the Pythian Priestess Ceases Her Oracles in Verse" (*Moralia* 3. 74) and which he quotes again in his Plutarch essay.[13]

Occasionally a sentence in Emerson shows a similarity in content and idea with one in Plutarch, and a classical term or a reference to "the Greeks" or "the ancients" gives us the clue; a reference to the "Delphian prophetess" in "Natural History of Intellect" (*CW* 12. 50) recalls Plutarch's two essays on the oracle at Delphi, essays which specially interested Emerson; he says here: "Reason does not keep her firm seat. The Delphian prophetess, when the spirit possesses her, is herself a victim." He had quoted in "Courage" the anecdote of the priestess who tried to "prophesy without command in the temple at Delphi" which he read in Plutarch's "Why the Oracles Cease to Give Answers"; he also knew well Plutarch's essay on love, in which Plutarch says that love is a "celestial rapture of the mind," and Plutarch adds, "What do we find equal to it in the Pythian prophetess, when she sits upon the tripod?" We can find another Plutarchan reminiscence in "English Traits." He remarks that to Sir John Herschel "London is the centre of the terrene globe," and gives examples of other nations which have claimed a central geographic position — Venice prided itself that it was midway between the pole and the equator and "Long of old, the Greeks fancied Delphi the navel of the earth, in their favorite mode of fabling the earth to be an animal." Plutarch had discussed the theory that the earth was an animal in *Moralia* 3. 133 and his essay "Why the Oracles Cease to Give Answers" (*Moralia* 4. 3) begins: "There is an old story . . . that heretofore eagles or swans, flying from the opposite bounds of the earth, met together where now stands the temple of Apollo Pythius, in the place now called the Navel." The same passage in the *Moralia* probably lies behind a metaphor in the essay on Shakespeare which without knowledge of this origin is puzzling in meaning: "The unaffected joy of the comedy, — he lives in a gale, — contrasted with the grandeur of the tragedy, where he stoops to no contrivance, no pulpiting, but flies an eagle at the heart of the problem; where his speech is a Delphi, — the great Nemesis that he is and utters." Here the two words "eagle" and "Delphi" probably give us the clue to the origin of the curious figure employed here.

In "Worship" he quotes an anecdote from "Of Garrulity" (*Moralia* 4. 231): "The son of Antiochus asked his father when he would join battle. 'Dost thou fear,' replied the king, 'that thou only in all the army will not hear the trumpet?'" The reference in *Journals* 4. 329 to "the Spartan maxim of fighting better in the shade" is a commonplace aphorism which is attributed to Leonidas in *Moralia* 1. 418; a reference in the essay on Swedenborg (*CW* 4. 112) is more likely to be the result of a reading of Plutarch. Emerson says: "He [Swedenborg] knows, if he only, the flowing of nature, and how wise was that old answer of Amasis to him who bade him drink up the sea, — 'Yes, willingly, if you will stop the rivers that flow in'." Emerson does not examine the background of the story; it is only partly correct that it is the answer of Amasis of Egypt to a problem set him by the king of Ethiopia; but Amasis, the legend goes, sent to Bias, one of the Seven Wise Men, for the solution; Emerson had read it in Plutarch's "Banquet of the Seven Wise Men" (*Moralia* 2. 14). In 1841 he writes in journal "G,"

"Parmenio loves the king, but Hephaestion loves Alexander" and probably recalls an aphorism in the "Apothegms of Kings," where however it is Craterus who is named instead of Parmenio, and a journal note "Xenophon says of Agesilaus, 'What youth was ever so gallant, but that *his* old age surpassed it?'" seems to come from "Whether an Old Man Ought to Meddle in State Affairs" (*Moralia* 5. 67).

Sometimes, without a classical name as a clue, we can still find traces of reminiscences of stray remarks of Plutarch: In "Nature" (*CW* 1. 71 72) occurs the sentence, "Now is man the follower of the sun, and woman the follower of the moon," in a long quotation from Emerson's "Orphic Poet." This may be a casual reminiscence of a sentence of Plutarch in the *Moralia* (4. 294): "We appear to be passionately in love with the sun"; the concept of woman as a follower of the moon is quite likely a natural parallel which would occur to Emerson's mind — it occurs all through Greek and Roman mythology; or again he may have recalled Plutarch's comparison of Venus to the moon in his dialogue "Of Love," especially since it occurs in a passage in which the god of love is compared to the sun (*Moralia* 4. 293).[14] If this is a recollection of Plutarch it may serve as another indication that Emerson's "Orphic Poet" of *Nature* is merely a figure of speech and that all this material, so mysteriously presented, is genuine Emerson.

A sentence in the short essay "Nature" in *Essays: Second Series* contains perhaps another echo of Plutarch. Emerson says (*CW* 3. 186): "Let the stoics say what they please, we do not eat for the good of living, but because the meat is savory and the appetite is keen." In the "Symposiacs" (*Moralia* 3. 341–345) one of the topics of discussion is "whether want of nourishment causeth hunger and thirst, or the change in the figure of the pores or passages of the body." Philo the physician expresses the physical and mechanical explanation of hunger. Plutarch rejects this: "I must confess this discourse seemed to carry in it some shadow of reason and probability; but in the main it is directly repugnant to the chief end of nature, to which appetite directs every animal. For that makes it desire a supply of what they stand in need of, and avoid a defect of their proper food." He concludes his argument by saying that plants get their nourishment from the air; "but as for us men, our appetites prompt us on to the chase and pursuance of whatsoever is wanting to our natural temperament." Plutarch rejects the physical explanation; Emerson rejects what we may call the teleological explanation; both adopt the more immediate and less recondite explanation — we eat because we have the urge to eat. Plutarch writes of plants first and man second; Emerson takes up man first and then (in the sentence after the one quoted) goes on to a parallel in "vegetable life." There is perhaps still another trace of Plutarch in "Character" (*CW* 3. 112). Emerson says: "Friends also follow the laws of divine necessity; they gravitate to each other, and cannot otherwise. . . . Their relation is not made, but allowed. The gods must seat themselves without seneschal in our Olympus, and as they can instal themselves by seniority divine." The last sentence has not much meaning until we connect it with the passage in the "Symposiacs" on the seating arrangements at the banquets of the gods (*Moralia* 3. 206–207) which he had noted in his journals in 1837.

Towards the end of "Man the Reformer" Emerson speaks of the power of love, and uses the mushroom as a symbol of it (*CW* 1. 254): "Have you not seen in the woods, in a late autumn morning, a poor fungus or mushroom, — a plant without any solidity, nay, that seemed nothing but a soft mush or jelly, — by its constant, total, and inconceivably gentle pushing, manage to break its way up through the frosty ground, and actually to lift a hard crust on its head?" This is a curious symbol and perhaps one that would not strike the modern reader as the best one here. But we cease to wonder why Emerson used it when we read Plutarch's second question of the fourth book of the "Symposiacs," "Why mushrooms are thought to be produced by thunder" (*Moralia* 3. 296); Plutarch says: "Some said that thunder did split the earth, using the air as a wedge for that purpose, and that by those chinks those that sought after mushrooms were directed where to find them; and thence it grew a common opinion, that thunder engenders mushrooms, and not only makes them a passage to appear." Plutarch was interested in the question of how mushrooms manage to come up through the earth, and it is probable that, as in so many other cases, Emerson here has read the passage in the "Symposiacs."

In "Wealth," Emerson's remark (*CW* 6. 95), "Kings are said to have long arms, but every man should have long arms, and should pluck his living, his instruments, his power and his knowing, from the sun, moon and stars," with its theme of the long arm, may have occurred to him after he had read the first sentence of Plutarch's "Of Love of Wealth" (*Moralia* 2. 294): "Hippomachus, a master of the exercises, when some were commending a tall man that had long hands as one that promised fair to be good at fisticuffs, replied, A fit man indeed, if the victor's laurels were to be hanged up aloft, and should be his that could best reach it and take it down."

Emerson does not always give the correct attribution of an aphorism when he recalls it from memory; so in 1832 in *Journals* 2. 450 he notes, "Diogenes was a true philosopher when he compared his shade and his sunshine to the alternate residence of the Persian king at Susa and Ecbatana." Plutarch gives this in *Moralia* 4. 501 but attributes it to Metrocles: "Metrocles laughs at thee, who sleeping in the winter amongst the sheep, and in the summer in the porches of the temples, challenged the king of the Persians, that wintered in Babylon and passed the summer in Media, to vie with him for happiness." This is certainly the kind of aphorism which would quite naturally be attributed to Diogenes and a sentence in "History" (*CW* 2. 21) may show that Emerson had read an improved version elsewhere: ". . . the Persian court in its magnificent era never gave over the nomadism of its barbarous tribes, but travelled from Ecbatana, where the spring was spent, to Susa in summer and to Babylon for the winter."

In his essay "How to Know a Flatterer from a Friend" Plutarch says (*Moralia* 2. 100) that we welcome the flatterer who appears in the guise of a friend because flattery appeals to our self-conceit. Emerson in "Gifts" (*CW* 3. 160; we have observed that there is in this essay a verse quotation from Plutarch) makes a reference to flattery in the form of a proverbial saying, the type of remark which he looked for in Plutarch: "Men use to tell us that we love flattery even though we are not deceived by it, because it shows that we are of importance enough to be courted." Perhaps here he adapts and modifies Plutarch; we are not deceived, as Plutarch would have it, but still we receive and welcome flattery.

Thus it is not always fanciful to see in remarks of Emerson reminiscences of his devoted reading of Plutarch's *Moralia*. But the *Lives* too provide classical references and anecdotes, though in the earliest cases only indirectly. Two early references come originally from the life of Brutus and are of interest since Brutus was a Roman Stoic and we may here have early indication of Emerson's attraction to the Stoic figures in ancient history. In a letter of about 1834 (*Letters* 1. 415) he refers to Brutus' appointment at Philippi with his "daemon"; but this anecdote is of course familiar in Shakespeare and in Bacon's "Of Prophecies." It is also the first reference in Emerson to the classical theory of the "daemon" or "genius" which as we have seen exerted its attraction on him. The second apothegm from Plutarch's life of Brutus is given in a letter of 1837 (*Letters* 2. 88) but here *Julius Caesar* is almost certainly the source: "Caius Ligarius would fain be well if there were anything for a man to do." This remark also has Stoic overtones; and the classical demonology appears again in *Journals* 1. 200, of the year 1822, where there is a passing reference to "the soothsayer's faithful account of Antony's guardian genius" which was subdued only by that of Caesar. *Antony and Cleopatra* is probably the source here, rather than the original life of Antony. It may be no coincidence that two of these passages on the daemon are crucial extracts for a knowledge of classical demonology, since they separate the daemon from the man himself and show the daemon beginning to pass over into the Christian and Oriental belief in the guardian angel.

At the end of "Art" (*CW* 7. 56) Emerson says that the great cathedrals and the great paintings arose out of some genuine enthusiasm "and never out of dilletanteism and holidays"; his illustration is the division of the Athenian people into political factions over the merits of the sculptor Phidias. He here probably recalls Plutarch's life of Pericles, which contains two passages on the jealousy of the Athenians for Phidias' friendship with Pericles, and his eventual trial, imprisonment, and death.

In 1862–63 (journal "VA") when Emerson says, "young Athenians sat whole days drawing the figure of Sicily in the dust," he evidently recalls Plutarch in the life of Alcibiades.

One of the earliest journal passages derived from Plutarch belongs to the year 1825. In *Journals* 2. 48 Emerson writes: "Of Tyrtaeus and his conquering elegies who has not heard? And Greek history has another more extraordinary instance to the purpose. When Lycurgus meditated the introduction into Sparta of his unprecedented political model, he prevailed on Thales, whom he met as he travelled in Asia Minor, to pass to Laconia and compose poems there of such a character as to prepare the minds of his countrymen for the novel schemes of the Reformer." [15] This is a paraphrase of a passage in Plutarch's life of Lycurgus, and it has an interest for us since it shows Emerson's early interest in the Spartans; we may conjecture that it also attracted him as a valuable illustration of the power and value of poetry. But the *Moralia* too mention Lycurgus, and it was here rather than in the *Lives* that Emerson obtained a Spartan aphorism: in "Politics" he outlines a theory of the history of politics; it is based on property and the ownership of property; the principle finally admitted is that which states that "property should make law for property and persons for persons": "At last it seemed settled that the rightful distinction was that the proprietors should have more elective franchise than non-proprietors, on the Spartan principle of 'calling that which is just, equal; not that which

is equal, just'." Plutarch refers to this Spartan principle in his question, "What is Plato's meaning when he says that God always plays
the geometer?" in the "Symposiacs" (*Moralia* 3. 403–404), an essay
with which, as we know from a passage in his journals, Emerson
was acquainted; Plutarch writes:

> For Lycurgus, I suppose you know, banished out of Sparta all arith-
> metical proportion, as being democratical and favoring the crowd; but
> introduced the geometrical, as agreeable to an oligarchy and kingly
> government that rules by law; for the former gives an equal share to
> every one according to number, but the other gives according to the
> proportion of the deserts. . . . The same proportion, my dear Tyndares,
> God introduceth . . . which teacheth us to account that which is just
> equal, and not that which is equal just.

Emerson seems to be quoting the last sentence of this paragraph;
in his essay on Plutarch he confirms this attribution by quoting this
passage verbatim.

Emerson employed a more familiar quotation in "Art and Criticism": "Speak with the vulgar, think with the wise. See how Plato
managed it, with an imagination so gorgeous, and a taste so pa-
trician, that Jove, if he descended, was to speak in his style." He
had already used this in *Representative Men* and Plutarch attributes
it to Cicero in his life of Cicero. In 1845 (journal "W"), however,
Emerson reads it again, this time in Ammianus Marcellinus. This
fact, that an aphorism or epigram was found in other writers besides
Plutarch, makes necessary the reminder that in the case of a few
of these "lustres," especially when they consist of a vivid epigrammatic expression, it is inadvisable to state categorically that we have
here another instance of a borrowing from Plutarch. But our knowledge of Emerson's long devotion to, and repeated reading of, Plutarch makes it in many cases more than probable that Plutarch is
the source.

Sometimes, as we have seen, it is a figure or metaphor which
catches Emerson's observant eye. It is significant that when in
"Poetry and Imagination" he writes of the great charm of "imagi-

native expressions" in poetry and adds, "a good symbol is the best argument, and is a missionary to persuade thousands," out of a number of examples of such symbols there is only one which is taken from "pagan literature" and this one comes from Plutarch: "Thus the Greek mythology called the sea 'the tear of Saturn'." This symbol had been noted in the journal in 1837 and comes from Plutarch's "Of Isis and Osiris." Further on in the same essay, Emerson concludes a paragraph (*CW* 8. 23): "Every healthy mind in a true Alexander or Sesostris, building a universal monarchy." We have seen above that Emerson uses an expression from Plutarch's "Of Isis and Osiris" and it is not likely to be coincidence that in this same essay (*Moralia* 4. 85) we find Sesostris and Alexander in a list of great rulers.

We have seen too that in 1837 Emerson was reading some of the essays in the *Moralia* and hence a "fable" in "The American Scholar," delivered in that year, may be Plutarchan in origin. Emerson refers to the story "that the gods, in the beginning, divided Man into men, that he might be more helpful to himself; just as the hand was divided into fingers, the better to answer its end." Harrison observes [16] that the original of this is in Plato's *Symposium* but that blended with this recollection of Plato Emerson must have read Plutarch's account of the use of brothers in "Of Brotherly Love" (*Moralia* 3. 37): "And Nature hath given us very near examples of the use of brothers, by contriving most of the necessary parts of our bodies double, . . . thereby telling us that all these were thus distinguished for mutual benefit and assistance, and not for variance and discord. And when she parted the very hands into many and unequal fingers, she made them thereby the most curious and artificial of all our members; . . ." Many years later Emerson used this figure again in his essay on Plutarch: "God divided man into men that they might help each other," attributing it to Seneca instead of to Plutarch himself.

Another interesting figure is quoted in a journal note of 1869 (10. 305); Emerson refers to the purpose of Simonides "to declare war against length of time" and seems to have found it in "Of Isis and Osiris" (*Moralia* 4. 84); the same essay of Plutarch produces a sentence in "Experience" (*CW* 3. 46); Emerson writes that often when we think ourselves idle we accomplish much. We acquire wisdom, poetry, virtue, but "not on any dated calendar day": "Some heavenly days must have been intercalated somewhere, like those that Hermes won with dice of the Moon, that Osiris might be born." He alludes to this myth again in 1841 in a letter to Margaret Fuller (*Letters* 2. 399). The source of both references is an extract which he made in 1839 (*Journals* 5. 287) from Plutarch's essay on Isis and Osiris (*Moralia* 4. 74), and it occurs behind a phrase in "The Preacher": "We want some intercalated days, to bethink us and to derive order to our life from the heart."

Occasionally the metaphor which attracts Emerson's eye and imagination in Plutarch is not Plutarch's own but one which had attracted Plutarch's attention also in his reading of Plato. Emerson's essay "The Comic" begins (in the form in which it was originally published in the *Dial*), "It is a nail of pain and pleasure, said Plato, which fastens the body to the mind." He found this figure in the "Symposiacs" (*Moralia* 3. 402) and quoted it again in his essay in Plutarch. In the same way he notes in journal "B," "Man is a heavenly plant &c as Plato says in Plutarch." This comes from "Of Banishment" (*Moralia* 3. 18–19 and 81) and Emerson used it (perhaps from Montaigne) in the essay on Montaigne in *Representative Men* and in "The Poet."

In 1835 also (*Journals* 3. 489) he writes of Cudworth: "Cudworth . . . has fed so entirely on ancient bards and sages that all his diction is redolent of their books. He is a stream of Corinthian brass in which gold and silver and iron are molten together out of ancient temples." This story of the discovery of brass comes from Plutarch's "Why the Pythian Priestess Ceases Her Oracles in Verse." Emerson evidently liked the symbolism of the story, for he used it in the lecture "Ethical Writers" in 1836 and again in 1845, speaking of the melting pot of America (*Journals* 7. 115–116).

Perhaps another simile may be the result of a recollection of a phrase of Plutarch. Emerson says (*CW* 12. 18): "There are viviparous and oviparous minds; minds that produce their thoughts complete men, like armed soldiers, ready and swift to go out to resist and conquer all the armies of error. . . ." The comparison to "armed soldiers" of course recalls the story of the birth of Athena fully armed from the head of Zeus, but Emerson may also have recalled a remark (recorded in his journal of 1834) in the familiar short Plutarchan life of Demosthenes in the "Lives of the Ten Attic Orators" (*Moralia* 5. 46): "He [Philip] used to compare Demosthenes's orations to soldiers, for the force they carried along with them."

We have seen Emerson in "Intellect" probably employing the figure of the lantern which Plutarch had used of Demosthenes; and again when Emerson says in "The Poet," "words are also actions, and actions are a kind of words," he may be thinking of Democritus' remark, "words are but the shadows of actions," given by Plutarch in *Moralia* 1. 22, but more probably of Demosthenes' more familiar description of oratory as "Action! action! action!" given both in the life of Demosthenes in the *Lives* and in the shorter life in the "Lives of the Ten Attic Orators."

In his description of the British universities in "English Traits" a Plutarch tag appears. Emerson is speaking of the knowledge and study of Greek and Latin in the universities; of the Englishman he says (*CW* 5. 207): "Access to the Greek mind lifts his standard of taste. . . . The great silent crowd of thoroughbred Grecians always known to be around him, the English writer cannot ignore. They prune his orations and point his pen." The phrase "prune his orations" is a recollection of Demosthenes' remark that Phocion was the "pruning-knife" of his speeches; it comes from Plutarch's "Political Precepts" and life of Phocion, and Emerson had set it down in his journals in 1834.

Twice in his poetry Emerson uses figures which seem to be Plutarchan in origin. It may be a curious adjective which catches his eye: in "The Poet" (*CW* 9. 309) occur the lines:

The pious wind took it away,
The reverent darkness hid the lay.

The editor notes that in his essay on Plutarch Emerson quoted a sentence of the "Several Hands" translation of the *Moralia*, from "Of Fortune" (*Moralia* 2. 477): "Were there not a sun, we might, for all the other stars, pass our days in the Reverend Dark, as Heraclitus calls it." Emerson noted this as an instance of unconscious humor in the old translation of the *Moralia* which, he observed, Goodwin did not retain since it was incorrectly translated. In the poem he has used "reverent" rather than "reverend" but it is more than likely that he recalled the expression from the old translation of Plutarch. Then, too, the motto poem for the essay "Heroism" contains the lines:

The hero is not fed on sweets,
Daily his own heart he eats.

Holmes noted that the image came from Pythagoras; it seems to be a Pythagorean apothegm given in *Moralia* 1. 28. Plutarch explains its meaning, "Eat not thy heart; which forbids to afflict our souls, and waste them with vexatious cares." Emerson may also have read it in Bacon's essay on friendship. These lustres in Emerson's poetry are the more obviously Plutarchan ones; there must be very many more, as yet undiscovered, but which can be traced by a study of the poems and of Emerson's reading at the time when they were taking shape. For example it has been clearly shown recently that the "Song of Nature" and "Cosmos" contain many ideas and expressions drawn from two favorite Plutarchan essays, "Of Isis and Osiris" and "Why the Oracles Cease to Give Answers." [17]

iv

Sometimes Montaigne may be the intermediary between Plutarch and Emerson, or else, because of their kinship in attitude and literary taste, both Emerson and Montaigne instinctively observe the same sentence in Plutarch. In "Poetry and Imagination" for example, Emerson employs a figure which has a long history in literature: "In poetry we say we require the miracle. The bee flies among the flowers, and gets mint and marjoram, and generates a new product, which is not mint and marjoram, but honey; . . . and the poet listens to conversation and beholds all objects in Nature, to give back, not them, but a new and transcendent whole." This figure appears in Plutarch and Seneca; Aeneas Sylvius Piccolomini popularized it in the time of the Renaissance and it was used also by Montaigne; indeed, Emerson's wording is very close to that of Montaigne in "Of the Education of Children" and this is probably his more immediate source. But Montaigne found it in Plutarch's "Of Hearing" (*Moralia* 1. 450). Plutarch uses the figure briefly elsewhere also (*Moralia* 1. 142; 2. 78, 83, 457) and in the last of these passages shows that the figure goes back long before his own time, to Simonides. It is from Simonides that Plutarch and Seneca obtain it, Montaigne borrows it from Plutarch and Emerson from Montaigne. Both Plutarch and Emerson use the figure in connection with poetry, while Montaigne uses it in reference to the transformation of the opinions of philosophers in the mind of the youth who is acquiring an education. But if Emerson and Plutarch use the figure in the same connection their purposes are different. Plutarch uses it for a hortatory purpose — for inculcating proper habits in the reading of poetry — while Emerson uses it to describe the creative process of the poet himself. While he follows Montaigne in his wording, he almost certainly is also familiar with at least one of the uses of it by Plutarch. But the use of this ancient figure by Emerson is a good illustration of his classicism. He dresses his novel, often revolutionary ideas with an old lustre or illustration; not because it is old but because, although it is old, it is still apt and striking.[18]

The use of the bee as symbolic of the poet also lies behind Emerson's poem "The Humble-Bee," which must be dated after 1837, "when a *Journal* entry described the experience and outlined the

idea behind the poem," [19] and it was also in 1837, as we have seen,
that Emerson made his most extensive journal entry of extracts
from the *Moralia*. In this poem the poet is like the bee for he
"gathers and distils the sweetness of nature for man, yet does so
almost by instinct, 'humbly,' without the pride of conscious intellect." [20] It will be observed that this is closely similar to the Plutarchan figure, while the instinctive and nonintellectual nature of
the poetic process stems from Emerson's Platonism and can be
found repeated in another Platonist, Plutarch.

There are more passages which may come from Plutarch by way
of Montaigne. In journal "DO" (1852) he notes, "Alexander the
Great had a natural perfume"; this comes from the life of Alexander, but Montaigne begins his "Of Smells" with it, and in *Journals*
6. 362 Emerson observes, "Aristo said, that neither a bath nor a
lecture did signify anything unless they scoured and made men
clean," a remark from Plutarch's "Of Hearing." But Emerson's
wording indicates that he used this at second hand, from Cotton's
translation of Montaigne's "Of Vanity." Plutarch by way of Montaigne may perhaps be the source of a passage which Edward
Emerson did not think was written by his father but whose source
eluded him; it is the epitaph of Sir Jenkin Grout which Emerson
gives in "Manners" (*CW* 3. 145): "Here lies Sir Jenkin Grout,
who loved his friend and persuaded his enemy: what his mouth ate,
his hand paid for: what his servants robbed, he restored: if a
woman gave him pleasure, he supported her in pain: he never
forgot his children; and whoso touched his finger, drew after it
his whole body." Edward Emerson noted that much search had
failed to determine the source of the epitaph, yet doubted that
Emerson himself composed it. It is just possible that this may be
Emerson's own; the curious last clause of the epitaph seems to be
an adaptation of a passage of Montaigne in "Of Vanity": "The
Stoicks say that there is so great a connexion and relation amongst
wise men, that he who dines in France, nourishes his companion
in Egypt; and that whoever does but hold out his finger, in what

part of the world soever, all the wise men upon the habitable earth feel themselves assisted by it." It has been noted [21] that Montaigne found this in Amyot's translation of "Of Common Conceptions, against the Stoics" (*Moralia* 4. 392): "If (say they) one wise man does but any way prudently stretch out his finger, all the wise men all the world over receive utility by it." Emerson was familiar with this apothegm for he uses it in *Journals* 2. 456 and 2. 466; he quotes it twice in sermons and if he composed the imaginary epitaph in "Manners" he is ringing the changes on an expression which he had read in Plutarch or in Montaigne.

In *Journals* 9. 26 (1856) Emerson makes a passing reference to "Menander's speech, 'that he had finished the comedy, all but the verses'." This comes from "Whether the Athenians Were More Warlike or Learned" (*Moralia* 5. 403–404); Montaigne refers to this anecdote in his essay on education. Two classical apothegms in the lecture on Martin Luther in the series "Biography" probably come from Plutarch by way of Montaigne, that of Epaminondas from Montaigne's "Of the Most Excellent Men" (and Montaigne found it in the "Apothegms of Kings" or in the life of Coriolanus); that of Agesilaus is given in Montaigne's essay on friendship and comes from the "Laconic Apothegms" or the life of Agesilaus.[22] Again in *Journals* 6. 84 Emerson observes, "Hippomachus knew a good wrestler by his gait in the street, and an old stager like myself will recognise the subtle Harlequin. . . ." This remark about Hippomachus comes from Plutarch's life of Dion, but Emerson may also have read it in Montaigne's "Of Three Kinds of Intercourse."

Near the beginning of his second essay entitled "Nature," Emerson writes of the forest and nature (*CW* 3. 170): "Here we find Nature to be the circumstance which dwarfs every other circumstance, and judges like a god all men that come to her. We have crept out of our close and crowded houses into the night and morning, and we see what majestic beauties wrap us in their bosom." Part of this recalls more or less closely a sentence near the beginning of Plutarch's "Of Banishment" (*Moralia* 3. 20) which Emerson had copied into his journals in 1837: "Nature in our first production sent us out free and loose; we bind and straiten and pin up ourselves in houses, and reduce ourselves into a scant and little room." But Montaigne had copied the passage (and the anecdote with which Plutarch follows it up) in "Of Vanity"; and it is certainly from this essay of Montaigne that Emerson (as other quotations in the same volume of the journals show) read another Plutarchan anecdote which appears in *Journals* 10. 243: "'Did you give Athens the best laws?' 'No,' replied Solon, 'but the best it would receive'," and which comes from the life of Solon. In *Journals* 5. 383 is a reference to the legend of the proclamation of Xerxes advertising for a new pleasure and offering a reward to the one who would discover it; Emerson perhaps recalls the "Symposiacs" (*Moralia* 3. 216) where however the reward is offered by "an Assyrian king," but the anecdote is also in Montaigne. Another classical aphorism is almost so much of a commonplace that it is impossible to give the source categorically: in the "Editors' Address" in the *Massachusetts Quarterly Review* Emerson speaks of the power, wealth, and resources of America. He adds (*CW* 11. 384): "Keep our eyes as long as we can on this picture, we cannot stave off the ulterior question, — the famous question of Cineas to Pyrrhus, — the WHERE TO of all this power and population. . . ." This is a reference to an anecdote found in Plutarch's life of Pyrrhus and Emerson gives it again in sermon 97. We may also note that Montaigne too found the story in Plutarch and used it in "Of the Inequality amongst Us." Almost equally familiar in Emerson's time is the story that Julius Caesar, when shipwrecked, swam to land carrying his writings between his teeth; Emerson gives it several times and it is in Plutarch and in Montaigne's "On the Means to Carry on a War According to Julius Caesar." In "Eloquence" (*CW* 7. 78) Emerson quotes Caesar's aphorism to Metellus, which he probably read in Plutarch's life of Julius Caesar or in the "Apothegms of Kings"; he follows it with the story of the capture of Caesar by pirates which is given in the same two Plutarchan works and which he himself used again in "Manners."

Much of Emerson's reading in Montaigne and in Bacon and other English writers of the seventeenth century led him to Plutarch; in reading an author like Montaigne he is instinctively drawn to the quotations from Plutarch, even if Montaigne does not always state that Plutarch is the source. In 1837 he is reading Montaigne and notes quotations under the heading "The Antique" (*Journals* 4. 197). The first quotation is: "The Lacedaemonians entering into battle sacrificed to the Muses, to the end that their actions might be well and worthily writ." Montaigne probably found this in the "Laconic Apothegms." Then, when Emerson himself read Plutarch in 1845, he observed that in the life of Lycurgus Plutarch attributes the institution of this custom to Lycurgus, and entered it once more in his journals.[23] Some years later again, in journal "NY" (1868–1870), he copied the anecdote verbatim once more, this time from the "Customs of the Lacedaemonians" (*Moralia* 1. 91). So, introduced to a Plutarchan apothegm by Montaigne, Emerson as it were recognizes it as an old friend when he comes to read it in Plutarch and makes a note of it once more.

Sometimes a Plutarchan apothegm may have reached Emerson by way of another favorite essayist, Bacon. Near the beginning of "Concord Walks" Emerson speaks of his purchase of his Concord farm and says: "Still less did I know what good and true neighbors I was buying." The curious expression "buying neighbors" sounds typically Emersonian but it gains point and precision if we suggest that Emerson here recalls an aphorism of Themistocles in Plutarch's *Lives* and in the "Apothegms of Kings": "Having a farm to sell, he bid the crier proclaim also that it had a good neighbor." Bacon used this in "Of Building" and Bacon's "Of Friendship" may have provided Emerson with another anecdote which he used in "Table Talk" in a series on American life. It is Themistocles' comparison of speech to tapestry and is again in the life of Themistocles and in the "Apothegms of Kings." One of Emerson's favorite apothegms,

the comparison of Timoleon's victories to Homer's verses, which
originates in Plutarch,[24] might have come from Bacon's "Of Fortune" but it was often quoted in Emerson's time and before and is
in the well-known textbook on ancient history by Rollin. Still
another Plutarchan aphorism is used in Emerson's quatrain (*CW*
9. 296):

> Well and wisely said the Greek,
> Be thou faithful, but not fond;
> To the altar's foot thy fellow seek, —
> The Furies wait beyond.

The editor observes (*CW* 9. 499) that Emerson gave a Latin expression *usque ad aras* as the source for "to the altar's foot"; this
apothegm of Pericles is given three times by Plutarch;[25] but the
Latin version comes from Gellius and Emerson very likely read it
in Bacon's *Advancement of Learning*, II, vii, 2. Emerson twice, in
"English Traits" and in "Manners," uses a curious figure "dry
light" which goes back to a simile of Heraclitus, "the wisest soul
is like a dry light," in Plutarch. But in both occurrences of this term,
Emerson shows that he has found it too in Bacon's *Advancement
of Learning* — in "English Traits" he quotes it from Bacon and in
"Manners" the phraseology shows that it comes from Plutarch
by way of Bacon.[26]

Then too Emerson could not fail to observe Jeremy Taylor's devotion to Plutarchan "sentences"; in 1831 (*Journals* 2. 412) he notes
at second hand a quotation from Plutarch which he has found in
this seventeenth-century devotee of Plutarch: "*Loquendi magistros
habemus homines, tacendi Deos, apud* Jeremy Taylor. And Plutarch
said excellently, *Qui generose et regio more instituuntur, primum
tacere, deinde loqui discunt.* ('To be taught first to be silent, then
to speak well and handsomely, is education fit for a prince')." The
Plutarchan quotation is from "Of Garrulity" (*Moralia* 4. 231); the
first quotation also, although Emerson does not so indicate, is from
the same work of Plutarch.[27]

The editor of Emerson's letters says of the influence of Plutarch on Emerson, "It is not surprising to find that this patron saint shed his influence on many an essay and lecture." [28] This influence can be found occasionally in the substance of an essay or in a title but its vast extent and long duration can best be observed in reading Emerson's writings, as he read those of Plutarch, for "lustres" in the form of moral "sentences," apothegms and epigrams, anecdotes or curious metaphors and symbols. Over and over again he turned the pages of the Plutarch of Langhorne and the "Several Hands" for illustration and adornment of his own essays and lectures by sentences which had "point and surprise." We may almost say of Emerson what he himself said of Montaigne, that he is "the best reader Plutarch has ever found."

v

It would be surprising if the literary style of Plutarch which Emerson so much admires has not also exerted an influence upon his own literary style. Here we must distinguish between two "styles" of Plutarch, his own characteristic style in the Greek original, the main elements of which, such as the use of anecdote and epigram, come through in translation, and the other "style," the English style of the "Several Hands" translation of the *Moralia* and the Langhorne style of the *Lives*, for Emerson knew his Plutarch almost entirely through the medium of these translations. Oliver Wendell Holmes says that the portrait of Plutarch which Emerson draws in his "Plutarch" essay might, *mutato nomine*, be that of Emerson.[29] Here Emerson says of Plutarch's mind and of the manner in which his thoughts found expression (*CW* 10. 297–298):

Whatever is eminent in fact or in fiction, in opinion, in character, in institutions, in science, — natural, moral or metaphysical, — or in memorable sayings, drew his attention and came to his pen with more or less fulness of record. He is, among prose writers, what Chaucer is among English poets, a repertory for those who want the story without searching for it at first hand, — a compend of all accepted traditions. And all this without any supreme intellectual gifts. He is not a profound mind; not a master in any science; not a law giver, like Lycurgus or Solon; not a metaphysician, like Parmenides, Plato or Aristotle; not the founder of any sect or community, like Pythagoras or Zeno; not a naturalist, like Pliny or Linnaeus; not a leader of the mind of a generation, like Plato or Goethe. But if he had not the highest powers, he was yet a man of rare gifts. He had that universal sympathy with genius which makes all its victories his own; though he never used verse, he had many qualities of the poet in the power of his imagination, the speed of his mental associations and his sharp, objective eyes. But what specially marks him, he is a chief example of the illumination of the intellect by the force of morals.

This combination of intellect and moral power is one of the elements which makes Plutarch exert a special appeal for Emerson; it is this which makes him seem as modern as the latest philosopher. Emerson sets this aspect of Plutarch before himself as a model in 1839 (*Journals* 5. 286): "Plutarch fits me better than Southey or Scott, therefore I say, there is no age to good writing. Could I write as I would, I suppose the piece would be no nearer to Boston in 1839 than to Athens in the fiftieth Olympiad. Good thought, however expressed, saith to us, 'Come out of time, come to me in the Eternal'." This quality of timelessness is what Emerson calls, wherever he finds it, "the oracular," the use of sayings and anecdotes which are always apt and relevant; and in his interest in "memorable sayings" and in collecting anecdotes and stories Emerson closely resembles Plutarch; Sanborn also observes that "Plutarch, in his genius and his influence, — nay, even in his style of writing, — was the prototype of Emerson." [30] Emerson's genre, the moral essay, is an old one — the moral essay of Bacon, Montaigne, and Plutarch [31] — and in his predecessors he finds topics, and from them he draws the device of copious illustration by epigram and anecdote, and he even, as we have seen, uses the same anecdotes, the same neat phrases which they have used. Emerson values highly the transitory, individual and single experience and this draws him toward the brief expression, the image, the anecdote. Canby speaks of "the Emersonian mosaic of apothegms."[32] The phrase might equally well be applied to numerous essays in Plutarch's *Moralia;* indeed, Maurice Morgan's introduction to the "Several Hands" translation of the *Moralia* says that Plutarch "appears like a piece of Mosaick Work, which consists of several parts, but all extremely beautiful." This addiction to the anecdote and to the epigram Emerson owes to his reading and to his method of composition. This is the style of Plutarch, most marked in the "Apothegms of Kings and Great Commanders," where the epigrams are simply strung together one after another, and, as Holmes says of Emerson: "We must not find fault with his semi-detached sentences until we quarrel with Solomon and criticize the Sermon on the Mount. The 'point and surprise' which he speaks of as characterising the style of Plutarch belongs eminently to his own."[33] In other classical moralists whom Emerson read he must have observed the same short, abrupt style — in the three Roman Stoics, Epictetus, Seneca, Marcus Aurelius, and later in Montaigne and Pascal. These writers adopt this style for the same reason Emerson did. The formal structure of their work is not important to them. They wish above all to be casual, to record their own thoughts without restrictions of form.

This abrupt, epigrammatic style which makes sentences and paragraphs vary greatly in length is also largely due to Emerson's method of composition. He decides on a theme and then searches through his journals and notebooks for fresh material which he thinks might be used here. Occasionally apparently the only criteria used in deciding whether a paragraph or anecdote should be included in an essay are a general coherence in topic and the fact that the paragraph has not been published already. This is especially the method used with the last essays of Emerson to be published. Often the connections between the paragraphs are very loose because he wishes to insert a quotation or an anecdote which he has not examined with sufficient care for its appositeness to the topic which he is discussing at this point.

But as recent studies have pointed out this lack of relevance in Emerson is often deliberate. The essay forms an organic whole; the relevance of a lustre may not be a relevance to the sentence immediately preceding or following it, but to a larger unit. He sometimes deliberately forfeits continuity and cultivates obscurity of style. In a journal passage of 1834, he finds sanction in Coleridge for an abandonment of orderly arrangement of topics and he writes to Carlyle just before the first series of essays was published: "In a fortnight or three weeks my little raft will be afloat. Expect nothing more of my powers of construction, — no shipbuilding, no clipper, smack, nor skiff even, only boards and logs tied together." To Carlyle also he says that the sentence is his unit, his paragraphs are only collections of "infinitely repellent particles." Here Matthiessen points out the influence of the early reading of Bacon's *sententiae* with the same intensification of the moment which Emerson cultivated,[34] and Bacon may well be one source of the aphoristic and proverbial element in Emerson's style. Emerson is, as Matthiessen shows, always torn between the common sense, the down-to-earth, the popular proverb on the one hand, and abstract philosophy on the other; as a consequence, says Matthiessen, his style is somewhere midway between Transcendentalism and Franklin's *Poor Richard*. The same mixture of the mystical and the practical is in his aunt Mary Moody Emerson, the sibyl of Concord, and she too may be another source, close at hand, for his sharp, aphoristic style.[35] Another journal passage of 1838 says about style (*Journals* 5. 63–64): "If you desire to arrest attention, to surprise, do not give me facts in the order of cause and effect, but drop one or two links in the chain, and give me with a cause, an effect two or three times removed." And the editor of the journals observes that this was Emerson's lecture method — "to keep attention on the stretch, and give the hearer the creative pleasure of supplying the link." [36]

There is little doubt that Bacon, Montaigne, Mary Moody Emerson, Coleridge all play some part in the development of Emerson's style, both in theory and practice, and it is becoming more obvious that no single source should be overstressed. But we should also add Plutarch to the list. Maurice Morgan said precisely the same thing of Plutarch's style in his preface to the "Several Hands" translation of the *Moralia*: ". . . for his Periods sometimes are to be supplied, great Casus to be fill'd up, nay Transitions are to be made for him, that may conduct him gently from one Thought to another. . . ." Emerson must have noticed that Montaigne rambles and that Plutarch is addicted to digression. He knew the autobiographical essay of Montaigne entitled "Of Vanity" and employs several Plutarch quotations which he read there; he could hardly have missed Montaigne's comment on Plutarch's style: "There are pieces in Plutarch, where he forgets his theme, where the proposition of his argument is only found by incidence; and stufft throughout with foreign matter. Do but observe his footing in the Daemon of Socrates. Good God, how beautiful then are his variations and digressions, and then most of all, when they seem to be fortuitous, and introduced for want of heed." Montaigne thus defends himself by the precedent of Plutarch: " 'Tis the indiligent reader that loses my subject, and not I; there will always be found some words or other in a corner that are to the purpose, though it lie very close. I ramble indiscreetly and tumultuously, my stile and my wit wander at the same rate; a little folly is tolerable in him that will not be guilty of too much, says both precepts: and more the examples of our masters."

The remarks in these quoted passages might equally well hold good of Emerson, and here where Montaigne draws precedent from Plutarch, he must have recognized his own feeling and attitude. Emerson says of Plutarch (*CW* 10. 301): "I admire his rapid and crowded style, as if he had such store of anecdotes of his heroes that he is forced to suppress more than he recounts, in order to keep up with the hasting history." Much of Plutarch's "rapid and crowded style" is simply the result of rapid composition, or even of careless translation, but Emerson can appreciate its effectiveness. It probably helped to develop his own style, not always rapid or crowded, but with a Plutarchan disregard for smooth transitions and connections.

We know too that Emerson liked oracles and the oracular and Plutarch's two essays which deal with oracles were familiar to him; he must have read a passage in "Why the Pythian Priestess Ceases Her Oracles in Verse" (*Moralia* 3. 99):

For the deity is not bound to observe that law of Euripides, where he says

> Phoebus alone, and none but he,
> Should unto men the prophet be.

Therefore, when he makes use of mortal prophets and agents . . . he does not altogether go about to suppress the truth, but only eclipses the manifestation of it, like a light divided into sundry reflections, rendering it by the means of poetic umbrage less severe and ungrateful in the delivery. For it is not convenient that princes or their enemies should presently know what is by Fate decreed to their disadvantage. Therefore he so envelops his answers with doubts and ambiguities as to conceal from others the true understanding of what was answered; though to them that came to the oracle themselves, and gave due attention to the deliverer, the meaning of the answer is transparently obvious.

This is what Emerson likes in the writers whom he calls "oracles" and perhaps he tries to imitate them; to quote a favorite Pindaric phrase of Emerson, his writing "sounds to the intelligent." Bacon and Montaigne on style point Emerson back to Plutarch and here in the master he finds obscurity again commended.[37]

As for the second element in Emerson's style, a matter of words and language rather than of transitions of thought and ideas, Emerson cultivates plainness and grandeur as one; for they can in a sense be combined — by the treatment of the commonest objects in an uncommon way. This is done by showing the symbolism which underlies everything and the result will be a new appreciation of the identity of all things. According to Emerson, only this unity of simplicity and grandeur will make a literary style alive and vital, and these are the qualities which above all he wishes to obtain. In *Representative Men* he says of Montaigne's style, "cut these words and they would bleed; they are vascular and alive," and he notes how close to life and ordinary experience is the conversational style of Montaigne; it is "a shower of bullets"; indeed, it is quite probable that in Montaigne Emerson finds during his years of development a direct exposition of stylistic qualities. In 1834 he writes in his *Journals* (3. 272), "Glad to read in my old gossip Montaigne some robust rules of rhetoric: I will have a chapter thereon in my book." He gives references to indicate what he is reading in Montaigne — it is several pages in "On Some Verses of Virgil" (including a passage which Emerson later quoted in his essay on Plutarch). Montaigne finds that "there is stuff enough in our language" but that it is "not sufficiently pliant and vigorous." Fresh and vivid expressions can be drawn from many fields of activity, for "the forms of speaking, like herbs, improve and grow stronger by being transplanted." Then, returning to the language of Vergil, Montaigne says:

Of some of the words I have pick'd out for my own use, we do not easily discern the energy, by reason that the frequent use of them hath in some sort embas'd their beauty, and render'd it common. As in our ordinary language there are several excellent phrases and metaphors to be met with, of which the beauty is wither'd by age, and the colour is sullied by too common handling; but that takes nothing from the relish to an understanding man: neither does it derogate from the glory of those antient authors, who, 'tis likely, first brought those words into that lustre.

He then goes on to say, in a passage which Emerson quoted in his Plutarch essay, that he can dispense with other books, which only interfere with his own style, but that he cannot be without Plutarch with his "not to be exhausted hand of riches and embellishments." Montaigne says that he plunders Plutarch frequently. It has been pointed out that the description of the style which Montaigne emulates is also an extraordinarily accurate statement of Emerson's stylistic aims and it is suggested that Montaigne became Emerson's preceptor in style as well as in literary form, that the combination of simplicity and grandeur which is peculiarly Emerson's, the new use of old words to impart life and sinew to style, is contributed to Emerson by his reading of Montaigne.[38]

But it is at once noticeable that in this passage, which may have been Emerson's youthful handbook of rhetoric, the name of Plutarch appears twice and Montaigne indicates that in the matter of style he is independent of all books — except Plutarch. A journal passage of 1850 indicates that when Emerson years later recalled this reading of Montaigne it was the references to Plutarch which remained with him [39] and when in the Plutarch essay he mentions Montaigne's love of Plutarch he quotes from this same part of "On Some Verses of Virgil." If Emerson adopted this passage of Montaigne as his preceptor of style, he noted at once that Montaigne's master was Plutarch and he would "raffle all day in Plutarch's *Morals*" with a new confidence that his teacher Montaigne would approve of this and had done the same thing in his own time.

But the English style of the seventeenth-century translation of the *Moralia* also exerted an influence upon Emerson. "Were I professor of rhetoric," he writes in his journals, "I would urge my class to read Plutarch's *Morals* in English, and Cotton's Montaigne for their English style." He complains, perhaps in the course of preparing his introductory essay for Goodwin's revised version, that the new translation removes the poetical style of the old version. As he admits in the Plutarch essay, the new version is often more accurate, but Emerson read for sound and language as much as for content and even after the new Plutarch has been in his hands for several years, he still tends to go back to his 1718 edition. In his essay on Plutarch he wrote:

. . . I yet confess my enjoyment of this old version, for its vigorous English style . . . it is a monument of the English language at a period of singular vigor and freedom of style . . . [the old volumes of the *Moralia*] show the wealth of [the English] tongue to greater advantage than many books of more renown as models. It runs through the whole scale of conversation in the street, the market, the coffee-house, the law courts, the palace, the college and the church. There are no doubt many vulgar phrases, and many blunders of the printer; but it is the speech of business and conversation, and in every tone, from lowest to highest.

This is a taste, not for Plutarch, but for the English style cultivated in the sixteenth and seventeenth centuries — in the "Several Hands," in Cotton, in Bacon, in Bunyan, Fuller, Browne, and Jeremy Taylor. Emerson states his admiration for the imaginative expressions in Plutarch and, as we have seen, many of the numerous extracts from Plutarch which he made in his journals were noted not primarily for their matter but for the vivid metaphor or striking expression — "the dirt of wine," "the sea is the tear of Saturn," "a dry light" — and that occasionally he incorporates into his own writing figures from Plutarch in translation — "enamelled in fire," "weaving like a spider out of its own bowels." It has often been observed how Emerson is given to familiar, coarse, rough or contemptuous words, how he likes words in their primary or classical sense, rather than in their later and more common sense; how he often strives to employ new word combinations. All these can be found in many of Emerson's favorite authors of the seventeenth century, but in the "Several Hands" translation of the essays they are extremely abundant[40] and there can be little doubt that Emerson's repeated reading of the *Moralia* in this translation contributed its share in influencing the development of his literary style, and helped to make his writing redolent of the seventeenth century and strange and novel to his contemporaries in the nineteenth.

   We must add, however, that Emerson's earthy expressions are not entirely the result of antiquarianism, of digging in Montaigne and the seventeenth-century writers. He wants to record the strong accents of everyday speech, to get away from an artificial literary style. Matthiessen has pointed out that this was also the aim of others of the Transcendentalists — of Theodore Parker and of Alcott — but that in Emerson the endeavor to write in the vital language of Montaigne or Bacon is sometimes inhibited by some

Puritan strain so that the homely language which appears occasionally in the journals is often missing from the published essays and,
when it does appear, takes the form of a "sudden colloquialism"
which surprises the reader by its incongruity with its surroundings.[41]
It is this, says Matthiessen, which makes us think not of everyday
speech but of some curious seventeenth-century expression which
Emerson has read and has inserted into ordinary literary prose.
This acute perception, like so many of Matthiessen's, is correct.
When it can be shown that besides the common words, there are
also in Emerson usages and meanings of words which were archaic
in his own time but which were current more than a century before
him,[42] his reading of old authors has great significance for his
style — authors like Bacon, Browne, Montaigne, and the Plutarch
of Langhorne and the "Several Hands."

VIII

EMERSON'S PLUTARCH

I must think we are more deeply indebted to him [Plutarch] than to all the ancient writers.

"Heroism"

In the preceding chapters I have endeavored to show that Emerson was very familiar with the writings of Plutarch, both the *Lives* and the *Moralia;* that throughout his long career he made in his journals many notations on the anecdotes and expressions which he found in Plutarch, and that since the published essays are based largely on the journals, traces of this reading of Plutarch appear constantly in Emerson's published works. Sometimes he quotes Plutarch directly; sometimes he retells an anecdote or borrows an idea which he had read in the *Moralia* or the *Lives;* occasionally he follows an essay of Plutarch rather closely in plan and in thought. In some cases, however, we cannot say definitely that he took an anecdote or maxim directly from Plutarch since he may have found it in the works of other writers like Montaigne and Bacon who read Plutarch for the same kind of plunder.

During his formative years Emerson read many of the writers whom we may call "moral essayists." This was especially true between 1820 when his journals begin and 1836 when, with the publication of "Nature," he indicated that the literary form which he was going to adopt as his own was that of the address and essay. Plutarch, Montaigne, and Bacon are prominent during this period [1] and as early as 1817 he was acquainted also with some of the eighteenth-century English essayists in Johnson's *Rambler*, while in 1818 we find the *Spectator* among his book borrowings. He knew Sir Thomas Browne's tracts and *Religio Medici*[2] and Cudworth, the "magazine of quotations" whose diction is "redolent of other books." Along with this reading of the "moral essayists" we can observe in Emerson's reading lists an appropriate interest in the sermon, which in his time was a moral essay illustrated by Biblical quotations or quotations from Christian and pagan moralists. We have seen that Jeremy Taylor is strongly classical and Plutarchan in anecdote and epigram; in 1827, 1828, and 1829 Emerson was reading Taylor and seems to have returned to his works again in 1831 and 1832.[3]

Emerson's taste for the moral essay, however, gives him a special devotion to Plutarch and his two closest imitators, Montaigne and Bacon.[4] To Emerson, Montaigne means Plutarch above all else. He frequently couples the two names together and writes in his journals (9.236), "We go to Plutarch and Montaigne for examples of character" and (8.126), "I look back over all my reading, and think how few authors have given me *things*—Plato has, and Shakspeare, and Plutarch, and Montaigne." He calls Plutarch and Montaigne "high oracles" and links Cotton's version of Montaigne and the "Several Hands" Plutarch together as fine examples of the best English style.[5] Or he writes in his Plutarch essay (*CW* 10. 300): "It is one of the felicities of literary history, the tie which inseparably couples these two names across fourteen centuries. Montaigne, whilst he grasps Etienne de la Boèce with one hand, reaches back the other to Plutarch. These distant friendships charm us, and honor all the parties, and make the best example of the universal citizenship and fraternity of the human mind." By 1828 Emerson seems to have been acquainted with Montaigne's lengthy tribute to Plutarch in his essay "Of the Education of Children"[6] and many years later, in his Plutarch essay, Emerson compares Seneca and Plutarch in a manner which recalls Montaigne's comparison of the same two in "Of Books."[7] In his formative years, then, Emerson read the moral essays of Plutarch, Montaigne, and Bacon and noted the close connection between Plutarch and Montaigne.

ii

But he did more than this. In his early years Emerson expressed the desire, sometimes the intention, of following at various times in the footsteps of each of his illustrious predecessors and of writing moral essays.[8] The young Emerson seems to be feeling his way towards the best medium for his own taste and special talents, but he never departs far from his predilection for the essay as a literary form. At one time he thinks of compiling a collection of epigrams and maxims with a moral content, at another time he is drawn to the more personal essay which would express his own ideas but which could at the same time have embedded in it his favorite "sentences" from other authors. But he never abandoned his masters Plutarch, Montaigne, and Bacon; he would either follow them as literary models or would collect attractive anecdotes or epigrams from them and from others. It is interesting to follow his thoughts on literary form during this period and to see how he found a solution for the dilemma.

He first expressed his feeling of vocation as a moral essayist in 1824 when he wrote in his journal under the heading "Books" (*Journals* I. 392–393):

There is another sort of book which appears now and then in the world, once in two or three centuries perhaps, and which soon or late gets a foothold in popular esteem. I allude to those books which collect and embody the wisdom of their times, and so mark the stages of human improvement. Such are the Proverbs of Solomon, the Essays of Montaigne, and eminently the Essays of Bacon. Such also (though in my judgment in far less degree) is the proper merit of Mr. Pope's judicious poems, the Moral Essays and Essay on Man. . . . I should like to add another volume to this valuable work. I am not so foolhardy as to write *Sequel to Bacon* on my title-page; and there are some reasons that induce me to suppose that the undertaking of this enterprise does not imply any censurable arrogance. . . . It may be made clear that there may be the Wisdom of an Age, independent of and above the Wisdom of any individual whose life is numbered in its years. And the diligence rather than the genius of one mind may compile the prudential maxims, domestic and public maxims current in the world and which may be made to surpass the single stores of any writer, as the richest private funds are quickly exceeded by a public purse.

Although Emerson is only twenty-one at this time, we can already see a strong indication of his calling to be a moral essayist. His aim is to be a compiler of current maxims resembling those which he had been noting in his commonplace books since he was sixteen years old. The reference to the Proverbs of Solomon probably comes to his mind from the frequent occurrence of "Salomon saith" in Bacon, for at this point in Emerson's career, Bacon is his great exemplar, and Montaigne comes next to Bacon.

Towards the end of that same year, 1824, there is another reference (*Journals* 2. 20–21) to Emerson's hope of writing essays, which he now calls "dissertations." To fortify his resolution he writes down some plans for systematic study and reading: ". . . to begin with solid labour at Hebrew and Greek; theological criticism, moral philosophy and laborious writing should succeed; then history; then elegant letters — that species of books which is at once the most elevated amusement and the most productive suggester of thought, of which the instant specimens are the bulk of Johnson's works, as Lives of Poets, Rambler, etc., Pope's Moral Essays, and conspicuously Montaigne's Essays." In *Journals* 6. 371–372 he recalled: "In Roxbury, in 1825, I read Cotton's translation of Montaigne. It seemed to me as if I had written the book myself in some former life, so sincerely it spoke my thought and experience. No book before or since was ever so much to me as that." Here Emerson's admiration for Bacon seems to give way momentarily and partially to admiration for another hero — Montaigne. Emerson had thought first of collecting some of the copybook wisdom of the past, but now the influence of Montaigne seems to modify this

desire to imitate and rather to encourage him towards self-reliance
and a spirit of inquiry which is personal and based on his own experience. In "Experience" (*CW* 3. 55) Emerson admits that his
taste changes: "Once I took such delight in Montaigne that I
thought I should not need any other book; before that, in Shakspeare; then in Plutarch . . . but now I turn the pages of either
of them languidly, whilst I still cherish their genius." Plutarch
is another favorite author and in 1828 we have seen him writing
to his brother Charles, talking of putting together "a Schoolmaster"
which would excel Ascham's celebrated book. He still entertains
the idea of entering the world of the literature of maxims and
anecdotes, and he is partially withdrawing from his resolution,
whose impertinence he had half questioned, of writing a "sequel to
Bacon." He now thinks of a less ambitious type of writing, a kind
of schoolbook in the classical tradition, using anecdotes of antiquity
(such as his favorite ones about Archimedes in Plutarch's life of
Marcellus) to impart moral and ethical quality to the young. Collections of maxims and adages of this type were the traditional
framework out of which essays were constructed, as for example
in the writing of Montaigne's essays. But this idea of collecting anecdotes of the Plutarchan type came to nothing. Instead, Emerson
turned to the higher ideal of writing fully developed moral essays
and Montaigne resumes his place as Emerson's model.

A later passage in the journals, in 1835 (*Journals* 3. 480), seems to
indicate once more that in writing his own essays Emerson thought
of emulating Montaigne, or even of improving on him:

When will you mend Montaigne? When will you take the hint of
nature? Where are your Essays? Can you not express your own conviction that moral laws hold? Have you not thoughts and illustrations
that are your own; the parable of geometry and matter; the reason why
the atmosphere is transparent; the power of composition in nature and
in man's thought; the uses and uselessness of travelling; the law of
Compensation; the transcendent excellence of truth in character, in
rhetoric, in things; the sublimity of self-reliance; and the rewards of
perseverance in the best opinion? Have you not a testimony to give

for Shakspeare, for Milton? One sentence of real praise of Jesus, is worth a century of legendary Christianity. Can you not write as though you wrote to yourself, and drop the token, assured that a wise hand will pick it up?

Emerson now aims at the fully developed essay on the model of Montaigne; he wants now to express his own convictions and thoughts, using his own illustrations. But even so, he does not succeed entirely in breaking away from his original idea of a compilation. At the beginning of the next year, 1836, in "Ethical Writers" he affirms his liking for collections of "moral sentences";[9] and to the end of his writing career there lies beneath the personal reflections a strong basis of traditional wisdom, of moral precept and example, drawn largely from Plutarch and his followers.[10] Although he wanted to embody "the wisdom of the age" and "the current wisdom," he continued to draw much of his sustenance from the older authors.

But Plutarch, Montaigne, and Bacon are not the only models worth following. In a letter of 1832 to his brother William (*Letters* 1. 357–358) Emerson speaks in somewhat vague terms of publishing a magazine; periodicals in general "depend on many contributors who all speak an average sense & no one of them utters his own individuality." An individual must speak out, and not the general community. He says no more than that on this subject, but when we take this remark in conjunction with the journal passage of 1835, I think we can see Emerson's aim and ambition more clearly. He would like to write periodical essays, but they would not be on trivial topics; rather they would "mend Montaigne," show that moral laws hold; they would deal with ethical topics and moral values, with the great qualities of the human character, such as self-reliance. Emerson can contribute his own new thoughts and illustrations on some of the topics of the moral essayists. The lecture "Ethical Writers" of 1836 shows that the English periodical essayists stand out in Emerson's mind; they exert a permanent influence for good when they are inspired by sound morality and can thus inspire it in others in an age when the moral qualities are often neglected for trivial subjects which merely entertain the reader. Along with the classical moralists Epictetus, Marcus Aurelius, Cicero, Seneca, Plato, and Plutarch Emerson would place a number of great English writers, for "an utterance out of the heart's conviction of a social right or of a moral sentiment" is eternal; "Moral science is that Muse who alone hath immortality." The English scholars and "the poets who write elegant trifles" are dismissed as having no permanent interest, but along with Bacon and Milton and the English Platonists and Clarendon stands Addison, whose sound morality, besides his significance as one who transmits the ideas of Plutarch, Lucan, Xenophon, Rabelais, and Montaigne, gives him a place among the ethical writers. Dr. Johnson receives special attention, for he is a man of principle and of a perfect "sympathy with virtue."

There are, then, a number of ethical writers, followers of the moral muse, and among them are essayists like Addison and Johnson who speak a good word for morality and who can take a place, and by no means a low one, among the great exemplars of the moral essayists. For Emerson at this time of searching for a model, Montaigne and Bacon seem to be, at most, patterns for style; their writings have the stamp of an individual, the stamp which is lacking in modern periodicals, but still their morality is not above suspicion; Montaigne requires mending, he has no "grace" and Bacon, as Emerson had remarked not long before, is open to "censure." Plutarch also at this time seems to Emerson's view to be a pattern of style rather than an expounder of ethical truth. His moral essays are for Emerson a source of ethical illustrations and anecdotes; he is a "tuning-key" who stimulates new thoughts.

Plutarch wrote not only the *Moralia*, but also the generally better-known *Lives*. Now that we can appreciate something of the degree of Emerson's debt to Plutarch's moral essays a journal entry of 1832 (2. 503–504) is of special interest to us as showing that he aspired to write biographies too:

The British Plutarch and the modern Plutarch is yet to be written. They that have writ the lives of great men have not written them from love and from seeing the beauty that was to be desired in them. But what would operate such gracious motions upon the spirit as the death of Lord Cobham and of Sir Thomas More, and a censure of Bacon, and a picture of George Fox and Hampden, and the chivalrous integrity of Walter Scott, and a true portrait of Sir Harry Vane, and Falkland, and Andrew Marvell? I would draw characters, not write lives. I would evoke the spirit of each, and their relics might rot. Luther, Milton, Newton, Shakspeare, Alfred, a light of the world, — Adams. I would walk among the dry bones, and wherever on the face of the earth I found a living man, I would say, here is life, and life is communicable. . . . Socrates I should like well, if I dared to take him. I should repeat Montaigne though. I wouldn't . . . . I would make Milton shine. I would mourn for Bacon. I would fly in the face of every cockered prejudice, feudal or vulgar, and speak as Christ of their good and evil.

Here in the list of those who have portrayed human character, Montaigne's name appears again. Bacon is here also, but apparently as a subject for a life, rather than a literary model.[11] The most interesting thing about this casual paragraph, however, is that here Emerson speaks of his wish to redo Plutarch's *Lives* for modern times. Plutarch's name, he indicates, has been bandied about in the titles of several contemporary or recent collections of lives until it means merely a collection of lives. Such lives have been dull and bare; they have not portrayed the real character of the individual, whereas Emerson "would draw character, not write lives." In other words, Emerson wants to select the really vital elements in a man's life, the elements which make life "communicable" to all people and at all times.

Two years later, looking for topics for addresses, Emerson's mind still turns to biography which inspires morality by example rather than by precept. In 1834 (*Journals* 3. 387), after noting several anecdotes of Demosthenes in Plutarch's "Lives of the Ten Attic Orators," he writes: "Last night, abed, I recollected four names for four lectures: Luther, Michel Angelo, Milton, George Fox; then comes question of Epaminondas, esteemed by the ancients greatest of the Greeks; Demosthenes for the sake of his oratory and the related topics; Alfred for his human character; Sam. Johnson for his genuineness; Phocion, More, and Socrates for their three renowned deaths. . . ." Here Emerson wants to speak of lives or rather "characters" again, and for the Greeks he selects Plutarch's heroes once more.

When, in the development of his interest in writing, Emerson thus turns briefly to the idea of writing biography, he thinks at once of Plutarch. Plutarch would be his example, since in his Greek heroes life was made communicable; the identity of all human life is felt more vividly when we read a life by Plutarch, who gives inspiring examples of the moral nature which have a relevance for modern man as well as for Plutarch's own times. This itself is one of the moral truths which Emerson himself wishes to deal with and emphasize afresh.

We may note in passing that in connection with Socrates and Phocion it is their "renowned deaths" which Emerson singles out as specially inspiring. The reason for the attractiveness of the story of the death of Socrates is obvious; it is that Socrates' death is that of a martyr; the parallels between the martyrdom of Socrates and the Crucifixion are observed by Emerson (*Journals* 3. 419) as they could not fail to be noticed by any thinking reader. In the Socrates story is recounted the record of a pagan martyrdom which could provide the same inspiration as that of Jesus, with the advantage that there are no overlaid theological or dogmatic complications. The Biblical stories come in "black cloth" and impose an air of reverence, while at the same time in their Biblical phraseology they have become too familiar and hence are trite and meaningless. In the death of Phocion, Emerson finds the same ethical content "without cant." Plutarch says at the end of the life of Phocion, "The death which was suffered by Phocion revived among the Greeks the memory of that of Socrates." Again in the same life Plutarch tells how Phocion said to another prisoner who was to be executed along with him, "You cannot be contented to die with Phocion?" and

how when he was asked whether he had any final message for
his son, Phocion said, "Yes, by all means, bid him bear no grudge to
the Athenians." Emerson nowhere says so, but we may hazard
a guess that he has noted the similarity between these two remarks
and two of the familiar "Seven Last Words" of Jesus and indeed
the parallel between the whole story of the death of Phocion and
that of the Crucifixion. He is attracted by the realization that there
are pagan martyrs as well as Christian saints; that Christianity has
no monopoly on inspiring and ennobling stories of martyrdom.

iii

When we consider Emerson's regard for Plutarch and Plutarch's
heroes it would be surprising if this dominant liking does not show
in his own biographical writings. Although he never wrote the
"modern Plutarch" of which he spoke in his early journals, the
lecture series "Biography" of 1835 and the several other biographical
essays written at various times may be examined briefly to see what
traces there are of Plutarch's biographical method and also to ascer-
tain whether Emerson's attitude to these modern heroes of his is
in any way accommodated to that of Plutarch. If Emerson's admiration for Plutarch is carried over into his sketches of persons, we
shall expect to find the biographical facts briefly stated, with the
chief emphasis laid on the character of the individual, which will be
illumined by quotation and anecdote. In the character there will
be indicated the qualities which Emerson admires in Plutarch's
heroes — the self-reliance, independence of fashion and opinion, the
integrity, sincerity, and manliness which Emerson sums up under
the term "Stoicism." The characters portrayed will tend to be treated
as heroes and given heroic stature.[12]

"Biography" shows that Emerson usually singles out for special
mention certain qualities in his subjects; these qualities are the same
ones which he admires in the Greeks and Romans. This does not
mean that he converts his subjects into classical types or that he

will not write about a great man if he does not meet the classical or Plutarchan yardstick. He uses the Plutarchan method of describing them and bringing out what he sees as their essential greatness, and he tends to single out details which accentuate the simplicity of the hero, or his devotion to high principle and ability to withstand public pressure or the pressure of events, his self-reliance and military bearing; or occasionally, as in the lecture on Burke, the classical eloquence. Emerson feels with Plutarch that aphorism and anecdote help to portray the real man and to illustrate succinctly one of these heroic qualities.

So in the lecture on Michelangelo, his solitude, industry, devotion to study are given mention; he is practical and dexterous, a man of action and toil; his devotion to work produces simplicity in his way of life. He is superior to the multitude and independent of it. He adheres to high principles which he derives from an inward inspiration with which all his outward life is consistent. Like Luther he is compared to George Washington for his self-reliance. He is completely good: "his was a soul so enamoured with grace that not possibly could it stoop to meanness or depravity."

Similarly, Martin Luther is a fighter of indomitable will, summoned by God, who strives boldly and confidently to overcome evil. His aims are spiritual, not material, and his chief weapon is the translation of the Bible; he is a man of energy, power, and "prodigious efficiency." At one point he is compared to a Hebrew prophet, at another he is what Homer was to the Greeks, Moses to the Hebrews, Alfred to the Saxons, and George Washington to America. But Luther is also a simple, honest man, aiming at the simplicity of the early Church, no philosopher; he stands in strong contrast to the present, imitative, artificial age; again his life is upright and his homely, affectionate temper and humor are compared with similar characteristics in Plutarch's portrayal of Epaminondas and Agis. He embodies the heroic self-reliance, indeed "no man in history ever assumed a more commanding attitude or expressed a more perfect self-reliance."

Milton too is a born leader; "the voice of the mob is silent and Milton speaks." As a fighter he never employs conciliation but demands liberty; like Luther he is "erect, commanding"; his eloquence is stressed, his "honest haughtiness and self-esteem." Again his virtues are simple and humane and Plutarch's apothegm on Timoleon's victories serves to bring this idea home. He is heroic with an "antique heroism" and portrays the heroic image to man. He is never deterred by labor or danger from working to advance the supreme interests of man.

The lecture on George Fox provides the opportunity for Emerson to demonstrate that greatness and grandeur sometimes make their appearance among ordinary people, far from the circumstances which the world thinks of as nurturing greatness. Fox cannot be made so easily to resemble a classical hero, but Emerson borrows a phrase of Hume to portray him as a representative of the religious element which opposes arbitrary government; he is thus a hero of liberty — the religious liberty of the individual. Like Luther, he has an inward source of infallible guidance and Emerson thinks of the classical daemon as a parallel. Fox's Quaker plainness, simplicity, and meekness, the complete absence in him of respect for convention and rank, give him something of the simple, good humanity of the Plutarchan hero; anecdotes and apothegms illustrate this. Like a physician he ministers to the human soul and like all the heroes he fortifies mankind.

The Greeks come more readily to mind when one thinks of Edmund Burke. "Grace is natural to him like the genius of the Greeks" and we naturally recall Demosthenes, for Demosthenes was Burke's favorite orator and Plutarch his favorite classical writer; all the great examples of the philosopher in action — the Stoic emperor Marcus Aurelius, Machiavelli, and Bacon — are briefly portrayed; all fall short of Burke. Again his prime qualities are those of the hero — virtuous sentiment, affection, devotion to duty, unselfishness, generosity, simplicity, neglect of reputation, absence of fear or pride. His eloquence is of course compared with that of Demos-

thenes, with the aid of anecdotes from Plutarch, and Burke remains
in the end superior to Demosthenes since his oratory has the narrow
and the comprehensive view together — besides the farsightedness
which enables him to forecast the course of the French Revolution
he has the ability to see the principle behind the immediate problem,
indeed he "brought principles to bear upon the public business of
England."

In all these lectures in the series on biography, the parallels from
Greek history or the passing references to the Greeks are only part
of the decoration of the essay. Of much greater significance is the
combination of qualities which Emerson singles out in them all —
the military virtues of the hero which inspire and strengthen other
men, and at the same time the simpler human qualities which are
also characteristic of real greatness and which evoke, besides reverence and admiration, affection and love.

The earliest journal reference to Plutarch, in 1822 (1. 162), connected the heroes of American history with those of Plutarch. Emerson's essay on Abraham Lincoln is not primarily biographical, but
rather takes the form of a eulogy, for it was written to be delivered
at a memorial service for Lincoln held in Concord in 1865. Emerson
adheres to the aim he expressed in the journals; he draws a character rather than writes a life, and the work, though short, still
conveys a sense of the essential character of Lincoln in a few
sketched outlines. Here Emerson has no space for the Plutarchan
apothegm, but he cannot restrain his taste for epigram and pointed
phrase in depicting Lincoln's character; it is in this connection that
he compares Lincoln with the ancients: "He is the author of a
multitude of good sayings, so disguised as pleasantries that it is
certain they had no reputation at first but as jests; and only later,
by the very acceptance and adoption they find in the mouths of
millions, turn out to be the wisdom of the hour. I am sure if this
man had ruled in a period of less facility of printing, he would have
become mythological in a very few years, like Aesop or Pilpay, or
one of the Seven Wise Masters, by his fables and proverbs." Lincoln

was the kind of man whom Emerson could call a hero of the Civil War: "There, by his courage, his justice, his even temper, his fertile counsel, his humanity, he stood a heroic figure in the centre of a heroic epoch." He was the "heroic deliverer"; his "good nature became a noble humanity"; he was "a plain man of the people"; he "did not offend by superiority"; he had a strong sense of duty and the hard-headedness of the farmer. These are the qualities which Emerson sees also in Plutarch's heroes and he would readily assent to the lines on Lincoln from Lowell's Harvard "Commemoration Ode" which he sets before this essay as its motto:

> Here was a type of the true elder race,
> And one of Plutarch's men talked with us face to face.

There are few direct references to Plutarch in Emerson's biographical essays themselves, but the address on Theodore Parker has a reference in the second paragraph to Plutarch's lives of Alexander and Pericles.

Emerson's best biographical essays, however, are those in which he writes about intimate friends, whose nature and character he knows better, such as Dr. Ezra Ripley, his aunt Mary Moody Emerson, Samuel Hoar, or Thoreau. Each of these essays begins with the biographical facts, the dates, the outline of the life of the subject put briefly. Then by anecdote and quotation the essential character is brought out. The traits of character which interest Emerson are the same in each of the four. He does not try to force his character into a preconceived pattern, that of Plutarch's heroes; instead he writes of these four because he feels that in them he sees the qualities which he likes to find and which they had in common with Plutarch's men — self-reliance, independence, sincerity, courage, honor. Emerson draws traits, some of them amusing, from Dr. Ripley's diary and adds anecdotes from his own memory; he was "a natural gentleman, no dandy, but courtly, hospitable, manly and public-spirited; his nature social, his house open to all men." He was "open-handed and just and generous"; his speech was "neat, natural,

terse," that is, like that of the Spartans. "His whole life and conversation were consistent." Emerson cannot compare Dr. Ripley
with a Greek hero, however, even though the traits which he describes in him are also those which Emerson thought characteristically Greek and Plutarchan. We can gather from Emerson's remarks
that Dr. Ripley was more feared than loved; he was a little too rigid
and severe for a Greek hero. Emerson feels this, and at the end of
the essay he compares him rather to a Hebrew prophet, "a modern
Israelite in his attachment to the Hebrew history and faith," and
refers to his "antique Hebraism." It almost seems as if Emerson
is momentarily at a loss. The Puritan cannot be compared with a
Greek; there are few traits of the Plutarchan hero about Dr. Ripley.
But if his character is not easily adapted to the Plutarchan pattern,
yet Plutarch's method of comparing is still valid; the comparison
with the ancient Hebrew rather than with the antique Hellene suits
exactly the character of the subject.

Mary Moody Emerson resembled Dr. Ripley in several ways, and
Emerson is able to give many anecdotes and quotations from her
journal. In this case it is difficult to distinguish between Plutarchan
classical traits contributed to the portrait by Emerson and Plutarchan
qualities of the subject herself, for her own journals and letters
demonstrate that she had many Stoic qualities. When Emerson
observes how the Greek genius always reappears in society, his
remark that "Aunt Mary is a Greek" [13] and his description of her
as "our Delphian," a Pythian priestess like that of Plutarch's essays,
who makes inspired, oracular pronouncements, are peculiarly apt.
She is a Cassandra, uttering "to a frivolous, sceptical time, the arcana
of the Gods." She is Greek in her simplicity; Emerson quotes her
own remark: "Our civilization . . . is sauced and spiced with our
complexity of arts and inventions, but lacks somewhat of the
grandeur that belongs to a Doric and unphilosophical age." She
had spent a solitary youth, yet commends solitude; she is severely
religious and ascetic and her religion is a direct communion with
the Infinite, requiring no mediator or revelation; joy, hope, and

resignation unite her with the Divine Will; there is a Puritan or Stoic taste for self-examination; her lifelong search is for superior virtue. She speaks of "the heroism of morals"; she scorns to shine and likewise scorns levity, anger, and trifles. She is in her own mind "the puny pilgrim, whose sole talent is sympathy." She cherishes the grandeur of humility and privation. Her "do what you are afraid to do" is Christian but also more than Christian — it is also Stoic and she reads the great Stoic Marcus Aurelius and sets a high value on fortitude and independence; she would prefer war to "private animosities," oppression, and corruption, for war is "among the means of discipline, the rough meliorators, and no worse than the strife with poverty, malice and ignorance." Like some of the heroes she delights in undermining vanity and her intentions are "disinterested, though uncontrolled by proper reverence for others." But yet she dislikes the Stoic mean, except the mean between wealth and poverty; too often, she thinks, mediocrity is "distant from eminent virtue." Her concept of fate has more of the Stoic than the Christian about it — it is "the order of things"; death is not merely inevitable but is even welcome.

All these traits in Mary Moody Emerson's own character, so Stoic-sounding, so military and Spartan, serve us as a reminder that Calvinist Puritanism in one who cherished Plato and Plotinus and who had been reared on the Bible and Plutarch produces a view of life which is naturally Stoic. We are also reminded that there must have been many others of her time in New England who were in the same tradition, less articulate and individual perhaps, but certainly no less Stoic for that. Just as she was, she made an ideal subject for a Plutarchan sketch.

It was much easier to find a Plutarchan hero for comparison with Samuel Hoar, and that hero is a Roman. The essay is preceded by Lucan's famous distich on Cato and by a sonnet of F. B. Sanborn on Hoar:

> Thy name on other shores may ne'er be known,
> Though Rome austere no graver consul knew.

The first paragraph introduces Samuel Hoar as "our old Roman" and he is compared again with Cato. Emerson then enlarges on Hoar's heroic qualities. When sent by Massachusetts to protect free Negro citizens of Massachusetts in South Carolina, Hoar walked openly in the street without fear, "unattended by his friends"; he refused protection and had to be removed forcibly by the state. His comment then was, " 'Well, gentlemen, since it is your pleasure to use force, I must go.' But his opinion was unchanged." "He was a very natural, but a very high character; a man of simple tastes, plain and true in speech, with a clear perception of justice, and a perfect obedience thereto in his action. . . . He combined a uniform self-respect with a natural reverence for every other man. . . ." "Though rich, of a plainness and almost poverty of personal expenditure, yet liberal of his money to any worthy use. . ." Among all these qualities of a Roman hero Emerson quotes none of Hoar's anecdotes, but he says that Hoar borrowed "the aid of a good story, or a farmer's phrase, whose force had imprinted it on his memory" and that many good stories were told of Squire Hoar in court. The comparison with Cato is not stressed, but all the qualities which Emerson outlines are those of a Roman. Hoar to Emerson is the Roman consul, practical and businesslike, impatient of philosophy or abstraction, with no love of poetry but with an inflexible devotion to his country, his duty, and his conscience.

The essay on Carlyle is not really biographical, but still one or two traits of the Plutarchan hero appear. "His guiding genius is his moral sense, his perception of the sole importance of truth and justice. . . ." "Carlyle has, best of all men in England, kept the manly attitude in his time"; he has stood for the people, "intrepidly and scornfully." Emerson depicts the character of George L. Stearns in much the same way, referring to his "high virtue," his "exclusive devotion . . . to public and patriotic interests," "his transparent singleness of purpose, his freedom from all by-ends, his plain good sense, courage, adherence, and his romantic generosity." Stearns was "no boaster or pretender, but a man for up-hill work, a soldier to bide the brunt; a man whom disasters, which dishearten other men, only stimulated to new courage and endeavor."

Emerson's biographical essay or character sketch of Thoreau has been called by Matthiessen "one of the finest brief biographies in the language." In it Emerson wrote of someone whom he knew better than anyone else; he had had opportunities to see every side of Thoreau's character. Thoreau was the most obviously Spartan or Stoic of all his friends, and it was natural that others besides Emerson should observe this; Bronson Alcott speaks of Thoreau's Stoic and Spartan virtues and says that "Plutarch would have made him immortal in his pages had he lived before his day." [14] If Emerson anywhere endeavors to emulate Plutarch or to see a Plutarchan hero in any of his contemporaries, we should expect here to see some indications of his wish to be the modern Plutarch and to draw characters rather than to write lives. The biographical facts and the dates of Thoreau's youth are given at the beginning of the essay; one of Thoreau's epigrams appears in the second paragraph. Emerson goes on to establish Thoreau as a real Spartan: "he had no temptations to fight against, — no appetites, no passions, no taste for elegant trifles." Thoreau's traits are Spartan or Stoic and are outlined by anecdote and epigram.[15] He is described as a "hermit and stoic"; he is a "speaker and actor of the truth"; like the ancient Stoics, "he chose to be rich by making his wants few." In the poll-tax affair he is a minority of one (like Phocion): "No opposition or ridicule had any weight with him. . . . It was of no consequence if every one present held the opposite opinion." He had strong common sense and "could give judicious counsel in the gravest private or public affairs"; he had an intense patriotism, in his case a strong devotion to and pride in his native Concord. When Emerson discusses Thoreau's poetry he observes the tenderness under "that triple steel of stoicism" and his comment on Thoreau's detachment from organized religion is a quotation of Aristotle, "one who surpasses his fellow citizens in virtue is no longer a part of the city. Their law is not for him, since he is a law to himself." The tone of this and the idea expressed is that of the Dandamis apothegm which Emerson had used in "New England Reformers"; and we are reminded of a passage on the wise man (Emerson uses the Stoic term) in "Politics" (*CW* 3. 216): "To educate the wise man the State exists, and with the appearance of the wise man the State expires. The appearance of character makes the State unnecessary. The wise man is the State." Emerson admits, however, that Thoreau's virtues ran to extremes; his austerity and his inexorable demand for exact truth made him a hermit. He deplores the loss of Thoreau's power of action, for "he seemed born for great enterprise and command," and he criticizes his lack of ambition. At the end of the essay he sets down a couple of pages of unpublished "sentences" or epigrams of Thoreau.

There are faults in this essay, mostly faults of exaggeration; perhaps the most glaring is his remark that a certain poem of Thoreau's is like one of Simonides "but is better than any poem of Simonides." Since Emerson feels that Thoreau has not been properly appreciated, he is laudatory, sometimes extravagantly so. Though he has caught Thoreau's character well, the references to Simonides and Aristotle grate upon the reader's ear, because Emerson tries to turn the Thoreau of the Concord streets and woods into a hero, a Stoic hero, above the law because of his superiority in virtue. Thoreau's "Stoicism," his supposed ability to command, his indifference to public opinion are details which fit well into the picture which Emerson wishes to give. But still there is occasionally a trace of disappointment in Emerson that Thoreau's talents are wasted. "Instead of engineering for all America, he was the captain of a huckleberry-party." Perhaps Emerson is so impressed by the antique heroism of Thoreau that he is unable fully to appreciate the real heroism exhibited in Thoreau's adherence to his preference for a private life of his own, and in his refusal to participate in public and national life. Thus, in spite of Emerson's excellent writing, the portrait in this case is distorted by Emerson's partly unconscious shaping of Thoreau as a classical hero; enthusiasm and affection have deprived him of the proper perspective.

Throughout his biographical writings, then, Emerson seems to borrow Plutarch's technique of writing lives as well as his interest in the hero and the heroic. He uses small points of comparison, likes an anecdote and a pointed phrase, devotes small space to biographical facts, and prefers the features which illumine the character of the subject. These features tend to be given a heroic coloring and to approximate Stoicism. In the subjects are always found self-reliance, sincerity, independence of thought, sometimes a scorn for others. Emerson shows his devotion to the Plutarchan concept of the hero and tries to make his contemporaries appear to his readers, as they really did appear to him, examples of the classical hero.

iv

We have seen that at one time Emerson wanted to write moral essays like those of Bacon, Montaigne, and Plutarch and that at another time he thought of writing lives of the Plutarchan style. What was the reason for this attachment to Plutarch, besides the neat epigram and illustrative anecdote which Emerson as well as Bacon and Montaigne found in the *Moralia* and in the *Lives*? The element in both these works of Plutarch which attracted Emerson was their emphasis on morality, their "moral sentiment." The *Moralia*, as their title shows, are principally concerned with the qualities of the human character, and their whole tendency is towards the production of right principles of conduct by precept and instruction, while in the *Lives* we are given, not purely historical narrative, but examples of goodness and nobility in the great men of Greece and Rome.

It should not be necessary to try to find a reason for Emerson's devotion to "the moral sentiment" or "the moral sense." There can be no doubt that it is of prime importance in his thinking when he says in "Nature" that "the moral law lies at the centre of nature and radiates to the circumference," or that the causal force in nature

is moral and "its other name is the Moral Sentiment." The perception of this supremacy of morals, a "commanding sense of right
and wrong," is the peculiarity of the Anglo-Saxon race, we are
told (*CW* 5. 311), and the moral sense, the immanent part of
Transcendentalism, must inevitably be strong in a descendant of
Puritans, especially in a descendant of a number of Calvinist ministers. Emerson himself is well aware of the power of the old creed
and himself expressed the debt of his generation "to that old religion
which, in the childhood of most of us, still dwelt like a sabbath
morning in the country of New England, teaching privation, self-
denial and sorrow!" [16] The new ideas may have liberated men
from the sorrow and from some of the old sanctions of morality,
but there is certainly in New England no deterioration in moral
standards, no subordination of moral sense to any other obligation,
no taking of morality less strenuously. It seems to me that Canby
sums up well the moral air of Emerson's generation: [17]

Emerson was living in the tradition of dedicated men and women who
had made conceptions of the right will dominant if not common in the
community. Speculation upon conduct was as natural to them as breathing. The will had been set free by the breakdown of Calvinism, made
free by the absorption of new and liberal ideas from science and philosophy and new and liberal ideas as to the rights of the individual, but
never for one instant was it freed from the necessity to think for the
spiritual benefit of man. . . . The dedicated individual in New England
breathed a moral air in which responsibility was a live and creative
thing.

This interest in morals accounts in large part for Emerson's devotion to Plutarch and also for the fairly extensive knowledge of
Plutarch in America during Emerson's time. Although Emerson
says of Montaigne: "No book before or since was ever so much to
me as that," he later declares in the Plutarch essay: "Plutarch had
a religion which Montaigne wanted, and which defends him from
wantonness; and although Plutarch is as plain-spoken, his moral
sentiment is always pure." And again he emphasizes the ethical side

of Plutarch: "But what specially marks him, he is a chief example of the illumination of the intellect by the force of morals. Though the most amiable of boon companions, this generous religion gives him *aperçus* like Goethe's." For Emerson intellect and morals belong together; "there is an interdependence of intellect and morals," and a new church will be founded upon "moral science, that is intellect applied to morals." In both these sentences on Plutarch, "religion" and "moral sentiment" or "morals" are synonymous to Emerson; religion and a sound morality belong together. Elsewhere, for example briefly in "Nature" and at length in his "Lecture on the Times," Emerson applies a more technical, specialized meaning to the term "moral sentiment"; it is here a term from the seventeenth-century theory of moral philosophy founded by Shaftesbury and developed by Hutcheson, a theory which derived man's moral perceptions from a special sixth sense, the Moral Sense, which provides men with moral principles which are innate, superhuman, and instinctive. Here, however, writing on Plutarch and Montaigne, Emerson means by "moral sentiment" simply morality or moral principles.

In his essay on Plutarch, Emerson quotes La Harpe, that "Plutarch is the genius the most naturally moral that ever existed." I have no doubt that Emerson would emphasize the word "naturally"; indeed "natural morality" would be an adequate definition of Emerson's own religion. The religion of cult, symbols, ceremonies, metaphysics, and dogma Emerson (and Carlyle) calls "cant": "The ethical writings of the Ancients are without cant. The ancients are no transcendentalists; they rest always in the spontaneous consciousness." Again, Emerson writes: "God never cants. And the charm of Plutarch and Plato and Thucydides for me, I believe, is that there I get ethics without cant." [18] He says the same thing again in *Journals* 4. 154:

In what I call the *cyclus* of orphic words, which I find in Bacon, in Cudworth, in Plutarch, in Plato, in that which the New Church would indicate when it speaks of the truth possessed by the primeval Church broken up into fragments and floating hither and thither in the corrupt church, I find myself addressed thoroughly. They do touch the intellect and cause a gush of emotion which we call the moral sublime; they pervade also the moral nature.

The intellect and the moral sentiment are together reached by the "orphic words," the spontaneous, natural inspiration of certain writers such as Plutarch and Plato. Such moral precepts are not given by revealed religion or imparted by dogma, but come from an "oracle" — Emerson likes the term — close to the source of inspiration. The great stories and ethical precepts were not intended to found an institution, just as the Lord's Supper was "never intended by Jesus to be the foundation of a perpetual institution" (*CW* 11. 12). That is cant, and "God never cants." Plutarch, too, Emerson must have observed, felt the same distaste for ritual and dogma. They are what Plutarch calls "superstition" or "indiscreet devotion" in the "Several Hands" translation. The theme of the essay "Of Superstition" is the folly of unreasoning worship of an unreasoning, blind deity. "Dogma" occupies only a minor place in the essay since it occupied only a minor place in Greek religion. But ritual and "canting words" are vigorously attacked and it was this emphasis on ritual, Plutarch says, which produced atheism (*Moralia* 1. 182):

No, it was the uncouth actions and ridiculous and senseless passions of superstition, her canting words, her foolish gestures, her charms, her magic, her freakish processions, her taborings, her foul expiations, her vile methods of purgation, and her barbarian and inhuman penances, and bemirings at the temples, — it was these, I say, that gave occasion to many to affirm, it would be far happier there were no Gods at all than for them to be pleased and delighted with such fantastic toys, and to thus abuse their votaries, and to be incensed and pacified with trifles.

Plutarch calls for a natural worship, not for one of "canting language" (*Moralia* 1. 171):

They that were careful to preserve good singing used to direct the practisers of that science to sing with their mouths in their true and proper postures. Should we not then admonish those that would address themselves to the heavenly powers to do that also with a true and natural mouth, lest, while we are so solicitous that the tongue of a sacrifice be pure and right, we distort and abuse our own with silly and canting language, and thereby expose the dignity of our divine and ancient piety to contempt and raillery?

The religion or philosophy of the pagan moralists was a natural one. Emerson is strongly drawn to it in contrast to orthodox Christianity. He is approaching this idea cautiously in a note on a stray page which is undated: "A critic of Christianity will examine the power exerted by its offices and teachers: then, how it was equivalented in the classic age, in Greece and Rome. Were there no preachers and pastors then? Was their method less searching? The philosopher undertook the education of the boy, and his salvation, and achieved it, I doubt not, quite as well as our best divines." In "The Preacher" he speaks almost with regret of the loosening hold of "the venerable and beautiful traditions in which we were educated" and thinks of his own time as a transitional one, "as when the Roman Church broke into Protestant and Catholic, or, earlier, when Paganism broke into Christians and Pagans." His own age is like that of Plutarch, when pagan philosophy was struggling for survival with a new and more appealing revelation. Now Christianity and the other current religions have become "either childish and insignificant or unmanly and effeminating" (*CW* 6. 207); religion has been corrupted into "a timid conservatism and believes in nothing"; the city population is godless, materialized and "the churches stagger backward to the mummeries of the Dark Ages." Like Plutarch he gives instances of people (and the Greeks are included) who blame all things on their gods; he attacks those who believe in luck and circumstances. His idea of true religion is like that of Plutarch; it must be based on the sublimity of the "simple and terrible" moral laws. It must be heroic and active and man must accept responsibility for his own fate. This theme recurs in "Worship" and in "The Sovereignty of Ethics." This is of course the Emersonian self-reliance again and repeatedly its active aspect is mentioned in various terms — "We are the builders of our fortunes" or "The way to mend the bad world is to create the right world." This too is Plutarch's view. In "Of Superstition" the reader is reminded that disaster came to the Athenians at Syracuse because Nicias was mastered by superstition at a time when reasoning and action were imperative. Plutarch then points out that a pilot falls to prayer in the storm but still holds the rudder (the vignette perhaps came from a Stoic sermon); [19] Hesiod, Plutarch recalls, advocates prayer for the farmer before ploughing.

Both Plutarch and Emerson condemn the current moral scepticism. Plutarch (*Moralia* 1. 168) has some sympathy with those who take virtue and vice to be "substantial bodies" but none for those who regard virtue only as a name, a word, not to be pursued if it means loss of wealth or decrease in one's pleasures; and Emerson writes (*CW* 6. 210): "Another scar of this skepticism is the distrust in human virtue. It is believed by well-dressed proprietors that there is no more virtue than they possess; that the solid portion of society exist for the arts of comfort: that life is an affair to put somewhat between the upper and lower mandibles." He develops this theme, the moral corruption of American society, at some length. He would believe with Plutarch and the Stoics that virtue is to be pursued for its own sake and is its own reward.

When weighed against the religion or at least against the philosophy of the classical world, Christianity is found wanting. In 1865 in his journals (10. 101) the criticism of contemporary Christianity becomes stronger and Emerson speaks more vigorously; but the feeling has always been in his mind:

It should be easy to say what I have always felt, that Stanley's *Lives of the Philosophers*, or Marcus Antoninus, are agreeable and suggestive books to me, whilst St. Paul or St. John are not, and I should never think of taking up these to start me on my task, as I often have used Plato or Plutarch. It is because the Bible wears black cloth. It comes with a certain official claim against which the mind revolts.

In the same year he said the same thing in "Character" (*CW* 10. 115):

This charm in the Pagan moralists, of suggestion, the charm of poetry, of mere truth (easily disengaged from their historical accidents which nobody wishes to force on us), the New Testament loses by its connection with a church. Mankind cannot long suffer this loss, and the office of this age is to put all these writings on the eternal footing of equality of origin in the instincts of the human mind. It is certain that each inspired master will gain instantly by the separation from the idolatry of ages.

The pagan moralists, Emerson thinks, must be restored to their rightful place alongside or even above the morality inspired by dogmatic religion.

In 1832 Emerson felt so strongly the unnatural character of contemporary Christianity that he left the pulpit. In the pages of his journals we can trace his changing attitude towards orthodox Christianity, and it is curious to note how often in that year of decision the "pagan moralists" and pagan religion occur to his mind in contrast with the religion of the present day Church. In the very week in which Emerson publicly expressed his repugnance to the current use and significance of the communion service his thoughts turned to the "pagans" (*Journals* 2. 491–492): "We worship in the dead forms of our forefathers. Were not a Socratic paganism better than an effete, superannuated Christianity?" A few days later the name of Jesus appears placed between those of two Greeks, one of whom is Emerson's favorite Plutarchan hero (*Journals* 2. 514): "Socrates believed in man's moral nature and knew and declared the fact that virtue was the supreme beauty. He was capable therefore of enthusiasm. Jesus Christ existed for it. He is its Voice to the world. Phocion felt it, recognized it, but was a man of action, true in act to this conviction." A journal passage of 1835 (3. 538–539) finds that Montaigne "pricks and stings the sense of virtue"; some of his writings "do wind up again for us the spent springs and make virtue possible without the discipline of Christianity."

Montaigne's virtue is a natural one, not imparted by some outside discipline. Emerson had said this before, in 1834 (*Journals* 3. 426–427): "The height of virtue is only to act in a firm belief that moral laws hold. Jesus and Saint Paul and Socrates and Phocion believed, in spite of their senses, that moral law existed and reigned, and so believing, could not have acted otherwise. The sinner lets go his perception of these laws, and then acts agreeably to the lower law of the senses. The logic of the sinner and of the saint is perfect. There is no flaw in either Epicureanism or Stoicism." He continues, "Does not Aristotle distinguish between Temperance for ends and Temperance for love of temperance? Each of these virtues becomes dowdy in a sermon. They must be practised for their elegance; the virtuous man must be a poet and not a drudge of his virtues, to have them perfect." And he had written something like this only a few days before (*Journals* 3. 418–419) in a passage in which he acknowledged his debt to "Greek art, or poetry, or virtue"; here he speaks of the "severe yet human beauty" in all the words, acts, and arts of the Greeks:

. . . especially animating the biography of their men with a wild wisdom and an elegance as wild and handsome as sunshine; the brave anecdotes of Agesilaus, Phocion, and Epaminondas; the death of Socrates, that holy martyr, a death like that of Christ; the purple light of Plato which shines yet into all ages, and is a test of the sublimest intellects — to receive the influences, however partial, of all this, and to speak of it as if it were nothing, or, like a fool, underpraise it in a sermon, because the worshippers are ignorant, and incapable of understanding that there may be degrees and varieties of merit, and that the merit of Paul shall not be less because that of Aristotle is genuine and great, — I call that mean-spirited, if it were Channing or Luther that did it.

In the "Divinity School Address" in 1838 Emerson said plainly what he found deficient in Christianity and what he would like to find there. In this address the moral sentiment reigns supreme. He defines it as "a reverence and delight in the presence of certain divine laws" or "an insight of the perfection of the laws of the soul" which cannot be adequately spoken or written but which shines in "every virtuous act and thought." It is in fact God in man himself. This sentiment, Emerson says (*CW* 1. 125), "corrects the capital mistake of the infant man, who seeks to be great by following the great, and hopes to derive advantage *from another*, — by showing the fountain of all good to be in himself, and that he, equally with every man, is an inlet into the deeps of Reason." Emerson implies that instead of following a great individual as an example of conduct — as, for instance, for so long Plutarch's heroes had been used for models of conduct — we read of and are inspired by great men simply because we perceive that they are one with us and that the same natural principles of morality operate in us as in them.

Such moral principles are found not merely in Jesus or in the Bible, but are also in "the sentences of the oldest time," in the East as well as in Palestine. Jesus is only the greatest of several sure indications of the universal presence of natural moral law, but (*CW* 1. 127): "because the indwelling Supreme Spirit cannot wholly be got rid of, the doctrine of it suffers this perversion, that the divine nature is attributed to one or two persons, and denied to all the rest, and denied with fury." Jesus perceived this moral law, and this was what He meant to show by his incarnation, but Christianity was perverted like Greek and Egyptian religion into cult and myth: "the language that describes Christ . . . is not the style of friendship and enthusiasm to a good and noble heart, but is appropriated and formal, — paints a demigod, as the Orientals or the Greeks would describe Osiris or Apollo." Christianity thus denies manliness to man; it does not permit a man to live according to the law that is in him, but he is required to subordinate his nature to Christ's nature. In contrast, Stoicism has merit. "The sublime is excited in me by the great stoical doctrine, Obey thyself. That which shows God in me, fortifies me." [20] Emerson is thinking of the Greeks when he writes: "The divine bards are the friends of my virtue, of my intellect, of my strength. They admonish me that the gleams which flash across my mind are not mine, but God's; that they had the like, and were not disobedient to the heavenly vision. So I love them. Noble provocations go out from them, inviting me to resist evil; to subdue the world; and to Be. And thus, by his holy thoughts, Jesus serves us, and thus only." Modern preaching harms Jesus by the lack of gladness and beauty in its portrayal of Him. Rather for Emerson in his "Divinity School Address" (*CW* i. 133), "When I see a majestic Epaminondas, or Washington; when I see among my contemporaries a true orator, an upright judge, a dear friend; when I vibrate to the melody and fancy of a poem; I see beauty that is to be desired. And so lovely, and with yet more entire consent of my human being, sounds in my ear the severe music of the bards that have sung of the true God in all ages." Then beginning his vigorous criticism of contemporary preaching and ministry he defines preaching as "the expression of the moral sentiment in application to the duties of life."

For Emerson, preaching has nothing whatsoever to do with either dogma or theology, and his definition applies equally to a church sermon and to a moral essay, the application of the law of morals to everyday life. He feels that preaching has become divorced from life. The remedy is "stoicism" again: "It wants nothing so much as a stern, high, stoical, Christian discipline, to make it know itself and the divinity that speaks through it."[21] Religion, Emerson thinks, wants a man rather than books: "See how nations and races flit by on the sea of time and leave no ripple to tell where they floated or sunk, and one good soul shall make the name of Moses, or of Zeno, or of Zoroaster, revered for ever." This good man to Emerson does not have "the virtue that glitters for the commendation of society": "There are persons who are not actors, not speakers, but influences; persons too great for fame, for display; who disdain eloquence; to whom all we call art and artist, seems too nearly allied to show and by-ends, to the exaggeration of the finite and selfish, and loss of the universal." Such men, the really good and great, have a "bold benevolence, an independence of friends" and "a certain solidity of merit, that has nothing to do with opinion." They are "the Imperial Guard of Virtue, the perpetual reserve, the dictators of fortune." As an example Emerson mentions Napoleon, and his adoption of a military hero and the military figures of speech recall his definition of heroism as "this military attitude of the soul" (*CW* 2. 250). Emerson is always attracted to the military hero, and he often uses as an example one of Plutarch's heroes, as in this address Epaminondas is mentioned. Indeed the new religion that Emerson calls for here is by every evidence the "wild stoicism" of Plutarch. He does not use the term "wild" here but in "Worship" Emerson does say of religion that it "cannot be grafted and keep its wild beauty." He puts it in the form of a quotation (*CW* 6. 214): " 'I have seen,' said a traveller who had known the extremes of society, 'I have seen human nature in all its forms; it is everywhere the same, but the wilder it is, the more virtuous'."

Thus in the "Divinity School Address" Emerson calls for a new, militant, heroic religion. Twice he describes it as "stoical," once he mentions Zeno the founder of the Stoic school, and he names as an example of his ideal of the really good and great man Plutarch's hero Epaminondas. In other places too we can find signs of the impact this loose Stoicism of Plutarch made upon Emerson as a better substitute for current religion. In a journal passage of the next year (*Journals* 5. 250) Emerson appeals again for Stoicism: "Yesterday Mr. Mann's Address on Education. It was full of the modern gloomy view of our democratical institutions, and hence the inference to the importance of schools. But as far as it betrayed distrust, it seemed to pray, as do all our pulpits, for the consolation of Stoicism. A Life in Plutarch would be a perfect rebuke to such a sad discourse. If Christianity is effete, let us try the doctrine of power to endure." A year later the same idea reappears (*Journals* 5. 395):

Yet how is the world better for Goethe? . . . There is Austria, and England, the old and the new, full of old effete institutions and usages, full of men born old, and the question still incessantly asked by the

young, "What shall I do?" with forlorn aspect. But let some strong
Zeno, some nervous Epaminondas, Moses or Isaiah come into our society, and see how he defies it, and enables us to brave it, to come out
of it, and re-make it from the corner-stone. There is hardly a life in
Plutarch that does not infuse a new courage and prowess into the youth
and make him gladder and bolder for his own work.

Here once more are the Stoic Zeno, the Plutarchan hero Epaminondas, and Plutarch himself.

That in his later years Emerson came to realize that his own
philosophy in many ways approaches Stoicism is demonstrated by
his more frequent use of the label "Stoic" or "stoic" and "Stoicism"
or "stoicism." In "The Sovereignty of Ethics," in a passage based
on a journal entry of 1863 (*Journals* 9. 500), he calls for a new
"asceticism, duty and magnanimity" (*CW* 10. 208): "How is the
new generation to be edified? How should it not? The life of those
once omnipotent traditions was really not in the legend, but in the
moral sentiment and the metaphysical fact which the legends en-
closed — and these survive. A new Socrates, or Zeno, or Swedenborg, or Pascal, or a new crop of geniuses like those of the Elizabethan age, may be born in this age, and, with happy heart and a
bias for theism, bring asceticism, duty and magnanimity into vogue
again." He goes on to complain that Stoicism "has now no temples,
no academy, no commanding Zeno or Antoninus. It accuses us that
it has none." The virile morality, the Stoic heroism and endurance
which are deficient in the Church are found in the pagan moralists;
and in "Worship" Emerson foresees a new religion, founded on
"moral science"; "it will fast enough gather beauty, music, picture,
poetry. Was never stoicism so stern and exigent as this shall be."

His contemporary critics who spoke of Emerson's "atheism" were
far from the mark. Those who talked of his "pantheism," if they
meant by that term the pantheism of the Stoics, seem to have perceived more accurately the trend of his thinking. "Emerson est bien
alors un Stoïcien classique à l'école de Montaigne," says Michaud,[22]
and the Stoicism of Montaigne is essentially that of Plutarch. We

have seen too that "Stoicism" is the word which Emerson uses, loosely enough, to describe the character of Plutarch's heroes. In "Heroism" Plutarch is the teacher of Stoicism and in the Plutarch essay Emerson describes Plutarch himself as "this Stoic in his fight with Fortune" and talks of Plutarch's "stoic resistance to low indulgence." This term no doubt Plutarch, the professed foe of the Stoic school, like his follower and imitator Montaigne, would have disliked extremely; but Emerson does not mean by this the classical academic Stoicism in all its details. He is quite well aware that Plutarch is not an academic Stoic; indeed Plutarch, Emerson points out (*CW* 10. 319), "held the balance between the severe Stoic and the indulgent Epicurean." Instead, Plutarch's pantheistic view of religion is roughly similar to that of the Stoics; his "power to endure" sounds Stoic, but it is "a wild courage, a Stoicism not of the schools but of the blood." Thus when Emerson despairs of the Church and of the contemporary religion of dogma, symbol, and institution and when he outlines, as he does in "Worship," what he means by "natural religion," he turns to what he thinks of as the religion of the Greeks, that is, the religion of Phocion and the Plutarchan Greeks.

One writer has described Emerson's religion as "the faith of a moralist," [23] and the term is apt because it brings in both the transcendental and the practical element in his thought; his faith is always linked with implications for action; it may be described as a "practical idealism," for in Emerson theory is never divorced from practice. In "The Scholar" he protests against the abusive use of the term "practical" to "lower activities": "The drygoods man, and the broker, the lawyers and the manufacturers are idealists, and only differ from the philosopher in the intensity of the charge." He would find nothing strange or unacceptable in the term "practical idealism" as applied to religion. It is Stoic and Emersonian. In "The Preacher" Jesus is called a hero and in Emerson's view of Sunday and its observance the same Stoic tone of practical idealism can be observed (*CW* 10. 236):

But certainly on this seventh [day] let us be the children of liberty, of reason, of hope; refresh the sentiment; think as spirits think, who belong to the universe, whilst our feet walk in the streets of a little town and our hands work in a small knot of affairs. We shall find one result, I am sure, — a certain originality and a certain haughty liberty proceeding out of our retirement and self-communion, which streets can never give, infinitely removed from all vaporing and bravado, and which yet is more than a match for any physical resistance.

This last sentence is a description of the Stoicism of the "military hero," that of Plutarch.

The term "practical idealism" suits to an extraordinary degree the Plutarch who was a devoted disciple of Plato, yet was at the same time the "physician of the soul." Plutarch, too, saw signs of divine governance everywhere in the world and divine commands transmitted to man by oracles and daemons. While Emerson makes Puritanism modern and rational, Plutarch's aim is to do exactly this for the dying classical Greek religion of his time.

The term "Stoicism," then, Emerson would probably select as one way of describing his own religion if he were required to state his own views thus briefly. But it has often been pointed out that two contrary forces operate in Emerson's philosophy. Sometimes they are summed up as Transcendental idealism and Yankee realism. Sometimes his thought is described as a dualism of Eastern mysticism and European realism and pragmatism, or a modified Platonic dualism of ideal and real. Perry Miller thinks that both elements, mysticism and practical reason, have a part in New England Puritanism and that we do not have to go beyond New England for the source of the tension in Emerson's thought;[24] the Puritans had a strong social sense of law and order and a practical morality, while at the same time enthusiasm, mysticism, and pantheism are not always heretical but occasionally come very close to adoption as orthodox.

One of these two forces in Emerson is the Christian, Transcendental one, and it constantly changes and is modified with time.

In his youth it is strong and can be seen operating in his poem to
"Grace" and in his tribute to the "old religion"; it is still present
when his doctrine of the "Over-Soul" is found pantheistic and is
called "the latest form of infidelity," or when he expresses his dis-
satisfaction with institutionalized, dogmatic Christianity and finds
his own ideas more akin to those of George Fox and the Quakers.
In 1834 Emerson admitted, "I believe I am more of a Quaker than
anything else. I believe in the 'still small voice,' and that voice is
Christ within us." [25]

But along with this Christian side of Emerson there is also
another force which produces what may be called the classical side
of his nature. As Emerson's Christianity has much of Quakerism
about it, so his classical side may perhaps justifiably be called Stoic.
If he rejected the formalized morality of religious orthodoxy, he
retained the Puritan belief in the possibility of a better order of
society based on an improved morality and on the Puritan linking
of practical affairs with religion. He tends to feel that the Christians
have no monopoly of virtue, and that the pagans, especially the
Stoic heroes, possessed qualities as valuable as those of the Christian
saints. It is the absence of the Christian element in Montaigne which
is the ground of Emerson's complaint that while Montaigne "pricks
and stings the sense of virtue in me," he has no "grace," the gift
only of religion; [26] and on the other hand, we have commented
above on Emerson's repeated complaint about the absence of the
Stoic, manly, practical element in current Christianity.

This loose Stoicism of Plutarch he seems to find most congenial
to him, and when he seeks for an example of the good man, he
would think first of one of Plutarch's heroes. Emerson found this
same Stoicism reinforced elsewhere also. We have observed that
the seventeenth-century English essay, cultivated in imitation of
Montaigne, Plutarch, and Seneca, adopts a Stoic attitude towards
life and that a kind of Neostoicism, introduced by Lipsius, was
prominent in English literature of the seventeenth century. I think
it would prove to be the same kind of "Stoicism" as that of which

Emerson writes. It is no more genuinely Stoic than Plutarch is. It has nothing to do with the physics, metaphysics, or cosmogony of academic Stoicism but is in accord with a general concept of Stoic ethics. It is the attitude which his readers saw in Plutarch's heroes, the pursuit of goodness in accordance with a natural moral law, endurance in the face of suffering, and a disregard for the pleasures and rewards of life, based upon a belief in the transient nature of the individual life itself. It is the attitude which Emerson attributes to the classical heroes in "New England Reformers": "The heroes of ancient and modern fame, Cimon, Themistocles, Alcibiades, Alexander, Caesar, have treated life and fortune as a game to be well and skilfully played, but the stake not to be so valued but that any time it could be held as a trifle light as air, and thrown up."

This kind of Stoicism Emerson met in Plutarch, Montaigne, and the seventeenth-century essayists, and in this loose use of the term he was not original but was very much a follower of his sources. In all his favorite reading Stoicism met his observant eye.

Nor can this Stoicism be found only in Emerson in the nineteenth century. Carlyle read the Stoic philosophers, and one writer thinks that a passage in Carlyle's *Life and Writings of Werner* gives in essence Carlyle's own Stoical theory.[27] Here Carlyle speaks of the principle of "Self-forgetfulness" as "a principle which reigns both in Stoical and Christian ethics, among all German philosophers, especially of the Transcendental class." According to this theory happiness is to be resisted "until it become obedient to love of God, which is only, in the truest sense, love of Goodness. . . ." This is hardly the natural inner law of Emerson, the moral sense which he finds in Plutarch's heroes, but a morality with a much more strongly Christian basis. Carlyle is far more of a Christian than a Stoic, but he uses the term loosely as Emerson does, and it may well be that there is a Stoicism of the nineteenth century which resembles its counterpart in the seventeenth century but which has not received as much attention as the latter.[28] If Emerson in writing essays consciously adopts the moral essay as a literary type and follows the example of Plutarch in the fundamental concept of the hero, in his own religion he again finds in Plutarch his master, a guide to the Stoic heroism which suits him better than the institutional religion of his own country.

V

Emerson had many teachers. All his writing discloses his wide reading and he draws references and quotations from a vast field. Among the manifold influences which might be traced, it is impossible to say that this or that single individual dominated Emerson more than another. The number of direct references to an individual in his writing gives only a very partial clue. Holmes many years ago put together statistics which showed that twenty-seven great names provided more than a thousand references.[29] Shakespeare leads with 112, Napoleon is second with 84, Plato is mentioned 81 times while Plutarch ranks fourth in frequency with 70 references. Shakespeare leads by reason of repeated references to him as one of the great, representative men; Napoleon is used as the example of the military hero. Plato and Plutarch are the first two names of men who might be called Emerson's literary sources. If we were to add to the total number of references to Plutarch the number of passages in which Emerson borrows an anecdote or an expression from Plutarch, consciously or unconsciously, without naming him, and the references to Plutarch's Greek heroes, Plutarch would move to a position in the list above that of Plato and probably above that of Napoleon. Then too at least some of Emerson's Platonism is derived from Plutarch, one of the first great Platonists. But besides these Plutarchan elements in Emerson we must also put the more subtle and intangible influence exerted by Plutarch's "heroism," by his attitude to history and the great men in history, by the form of the essay which he used in the *Moralia*, by his literary style, and, since Plutarch to Emerson means the

English translations, by the special style and expressions of the translators.

The influence of Plutarch remains fairly constant throughout Emerson's career. He knew his name and a number of stories from Plutarch when he was a boy; he thought of Plutarch repeatedly during the years when he was contemplating a literary career and was uncertain as to which literary form he should adopt. His influence seems greatest between 1837 and 1840 and during that period, besides many journal notes on Plutarch, the two essays "Love" and "Friendship" which are most strongly Plutarchan were written. Thereafter, if the reading of Plutarch does not always show obviously in his writing, still there are few essays which do not refer to him or make use of Plutarch in one way or another. Finally, in his old age, the request to write the Plutarch essay turned Emerson to his old favorite and the journal references and quotations again become more numerous. His liking for the Plutarchan hero and for the style of the "Several Hands" translation, his predilection for Plutarch's "Stoicism" over Christianity find expression from time to time over a space of many years. The natural morality of Plutarch had a perennial appeal.

The links which connect Plutarch the moralist of Chaeronea, where Greece's last battle for liberty was lost, with Emerson the moralist of Concord, where the fight for America's freedom was begun, are manifold. While many people, contemporary, nearly contemporary, or of the distant past, exerted their respective influences upon America's nineteenth-century oracle, it looks very much as though Emerson was speaking personally and for himself when he wrote, "we are more indebted to him than to all the ancient authors."

BIBLIOGRAPHY
NOTES
INDEX

BIBLIOGRAPHY

I list here all the more significant works used in writing this book, the titles omitted being several works only remotely connected with Plutarch or Emerson, which are referred to once or twice in the notes to the chapters.

Alcott, Bronson, *Emerson: An Estimate of His Character and Genius* (Boston, 1882).

Arnold, E. V., *Roman Stoicism* (Cambridge, 1911).

Barker, Sir Ernest, *Traditions of Civility* (Cambridge, 1948).

Brown, Stuart G., "Emerson's Platonism," *New England Quarterly*, 18: 325–345 (September 1945).

Bush, Douglas, *English Literature in the Earlier Seventeenth Century*, Oxford History of English Literature (Oxford, 1945).

Cabot, James E., *A Memoir of Ralph Waldo Emerson*, 2 vols. (Boston, 1887).

Cameron, Kenneth W., *Ralph Waldo Emerson's Reading* (Raleigh, N. C., 1941).

—— *Emerson the Essayist*, 2 vols. (Raleigh, N. C., 1945).

—— "Emerson's Early Reading List, 1819–1824." *Bulletin of the New York Public Library*, 55: 315–324 (July 1951).

Canby, Henry Seidel, *Classic Americans* (New York, 1931).

Carpenter, Frederick I., *Emerson Handbook* (New York, 1953).

Celières, André, *The Prose Style of Emerson* (Paris, 1936).

Christy, Arthur E., *The Orient in American Transcendentalism* (New York, 1932).

Croiset, A., and Croiset, M., *Histoire de la Littérature Grecque*, 2nd ed., 5 vols. (Paris, 1901).

Dill, Samuel, *Roman Society from Nero to Marcus Aurelius* (London, 1905).

Dobree, Bonamy, *The Broken Cistern* (London, 1954).

Elliott, George Roy, "On Emerson's 'Grace' and 'Self-Reliance'," *New England Quarterly*, 2: 93–104 (January 1929. Reprinted in *Humanism and Imagination* [Chapel Hill, 1938]).

Firkins, Oscar W., *Ralph Waldo Emerson* (Boston, 1915).

Foerster, Norman, *American Criticism* (Boston, 1928).

Foster, C. H., "Emerson as American Scripture," *New England Quarterly*, 16: 91–105 (March 1943).

Frothingham, Octavius B., *Transcendentalism in New England* (Boston and New York, 1876).

Garrod, Herbert W., *Poetry and the Criticism of Life* (Cambridge, Mass., 1931).

Glover, Terrot R., *Conflict of Religions in the Later Roman Empire*, 9th ed. (London, 1930).

Goddard, Henry C., *Studies in New England Transcendentalism* (New York, 1908).

Hale, Edward Everett, ed., *Ralph Waldo Emerson: Two Unpublished Essays* (Boston, 1896).

Harrison, John S., *The Teachers of Emerson* (New York, 1910).

Hickes, R. Dawes, *Stoic and Epicurean* (New York, 1910).

Highet, Gilbert, *The Classical Tradition* (Oxford, 1949).

Hirzel, Rudolf, *Plutarch* (Leipzig, 1912).

Holmes, Oliver Wendell, *Ralph Waldo Emerson*, American Men of Letters Series (Boston, 1884).

Hopkins, Vivian, "Emerson and Bacon," *American Literature*, 29: 408–430 (January 1958).

—— "Emerson and Cudworth," *American Literature*, 23: 80–98 (March 1951).

——*Spires of Form: A Study of Emerson's Aesthetic Theory* (Cambridge, Mass., 1951).

Houghton, Walter E., Jr., *The Formation of Thomas Fuller's "Holy and Profane States"* (Cambridge, Mass., 1938).

Kirk, Rudolf, ed., *Joseph Hall: "Heaven upon Earth" and "Characters of Vertues and Vices"* (New Brunswick, 1948).

Mahaffy, John P., *The Silver Age of the Greek World* (Chicago and London, 1906).

Matthiessen, Frank O., *American Renaissance* (New York, 1941).

McCormick, J. O. "Emerson's Theory of Human Greatness," *New England Quarterly*, 26: 291–314 (September 1953).

McGiffert, Arthur C., Jr., *Young Emerson Speaks* (Boston, 1938).

McNulty, John B., "Emerson's Friends and the Essay on Friendship," *New England Quarterly*, 19: 390–394 (September 1946).

Michaud, Régis, *Mystiques et Réalistes Anglo-Saxons* (Paris, 1918).

Miller, Perry, *The American Transcendentalists: their Prose and Poetry* (New York, 1957).

———— "Emersonian Genius and the American Democracy," *New England Quarterly*, 26: 27–44 (March 1953).

———— "From Jonathan Edwards to Emerson," *New England Quarterly*, 13: 589–617 (December 1940. Reprinted in *Errand into the Wilderness* [Cambridge, Mass., 1956]).

———— *The Transcendentalists: an Anthology* (Cambridge, Mass., 1950).

Murdock, Kenneth B., *Literature and Theology in Colonial New England* (Cambridge, Mass., 1949).

Norton, Charles Eliot, ed., *The Correspondence of Thomas Carlyle and Ralph Waldo Emerson, 1834–1872*, 2 vols., (London, 1883).

Norton, Grace, *Le Plutarque de Montaigne* (Boston and New York, 1906).

Oakesmith, John, *The Religion of Plutarch* (London, 1902).

Paul, Sherman, *Emerson's Angle of Vision: Man and Nature in American Experience* (Cambridge, Mass., 1952).

Rusk, Ralph L., *The Life of Ralph Waldo Emerson* (New York, 1949).

Sanborn, Franklin B., ed., *The Genius and Character of Emerson* (Boston, 1885).

Schneider, Herbert W., *A History of American Philosophy* (New York, 1946).

Seybold, Ethel, *Thoreau: The Quest and the Classics* (New Haven, 1951).

Spiller, Robert E., "Ralph Waldo Emerson," *Literary History of the United States*, eds. Spiller *et al.* (New York, 1948), I, 358–387.

———— *The Cycle of American Literature* (New York, 1955).

Strauch, Carl F., "Emerson's Sacred Science," *PMLA*, 73: 237–250 (June 1958).

———— "Gérando: Source for Emerson," *Modern Language Notes*, 58: 64–67 (January 1943).

———— "The Importance of Emerson's Skeptical Mood," *Harvard Library Bulletin*, 11: 117–139 (Winter, 1957).

———— "The Year of Emerson's Poetic Maturity: 1834," *Philological Quarterly*, 34: 353–377 (October 1955).

———— "The Sources of Emerson's 'Song of Nature'," *Harvard Library Bulletin*, 9: 300–334 (Autumn 1955).

Sutcliffe, Emerson G., "Emerson's Theories of Literary Expression," *University of Illinois Studies in Language and Literature*, 8: 9–143 (1923).

Trench, Richard C., *A Popular Introduction to Plutarch* (London, 1873).

Trevelyan, Humphry, *Goethe and the Greeks* (Cambridge, 1941).

──── *The Popular Background of Goethe's Hellenism* (London, 1934).

Villey, Pierre, *Les Sources et L'Evolution des Essaies de Montaigne*, 2 vols. (Paris, 1908).

Wellek, René, "Emerson and German Philosophy," *New England Quarterly*, 16: 41–62 (March 1943).

Whicher, Stephen, *Freedom and Fate: an Inner Life of Ralph Waldo Emerson* (Philadelphia, 1953).

Williamson, George, *The Senecan Amble* (Chicago, 1951).

Young, Charles Lowell, *Emerson's Montaigne* (New York, 1941).

Ziegler, K., *Plutarchos von Chaironeia* (Stuttgart, 1949).

NOTES

1. The most recent and most scholarly study of Plutarch is K. Ziegler, *Plutarchos von Chaironeia* (Stuttgart, 1949); the only single work on Plutarch in English is R. C. Trench, *A Popular Introduction to Plutarch* (London, 1873); S. Dill, *Roman Society from Nero to Marcus Aurelius* (London, second edition 1905 and later reprints) is useful and the best essay on Plutarch in English is the chapter in T. R. Glover, *Conflict of Religions in the Early Roman Empire* (London, 9th edition 1930); see also J. P. Mahaffy, *The Silver Age of the Greek World* (Chicago and London, 1906). A. and M. Croiset discuss Plutarch the writer in the fifth volume of *Histoire de la Littérature Grecque* (Paris, second edition 1901); one aspect of Plutarch is dealt with by John Oakesmith, *The Religion of Plutarch* (London, 1902); on his demonology and religion see also U. von Wilamowitz-Moellendorf, *Der Glaube der Hellenen* (Basel, 1956), II, 489–497. R. Hirzel, *Plutarch* (Heft 4 of "Das Erbe der Alten," eds. Crusius, Immisch, and Zielinski [Leipzig, 1912]), traces the history of the study and use of Plutarch in literature down to modern times and collects all the more significant references to Plutarch in later literature; however, Hirzel was unfamiliar with Plutarch in America in the nineteenth century and especially with his influence on Emerson. See also Gilbert Highet, *The Classical Tradition* (Oxford, 1949).

2. Thoreau quotes from the *Moralia* a number of times; see Ethel Seybold, *Thoreau: The Quest and the Classics* (New Haven, 1951), p. 38 and fn. 9. In American schools the *Lives* were commonly used in the teaching of history; see, for example, Julian Hawthorne, *Hawthorne and his Wife*, 2 vols., (Boston and New York, 1884), I, 61.

3. Croiset, *Littérature Grecque*, V, 513.

4. For a good recent account of English Neostoicism see Rudolf Kirk's introduction to his edition of Joseph Hall's *Heaven upon Earth and Characters of Vertues and Vices* (New Brunswick, 1948). See also Douglas Bush, *English Literature in the Earlier Seventeenth Century*, vol. 5 of the Oxford History of English Literature (Oxford, 1945), pp. 314–315. Bush quotes (p. 339) Sir Thomas Browne: "truly there are singular pieces in the Philosophy of Zeno, and doctrine of the Stoics, which I perceive, delivered in a Pulpit, pass for current Divinity." On Christian Stoicism see also F. P. Wilson,

Elizabethan and Jacobean (Oxford, 1945), pp. 28ff. where the Christian Stoicism of Joseph Hall is discussed, and P. A. Smith, "Bishop Hall, 'Our English Seneca'," *PMLA* 63: 1191–1204 (December, 1948); A. Chew, "Joseph Hall and Neo-Stoicism," *PMLA* 65: 1130–1145 (December, 1950), argues that Hall's Neostoicism is not Senecan, but English and traditional.

5. Emerson in his essay on Plutarch says: ". . . it is curious that the Lives were translated and printed in Latin . . . more than a century before the original Works were yet printed. For whilst the Lives were translated in Rome in 1470, and the Morals, part by part, soon after, the first printed edition of the Greek Works did not appear until 1572." There is really nothing curious, for Emerson is incorrect here in the date of the first printed edition of Plutarch in Greek. It is true that in 1572 the first printed edition of the complete works together (that of Stephanus) appeared, but the *Lives* were printed in Greek in 1517 at Florence and the *Moralia* had been printed by the Aldine Press in 1509, the same year in which a portion of the *Moralia* became the second Greek book to be printed in France.

6. See W. G. Crane, *Wit and Rhetoric in the Renaissance* (New York, 1937), chapters 8–10.

7. Pierre Villey, *Les Sources et L'Evolution des Essaies de Montaigne*, 2 vols. (Paris, 1908), II, 107. See also Highet, *Classical Tradition*, pp. 185ff.

8. The quotation is from the dedicatory epistle of 1612 which was replaced by another epistle in the printed work. See the edition of W. Aldis Wright (*Bacon's Essays* [London and New York, 1887]), p. xii.

9. Bacon says in "Of Truth" (*Works*, eds. Ellis, Spedding, Heath [London, 1858], VI, 378–379): "There is no vice that doth so cover a man with shame as to be found false and perfidious. And therefore Montaigne saith prettily, when he inquired the reason, why the word of the lie should be such a disgrace and such an odious charge? Saith he, *If it be well weighed, to say that a man lieth, is as much as to say, as that he is brave towards God and a coward towards men.* For a lie faces God, and shrinks from man." In "Of Giving the Lye" Montaigne writes (*All the Essays of Michael Seigneur de Montaigne* [Cotton's translation, reprinted from the 3rd English ed.] London, 1869), p. 562: "Lying is a base unworthy vice; a vice that one of the ancients pourtrays in the most odious colours, when he says, 'that it is to manifest a contempt of God, and withal a fear of men'."

10. R. C. Trench, *Plutarch*, p. 135.

11. Sir Ernest Barker, *Traditions of Civility* (Cambridge, 1948), p. 26.

12. See Walter E. Houghton, Jr., *The Formation of Thomas Fuller's "Holy and Profane States"* (Cambridge, Mass., 1938), pp. 170–171. The translator of *The French Academie* in 1586 expressed as the object of the book "the practice of vertue in life, and not the bare knowledge and contemplation thereof in braine," and the title page of the work reads: "The French Academie, wherein is discoursed the institution of manners, and whatsoever els concerneth the good and happie life of all estates and callings, by preceptes

of doctrine, and examples of the lives of ancient Sages and famous men."
Houghton points out that in 1623 Degory Wheare in his opening lecture
at Oxford indicates that biography is "the history of persons" whose ultimate
end was "Practice, and not Knowledge or Contemplation." Therefore history
should "gather, note and lay up . . . Moral, Oeconomick, and Politick
Examples, that the Reader may thereby be enabled to act prudently,
and to form his life by the Rules of Vertue."

13. See Trench, *Plutarch*, pp. 75–78 and Bush, *Seventeenth Century*, p. 384.
The well-known lines in a sonnet

> . . . and the repeated air
> Of sad Electra's poet had the power
> To save the Athenian walls from ruin bare

are an allusion to a passage in the life of Lysander. At least one passage in
Paradise Lost (I, 549–559) owes something to the life of Lycurgus. The cata-
logue of the pagan gods seems influenced by "Why the Oracles Cease to
Give Answers" and "Of Isis and Osiris." See also George L. Whiting, *Milton's
Literary Milieu* (Chapel Hill, 1939), pp. 176–185.

14. K. B. Murdock, *Literature and Theology in Colonial New England*
(Cambridge, Mass., 1949), p. 68.

15. Cotton Mather, *Magnalia Christi Americana*, quoted by Murdock,
Literature and Theology, pp. 68–69. In this century, when modern science
was developing, it is interesting to see that Plutarch's works on natural
science were still considered reliable scientific documents. Kepler, the German
astronomer, translated Plutarch's "Of the Face in the Orb of the Moon" and
tried to emend and complete the text. He wrote in a letter of 1630: "I have
supplemented some lacunae to make sense of the whole, as this was impossible
to Xylander, who was not an astronomer by profession." Xylander was the
editor of Plutarch and his text was standard until the nineteenth century.
See Carola Baumgardt, *Johannes Kepler: Life and Letters* (New York, 1951),
pp. 175, 187. Baumgardt observes (p. 175, fn. 32) that Xylander's edition was
used by Karl Marx in his doctoral dissertation.

16. *Werke*, 60 vols. (Weimar, 1887–1919), XLI, 265.

17. Barker, *Traditions of Civility*, p. 153, fn. 1. Emerson knew another
British Plutarch, that of Francis Wrangham (1816).

18. Highet, *Classical Tradition*, p. 395.

19. Lessing speaks of "the dazzling antithesis of the Greek Voltaire, that
painting is silent poetry and poetry vocal painting" which he read in
Moralia 5. 402 or 2. 50; Emerson also noted and quoted this apothegm (*CW*
7. 52).

20. In his rectorial address at Edinburgh University, Carlyle deplores
rushing after "fine speech" and chooses the silence of Phocion against the
oratory of Demosthenes, which he makes fun of, quoting several of Plutarch's
anecdotes of Phocion.

21. Hirzel, *Plutarch*, pp. 177–178, 190.

22. See *Causeries du Lundi*, 5th ed. (Paris, n.d.), I, 289–290; IV, 450–470; XII, 313–314.

23. Pierre Villey, *Sources*, II, 93–113. See also Highet, *Classical Tradition*, pp. 185ff.

24. On the "moral discourse" in the sixteenth century see Crane, *Wit and Rhetoric*, chapter 8.

25. On the debt of English literature and especially of the essay to Senecan and Stoic influences see Douglas Bush, *Seventeenth Century*. Bush says (p. 182): "Senecan or Lipsian prose, loose or curt or a mixture of both, was frequently wedded to Stoic thought, and among the offspring of the marriage were the English essayists, whose moral didacticism and studied informality made them the natural exponents of the new modes." There is a strong current of anti-Ciceronianism and a call for the short, pithy, axiomatic style evident in stylistic discussions of the seventeenth century; see George Williamson, *The Senecan Amble* (Chicago, 1951). Cicero and Tacitus were the representatives of "Asianism" and elaborate style; Seneca and Plutarch are adduced as examples of the casual, conversational style. Seneca is usually given first place because of his supposed influence on Montaigne and Bacon, but consideration of the debt of both these to Plutarch, and especially considering Montaigne's remarks on Plutarch's style, I think that Plutarch should be given more prominence in the stylistic controversy. For Plutarch as a model of the short style, see, for example, Williamson, *Senecan Amble*, pp. 106, 108, fn. 2.

26. John Wilkins' *Ecclesiastes* includes some of the "heathen moralists" among "authors proper for a Divine." He gives first place to the Stoics, adding Bacon and Lipsius. At the same time he says of Plutarch, "De moribus nemo felicius scripsit quam Plutarchus." See Williamson, *Senecan Amble*, p. 255, fn. 1.

27. R. C. Trench, *Plutarch*, p. 71.

28. Leon Howard, *Herman Melville* (Berkeley, 1951), p. 334. The poem is in H. P. Vincent, *Collected Poems of Herman Melville* (Chicago, 1947), pp. 209–215.

29. *The Letters of Theodore Roosevelt*, ed. E. E. Morison, 8 vols., (Cambridge, Mass., 1951), III, 606.

CHAPTER II. EMERSON'S ACQUAINTANCE WITH PLUTARCH

1. *CW* 10. 569–570. It is interesting to see his father's classical training appearing in the writings of Emerson's son, brought up on Plutarch. His writings (*The Essays, Addresses and Poems of Edward W. Emerson* [Cambridge, Mass., 1930]) contain many references to classical literature, art, and mythology; he mentions his father's interest in Plutarch (p. 211) and his classicism (pp. 227, 230–231, 242) and quotes from the *Moralia* (pp. 16,

243; the latter quotation he may have found in his father's essay on Plutarch).

2. *Journals* 3. 546; *CW* 6. 312, 7. 119–120, 368; J. E. Cabot, *A Memoir of Ralph Waldo Emerson*, 2 vols. (Boston and New York, 1887), I, 57; *Journals* 8. 147; *Letters* 2. 9.

3. *Letters* 6. 330–332.

4. *Letters* 1. 67.

5. *Letters* 5. 164.

6. Emerson is quite frank about his use of the classical languages in translation and a well-known passage in "Books" has often been quoted as an indication that he is not friendly towards the study of the classical languages. We should remember, however, that he was able to read at least ordinary Greek and Latin fairly easily when it was necessary. Translations save time and give him the central idea and the meaning which in many cases was all that he required. In "New England Reformers" for example, he protests against the amount of time and labor devoted in the American colleges to the ancient languages when very few of the students will ever have occasion to use them. Yet sometimes he changes his attitude and feels that the continual use of translations works harm (*Journals* 8. 289–290). He expresses a more balanced view and one which was probably his own final conclusion when he advises the scholar (quoted in notes to "Books," *CW* 7. 408): "I am glad you have so many of the Greek Tragedies. Read them largely and swiftly in translation to get the movement and flow; and then a little in the original every day. For the Greek is the fountain of language. The Latin has a definite shore line, but the Greek is without bounds." A single reference, or even several references to or quotations from a classical author, does not by any means indicate, however, that Emerson read even a complete translation of that author; a journal reference to Tertullian he finds in Clarkson's *Life of William Penn*, he quotes Vegetius from Burton, and so on. Many of the quotations from the Greek poets were found in Plutarch or in Kennett's *Greek Poets*. Montaigne, Cudworth, and Thomas Taylor provide other classical quotations, either in the original or in translation.

Emerson can of course handle Greek or Latin well enough to note down in his journals a line or two of Homer, a phrase of Pindar, or to write in fair Latin a more private and personal paragraph, but when Greek or Latin appear in the journals it is usually a familiar tag which appears again and again.

Emerson's direct acquaintance with classical literature was not as deep as that of Thoreau or Theodore Parker or Convers Francis but it was almost certainly wider. The lists of books which he borrowed from libraries over the years give some indication of his classical reading. The Greeks far outnumber the Romans. In translation he read at various times Aristophanes, Arrian, Plato, Eusebius, Sophocles, Aristotle (the *Ethics* and *Politics*), Herodotus, Euripides, Homer, Hesiod, Plutarch, Marcus Aurelius, Aeschylus,

Demosthenes, Callimachus and Theognis, Plotinus, Iamblichus, Porphyry, Proclus, Pliny, Ovid, Vitruvius. In the original he read Demosthenes in 1830, Cicero in 1831, Sophocles in 1836; Plato was read in 1846 and in the next year Emerson evidently read Martial (and he said that he often took a Horace or Martial in his pocket on a train journey). There is then a gap of some years in Emerson's reading in the classics, but Homer appears in the book list for 1866, Pindar in 1870, Horace in 1871. See K. W. Cameron, *Ralph Waldo Emerson's Reading* (Raleigh, N.C., 1941).

7. The college prize essays were published with an introduction by Edward Everett Hale (*Ralph Waldo Emerson: Two Unpublished Essays* [Boston, 1896]). We are prevented from making a categorical statement about Emerson's acquaintance with Plutarch during his college career by the fact that no journals of these years are extant and, if the list of books which he borrowed from libraries is now fairly complete, Plutarch does not appear there at this time. The journals for 1820–1821 show a remarkable range of reading and over twenty of the quotations are classical, but Plutarch is not mentioned.

8. In "The Present State of Ethical Philosophy" Emerson says of Socrates' attribution of his successes to his daemon: "It is probable that the philosopher adopted the successful artifice of Lycurgus, referring his instinctions to higher agents in order to enforce their obedience." This might have been recalled from Plutarch's life of Lycurgus but Emerson could have found the name elsewhere.

9. In the journals of 1823 the single trace of Plutarch is in Emerson's motto for this year's journal. The motto is the Greek *dos pou stō* and is the first part of Archimedes' famous remark, "Give me a place to stand on and I shall move the universe." This too is a familiar Greek tag and we could not, on this evidence alone, say that Emerson had read Plutarch in Greek. It occurs in the life of Marcellus which is first definitely referred to in a letter of 1828; however Emerson's son remembered the stories of Archimedes from his youthful reading of this life with his father, and Emerson at least knew this epigram in Greek (*Journals* 2. 271; *Letters* 1. 358). In 1825 (*Journals* 2. 48) there appears a passage on Tyrtaeus which recalls the *Lives* fairly closely, see below, p. 227.

10. K. W. Cameron, *Emerson the Essayist* (Raleigh, N.C., 1945), II, 161–163.

11. Cameron, *Ralph Waldo Emerson's Reading*, p. 46.

12. C. L. Young in *Emerson's Montaigne* (New York, 1941), p. 111, fn. 3, notes the minor changes in Langhorne's wording which Emerson made; he observes that Montaigne quotes this passage in the third book of the *Essays* but there can be no doubt that Emerson used Langhorne here. He used this anecdote also in sermon no. 22 and in the lecture "Truth" in 1861.

13. The letters of this year (*Letters* 1. 193) contain another Plutarch tag, the remark of Julius Caesar to the sailors, "You are carrying Caesar and his

fortunes"; Emerson quotes the Latin, which indicates that his source was Suetonius or some collection of aphorisms; Plutarch gives it in the life of Caesar and twice in the *Moralia*, 1. 247, 4. 205, but it is also in Suetonius, Appian, Dio Cassius, Lucan and Valerius Maximus; Bacon gives a Latin version in "Of Fortune" and in the second book of *The Advancement of Learning*.

14. In a letter of 1829 (*Letters* 1. 279) he writes that "in New Hampshire generally is a most Catonic desire that houses should be houses & not *seem* such." Rusk suggests that this passing reference to the simplicity of Cato may come from Plutarch, but prefers as a source Bacon's essay "Of Building"; Emerson may also have read Seneca's essay on Cato's house.

15. *Letters* 1. 254 (December 1828). We may here mention the volumes of Plutarch which Emerson actually owned; in his library at Concord or in the Houghton Library of Harvard University there are still extant the following:

(1) Two volumes only (vol. III and one which contains parts of original vols. I and V) of the fifth edition of the *Moralia*, in the "Several Hands" translation, published in London in 1718.

(2) Vols. I–VI and VIII of Langhorne's *Lives*, published in Philadelphia, 1822.

(3) *The Beauties of Plutarch*, by Alfred Howard, published in Boston, 1831.

(4) Vols. I, II, and IV of Goodwin's edition of the *Moralia* in the "Several Hands," translation, Boston, 1870. This is the revision for which Emerson's Plutarch essay was written as an introduction, and the first volume is a presentation copy from the publishers.

(5) Six volumes of the Tauchnitz edition of the Greek text of the *Moralia*; vols. I–III and V are dated 1829 and vols. II and VI belong to the new edition of 1866; Cabot says that Emerson bought this set for the purpose of comparing the Greek text with Goodwin's revision of the translation when he was writing the introduction.

16. The passage is reproduced in Cameron, *Emerson the Essayist*, I, 19–36; a second quotation from Plutarch (on Anaxagoras) in the same section of the *Journals* (2. 337) comes also from Gérando, who found it in Plutarch's life of Pericles.

17. See C. F. Strauch, "Gérando: a Source for Emerson," *Modern Language Notes*, 58: 64–67 (January 1943), and "The Year of Emerson's Poetic Maturity: 1834," *Philological Quarterly* 34: 353–377 (October 1955).

18. O. W. Holmes, *Ralph Waldo Emerson*, American Men of Letters Series (Boston, 1884), p. 380.

19. *Moralia* 1. 208, 296, 2. 471; 5. 101–102; life of Themistocles.

20. *Moralia* 1. 166; there is another echo of the Plutarchan phrase in "Nature": Emerson says that in the woods "a perennial festival is dressed." Emerson used this in a variant version of the lecture "Ethical Writers" (1836); see *The Early Lectures of Ralph Waldo Emerson*, eds. Stephen E.

Whicher and Robert E. Spiller (Cambridge, Mass., 1959), I, 526; he used it also in sermon no. 136.

21. Quoted by H. C. Goddard, *Studies in New England Transcendentalism* (New York, 1908), p. 71.

22. *Letters*, 2. 77, fn. 92; Rusk in *Letters* 4. 99, fn. 356.

23. H. W. Garrod, *Poetry and the Criticism of Life* (Cambridge, Mass., 1931), pp. 111–112.

24. For Emerson's acquaintance with Montaigne on Plutarch, see *Journals* 4. 406 and *Letters* 2. 123. Rusk, in his notes on this passage in the Letters, points to Montaigne's "Defence of Seneca and Plutarch" but adds that it does not fit Emerson's comment well; the "Defence" has three references to Cicero, but none of them could be called "railing at Cicero." But in "Of Books" the paragraph on Seneca and Plutarch is immediately followed by two paragraphs which vigorously attack Cicero's style and method. In this letter, then, Emerson refers to "Of Books." In writing the letter he recalled the comparison of Seneca and Plutarch and in error referred to the essay, not by its title, but by the confusing words "On Seneca and Plutarch." He mentions both essays of Montaigne together in *Journals* 3. 538–539.

25. This was used also in "The Comic"; see below, pp. 217–219.

26. The references to and quotations from specific passages in the *Moralia* may be found in the following places in Goodwin's edition: *CW* 10. 298: *Moralia* 5. 391–392; 303: 5. 405 (*cf.* 2. 44); 304: 3. 74, 2. 399; 305: 1. 179; 307: 4. 13, 3. 82, 4. 56, 1. 478, 5. 426; 308: 2. 388, 3. 402, 3. 403, 2. 371; 309: 1. 451, 4. 166; 310: 3. 152, 3. 160–161, 3. 252, 4. 73, 5. 65; 312: 3. 200, 4. 65; 313: 4. 74, 2. 56, 4. 404, 4. 170, 4. 170, 2. 193; 314: 2. 199, 5. 393, 5. 394, 1. 69; 315: 4. 201, 1. 475–516, 4. 207–208, 1. 49, 1. 35, 3. 38; 316: 2. 374, 1. 59, 3. 374, 3. 373, 3. 374; 318: 1. 478–479; 319: 1. 479, 3. 383; 320: 3. 394; 321: 2. 477.

27. See below, p. 98.

28. For the Seneca epigram, see J. S. Harrison, *The Teachers of Emerson* (New York, 1910), p. 226; for the incorrect dating, see above, Chapter I, fn. 5.

CHAPTER III. GREEK SIMPLICITY

1. *Gedanken über die Nachahmung der Griechischen Werke* . . . (1755), p. 21.

2. *Classical Tradition*, p. 374.

3. See Humphry Trevelyan, *Goethe and the Greeks* (Cambridge, 1941), for a picture of Goethe's changing attitude toward the classical world.

4. *CW* 2. 26.

5. *CW* 2. 24, 26.

6. *Journals* 8. 525.

7. *Early Lectures*, eds. Whicher and Spiller, I, 257.

8. *Journals* 8. 360–361. That Emerson is more interested in the occult or spiritual meaning than in the actual story of the myth and that in this he follows the example of Plutarch, has been pointed out by C. F. Strauch, "The Sources of Emerson's 'Song of Nature'," *Harvard Library Bulletin*, 11: 319–320 (Autumn, 1955).

9. *CW* 2. 24–26.

10. *Early Lectures*, I, 192, and note 8.

11. In a penetrating analysis of Emerson's Hellenism, Norman Foerster (*American Criticism* [Boston and New York, 1928], pp. 81ff.) shows how Emerson's concept of the "naturalness," "boyishness," and "the engaging unconsciousness of childhood" is a false Hellenism which fails to take into consideration the Greek "humanistic control" or concern with moral principles and thinks that the source of Emerson's fallacy was that, dominated by an Oriental and Christian sense of the supernatural, when he found that the Greeks did not have this sense developed, he ascribed to them the false spontaneity of the Romantic Movement. This is a helpful observation when applied to the Greeks of the fifth century B.C. The trouble seems to be that Emerson attributes this "naturalness" and spontaneity to all the Greeks, for example in "History" to the Greeks of both Homer and Xenophon. Foerster's "humanistic control" or insight into moral principles is certainly an important element in the Greek view of life from the sixth century on, but the morality of Homeric times, while by no means primitive or "childlike" may not unfairly be called "natural" in the sense that is it not based on a developed metaphysical or ethical system. Emerson's fallacy of Greek spontaneity is based upon his inability to see any development in Greek humanism and is clearly connected with his failure to understand the elaborate skill of Greek artistic accomplishment and the high civilization which Greece possessed.

Foerster (p. 81) finds Emerson totally free from what he calls the "formalistic deviation" of nineteenth century pseudo-Hellenism. But, as we shall see, Emerson's essays are really moral essays of the classical type.

12. *Journals* 3. 419.

13. *CW* 2. 248.

14. The story of Thales measuring the pyramid is in *Moralia* 2. 5; the couplet on Pythagoras is quoted several times in the *Moralia*; Emerson here uses the "Several Hands" version of *Moralia* 2. 174 but is probably quoting from memory, for he uses "hecatomb" for the "Several Hands" version "splendid ox"; he notes this in his journals in 1865 (*Journals* 10. 103). The story of the advice of the oracle to double the altar at Delos (Emerson wrote "Delphian" for "Delian") and the explanation of its meaning are given by Plutarch in *Moralia* 2. 385–386 and the anecdote is referred to in *Moralia* 4. 482. In journal "RS" Emerson notes that the story is also in Valerius Maximus, in Webster's *Orations*, and in Tennemann's *Life of Plato*.

15. Emerson indicates that he read this in Goodwin's version of *Moralia*

2. 97–98. It is a well-known passage; Rollin quotes it from Plutarch and Montaigne refers to it in "Of Physiognomy."

16. *Journals* 4. 213.

17. *Journals* 6. 41.

18. Towards the end of "Intellect" a conventional classical theme recurs: "The ancient sentence said 'Let us be silent, for so are the gods'." Emerson's habit of referring to "the ancients" a remark which he has read in Plutarch warns us that this probably came to him from Plutarch; he may have been thinking of "we have men to teach us to speak, but the Gods are they that teach us silence" (*Moralia* 4. 230); in 1830 he had noted it in Jeremy Taylor (*Journals* 2. 412; see below, p. 238). In "Circles" (*CW* 2. 311) Emerson wrote, "good as is discourse, silence is better, and shames it."

19. The source of the comment on Aristides in "Domestic Life" is the "Apothegms of Kings," *Moralia* 1. 210 and perhaps also the life of Aristides. The references in "Manners" to the poverty of Socrates, Diogenes, and Epaminondas are probably from Plutarch. The frugality of Socrates' fare is mentioned in *Moralia* 1. 150 (Emerson quoted this passage in a lecture at Manchester, England), 2. 390, 472; there is an anecdote of Epaminondas' self-denial and simplicity in the "Apothegms," *Moralia* 1. 222, and the familiar anecdotes of Diogenes the Cynic are in *Moralia* 1. 67, 283; 2. 458.

20. I owe this observation about Emerson's agrarianism to Professor S. E. Whicher, who referred me to the doctrines of John Taylor in A. M. Schlesinger, Jr., *The Age of Jackson* (Boston, 1946); see also A. I. Ladu, "Emerson: Whig or Democrat," *New England Quarterly*, 13: 419–441 (September 1940), and A. C. Kern, "Emerson and Economics," *New England Quarterly*, 13: 678–696 (December 1940).

21. In speaking of "fair water" in "Heroism" (*CW* 2. 254) Emerson seems to recall Plutarch's statement about Demosthenes (*Moralia* 5. 53): "He says of himself that he always drank fair water." In 1834 Emerson had noted this in his *Journals* (3. 386–387) among a number of extracts from this work, the life of Demosthenes in the "Lives of the Ten Attic Orators." See below, Chapter IV, note 22.

22. Thinking of Henry Thoreau's trial of a life of complete self-sufficiency, Emerson notes in journal "ST": "Good Thoreau in Goodwin's Plutarch, vol. V, 419–20." This is a passage in "Against Running in Debt" in which, as Emerson seems to indicate, Plutarch's remarks on the man who is free from debt provide a good description of Thoreau; Plutarch asks, "Dost thou not see how many occasions the land, and how many the sea affords thee for thy maintenance?" This indeed might be an adequate motto for *Walden* and the last sentence of the paragraph is pure Thoreau: "How great and generous was the courage of this man, who, coming from the mill and the kneading-trough, did with the same hand which had been employed in turning the stone and moulding the dough, write of the nature of the Gods, moon, stars and sun!"

CHAPTER IV. THE PLUTARCHAN HERO

1. See above, Chapter II, p. 36; *Letters* 1. 363, 365; *Journals* 3. 387, 419, 427.

2. See G. R. Elliott, "On Emerson's 'Grace' and 'Self-Reliance'," *New England Quarterly*, 2: 92–105 (January 1929).

3. *Ibid.*, p. 156. For the quotations in this paragraph see *Early Lectures*, I, pp. 324, 99, 143, 190, 149, 156.

4. See J. O. McCormick, "Emerson's Theory of Human Greatness," *New England Quarterly* 26:297–299 (September 1953).

5. The Delphic maxim *gnôthi seauton*, "know thyself," has a long history of changing interpretations. It attracted Plato, the Neoplatonists, Plutarch; it was very influential in Renaissance literature and was used and commented on by Montaigne (for whom it might almost be a motto), Elyot, Bacon, Hobbes, Browne, Emerson, Jones Very. See E. G. Wilkins, *The Delphic Maxims in Literature* (Chicago, 1929). Juvenal's "e caelo descendit *gnôthi seauton*" is a favorite of Coleridge (Wilkins, *Delphic Maxims*, pp. 163, 169, and Gilbert Highet, *Juvenal the Satirist* [Oxford, 1954], p. 220) who quotes it in "The Friend" (*Works*, ed. Shedd [New York, 1868], 2. 460). The maxim in its meaning of "God within us" and in its kinship with his own "Over-Soul" could not fail to attract Emerson; perhaps Coleridge is his most direct source but the Stoics said that this motto is the sum and substance of philosophy and this may well stand for another instance of Emerson's affinity for Stoic concepts; the poem "Astraea" (*CW* 9. 80–81 and notes, 9. 428) is said to have had the maxim *gnôthi seauton* as its original title, and in *Journals* 2. 395–399 there is a poem with this title. See Cameron, *Emerson the Essayist*, I, 161, 175–179, and Cameron's index. For Persius' "ne te quaesiveris extra" see *Journals* 3. 337, 338, 466; 4. 110, and Cameron, *Emerson the Essayist*, I, 332, and fn. 10.

6. McCormick, "Emerson's Theory," p. 308.

7. *Ibid.*, p. 302.

8. Perry Miller, "Emersonian Genius and the American Democracy," *New England Quarterly* 26:27–44 (March 1953).

9. *Journals* 8. 145. See below, p. 203.

10. Perhaps a recollection of *Moralia* 2. 55.

11. From the life of Marcus Cato. Also in *Moralia* 1. 235–236 and 5. 112. Emerson used this in the lecture "Greatness" in a series delivered in Boston in 1868.

12. Journal "BO" (1851–52) from the Langhorne version of the life of Demetrius.

13. See below, p. 232.

14. *Moralia* 1. 479–480.

15. *Journals* 2. 240–241; 527–528. See H. N. Smith, "Emerson's Problem of Vocation," *New England Quarterly*, 12:61 (March 1939).

16. Stephen E. Whicher, *Freedom and Fate: an Inner Life of Ralph Waldo Emerson* (Philadelphia, 1953), p. 83.

17. *CW* 2. 260; the anecdote comes from *Moralia* 1. 215, and, in a slightly different form, occurs in the lives of Phocion and Timoleon.

18. Because of his self-reliance the great man can endure the laughter of the masses; this is probably what attracted Emerson's attention in an anecdote which he found in *Moralia* 5. 110 and copied into his journals in 1830 (2. 281–282): "I read in Plutarch's Political Precepts, that when Leo Byzantinus went to Athens to appease the dissentions in that city, when he arose to speak, he perceived that they laughed on account of the littleness of his stature. 'What would you do,' he exclaimed, 'if you saw my wife who scarce reaches to my knees?' And they laughing the more he said, 'Yet as little as we are, when we fall out, the city of Byzantium is not big enough to hold us'." The man who possesses real power can afford to disregard popular opinion or even the laughter and scorn of the people.

19. "Tread the floors of hell" is borrowed from Pindar in Plutarch. See below, pp. 218, 219.

20. *Letters* 1. 365; *Journals* 4. 40; *CW* 12. 263.

21. Emerson referred to this again in *CW* 11. 226; the Euripides quotation, without the attribution to Brutus, is given in *Moralia* 1. 168. Emerson may also have met it in Browne's *Anatomy of Melancholy*, II, iii, 7. Incidentally, modern scholarship no longer assigns the lines definitely to Euripides.

22. Emerson says of self-sacrifice: "its own majesty can lend a better grace to bannocks and fair water than belong to city feasts" (*CW* 2. 254). The expression "fair water" is probably an echo of a remark about Demosthenes in *Moralia* 5. 53; see note 21 to Chapter III.

23. In a journal note of 1834 (3. 333) Emerson notes the story of Socrates' kindness to the humble told in Plutarch's "Of the Tranquillity of the Mind"; Emerson's son in his notes on this passage of "Courage" (*CW* 7. 428) points to a Plutarchan anecdote of Aristides which Emerson used also in "Domestic Life." See note 19 to Chapter III.

24. The reference to Pericles' wariness may come either from the life of Pericles or from *Moralia* 5. 67; Plutarch mentions Aemilius Paulus' opinion in the life of Aemilius Paulus. For Stoic caution, see Arnold, *Roman Stoicism*, pp. 323–324.

25. McCormick, "Emerson's Theory," p. 310.

26. H. Trevelyan, *The Popular Background to Goethe's Hellenism* (London, 1934), p. 82.

27. Dryden's introduction to the *Lives* quotes this passage to refute the idea that Plutarch believed in evil daemons. On Emerson's use of this passage again see below, p. 221.

28. *CW* 8. 303; 7. 6. In *Journals* 7. 429 Emerson used another story of Archimedes' concentration (from *Moralia* 5. 71) and incorporated it in a lecture "Health" in 1862. Yet another sentence in the life of Marcellus gave Emerson a different aspect of this concentration (*CW* 12. 113–114): "Archi-

medes disdained to apply himself to the useful arts, only to the liberal or causal arts." This appears in the journals in 1832 where he refashions the idea into an epigram with the aid of an apothegm which Plutarch quotes from Bias; see below, pp. 215–216.

29. F. O. Matthiessen, *American Renaissance* (New York, 1941), p. 17.

30. *CW* 7. 63–64. For Antiphon's definition see *Moralia* 5. 19; for that of Isocrates see *ibid.*, 31. Emerson used the latter again in "Art and Criticism" (*CW* 12. 300) and in *CW* 7. 98.

31. The picture of the orator with foot forward recalls the well-known Vatican statue of Demosthenes which was familiar in the nineteenth century, and the three-times repeated reference to action recalls a famous remark of Demosthenes in Plutarch (*Moralia* 5. 45).

32. *CW* 8. 118. See *Moralia* 5. 25 for rewards paid to orators.

33. The first comes from the life of Pericles or (more probably) from *Moralia* 5. 106 and was used also by Montaigne in "Of the Vanity of Words"; in *Journals* 3. 557 Emerson uses the name of Themistocles in error. The second aphorism comes from *Moralia* 5. 46 and was used in the lecture on Burke. Both aphorisms are in Rollin.

34. Julius Caesar's remark to Metellus (*CW* 7. 78) is in the life of Julius Caesar and in the "Apothegms of Kings"; Julius Caesar and the pirates are referred to in the same two works and Emerson had used the reference in "Manners." In the Metellus story Emerson's use of "easier" for the Dryden "more disagreeable" may be the result of his reading the anecdote in another passage of Plutarch, the life of Pompey in both the Langhorne and "Dryden" versions where this word is used; but the story is also in Appian, Dio Cassius, Cicero, and Lucan; Bacon gives it in *The Advancement of Learning*, I, vii, 28.

35. *CW* 7. 79 on the Spartan generals. See above, p. 65.

36. *CW* 7. 85: "The several talents which the orator employs, the splendid weapons which went to the equipment of Demosthenes, of Aeschines, of Demades the natural orator, of Fox, of Pitt, of Patrick Henry, of Adams, of Mirabeau, deserve a special enumeration." In this list the names are all familiar with the exception of that of Demades, a little-known Greek orator whom Emerson feels obliged to describe a little more closely as "the natural orator." Almost certainly Emerson met his name in Plutarch; there are several references in the *Moralia*, a brief anecdote of his ingenuity in oratory (5. 141, 145) and one in *Moralia* 2. 298 where he is mentioned along with Phocion; his name occurs a number of times in the life of Phocion. Plutarch attributes to him one apothegm which is well known — the Athenians are not to believe the stories of Alexander's death "for were it true, the whole world would ere this have stunk with the dead body." Plutarch seems to say nothing of Demades' natural ability as an orator; perhaps Emerson is thinking of his gift at extempore epigram and apothegm of which there is some slight indication in the life of Phocion.

37. See "The Assault upon Mr. Sumner" (*CW* 11. 251): "When the same

reproach was cast upon the first orator of ancient times by some caviller of his day, he said, 'I should be ashamed to come with one unconsidered word before such an assembly'." The orator is Demosthenes (see *Journals* 3. 386, *Moralia* 1. 15, and the longer life of Demosthenes); there is a rather similar anecdote about Pericles in the life of Pericles and in *Moralia* 1. 15 and 5. 109–110; Emerson had noted this in journal "GH" and in the *Lives* it occurs immediately after an anecdote which he used in his first essay on eloquence (*CW* 7. 73).

Two journal anecdotes on oratory stem from Plutarch. In journal "E" (1839–1842) Emerson writes, "Epaminondas told the Lacedaemonian orators that he was glad he brought them out of their short speeches." He read this in *Moralia* 2. 319. A journal note of 1835 (*Journals* 3. 504) remarks, "I see that the young men like to speak at public meetings just as they would take exhilarating gas, 'tis so pretty an intoxication. Oh, for the days of the Locrian halters again." This is a reference to the ancient practice of making public speakers wear a halter so that they might be checked at any time; it is attributed to several different lawgivers who are said to have instituted it. The editor of the journals identifies this as "a story of Plutarch" but I cannot find it and think that he may rather have confused it with a similar anecdote of the Locrians which Plutarch gives in "Of Inquisitiveness" (*Moralia* 2. 434–435).

38. *Moralia* 2. 412. *Journals* 5. 165 notes the "Several Hands" translation verbatim. The anecdote is also in *Moralia* 1. 444–445 and in Montaigne's "Of the Greatest Men."

39. Timoleon, Plutarch tells us, modeled himself on Epaminondas. If in his life of Timoleon, Plutarch is not entirely uncritical of him, yet he turns out a heroic soldier, the liberator of Sicily from the tyrants. At the beginning of the biography Plutarch indicates that he considered him heroic by saying that his purpose in writing the *Lives* is to find ennobling examples for himself to follow. Throughout, Timoleon's prudence and courage are mentioned; his devotion to principle is illustrated in the murder of his brother (and Emerson made a note on this in his journals). Constant signs of divine favor attend him; although he is "lucky," this does not detract from his bravery, courage, and assurance. He inspires popularity and even reverence and awe. After the expulsion of the tyrants he shows himself a practical reformer, "building popular government on the fall and ruin of tyranny." His achievements seemed "easy" (Emerson several times repeats the Plutarchan comparison of his victories with the smoothness and ease of Homer's verses); in other words, he has Emerson's "reserve of power after he has hit the mark." Timoleon has an incorruptible integrity and simplicity too, because he surrenders his power as soon as he has expelled the tyrants and established democracy.

Epaminondas has the same Stoic tinge. He is lordly, refusing to give an account of his actions to the people (*Moralia* 5. 101); he is honest and incorruptible; his tenure of a lowly office brings that office into great repute. Epaminondas also takes seriously his responsibilities as an ordinary citizen — this is what Emerson evidently found attractive in a passage which he noted in his journals under the heading "voting" (journal "NY" taken from *Moralia* 5. 458): "I read in Plutarch, Morals V, 419, that Epaminondas left his army, when fighting against the Spartans, to go to Thebes to be present at a public Election of Magistrates." A great and skillful general with a deep patriotism, he possesses Stoic consistency of character and remained the same toward everyone (*Moralia* 2. 109). His way of life is simple. He thinks that refusal of a gift is more honorable than acceptance of it; he pursues the mean and he has a certain ascetic turn of mind (*Moralia* 1. 223). Thus, though he lived before Stoicism was known, Plutarch gives Epaminondas the qualities which have loosely been called "Stoic."

CHAPTER V. THE PLUTARCHAN PHILOSOPHY

1. Quoted by Perry Miller, *The American Transcendentalists: their Prose and Poetry* (New York, 1957), pp. 36–37.

2. René Wellek, "Emerson and German Philosophy," *New England Quarterly*, 16:41 (March 1943).

3. *Ibid.*, p. 62.

4. "Jonathan Edwards to Emerson," *New England Quarterly*, 13:589–617 (December 1940); reprinted in *Errand into the Wilderness* (Cambridge, Mass., 1956), chapter 8.

5. Whicher, *Freedom and Fate*. Charles Eliot Norton partially saw Emerson's Stoic tone, but did not agree with him any the more because of it. He wrote to Moorfield Story: "What you say of getting comfort from Emerson's 'Diary' interests me much. I doubt if such comfort as one may derive from such faith as his and such doctrine is other than a modified Stoical attitude of mind, at least for one who does not, like Emerson, indulge in an optimism that rejects the evidence of facts. . . ." From *Letters of Charles Eliot Norton*, II, 335–336 (quoted by Edward Madden, "Charles Eliot Norton on Art and Morals," *Journal of the History of Ideas*, 18:438 [June 1957]).

6. S. G. Brown, "Emerson's Platonism," *New England Quarterly*, 18:344 (September 1945). It seems to me that Brown overestimates the Platonic and Neoplatonic element in Emerson, but on the other hand Herbert Schneider in his *History of American Philosophy* (New York 1946), p. 284, is equally wrong when he says, "Emerson's idealism was neither Platonic nor Berkeleyan, though he knew a little of both."

7. See Vivian Hopkins, "Emerson and Cudworth," *American Literature*, 23:82 (March 1951).

8. What Robert Spiller says of Emerson (*The Cycle of American Literature*, [New York, 1955], p. 55), is equally true of Plutarch; his best essays deal with ethical rather than metaphysical questions.

9. This work is one of several formerly attributed to Plutarch but now believed not to be genuinely Plutarchan. Emerson was not aware of this doubt as to its genuineness.

10. *Journals* 2. 330–331.

11. *De Augmentis Scientiarum*, Book III, chapter 4.

12. Emerson finds the reference to Anaximenes' doctrine in *Moralia* 3. 107–108; the second sentence comes from *Moralia* 3. 138; the direct quotation comes from 3. 144; the second opinion of Thales from 3. 146; the reference to the moon's eclipse he found in 3. 146–147; the last sentence is a quotation of 3. 132. That both passages, in the journals and in "Fate," are based on Plutarch could be determined, even if we did not have Emerson's reference in the journals, by the presence of the name of an unfamiliar philosopher, Oenopides; his name is given by Plutarch, *Moralia* 3. 138.

13. "Circles," *CW* 2. 301; see Sherman Paul, *Emerson's Angle of Vision: Man and Nature in American Experience* (Cambridge, Mass., 1952), pp. 97–98.

14. *Moralia* 4. 13.

15. *CW* 12. 350; *Moralia* 1. 179.

16. See below, p. 238 and note 26 to Chapter VII.

17. It is interesting to notice that although the Plutarch essay was written as an introduction to Goodwin's revision of the "Several Hands" translation, Emerson preserves the old "fucused" from the version he had used in "Ethical Writers" in 1836 instead of checking Goodwin's version, where he would have found "bespiced."

18. *CW* 8. 200 (see also *Journals* 8. 519, 9. 220); the editors in their notes on this passage comment on the repeated references to Heraclitus' flux, especially in Emerson's poems. In an undated but apparently early prose fragment (Rusk, *Letters*, 6. 333), Emerson writes, "I do not know if the occasion demands Heraclitus or Democritus." He means, "I do not know whether I should weep or laugh" and uses the names as Montaigne does ("Of Democritus or Heraclitus") or Seneca (*De Tranquillitate Animi*) or Browne (*Anatomy of Melancholy*, III, iv, 1).

19. C. F. Strauch, "The Sources of Emerson's 'Song of Nature'," pp. 300–334.

20. Strauch quotes Gérando's statement of Heraclitus' doctrine of unity in change in "The Year of Emerson's Poetic Maturity: 1834," *Philological Quarterly*, 34:365 (October 1955).

21. Montaigne inserted similar opinions from Plato, Pythagoras, the Stoics, and Epicharmus. Years later, in his Plutarch essay, Emerson used the apothegm of Epicharmus which Montaigne gives here. This may indicate that he followed Montaigne's version in "Illusions" also and merely substituted for Montaigne's names of philosophers those of Xenophanes, Diogenes, and "the Hindoos."

22. Whicher, *Freedom and Fate*, pp. 165–166.

NOTES TO PAGES 136–150 309

23. See Strauch, "The Year of Emerson's Poetic Maturity: 1834," p. 366. Emerson evidently recalls a collection of the opinions of the philosophers, perhaps that of Plutarch via Gérando, when he writes (*CW* 6. 324): "The early Greek philosophers Heraclitus and Xenophanes measured their force on this problem of identity. Diogenes of Apollonia said that unless the atoms were made of one stuff, they could never blend and act with one another."

24. C. F. Strauch, "Emerson's Sacred Science," *PMLA* 73:248 (June 1958), shows that the last phrase is Plotinian in origin.

25. J. S. Harrison, *The Teachers of Emerson*, pp. 241ff.

26. See C. F. Strauch, "The Importance of Emerson's Skeptical Mood," *Harvard Library Bulletin*, 11:117–139 (Winter, 1957), especially pp. 118 and 128–134.

27. See Whicher, *Freedom and Fate*, pp. 144–145.

28. Matthiessen, *American Renaissance*, p. 69. For example, see Karl Bapp, *Aus Goethes griechischer Gedankenwelt* (Leipzig, 1921), pp. 1–60, for evidence of Goethe's thorough knowledge of Heraclitus and extensive parallelism of idea and expression.

29. Edward Emerson (*CW* 1. xxvii) mentions Xenophanes as well as Heraclitus as philosophers who influenced Emerson; see note 21 to Chapter V and *CW* 1. 409–410. The poem is in *Journals* 2. 395–399; Emerson writes:

There is nothing else but God.
Where'er I look
All things hasten back to Him.

Surely this recalls a passage in "Nature" (*CW* 1. 43): "Xenophanes complained in his old age that, look where he would, all things hastened back to Unity." It is also in *CW* 8. 7: "All multiplicity rushes to be resolved into unity." On Emerson's use of Xenophanes in Gérando see Strauch, "The Year of Emerson's Poetic Maturity: 1834," pp. 353–377. Strauch shows that much of Emerson's idea of unity among Heraclitean diversity comes from Xenophanes and Empedocles.

30. C. A. Bartol, quoted by Frothingham, *Transcendentalism in New England* (New York, 1876), p. 342.

31. Whicher, *Freedom and Fate*, p. 141.

32. *Ibid.*, p. 31.

33. Varro, quoted by E. V. Arnold, *Roman Stoicism* (Cambridge, 1911), p. 185.

34. C. H. Foster, "Emerson as American Scripture," *New England Quarterly*, 16: 103 (March 1943).

35. Plutarch's remark is quoted in *CW* 10. 313.

36. R. D. Hicks, *Stoic and Epicurean* (New York, 1910), p. 26.

37. See notes 24 and 26 above.

38. See Strauch, "The Year of Emerson's Poetic Maturity: 1834," p. 367, and "Emerson's Sacred Science," p. 244. C. E. Jorgenson, "Emerson's Para-

dise under the Shadow of Swords," *Philological Quarterly*, 11: 274–292 (July 1932), finds (p. 281) a number of passages in Emerson which show that self-reliance is reliance upon God, or upon "Beneficent Tendency." For Whicher's helpful image of a polarity in Emerson's thought see *Freedom and Fate*, pp. 57–58, 157.

39. Whicher, *Freedom and Fate*, p. 37.

40. See above, Chapter II, note 20.

41. For a good brief account of classical demonology, see J. A. K. Thomson, *Shakespeare and the Classics* (London, 1952), pp. 195ff., and T. R. Glover, *Greek Byways* (Cambridge, 1932), pp. 260–274.

42. Quoted in *CW* 9. 411 from *Letters from Ralph Waldo Emerson to a Friend*, ed. C. E. Norton (Boston, 1899), p. 44.

43. Harrison, *Teachers*, pp. 148ff.

44. In "The Powers and Laws of Thought" (*CW* 12. 35–36), Emerson speaks of mythology and its close connection with nature. Pan is mentioned and here Emerson identifies Pan with nature. When he says that "the action of the Instinct is for the most part negative, regulative, rather than initiative or impulsive" he seems to be thinking of the negative impulse of the daemon of Socrates as described by Plato, and by Plutarch in "A Discourse concerning Socrates's Daemon."

45. Harrison, *Teachers*, pp. 148–149.

46. *CW* 8. 284, from "Why the Oracles Cease to Give Answers" (*Moralia* 4. 56); he had used this in his journals in 1839 (5. 287) and again in the Plutarch essay. It was from the same Plutarchan essay that Emerson took the story of the Pythian priestess forced to prophesy against her will, which he used in "Courage." See above, Chapter IV, pp. 108–109. We may note here that *Journals* 6. 310 contains a mythological story which the editors say was possibly composed by Emerson himself; the two characters are named Theanor and Amphitryon; perhaps Emerson recalled the name Theanor from the "Discourse concerning Socrates's Daemon," which also contains a single reference to Amphitryon. The journal passage is quoted by the editors in *CW* 3. 351–352.

47. The quotation from Epictetus is given by Arnold, *Roman Stoicism*, p. 228. For another passage on the daemon or genius see Epictetus 1.14. The translation of Marcus Aurelius (5.27) is that of Sir Ernest Barker, *From Alexander to Constantine* (Oxford, 1956), p. 318.

48. *Moralia* 4.51, 224.

49. The last two sentences, with two minor changes, were used in the lecture on Bacon in 1835.

50. See below, pp. 271–273.

51. Epictetus, fragment 48, translation of P. E. Matheson (Oxford, 1916), II, 235.

52. Bonamy Dobree, *The Broken Cistern* (London, 1954), introduction and pp. 9ff.

CHAPTER VI. BUILDING ON PLUTARCHAN THEMES

1. *CW* 3. 233.
2. O. W. Firkins, *Ralph Waldo Emerson* (Boston, 1915), pp. 179–180.
3. *Moralia* 4. 300; this borrowing was noted by Harrison, *Teachers*, p. 181.
4. *CW* 2. 410.
5. Harrison (p. 168) noticed that Emerson follows Plutarch, but did not observe the verbal similarities; Emerson says: ". . . but if, accepting the hint of these visions and suggestions which beauty makes to his mind, the soul passes through the body and *falls to admire* strokes of character, and the lovers *contemplate one another in their discourses and their actions,* then they pass to the *true palace of beauty,* more and more inflame their love of it, and by this love extinguishing the base affection . . . they become *pure and hallowed.*" This is simply a compression of two sentences of Plutarch which are in the Goodwin revision two pages apart (*Moralia* 4. 295–296; 297–298): "But as many as by sober and modest ratiocination have sincerely extinguished the raging heat of the fire . . . these, I say, in a short time passing by the bodies of those whom they love, penetrate more inwardly and *fall to admire* their manners and dispositions; and calling off their eyes from the body, they converse together and *contemplate one another in their discourses and in their actions* (295–296) . . . . whereas a lover truly chaste and amorous, being got to the *true mansion of beauty,* and there conversing with it as much as it is lawful for him to do, mounted upon the wings of chaste desire, *becomes pure and hallowed*" (297–298). I have printed in italics the words which Emerson takes over verbatim from the "Several Hands" translation of Plutarch.
6. Ralph L. Rusk, *The Life of Ralph Waldo Emerson* (New York, 1949), p. 281.
7. *The Correspondence of Thomas Carlyle and Ralph Waldo Emerson,* ed. C. E. Norton (London, 1883), I, 87–88.
8. J. R. Lowell, "Emerson the Lecturer" in *My Study Windows* (*The Complete Writings of James Russell Lowell*) 16 vols. (Elmwood Edition, Boston and New York, 1904), II, 392, 397.
9. See Perry Miller, *The Transcendentalists: an Anthology* (Cambridge, Mass., 1950), p. 418.
10. J. B. McNulty, "Emerson's Friends and the Essay on Friendship," *New England Quarterly* 19: 390–394 (September 1946). Sherman Paul, *Emerson's Angle of Vision,* studies Emerson's view of friendship in detail and traces its development; thus the essay "Friendship" becomes the result of an "experiment in letter-friendship" (p. 181) and a "manifesto to both the reformers and his correspondents" that he will be tied to neither group (p. 182).
11. Rusk, *Life,* p. 282.
12. Paul, *Emerson's Angle of Vision,* p. 180.

13. E. V. Arnold, *Roman Stoicism*, p. 366.

14. Perhaps there is a verbal reminiscence here; Emerson demands "leave this touching and clawing" (p. 210) and Plutarch in *Moralia* 2. 125 calls flatterers "such as claw and please."

15. Bacon in "Of Friendship" criticises the proverb "a friend is another self" because he takes it to indicate a use of friendship or "aid, and bearing a part in all actions and occasions"; he misunderstands the proverb to mean that friendship is a practical convenience; in his quotation of the proverb Bacon is probably thinking of it as he met it in Plutarch's "Of Large Acquaintance" (*Moralia* 1. 465). In his three "fruits of friendship" Bacon follows Plutarch; his three are "peace in the affections," "support of the judgment," and "aid." His misunderstanding of the proverb probably arose because he thought that Plutarch used it to illustrate his third "fruit." While Plutarch does not deny the usefulness of friends, in quoting the proverb that a friend is another self he wishes to indicate, as Emerson does, not practical ability but the closeness, almost the identity, of friends with ourselves. See the note on this passage of Bacon in S. H. Reynolds' edition of the *Essays* (Oxford, 1890), pp. 198–199.

16. *Moralia* 3. 39; for the journal passage, see below, p. 217.

17. *Moralia* 3. 198; 5. 31.

18. *CW* 7. 248.

19. *Moralia* 3. 339.

20. See below, pp. 217–218; that Emerson's attitude to the comic and to humor is essentially classical may be illustrated by an anecdote which he relates (*CW* 8. 167–168) as a personal experience. He says that he has come upon "an odd illustration of the remark I had heard, that the laws of disease are as beautiful as the laws of health": "I was hastening to visit an old and honored friend, who, I was informed, was in a dying condition, when I met his physician, who accosted me in great spirits, with joy sparkling in his eyes. 'And how is my friend, the reverend Doctor?' I inquired. 'O, I saw him this morning; it is the most correct apoplexy I have ever seen: face and hands livid, breathing stertorous, all the symptoms perfect.' And he rubbed his hands with delight, for in the country we cannot find every day a case that agrees with the diagnosis of the books." I wonder whether Emerson is not perhaps unconsciously thinking of an anecdote in Montaigne's "Of the Resemblance of Children to Their Fathers," which runs along the same lines and which Montaigne admits comes from Aesop: ". . . for he tells us, that a sick person, being ask'd by his physician what operation he found of the potion he had given him, 'I have sweat very much,' says the sick man; 'that's good,' says the physician; another time, having ask'd him how he felt himself after his physick, 'I have been very cold, and have had a great shivering upon me,' said he; 'that is good,' reply'd the physician: after the third potion, he ask'd him again how he did, 'Why, I find myself swell'd, and puff'd up,' said he, 'as if I had a dropsie.' 'That is very well,'

said the physician. One of his servants coming presently after to inquire how he felt himself, 'Truly, friend,' said he, 'with being too well, I am about to die.' "

21. *Moralia* 3. 239; *CW* 8. 395.

22. *Journals* 4. 141–142.

23. It is worth observing that the essay "Manners" begins and ends in the style of a classical moral essay. Emerson begins with an anthropological fact about a foreign tribe, the Fiji islanders, as Plutarch tends to begin a number of his essays with a historical or archaeological fact as in "Of Brotherly Love" or "Of Natural Affection." Emerson ends the essay with a "myth," apparently of his own invention, and in this he is following the Platonic example. Plutarch was also a good Platonist and ends "Concerning Such Whom God Is Slow to Punish" with a Platonic myth, while at the end of the "Consolation to Apollonius" he gives in quotation the myth of Plato's *Gorgias*.

24. *Moralia* 5. 87–88.

25. *Moralia* 5. 74, 79.

CHAPTER VII. READING PLUTARCH FOR "LUSTRES"

1. Garrod, *Poetry and the Criticism of Life*, pp. 101, 106.

2. *CW* 8. 178.

3. *CW* 8. 180.

4. Rusk (*The Life of Ralph Waldo Emerson*, p. 458) quotes from a notebook of Emerson a question and answer, "Who is he that sleeps at Philae?" "Osiris"; and suggests (p. 547, notes on p. 469) that Emerson was familiar with Plutarch's "Isis and Osiris." This reference to Philae is (in Goodwin's edition) on the page after that from which Emerson borrowed the expression about the spider (*Moralia* 4. 83). Emerson used it as early as 1833 (*Journals* 3. 188) and probably took it from Bacon, *Advancement of Learning*, I, iv, 5. See Vivian Hopkins, "Emerson and Bacon," *American Literature* 29: 422–423 and note 74 (January 1958).

5. See *Early Lectures*, I, 360, 361, 369.

6. A. C. McGiffert, Jr., *Young Emerson Speaks* (Boston, 1938), pp. 248–249, gives a list of 38 writers ancient and modern who are quoted in the sermons, adding that it is only a partial list. In the sermons there are a number of Plutarchan anecdotes and remarks; the numbering is that used by McGiffert, pp. 263–271:

(1) In sermon no. 96 Emerson gives an anecdote of Chilon which his son thought came from Plutarch (*CW* 1. 432), but I am unable to locate it.

(2) Sermon no. 117 contains an anecdote of Phocion which is in the life of Phocion and in *Moralia* 1. 214.

(3) Sermon no. 130 has an anecdote of Themistocles from *Moralia* 1. 208.

(4) Sermon no. 150 has the familiar anecdote of the Spartan boy which is

in the life of Lycurgus and *Moralia* 1. 435; the reference in this sermon to Pythagorean vegetarianism probably drew on Plutarch's "Of the Eating of Flesh."

(5) Sermon no. 164 has the well-known anecdote of the Roman and his house. See *Moralia* 5. 103.

7. See Carl Strauch, "Emerson's Sacred Science," pp. 241, 243.

8. *Journals* 3. 567–568; *Moralia* 3. 97, 98, 103. See above, pp. 163–164.

9. Several of these quotations are given in a slightly different wording in Goodwin. Some of them appear and reappear in Emerson's writings. They come from *Moralia* 4. 285, 150, 154, 170, 404, 325, 65, 146; 3. 20, 38–39, 42, 43, 81, 200, 320, 362; 1. 303, 56; 3. 21; 4. 93; 3. 215. Emerson used no. 2 in *Letters* 2. 84, no. 3 is probably the source of "bad counsel confounds the adviser" in *CW* 2. 109, no. 4 is in *CW* 10. 313, no. 5 in *CW* 3. 72; 10. 313, no. 7 in *CW* 10. 312–313, no. 9 seems to have influenced a passage in *CW* 3. 170 (see below, p. 235), no. 13 is in manuscript journal "B," no. 14 is in *CW* 10. 312, no. 17 in *CW* 3. 274; 4. 17; 8. 231–232, no. 20 in *CW* 8. 14, no. 21 in *CW* 8. 289.

10. In 1847 he takes as his motto for his journal a line of Pindar in Greek which is quoted by Plutarch in *Moralia* 3. 93; in the "Several Hands" version it is: "Were it the will of heaven, an osier bough Were vessel safe enough the seas to plough." It is quoted again in journal "ZO" in 1856, and in a notebook labeled "Morals" both the Greek and the "Several Hands" translation are set down under the heading "Immortality." Emerson here adds that it is "quoted doubtfully from Pindar."

11. Goodwin's revision gives a different translation, "If Gods do wrong, surely no Gods there are" and Emerson's quotation differs slightly from that of the original "Several Hands." He seems to be quoting from memory.

12. The remark about Protogenes was used in a temperance address in 1843 and a lecture on books in 1871 refers to "Plutarch's story of the Lacedaemonian who resembled Hector."

13. The ledgers or commonplace books in which in his later years Emerson noted down ideas of his own or quotations which attracted him indicate that, as we should expect, he now used Goodwin's revised edition of the familiar translation of the *Moralia*. Emerson now read in Goodwin, for instance, Heraclitus' remark, which Emerson puts into his own words, "there is one world common to all men who are awake; but of sleepers, each one betakes himself to a peculiar world of his own"; he noted this in ledger "IT" from *Moralia* 1. 171 and had used it in "Demonology." Always interested in curious etymologies, he noted in ledger "IL" from *Moralia* 4. 137 that "the Egyptians call myrrh *Bal*, and the most proper signification of that word is *scattering away melancholy*." He observes, "this adds some testimony to our account of the reason why they burn it," and adds to this another note, "Burn sweet scented woods, such as cypress, juniper and pine" from the same

passage of Plutarch. In ledger "PY" he quotes a sentence from "Of the Eating of flesh" (*Moralia* 5. 4) in the old translation and in Goodwin's version.

Emerson's published essays and addresses were put together from material in the journals and in the manuscripts of the lectures which are now in the Houghton Library of Harvard University. Consequently most of the allusions to remarks of, and quotations from Plutarch which are mentioned in this book occur in these manuscripts and I have noted above instances of "lustres" which recur in notebooks, journals, lectures, and sermons; here are a number of such allusions and quotations which occur in works which have not been published and which I have not alluded to in the preceding chapters:

(1) In pages entitled "Temperance" Emerson quotes the Greek of an apothegm of Cato from the life of Marcus Cato, or from *Moralia* 5. 10.

(2) In the lecture "The Heart" in the series "Human Culture," 1838, Emerson gives an anecdote of Laelius and Blossius which is in the life of Tiberius Gracchus.

(3) In the lecture "Comedy" in the series "Human Life," 1839, Emerson gives a remark of Alexander which is in *Moralia* 2. 138; also in Montaigne, "On Some Lines of Virgil."

(4) In the lecture "Art" in the series "Life and Literature," 1861, Emerson quotes Lysippus on Apelles from *Moralia* 4. 85–86.

(5) In the lecture "Table Talk" in the series "American Life," 1864, Emerson gives an apothegm of Themistocles which is in the life of Themistocles and in *Moralia* 1. 210, but Emerson here quotes it indirectly, from Bacon's "Of Friendship."

(6) In the lecture "Conduct of the Intellect" in the series "Philosophy of the People," 1866, Emerson has a remark on Pericles and Anaxagoras which seems to draw on the life of Pericles.

(7) In his notes for his essay on Plutarch, 1870, Emerson set down a number of anecdotes and quotations from Plutarch; these are taken from *Moralia* 1. 292, 388, 389, 389, 390, 405, 410, 416, 434, 418, and 84–85 or 93. All except the first are anecdotes of or comments on the Spartans.

(8) One sheet of a piece entitled "Parnassus" is subtitled "Plutarch's poetic citations"; here Emerson collected a number of poetic fragments from the "Several Hands" *Moralia*. These are the verse quotations in *Moralia* 2. 57, 63, 92, 181, 193; 5. 395; 2. 304, 321, 413; 3. 9, 42, 93; 4. 59, 150.

(9) In the lecture "Art," 1871, Emerson quotes the Persian king Darius. Compare *Moralia* 1. 186.

(10) On a sheet containing a list of some English words and their derivations Emerson notes Plutarch's derivation of the word "ethics," *Moralia* 1. 7, and adds, "Plutarch says, Plato thinks by the name as it were by tracks to discover the powers of the gods." See *Moralia* 3. 455.

14. The Plutarchan sources of this remark were noted by Harrison, *Teachers*, pp. 249–250.

15. In the manuscript of the lecture "Some Good Books" in a series entitled "Life and Literature," delivered in 1861, Emerson tells the story of the summoning of Tyrtaeus by Sparta in the Messenian War.

16. See Harrison, *Teachers*, pp. 222ff. See also *Moralia* 5. 128.

17. See C. F. Strauch, "The Sources of Emerson's Song of Nature," pp. 300–334. Strauch's study is a model for research into Emerson's literary sources and his method of handling them.

18. A French Emerson scholar applied the remark to Emerson and noted that he had obtained the figure from Montaigne; see *CW* 9. 418–419. For something of the history of this figure in literature see J. W. H. Atkins, *English Literary Criticism: the Renascence* (London, 1947), p. 30.

19. F. I. Carpenter, *Emerson Handbook* (New York, 1953), p. 83.

20. *Ibid.*

21. See Grace Norton, *Le Plutarque de Montaigne* (Boston and New York, 1906), p. 167.

22. See *Early Lectures*, I, 140.

23. See above, p. 65.

24. See above, pp. 105–106.

25. *Moralia* 1. 66, 211; 5. 119.

26. *CW* 5. 240–241; 3. 140; *Moralia* 5. 9. Emerson noted the Heraclitean phrase again in journal "Z." For the correct translation (for "dry light" does not seem to be what Heraclitus said) see the notes in *CW* 3. 320–321 and 5. 380–381. Bacon uses it in *Advancement of Learning*, II, xii, 2, in "Of Friendship," and in the *Apothegms*. Emerson's use of "offend" in the "Manners" passage shows that he is quoting Bacon. For another "lustre" from Plutarch by way of Bacon, see note 4 above.

27. Finally, in order to round out the picture of Emerson's reading of Plutarch for quotable "lustres" we may note a few verbatim quotations, most of them set down in the journals between the years 1868 and 1870. Some come from the "Several Hands" *Moralia*, a few from the Langhorne *Lives*. In 1868 he evidently read "Whether an Aged man Ought to Meddle in State Affairs" (*Moralia* 5. 84) for he quoted from this work (*Journals* 10. 242): "Dionysius the elder, when some one asked him if he was at leisure, replied, 'May that never befall me'." Or he wrote in *Journals* 7. 512 (quoting *Moralia* 2. 202): " 'God's having tasted the sweet of Eternity occasions him to demean himself enviously in it,' says the old translator of Plutarch, quoting Herodotus, *Thalia*." In journal "NY" he noted: "Much that is truly spoken is untruly heard. 'Theodorus who was called the Atheist, — for decrying the existence of the gods, — was used to say, that he reached out his instructions with his right hand, but his hearers received them with their left hands'." Emerson copied this verbatim from "Of the Tranquillity of the Mind," inserting only the words between the dashes; and in 1841 he read Plutarch's life of Cleomenes in Langhorne and noted down " 'War,' said Cleomenes, 'cannot be kept at a set diet'." In 1870, under the heading "Great-

ness" (*Journals* 10. 336), he quoted Plutarch's "Of the Cure of Anger" (*Moralia* 1. 51): "'They deride thee, O Diogenes!' He replied, 'But I am not derided'," and two years before this, in a lecture on "Hospitality and Homes," he spoke of "the modern terror of reporters and reviewers"; the Greeks and Romans were subject to the same torment and Emerson makes use of a Plutarch passage which he later took down verbatim from Plutarch (*Journals* 10. 339 from *Moralia* 3. 197): ". . . and the ancients used to consecrate Forgetfulness, with a ferula in hand, to Bacchus, thereby intimating that we should either not remember any irregularity committed in mirth and company, or should apply a gentle and childish correction to the faults." He then added some brief notations on several remarks of Plutarch, such as, "Plutarch of philosophy, see especially Plutarch, *Moralia* I, 448–9," a passage on the need for critical rather than lavish admiration or adulation of a philosopher's ideas or style. Or he referred, without quotation, to a passage in Plutarch, as when in *Journals* 10. 32–33 he remarked the caution which Plutarch and Plato require in reading of the poets by young people. He apparently recalled "How a Young Man Ought to Hear Poems."

28. Rusk in *Letters* 1, xxxii.

29. O. W. Holmes, *Emerson*, pp. 299–302.

30. F. B. Sanborn, in *The Genius and Character of Emerson*, ed. F. B. Sanborn (Boston, 1885), p. 182.

31. Similarity of title among the essays of Emerson, Bacon, Montaigne, and Plutarch is not of great significance; it may, however, show that Emerson is drawn to write essays on topics which his three predecessors in the moral essay had handled. So Emerson's "Friendship," Bacon's "Of Friendship," Montaigne's "Of Friendship," and Plutarch's "Of Large Acquaintance"; Emerson's "Education" and lecture "Public and Private Education" are parallel with Bacon's "Of Custom and Education," Montaigne's "Of the Education of Children," and Plutarch's "Of the Training of Children"; Emerson wrote "Old Age," Bacon "Of Youth and Age," Montaigne "Of Age," and Plutarch "Whether an Aged Man . . ."; Emerson's "Domestic Life" may be compared with Bacon's "Of Parents and Children" and "Of Marriage and Single Life," with Montaigne's "Of the Affections of Fathers for Their Children," and with Plutarch's "Of Natural Affection," "Of Brotherly Love," and "Conjugal Precepts." Emerson's "Demonology" may perhaps be compared with Bacon's "Of Superstition," with Montaigne's "Of Prognostications," and with Plutarch's "Of Superstition" and the essays which deal with oracles. Emerson's lecture title "Health" resembles Bacon's "Of Regiment of Health" and Plutarch's "Rules for the Preservation of Health"; Emerson, Bacon, and Plutarch all wrote essays entitled "Love" or "Of Love"; Emerson's "Society and Solitude" may be compared with Montaigne's "Of Solitude" and Plutarch's "Whether It Were Well Said, Live Concealed" and "Of Banishment." Emerson's "Greatness" recalls Bacon's "Of Great Place" and "Of the True Greatness . . ." and Montaigne's "Of the Inconvenience of Greatness." All

except Bacon have essays on woman and the virtues of women. Emerson's sermon "Consolation to the Mourner" is matched by Plutarch's two consolatory essays, and his "Fortune of the Republic," with Plutarch's "Concerning the Fortune of the Romans." Emerson's several essays on books and the scholar can be compared with Bacon's "Of Studies" and Montaigne's "Of Books," perhaps with Plutarch's "Discourse to an Unlearned Prince" and "How a Young Man Ought to Hear Poems," etc. It appears that there are a number of traditional topics for the moral essayist.

32. H. S. Canby, *Classic Americans* (New York, 1931), p. 152.

33. Holmes, *Emerson*, p. 405.

34. *American Renaissance*, p. 64–65. Matthiessen gives the journal quotation and the quotation from the letter to Carlyle (from *The Correspondence of Thomas Carlyle and Ralph Waldo Emerson*, I, 320).

35. See the remarks of R. E. Spiller in *Literary History of the United States*, eds. Spiller, Thorp, Johnson, and Canby (New York, 1948), I, 360.

36. *Journals* 5. 64, footnote 1. André Celières, *The Prose Style of Emerson* (Paris, 1936), pp. 30–31, takes as a specimen of this kind of writing a passage of "The Over-Soul" and shows how the "links" or transitions are left to be supplied by the reader.

37. At least one of those who want to find an Oriental source for Emerson's thought has gone also to the Orient, quite mistakenly in my opinion, for a source of his abrupt, inconsecutive style and his interest in "sentences." See Arthur Christy, *The Orient in American Transcendentalism* (New York, 1932), p. 57.

38. E. G. Sutcliffe, *Emerson's Theories of Literary Expression*, University of Illinois Studies in Language and Literature, VIII (Urbana, 1923), p. 137.

39. In *Journals* 8. 126–127 Emerson writes: "For Amount, I look back over all my reading, and think how few authors have given me *things*: Plato has, and Shakspeare, and Plutarch, and Montaigne, and Swedenborg. . . . Goethe abounds in things. . . ." This passage seems to be based on the sentence in Montaigne which Emerson quotes in *CW* 10. 300: "What better praise has any writer received than he whom Montaigne finds 'frank in giving things, not words,' dryly adding, 'it vexes me that he is so exposed to the spoil of those that are conversant with him'."

40. Emerson in the Plutarch essays speaks of the "vulgar phrases" which for him enliven the original "Several Hands" translation of the *Moralia*. Celières (*Prose Style*, pp. 12–14) has studied Emerson's own deliberate use of familiar or coarse or rough or contemptuous words. I have looked into several volumes of the original "Several Hands" translation and it is not difficult to find words which are Emersonian in this sense. Some of them reappear in Emerson: "shank and shin," "pudding-pies," "guts," "howl" for "wail," "putrid ulcers," "vomiting," "porridge-pot," "stuck" for "stabbed," "dunghills." Celières also speaks of Emerson's liking for words in their primary sense. Hundreds of such terms may be found in the "Several Hands"

and I give a few of them: "aliment" for "diet," "acrimony" used of a physical malady, "crude" for "undigested," "raillery" for "jest" (Celières notes Emerson's use of this word), "rallied" for "teased," "commerce" for "association," "auditory" for "audience," "suddenly" for "quickly," "expect" for "await," "delicate" for "fussy" or "luxurious," "eruption of his breath," "horror" for "shivering," "exasperates" for "roughens," "fondly" for "foolishly," "admiring" for "wondering," "suddenly" for "soon," "forward" for "eager," "decent" for "proper" or "fitting," "saucy" for "insolent" (Celières quotes Emerson), "mollified" for "softened," "eligible" for "worth choosing," "credence" for "belief," "consist with" for "be consistent with" (Celières quotes Emerson), "constipation" for "condensation," "discretion of " for "distinction between." Emerson, like the seventeenth-century translation, uses "generous" in the sense of "noble" and "expensive" for "extravagant." On this element in Emerson's style see also Matthiessen, *American Renaissance*, p. 39.

Celières also mentions (p. 12) Emerson's "curiosity in new word-combinations," his peculiar use of preterites and participles, of odd comparatives or superlatives, split infinitives and solecisms, or his use of archaisms and Latinisms. Many specimens of unusual usages of this kind can be found in the "Several Hands" translation, for example: "extasied," "dirted," "superstitionist," "super-adds," "strook with horror," "had stole," "sprung" for "sprang," "sunk" for "sank," "had spoke," "rigidest," "severer," "ancienter," "chiefest," or the title of the essay, "Which Are the Most Crafty, Water or Land Animals"; in addition, "more irremediable," "shall us admit," "might" for "may," "you was present," "may" for "might," "those kind of harangues," "extream" for "extremely," "breathing-while" for "breathing space," "screeking," "mischief" as a verb, "land-bounding ocean," "insectible" for "indivisible," "ambient sea," "reluctancy," "undecent," "unimitable," "primitude," "concernment."

41. *American Renaissance*, p. 38. For another theory, that Emerson's homely imagery is Puritan in origin, see K. B. Murdock, *Literature and Theology in Colonial New England*, p. 183; his liking for the English style of the seventeenth century may be hereditary as well as based on his own predilection.

42. See note 40 above for examples.

CHAPTER VIII. EMERSON'S PLUTARCH

1. In 1821 (*Journals* 1. 83) "Montaigne's Essays" appears in a list of "Books Inquirenda." In 1825–1829 Emerson borrowed volumes 2, 3, 4, and 5 of the "Several Hands" translation of the *Moralia*; between 1826 and 1828 volumes 4, 14, 15, and 19 of Amyot; and between 1823 and 1827 the three volumes of Montaigne in translation; but in 1820 he had used the first volume of a French edition of Montaigne. See Cameron, *Ralph Waldo Emerson's Reading*, pp.

45–47, and *Emerson the Essayist*, II, 157, 161–162. This puts Emerson's first acquaintance with Montaigne as early as 1820; Young (*Emerson's Montaigne*, pp. 84–86), without access to Emerson's list of book borrowings, had put it in 1824. In 1820 also there occurs in a letter (*Letters* 1. 91) the first reference to one of Bacon's essays; in the journals for 1820 there is a long passage in praise of the *Novum Organum* (*Journals* 1. 26–27); and in both of the prize essays of 1820 and 1821 there are references to Bacon. For Bacon in Emerson's book borrowings of 1820 and 1821 see Cameron, *Emerson the Essayist*, II, 156, and "Emerson's Early Reading List, 1819–1824," *Bulletin of New York Public Library*, 55: 318 (July 1951). In 1824 Emerson borrowed the first volume of an English edition of Bacon, containing the *Advancement of Learning* and the *Natural History;* in 1825 he borrowed the fourth volume of the same edition, containing the *Apophthegms, Miscellaneous Writings* and the second part of the *De Augmentis Scientiarum* (the much enlarged Latin version of the *Advancement of Learning*). See Cameron, *Emerson the Essayist*, II, 160, 161.

2. Cameron, *Ralph Waldo Emerson's Reading*, pp. 17–18; for the *Rambler* see *Letters* 1. 40 and *Emerson the Essayist*, II, 153; for the *Spectator*, II, 154.

3. Cameron, *Ralph Waldo Emerson's Reading*, pp. 50, 18.

4. Sometimes we can find the same apothegm in all four — Plutarch, Montaigne, Bacon, and Emerson. For example the Dandamis apothegm of "New England Reformers" is in Bacon's *Advancement of Learning*, II, xxv, 3, and in Montaigne's "Of Profit and Honesty" and in Plutarch's life of Alexander. The aphorism of Solon quoted above (p. 236) occurs in the *Advancement of Learning*, I, iii, 5, in *The Colours of Good and Evil*, I, iii, 15, and in Montaigne, "Of Vanity."

5. *Journals* 10. 320. See also the journal passage quoted in *CW* 4. 341 (1840): "I know nobody among my contemporaries except Carlyle who writes with any sinew and vivacity comparable to Plutarch and Montaigne."

6. In 1828 he wrote in his journals (2. 251): "I read things in Montaigne, Caius, that you cannot; much as he said himself. I will give you Scougal and you shall not find anything in it valuable to you. 'It sounds to the intelligent.' The lapidary will let you choose a stone from a handful of chrystals, knowing that your eye is not skilful enough to detect the unpolished diamond." This passage, according to Young (*Emerson's Montaigne*, pp. 114–115), refers to a remark in "Of the Education of Children"; and in his Plutarch essay, furthermore, Emerson sets down the saying of Plutarch which is used by Montaigne in the same passage; Emerson gives it as, "He [Plutarch] thinks that the inhabitants of Asia came to be vassals to one, only for not having been able to pronounce one syllable; which is, No." Again, in the Plutarch essay Emerson refers to a passage from Plutarch ("Of the Fortune of Alexander the Great") to which Montaigne also evidently refers when he writes in this same essay: "I am of Plutarch's mind, that Aristotle did not so much trouble his great disciple with the knack

of forming syllogisms, or with the elements of geometry, as with infusing into him good precepts concerning valor, prowess, magnanimity, temperance, and the contempt of fear."

7. Emerson's comparison of Seneca and Plutarch seems to be an expanded version of Montaigne's comparison of the same two and he apparently referred to Montaigne's remarks in a letter of 1838 (*Letters* 2. 123). The general picture in the paragraphs of Montaigne and Emerson is the same; perhaps Emerson read Montaigne at this point, and Montaigne's curious term " the cream of philosophy" may have recalled to him Plutarch's equally curious one, "the top of philosophy," and induced him to add to his comparison the apt sentence of Plutarch which contained this expression.

8. All of Emerson's earlier biographers observed his interest in Plutarch; so Holmes, Sanborn, Cabot. But, curiously enough, it seems to have been Bronson Alcott alone who observed that Emerson may be called a moral essayist; he writes in *Emerson: An Estimate of his Character and Genius* (Boston, 1882), pp. 22–23: "We characterize and class him with the moralists who surprise us with an accidental wisdom, strokes of wit, felicities of phrase — as Plutarch, Seneca, Epictetus, Marcus Antoninus, Saadi, Montaigne, Bacon, Sir Thomas Browne, Goethe, Coleridge." Alcott thinks of Plutarch's *Moralia* in connection with Emerson in another way; speaking of the value of Emerson's addresses, he says (pp. 22–23): "And, besides this, its immediate value to his auditors everywhere, it has been serviceable in ways they least suspect; most of his works, having had the first readings on its platform, were here fashioned and polished in good part, like Plutarch's *Morals*, to become the more acceptable to readers of his published works." Alcott knew the *Moralia* perhaps through Emerson. He paraphrases Plutarch (*Moralia* 3. 8–9) when he writes (p. 53), "Plutarch tells us that of old they were wont to call men *phōta*, which imports light, not only for the vehement desire men have to know, but to communicate also." The passage is marked in the margin of Emerson's copy of the 1718 edition of the *Moralia*.

9. See above, p. 210.

10. Sutcliffe, *Emerson's Theories*, p. 109, quotes another journal passage of 1835 (*Journals* 3. 518–519): "By and by, books of condensed wisdom may be writ by the concentrated lights of thousands [of] centuries which shall cast Bacon and Aristotle into gloom," and thinks that Emerson modified this plan "in the fact that now his contribution is to be self-derived or at least self-tested" and that its long persistence in Emerson's mind is shown in the course of lectures which he delivered at Harvard in 1870 and published as "Natural History of Intellect."

11. The reference to "the British Plutarch" is probably occasioned by a specific work, Wrangham's *British Plutarch*, which Emerson at least looked into in the period 1819–1824. See Cameron, *"Emerson's Early Reading List,"* p. 318.

12. Here, as so often, Matthiessen has observed something unnoticed be-

fore — that Emerson tends to make all his biographical subjects over into "heroes" (*American Renaissance*, pp. 71–75). Matthiessen stresses the influence of the seventeenth-century mode of presenting "type characters" but this is, as I have tried to show, in turn Plutarchan.

13. *Journals* 4. 145.

14. "Concord Days," quoted by Perry Miller in *The American Transcendentalists* (New York, 1957), p. 94.

15. Thoreau, Emerson says, declined invitations to dinner parties because there each was in everyone's way and he could not meet the individual to any purpose. "They make their pride," he said, "in making their dinner cost so much; I make my pride in making my dinner cost little." One may wonder whether there is any connection between this remark and Epaminondas' statement (in Plutarch's "Apothegms of Kings and Great Commanders") when departing from an elaborate and expensive dinner, "I thought you were sacrificing and not displaying your luxury." Another anecdote of Thoreau given by Emerson recalls a famous story of Diogenes the Cynic. Emerson says, "When asked at table what dish he preferred, he answered, 'the nearest'." Surely this is Thoreau's turn to the story of Diogenes, "'What food do you like best, O Diogenes?' 'Another's'." Emerson gives another illustration of Thoreau's classical Stoic limitation of desires: "There was somewhat military in his nature, not to be subdued, always manly and able. . . . It cost him nothing to say No; indeed he found it much easier than to say Yes." This recalls Emerson's quotation of Plutarch (*CW* 10. 314) given in note 6 above.

16. *CW* 1. 220, quoted by Perry Miller in "Jonathan Edwards to Emerson," p. 615.

17. Canby, *Classic Americans*, pp. 147–148.

18. *Journals* 4. 197, 266.

19. Emerson's prayer of the sailor to Neptune in "Demonology" (*CW* 10. 14), "O God, thou mayst save me if thou wilt, and if thou wilt thou mayst destroy me; but, however, I will hold my rudder true" is taken from Montaigne, but Montaigne obtained it from the Stoic Seneca (Epistle 85) and Seneca may perhaps also be the source of this sentence of Plutarch.

20. *CW* 1. 131–132.

21. *CW* 1. 142. There is an apparent inconsistency here. Elsewhere Emerson talks of a "wild stoicism" but here is a "stoical discipline." But, as has been pointed out by Stephen Whicher ("The Lapse of Uriel" [Harvard dissertation, 1942], pp. 210–211) there are to Emerson two separate kinds of discipline, that imposed by the world (and by the dogma of the Church or any dogma) and a self-imposed discipline, as asceticism, that of self-trust. Emerson rejects the former but would still retain the latter.

22. Régis Michaud, *Mystiques et Réalistes Anglo-Saxons* (Paris, 1918), p. 9.

23. Canby, *Classic Americans*, p. 155.

24. See "Jonathan Edwards to Emerson."

25. E. W. Emerson, *Emerson in Concord* (Boston and New York, 1889), p. 48; quoted by Whicher, *Freedom and Fate*, p. 28.

26. *Journals* 3. 538f.

27. William S. Johnson, *Thomas Carlyle: A Study of His Literary Apprenticeship* (New Haven, 1911), p. 32.

28. The Stoicism of Matthew Arnold has received some study; see, for example, John Hicks, *The Stoicism of Matthew Arnold*, University of Iowa Humanistic Studies, VI, no. 1 (1924).

29. O. W. Holmes, *Emerson*, pp. 381–382.

INDEX

Under *Journals*, *Letters*, and "Sermons" in this index are included all references to these works of Emerson, in the notes as well as in the text.

231; martyrdom of, 257–258; Thoreau
compared with, 266; and Jesus, 274;
life of (Plutarch), 34, 36, 84, 104, 116
Pindar, 84, 214, 219; "floors of hell," 218
Plato, 2, 9, 20, 44, 47, 72–73, 88, 129,
138, 150, 175, 205, 206, 209, 214, 218,
220; myth of cave, 73; demonology,
158; references in Emerson, 284;
Emerson's Platonism Plutarchan, 284;
language, 228; metaphors from, in
Emerson, 230; *Phaedo*, 138; *Phaedrus*,
181–182; man a plant, 217, 230;
Republic 78; *Symposium*, 46, 182, 229;
Timaeus, 126; theology, 8
"Platonic Questions" (Plutarch), 43
"Pleasure not Obtainable, That . . ."
(Plutarch), 42
Pliny, 88
Plotinus, 72, 119, 124–125, 150, 209
Plutarch: anti-Stoicism of, 171–172; and
Plutarchan tradition, 1–34; anecdote
and apothegm, 4, 13; not academic,
171–172, 280; biographer, 3; no cant
in, 70; commonsense of, 7, 69–70;
criticized, 84; reference in Donne, 13;
eclecticism, 8, 280; on eloquence,
110–114; Emerson's acquaintance with,
35–54; Emerson on Plutarch's style,
239–240; and morality, 239–240; "better than Southey," 240; resembles
Emerson, 240; used to start a work,
255, 273; Emerson's tribute to, 48–53;
97; concept of fate, 7; concept of God,
7–8; on Greek gods, 61–62; on Greek
philosophy, 3–4; Hellenism of, 6; debt
to Heraclitus, 8–9; historical method,
86–87; humanity of his heroes, 23,
68–69; heroism, 2, 10, 83–116; as historian, 3, 20, 86; linked with Montaigne, 250; *Moralia* influences biography, 22; in nineteenth century, 3, 29;
pantheism of, 8, 14, 280; philosophy
of, 6–11, 117–172; Platonism of, 2, 3,
7, 8, 9; religion, 20; in Renaissance, 2,
15–18; read by schoolboys, 36; simplicity of, 68; likes the Spartans, 64,
110; Stoicism of, 8–10, 80–81, 171–
172, 279–280; style, 243; Emerson on
his style, 239–240; on superstition 20,

165, 271–272; works translated, 16;
transmits Platonism, 123–124; concept
of virtue, 7; known to Wordsworth,
13
"Plutarch" (Emerson), 1, 48–53, 90, 117,
120, 123, 128, 229, 230, 239; on Plu-
tarch's style, 243; English style of
Plutarch mentioned, 246–247
"Poems, How a Young Man Ought to
Hear" (Plutarch), 42, 200, 212–213,
233
"Poet, The" (Emerson), 129, 211, 212,
213, 230, 231–232
"Poetical Essay" (Emerson), 36
"Poetry and Imagination" (Emerson),
129, 212, 228–229, 233
Poetry: figure of the bee used in, 233; in
Emerson, 233; spontaneity of, 234;
quotations from, in Plutarch, 216–220
"Political Precepts" (Plutarch), 41, 231
"Politics" (Emerson), 108, 227, 267
Pope, Alexander, 23
Poverty: Emerson on, 73ff; Plutarch on,
73ff
"Power" (Emerson), 95, 109–110
"Praise Himself, How a Man May" (Plu-
tarch), 42
"Preacher, The" (Emerson), 230, 272,
280–281
Preaching: criticized, 277; Emerson's defi-
nition of, 277
Presocratics, 119, 120, 122, 125ff, 142–
143, 205
Proclus, 119, 150
Prometheus, 62
Property, Spartan law of, 227
Proteus, 62
Protogenes, 220
Prudence: classical term, 107, 168–169;
two types in Emerson, 167–168
"Prudence" (Emerson), 166–169
"Punish, Concerning Such Whom God Is
Slow to" (Plutarch), 31, 41, 147, 214
Puritanism, 118, 119, 199; modernized by
Emerson, 281; source of dualism in
Emerson, 281; elements in, rejected by
Emerson, 282; and the Old Testament,
22–23
Pyrrhus, 70, 236; life of (Plutarch), 236

Silence: in Jeremy Taylor, 238; Pythagorean, 70–71
Simonides, 229–230, 233, 267
Smith, John, 210
Society and Solitude (Emerson), 111, 194, 199
"Social Aims" (Emerson), 196, 197, 198
Socrates, 20, 73, 90, 107, 108, 213; daemon of, 153ff; martyrdom of, 257, 275
"Socrates, Discourse concerning the Daemon of" (Plutarch), 37, 42, 46, 154ff, 162–163, 243
Solon, 2, 23, 24, 83, 206; aphorism of, 236; life of (Plutarch), 236
"Song of Nature" (Emerson), 130, 232
Sophocles, 64, 192
Sophron, 206
"Sovereignty of Ethics, The" (Emerson), 140, 215, 272, 279
Spartans, the, 55, 77, 105, 110, 115, 171; language of, 17, 67; Emerson's liking for, 64; generals, 65; discipline, 67; early references to in Emerson, 227; sacrificed to Muses, 237
"Spartans, Apothegms of" (Plutarch), 4, 31, 41, 52, 65, 215, 237; in "Luther," 235
Spectator, The, 33, 250
Spencer, Herbert, 141
Spencer, Edmund, 210
Spinoza, Benedictus de, 13, 141
"Spiritual Laws" (Emerson), 105
Spontaneity, 105
Stearns, G. L., Emerson's essay on, 265–266
Steele, Sir Richard, 33
Stoics, Stoicism, 51, 53, 55; brotherhood of man, 11, 93, 100; in Emerson's biographical essays, 258; called for by Emerson, 278; in Carlyle, 283–284; characteristics of, 13–14; and Christianity, 11–13, 276, 278, 282, 285; not cultivated now, 279; demonology of, 11, 154; Emerson's use of the term, 14, 279–280; Emerson's Stoicism that of Montaigne, 279; in Emerson's religion, 281; Emerson's affinity for, 14, 167–168; in England, 13; fate, 10, 151; no flaw in, 275; apothegm of finger,

234; friendship, 190–191; Greek Stoicism, 8; adapted Heraclitus, 131; Stoic hero, 13, 101–104; indifference, 10; limitation of desires, 79–80; aids Montaigne, 18; Montaigne's polemic against, 31; Emerson's Stoicism Plutarchan, 279; in nineteenth century, 283; of Plutarch, 8, 9, 52, 171–172, 280, 282; Emerson's Stoicism not academic, 8, 280; Plutarch's debt to Greek Stoicism, 9; practical, 2; public theme in literature, 172; Roman Stoicism, 8–10; missing in religion, 282; remedy for defects in religion, 277; of Seneca, 9–10, 12; in English sermons, 32; in seventeenth century, 13, 282–283; in Jeremy Taylor, 19; "wild" Stoicism, 66–67. *See also* Lipsius; Noestoicism; Seneca; Zeno
"Stoics, Against the" (Plutarch), 41
Strauch, Carl F., 130, 148
Study, Emerson's plans for, 252
Style, Emerson's, 242–248
Sulla, 162; life of (Plutarch), 39
"Sumner, Charles" (Emerson), 113
"Superlative, The" (Emerson), 67
Superstition: Emerson attacks, 163; Plutarch on, 271–272
"Superstition, Of" (Plutarch), 127, 165–166, 271–272, 273
Swedenborg, Emanuel, 110, 119, 211, 222
"Swedenborg" (Emerson), 129
Symbolism: Emerson on, in literature, 62, 228–229; in Neohellenism, 56. *See also* Allegory
"Symposiacs" (Plutarch), 41, 42, 43, 61, 124, 197, 198, 199, 200, 223, 224, 228, 230, 236
Symposium, The (Plato), 46, 175, 181–182, 184, 229

"Table-Talk" (Emerson), 196, 237
Tales of Demonology and Witchcraft (Scott), 156
Tantalus, 62
Tatler, The, 33
Taylor, Jeremy, 19, 210, 211; classicism of, 250; read by Emerson, 250; devoted to Plutarch, 238; on silence, 238